AN AUSTRALIAN
PRAYER BOOK

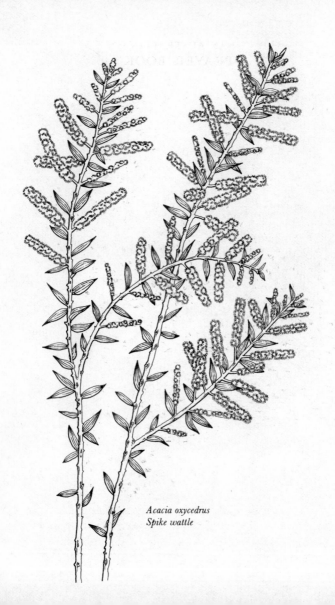

Acacia oxycedrus
Spike wattle

AN AUSTRALIAN
PRAYER
BOOK

for use together with
The Book of Common Prayer, 1662

1978

THE STANDING COMMITTEE
OF THE GENERAL SYNOD
OF THE CHURCH OF ENGLAND IN AUSTRALIA
SYDNEY

First Published 1978

Published by the Standing Committee of the Church
of England in Australia, General Synod Office,
St. Andrew's House, Sydney Square, NSW, 2000,
Australia. Distributed by the Anglican Information
Office, Sydney.

National Library of Australia ISBNo. 0 909827 79 6

Contents

CONTENTS

The Preface

This book is AN AUSTRALIAN PRAYER BOOK 1978 FOR USE TOGETHER WITH THE BOOK OF COMMON PRAYER 1662. It is supplementary to *The Book of Common Prayer* and not a replacement of it. *The Book of Common Prayer* remains, together with the *Thirty-nine Articles*, our controlling standard of doctrine and worship. It is expected that both *The Book of Common Prayer* and AN AUSTRALIAN PRAYER BOOK will continue in use. The status of AN AUSTRALIAN PRAYER BOOK is such that if the Church wishes to make necessary revisions it will be possible to do so.

It is important to recognise in any time of revision that people will vary in their attitudes. Some will prefer no revision, others only limited, and others more comprehensive revision. Many change their views. People respond to the wonder of God's love in different ways. If we listen to one another with patience and understanding, our love for God and our neighbour can be enriched and enlarged.

Aim

The Preface to *The Book of Common Prayer 1662* recognises that in the course of history changes in the liturgy of the Church may become necessary. Language alters, needs of ministry vary. But any change must be governed by the recognition that fundamental doctrines shall not be disturbed. The revisers of 1662 expressed their purpose in these words:

> Our general aim therefore in this undertaking was, not to gratify this or that party in any their unreasonable demands; but to do that, which to our best understandings we conceived might most tend to the preservation of peace and unity in the Church; the procuring of reverence, and exciting of piety and devotion in the publick worship of God.

Revision of liturgy may be taken as a response to renewal of life in the Church and the recognition that as the worship of God has to be expressed 'not only with our lips but in our lives', so the

7

language used must be 'alive' for our times. Public worship must also express the fact that the Church is the body of Christ, requiring in its members participation, responsibility, and commitment to the gospel it proclaims and by which it professes to live.

Authority

Such stirrings were taking place in the Church of England in Australia in the 1950s. When the Constitution, binding together the dioceses, had been accepted, it was not surprising that the first General Synod, meeting under a new Constitution in 1962, passed the following resolution:

> That this Synod appoints a Commission to explore the possibilities of revision of, and addition to, The Book of Common Prayer for the Church of England in Australia, and to report to the next session of Synod.

This first Commission with its large membership of 32 drew upon a wide range of experience in the Church. It prepared a Report, presented in book form, *Prayer Book Revision in Australia*, to the General Synod of 1966. The work of this first Commission was quite a remarkable achievement; not only did it produce a far ranging report which revealed the possibilities of effective Prayer Book revision; it also saw clearly the necessary disciplines that would have to be followed if the renewal in worship that the Church desired was to be effectively achieved.

The Right Reverend R. G. Arthur, then Bishop of Grafton, presented that first report to General Synod in 1966 as chairman of this first Commission. He was subsequently appointed chairman of the continuing Liturgical Commission, and this is a fitting point to pay tribute to his wisdom and leadership, and the very significant contribution he made to the worship and life of the Church of England in Australia through his chairmanship of the Commission from 1963 to 1974. His mind and manner were such that in his relationships with the members of the Commission and with the Church at large a pattern of revision developed that has met the needs both liturgically and pastorally of the Church of England in Australia for two decades.

In his report to the 1966 General Synod, Bishop Arthur drew the Church's attention to the fact that to revise forms of public worship is an accepted Anglican principle, but that any such revisions must be for good reason and sound both in doctrine and ceremony. He quoted both from the thirty-fourth *Article of Religion* and the Ruling Principles in the *Constitution* of the Church of England in Australia.

> It is not necessary that the traditions and ceremonies be in all places one, and utterly like; for at all times they have been divers, and may be changed according to the diversities of countries, times, and manners, so that nothing be ordained against God's word ... Every particular or national Church hath authority to ordain, change, and abolish, ceremonies or rites of the Church ordained only by man's authority, so that all things be done to edifying. *Article 34*

> This Church, being derived from the Church of England, retains and approves the doctrine and principles of the Church of England embodied in *The Book of Common Prayer together with The Form and Manner of Making, Ordaining, and Consecrating of Bishops, Priests, and Deacons* and in the *Articles of Religion* sometimes called the Thirty-nine Articles but has plenary authority at its own discretion to make statements as to the faith ritual ceremonial or discipline of this Church and to order its forms of worship and rules of discipline and to alter or revise such statements, forms and rules, provided that all such statements, forms, rules or alteration or revision thereof are consistent with the Fundamental Declarations contained herein and are made as prescribed by this Constitution. Provided, and it is hereby further declared, that the above-named *Book of Common Prayer*, together with the *Thirty-nine Articles*, be regarded as the authorized standard of worship and doctrine in this Church, and no alteration in or permitted variations from the Services or Articles therein contained shall contravene any principle of doctrine or worship laid down in such standard.
>
> Provided further that until other order be taken by canon made in accordance with this Constitution, a Bishop of a Diocese may, at his discretion, permit such deviations from the existing Order of Service, not contravening any principle of doctrine or worship as aforesaid, as shall be submitted to him by the Incumbent and Churchwardens of a parish. *Constitution, ch. 2, § 4.*

These quotations illustrate both the possibilities and necessary limitations of revision.

As Bishop Arthur also pointed out, it is essential that a Commission be not only sensitive to the need to make services flexible enough to meet the pastoral situations of parishes, in a language that is clear for people of our day, and that expresses the corporate nature of worship, it must also provide full opportunity for clergy and people to test these forms of worship by experience. Changes that may be liturgically and theologically correct must stand up to practical use. 'Trial use' has in fact become an essential part of the method of revision in Australia.

Sunday worship

Since the Synod of 1966, revision has continued systematically on two lines: that of conservative and of radical revision, represented in this book by first and second forms of service respectively. Attention was first given to the main services for Sunday worship. Not only was there need to bring language and style into contemporary idiom and to be sensitive to the 'liturgical movement' of this century, with its emphasis on the corporate nature of worship, it was important also to recognise that these were aims of Archbishop Cranmer himself and the framers of our Prayer Book. 'Radical' revision became for the Commission a real searching for the roots of worship in *The Book of Common Prayer*. The Prayer Book envisaged a balance of Sunday morning worship that was expressed in Morning Prayer, Litany, and Holy Communion. The balance was right, the time needed too long. Cranmer's pattern of Sunday worship had become impracticable even by the time of the industrial revolution, but as the Church lacked a method of responding to the actual needs of congregations no authorized changes took place and in practice the pattern was broken. Morning Prayer and Holy Communion became separated services and the Litany almost vanished from ordinary worship. In the context of a society which once more is looking for one main act of Sunday worship, it became clear to the Commission that it should concentrate on restoring the balance of worship envisaged in the Prayer Book within a time span that would be realistic for contemporary Australian Church life.

A Modern Liturgy (1966), *A Service of Holy Communion for Australia 1969*, and *A Service of Holy Communion for Australia 1973* were all part of a sequence of services for trial use which attempted to give practical expression to the Cranmerian pattern and balance of worship.

Countless people throughout Australia participated in the making of *Australia 73* which was widely used, but the Commission still had to listen carefully to those in the Church who had been using the English alternative services of Holy Communion, *Series Two* and *Series Three*. Further revision has been made, and the second Order of the Holy Communion in this Book is the result of this growth through liturgical use and comment.

Language of revision

Many congregations have wished to keep to the form of service as set out in *The Book of Common Prayer* but expressed in contemporary English. The work of conservative revision sought to provide for this need and in 1972 the Commission published *Sunday Services Revised*. Bishop Arthur's preface to these states the purpose and method of conservative revision, not only for *SSR* but also for the other conservatively revised services in this Book:

> These services are a contemporary 'translation' of Morning and Evening Prayer, the Litany, and Holy Communion from *The Book of Common Prayer 1662*, which is 'the standard of worship and doctrine in this Church' according to the Constitution of the Church of England in Australia. Many Anglicans are content gratefully to continue using that Book, more or less as it was published . . . For them, the Tudor English and style, coming directly from the classic period of Anglicanism, is still the most fitting for corporate worship. However, an increasing number of Anglicans are feeling that the worship of the Church today should be in more truly contemporary language.
>
> When the services of the Church of England in the 16th century were first put into English, Archbishop Cranmer was concerned to use 'the best and clearest English of his time'. Then, in the revision of the following century which gave us the 1662 *Book of Common Prayer*, the revisers stated that one of their aims was 'the more proper expressing of some words and phrases of ancient usage in terms more suitable to the language of the present time'. This has been the aim of the Australian Liturgical Commission in the translation of these four services.
>
> *Preface to SSR*

Contemporary needs

Since 1972 careful revision has been made to the services in *Sunday Services Revised* to improve phrasing and the flow of expression generally. 'Another Order of Service for Prayer and Hearing God's

11

Word' is also included in this Book for public worship on less formal occasions.

Not only did the pattern of Sunday worship envisaged by Archbishop Cranmer break down and become the separate services of Morning Prayer and Holy Communion at different times of day, but the practice of both clergy and people using Morning and Evening Prayer daily had also diminished considerably through the lack of any method of revision or any alternative order. In the second form of Morning and Evening Prayer in this Book a shorter form has been provided for each day with a variety of canticles, prayers, and intercessions. Trial use has indicated that this has begun to meet a need both in public and private use for lay people as well as for the clergy, who are in fact enjoined in the introduction to *The Book of Common Prayer* to 'say daily Morning and Evening Prayer either privately or openly, not being let by sickness or some other urgent cause'. To assist in and encourage the daily offering of prayer to God, a form of Prayer at the End of the Day has been provided and the Psalms have been given devotional headings.

The hearing and intelligent understanding of the Scriptures is fundamental to Anglican worship. The Commission's concern more adequately to meet this need in public worship finds expression in a number of ways. Among these are the fuller selection of readings from the Scriptures provided for the Holy Communion, together with the headings and themes supplied with them.

The Pastoral Services are in both first and second forms, except for the Funeral Services and the Ministration to the Sick, in which it was found that the needs of both forms of revision could be met by one order of service. The Ordinal was prepared in both radical and conservative revisions, but canonical and legal requirements showed that it was not possible to include the radical version in this Book. Similarly, the Ministration to the Sick has been limited by current canonical and legal requirements to the provisions of ministry in the 1662 Visitation of the Sick.

Talks with other Christians in Australia as well as Anglicans have shown that for a number of years yet at least two versions of the Lord's Prayer are likely to be in use. In this Book there are two versions. One is a contemporary English version approximating to that proposed by the International Commission on English

Texts (I.C.E.T.). This version is printed in all services, but the traditional version is printed at the beginning of the Book and is available as a constant alternative.

The versions of the Creeds, Sanctus, Gloria in excelsis, and the Canticles have been examined in the light of the I.C.E.T. texts.

The new and the old

The 'Ruling Principles' of the *Constitution* have at times been regarded by many in the Church as restrictive, but increasingly their wisdom has been appreciated. Divergent theological interpretations of fundamental Christian truths are bound to flow from finite minds. The Liturgical Commission has been a microcosm of the Church, with the different traditions of Anglicanism represented in its membership. Where there has been a difference of interpretation, the Commission has sought to find a common ground behind divergences of tradition. Respect for truth and for one's fellow Anglicans' understanding of the truth has been a matter of fundamental importance in the work of the Commission. Close and constant re-examination of *The Book of Common Prayer* has revealed afresh the extraordinary wisdom of Archbishop Cranmer and the revisers a century later in presenting a Prayer Book which could be used with integrity by people holding the same gospel but having different emphases in faith and worship.

We are living in a time of development in Christian awareness theologically, liturgically, and pastorally, and still need a recognised and ordered means for experiment in liturgy, so that the legitimate needs of congregations may be met and the necessary trial use take place. Then at a later date revisions of and additions to this Book can be made. AN AUSTRALIAN PRAYER BOOK 1978 may be expected to have a life of at least three sessions of General Synod (10 to 15 years). May it help the different traditions within the Church better to understand one another, be a teaching and devotional manual in contemporary language, and supply the confidence and stability in worship that can strengthen the unity and witness of the Church's worshipping members.

AN AUSTRALIAN PRAYER BOOK 1978 is a people's book, not just a Commission's production. It owes a great deal to individual comment, to provincial and diocesan liturgical committees, and to consultants in various parts of Australia. All have recognised the force of a sentence Bishop Arthur wrote in his preface to *Australia 73*, 'A form of words is only a means to an act of worship'. This Book is humbly offered to the Church with the prayer that it will enable her people more effectively to fulfil their high calling to worship God in spirit and in truth.

John Grindrod

Bishop of Rockhampton
Chairman of the Liturgical Commission

NOTES FOR THE CONDUCT OF SERVICES

1 The rubrics (rules governing the ordering of services) of *The Book of Common Prayer* apply unless separate provision has been made in this Book.

2 Where they occur, the directions to stand, sit, or kneel are suggestions only.

3 Words in square brackets may be omitted.

4 Sections marked ‡ are optional.

5 Words in **bold type** are said or sung by the congregation.

6 Where parts of the service are sung to a musical setting, the words for which these settings were composed may by used.

7 Hymns may be sung with these services otherwise than where provision is made for them. In the selection of hymns, careful attention should be given both to the appropriateness of the words to the themes of the service and also to the relation of the hymn chosen to its position within the service.

8 Additional notes for the conduct of these services will be found at the end of each service.

9 An explanation of the symbols used in the pointing of the psalms and canticles will be found on page 306.

THE LORD'S PRAYER

Wherever the Lord's Prayer is ordered to be said in this Book, the following traditional form may be used.

Our Father, who art in heaven,
  hallowed be thy Name,
  thy kingdom come,
  thy will be done
    on earth as it is in heaven.
Give us this day our daily bread.
And forgive us our trespasses
  as we forgive those who trespass against us.
And lead us not into temptation,
  but deliver us from evil.
For thine is the kingdom, the power, and the glory
  for ever and ever.   Amen.

THE ORDER FOR
Morning and Evening Prayer
FOR DAILY USE
THROUGHOUT THE YEAR

Callistemon rigidus
Stiff bottlebrush

Morning and Evening Prayer

FIRST FORM

INTRODUCTION

‡1   The minister may read aloud one or more of these verses from the Bible

You are worthy, our Lord and God, to receive glory and honour and power, for you created all things, and by your will they existed and were created.   Revelation 4.11

God is spirit, and those who worship him must worship in spirit and truth.   John 4.24

The Lord is in his holy temple; let all the earth keep silence before him.   Habakkuk 2.20

Christmas   Behold, I bring you good news of a great joy which will come to all the people; for to you is born this day in the city of David a Saviour, who is Christ the Lord.   Luke 2.10,11

Easter   Blessed be the God and Father of our Lord Jesus Christ! By his great mercy we have been born anew to a living hope through the resurrection of Jesus Christ from the dead.   1 Peter 1.3

Ascension   God has highly exalted Christ Jesus and bestowed on him the name which is above every other name, that at the name of Jesus every knee should bow, in heaven and on earth and under the earth, and every tongue confess that Jesus Christ is Lord, to the glory of God the Father.   Philippians 2.9-11

Whitsun   God's love has been poured into our hearts through the Holy Spirit who has been given to us.   Romans 5.5

2 The minister then reads one or more of these or other suitable
verses from the Bible

To the Lord our God belong mercy and forgiveness; though
we have rebelled against him, and have not obeyed the voice
of the Lord our God by following his laws which he set before
us.   Daniel 9.9,10

When a wicked man turns away from the wickedness he has
committed and does what is lawful and right, he shall save
his life. For I have no pleasure in the death of anyone, says
the Lord God; so turn, and live.   Ezekiel 18.27,32

The sacrifice acceptable to God is a broken spirit; a broken
and contrite heart, O God, you will not despise.   Psalm 51.17

Enter not into judgment with your servant, O Lord, for no
man living is righteous before you.   Psalm 143.2

Return to the Lord your God, for he is gracious and merciful,
slow to anger, and abounding in steadfast love.   Joel 2.13

The kingdom of God is at hand; repent, and believe in the
gospel.   Mark 1.15

I will arise and go to my Father, and I will say to him,
'Father, I have sinned against heaven and before you; I am
no longer worthy to be called your son'.   Luke 15.18,19

If we say we have no sin, we deceive ourselves, and the truth
is not in us. But if we confess our sins, God is faithful and
just, and will forgive our sins and cleanse us from all un-
righteousness.   1 John 1.8,9

3 The minister turns to the congregation and says this Exhortation.
He may omit the second paragraph.

Dear friends, the Scriptures urge us to acknowledge our
many sins, and not to conceal them in the presence of God
our heavenly Father, but to confess them with a penitent and
obedient heart, so that we may be forgiven through his
boundless goodness and mercy.

19

We ought always humbly to admit our sins before God, but chiefly when we meet together to give thanks for the benefits we have received at his hands, to offer the praise that is due to him, to hear his holy word, and to ask what is necessary for the body as well as the soul.

Therefore, let us draw near to the throne of our gracious God, and say together:

4 All kneeling, this general Confession is said by the congregation and minister together

Almighty and most merciful Father,
we have strayed from your ways like lost sheep.
We have left undone what we ought to have done,
and we have done what we ought not to have done.
We have followed our own ways and the desires of our own
   hearts.
We have broken your holy laws.
Yet, good Lord, have mercy on us;
restore those who are penitent,
according to your promises declared to mankind in Jesus
   Christ our Lord.
And grant, merciful Father, for his sake,
that we may live a godly and obedient life,
to the glory of your holy name.   Amen.

5 The Absolution or declaration of forgiveness is pronounced by the priest alone standing; the congregation still kneeling

The God and Father of our Lord Jesus Christ pardons and absolves all who truly repent and believe his holy gospel.
For God desires, not the death of a sinner, but rather that he should turn from his wickedness and live, and has given authority and commandment to his ministers to declare to his people, when they repent, the forgiveness of their sins. Therefore let us ask him to grant us true repentance, and his Holy Spirit, that what we do now may please him, and that

the rest of our life may be pure and holy, so that at the last we may come to his eternal joy; through Jesus Christ our Lord.

The congregation answer

Amen.

Or instead of the Absolution the minister may say this prayer

Merciful Lord, grant to your faithful people pardon and peace, that they may be cleansed from all their sins, and serve you with a quiet mind; through Jesus Christ our Lord.
Amen.

Or he may say the Word of Assurance, page 44.

Except on Sundays, this service may begin here or at §7, and end with the Collects and the Grace.

‡6   The Lord's Prayer may be said by all, kneeling

Our Father in heaven,
   hallowed be your Name,
   your kingdom come,
   your will be done
      on earth as in heaven.
Give us today our daily bread.
Forgive us our sins
   as we forgive those who sin against us.
Lead us not into temptation,
   but deliver us from evil.
For the kingdom, the power, and the glory are yours
   now and for ever.   Amen.

Evening Prayer continues on page 29.

Morning Prayer

FIRST FORM

Except on Sundays, when the Introduction is to be used, the service may begin here or with the Lord's Prayer as on page 21.

7   The minister says

Open our lips, O Lord;
        And the congregation answers
And we shall declare your praise.

O God, make speed to save us.
O Lord, make haste to help us.
        All stand, and the minister continues

Glory to God; Father, Son, and Holy Spirit,
as in the beginning, so now, and for ever.   Amen.

Let us praise the Lord.
The Lord's name be praised.

8   Psalm 95 is said or sung

1 O come let us sing | out · to the | Lord:
   let us shout in triumph to the | rock of | our sal|vation.

2 Let us come before his | face with | thanksgiving:
   and cry | out to · him | joyfully · in | psalms.

3 For the Lord is a | great | God:
   and a great | king a·bove | all | gods.

4 In his hand are the | depths · of the | earth:
   and the peaks of the | mountains · are | his | also.

†5 The sea is his and | he | made it:
   his hands | moulded | dry | land.

6 Come let us worship and | bow | down:
   and kneel be|fore the | Lord our | maker.

7 For he is the | Lord our | God:
   we are his | people · and the | sheep of · his | pasture.

8 Today if only you would | hear his | voice:
   'Do not harden your hearts as | Is|rael · did in the | wilderness;

9 'When your | fathers | tested me:
put me to proof though | they had | seen my | works.

†11 'Of whom I | swore · in my | wrath:
"They | shall not | enter · my | rest." '

Glo|ry to | God: Father | Son and | Holy | Spirit;
As in the be|ginning · so | now: and for | ever | A|men.

Or, especially in Eastertide, this Hymn of the Risen Christ

1 Christ our passover has been | sacri·ficed | for us:
so let us | cele|brate the | feast,

2 not with the old leaven of cor|ruption · and | wickedness:
but with the unleavened | bread of · sin|cerity · and | truth.

3 Christ once raised from the dead | dies no | more:
death has no | more do|minion | over him.

4 In dying he died to sin | once for | all:
in | living · he | lives to | God.

5 See yourselves therefore as | dead to | sin:
and alive to God in | Jesus | Christ our | Lord.

6 Christ has been | raised · from the | dead:
the | first fruits · of | those who | sleep.

7 For as by | man came | death:
by man has come also resur|rection | of the | dead;

8 For as in | Adam all | die:
even so in Christ shall | all be | made a|live.

Glo|ry to | God: Father | Son and | Holy | Spirit;
As in the be|ginning · so | now: and for | ever | A|men.

9   The Psalm or Psalms of the day are said or sung.
     After the last psalm is said or sung

Glory to God; Father, Son, and Holy Spirit:
as in the beginning, so now, and for ever.   Amen.

10   The First Reading from the Old Testament.
     The readings are announced, The first/second reading from . . .,
     chapter . . ., beginning at verse . . . .
     At the end of the readings, the reader says, Here ends the reading.

11   This Hymn (Te Deum) or a similar hymn of praise is said or sung

1   We praise | you O | God:
    we acknowledge | you to | be the | Lord.

2   All creation | worships | you:
    the | Father | ever|lasting.

3   To you all angels | cry a|loud:
    with | all the | powers · of | heaven,

4   Cherubim and | Sera|phim:
    ever | sing in | endless | praise,

5   Holy holy holy   Lord God of | power and | might:
    heaven and | earth are | full of · your | glory.

6   The glorious company of a|postles | praise you:
    the goodly | fellowship · of | prophets | praise you.

7   The noble army of | martyrs | praise you:
    through all the world your | holy | Church ac|claims you,

8   Father of | majesty · un|bounded:
    your true and only Son
        and the Holy | Spirit | advocate · and | guide.

9   You Lord Christ are the | King of | glory:
    the e|ternal | Son · of the | Father.

10 When you became man to | set us | free:
    you did not dis|dain the | virgin's | womb.

11 When you overcame the | sting of | death:
    you opened the kingdom of | heaven to | all be|lievers.

12 You are seated at God's right | hand in | glory:
    we believe that you will | come to | be our | judge.

13 Come then Lord and | help your | people:
    bought with the | price of | your own | blood;

14 and bring us | with your | saints:
    to | glory | ever|lasting.

        The Te Deum may end at this point.

15 Save your people Lord   and | bless · your in|heritance:
    govern and up|hold them | now and | always.

16 Day by | day we | bless you:
 we | praise your | name for | ever.

17 Keep us today Lord from | all | sin.
 Have mercy | on us | Lord have | mercy.

18 Lord show us your | love and | mercy:
 for we | put our | trust in | you.

19 In you Lord | is our | hope:
 let us not be con|founded | at the | last.

> Other suitable hymns and canticles for use at Morning Prayer are
> to be found in the Second Form for Morning Prayer to be found
> on pages 43-91.

12 The Second Reading, from the New Testament

13 The Song of Zechariah at the naming of John the Baptist, or
    another hymn, is said or sung

1 Blessed be the Lord the | God of | Israel:
 for he has come to his | people · and | set them | free.

2 He has raised up for us a | mighty | saviour:
 born of the | house · of his | servant | David.

3 Through his holy prophets he | promised · of | old:
 that he would save us from our enemies
        from the | hands of | all that | hate us.

4 He promised to show | mercy · to our | fathers:
 and to re|member · his | holy | covenant.

5 This was the oath he swore to our | father | Abraham:
 to set us | free · from the | hands of · our | enemies,

6 free to worship him with | out | fear:
 holy and righteous ‿
        in his sight | all the | days of · our | life.

7 And you my child shall be called the prophet of ‿
        the | Most | High:
 for you will go before the | Lord · to pre|pare his | way,

8 to give his people knowledge | of sal|vation:
 by the for|giveness · of | all their | sins.

25

9 In the tender compassion | of our | God:
   the dawn from on | high shall | break up|on us;
10 to shine upon those who dwell in darkness and ⌣
      the | shadow · of | death:
   and to guide our feet | into · the | way of | peace.

Glo|ry to | God: Father | Son and | Holy | Spirit;
As in the be|ginning · so | now: and for | ever | A|men.

14   The Apostles' Creed is said or sung by all standing

I believe in God, the Father Almighty,
maker of heaven and earth;
and in Jesus Christ, his only Son our Lord,
who was conceived by the Holy Spirit,
born of the virgin Mary,
suffered under Pontius Pilate,
was crucified, dead, and buried.
He descended into hell.
The third day he rose again from the dead.
He ascended into heaven,
and is seated at the right hand of God the Father
   almighty;
from there he shall come to judge the living and the dead.
I believe in the Holy Spirit;
the holy catholic church;
the communion of saints;
the forgiveness of sins;
the resurrection of the body,
and the life everlasting.   Amen.

   The Litany (page 98) may be said or sung here. When this is done,
   the remainder of Morning Prayer may be omitted.

15   The Prayers follow. The minister first says
The Lord be with you.
   And also with you.

All kneel, and the minister continues

Let us pray.

If the Lord's Prayer has already been said, this section may continue at Lord, show us your mercy.

Lord, have mercy on us.
  Christ, have mercy on us.
Lord, have mercy on us.

Our Father in heaven,
  hallowed be your Name,
  your kingdom come,
  your will be done
    on earth as in heaven.
Give us today our daily bread.
Forgive us our sins
  as we forgive those who sin against us.
Lead us not into temptation,
  but deliver us from evil.
For the kingdom, the power, and the glory are yours
  now and for ever.   Amen.

Lord, show us your mercy,
  and grant us your salvation.

Lord, save the Queen,
  and mercifully hear our prayers.

Clothe your ministers with righteousness,
  and make your chosen people joyful.

Lord, save your people,
  and bless your inheritance.

Give peace in our time, O Lord,
  for you are our help and strength.

Create in us clean hearts, O God,
  and renew us by your Holy Spirit.

27

16   Then are said the three Collects.

The first Collect, of the day.

The second Collect, for peace

O God, the author and lover of peace, in knowledge of whom stands our eternal life, whose service is perfect freedom; defend us your servants in all assaults of our enemies, that, surely trusting in your defence, we may not fear the power of any adversaries, through the might of Jesus Christ our Lord.
Amen.

The third Collect, of the morning.

Lord our heavenly Father, almighty and everlasting God, we thank you for bringing us safely to this day: keep us by your mighty power, and grant that today we fall into no sin, neither run into any kind of danger, but lead and govern us in all things, that we may always do what is righteous in your sight; through Jesus Christ our Lord.
Amen.

Or

Eternal God and Father, by whose power we are created and by whose love we are redeemed: guide and strengthen us by your Spirit, that we may give ourselves to your service, and live this day in love to one another and to you; through Jesus Christ your Son our Lord.
Amen.

‡17   An *Anthem* or hymn may be sung here.

Except on Sundays, when the Prayers on page 34 are to be used, the service may end with the Grace.

Evening Prayer

FIRST FORM

Except on Sundays, when the Introduction (page 18) is to be used, the service may begin here or at §7.

‡6   The Lord's Prayer may be said by all, kneeling

Our Father in heaven,
   hallowed be your Name,
   your kingdom come,
   your will be done
     on earth as in heaven.
Give us today our daily bread.
Forgive us our sins
   as we forgive those who sin against us.
Lead us not into temptation,
   but deliver us from evil.
For the kingdom, the power, and the glory are yours
   now and for ever.   Amen.

7   The minister says

Open our lips, O Lord;
         And the congregation answer
And we shall declare your praise.

O God, make speed to save us.
O Lord, make haste to help us.
      All stand, and the minister continues
Glory to God; Father, Son, and Holy Spirit:
   as in the beginning, so now, and for ever.   Amen.

Let us praise the Lord.
The Lord's name be praised.

8   The Psalm or Psalms of the day are said or sung.
     After the last psalm is said or sung

Glory to God; Father, Son, and Holy Spirit:
as in the beginning, so now, and for ever.   Amen.

9   The First Reading, from the Old Testament.
The readings are announced, **The first/second reading from . . .,
chapter . . ., beginning at verse . . . .**
At the end of the readings, the reader says, **Here ends the reading.**

10   The Song of Mary, extolling God's plan of salvation, or another hymn

1 My soul proclaims the | greatness · of the | Lord:
    my spirit re|joices · in | God my | Saviour;

2 for he has looked with favour on his | lowly | servant:
    from this day all gener|ations · will | call me | blessed;

†3 the Almighty has done | great things | for me:
    and | holy | is his | name.

4 He has mercy on | those who | fear him:
    in | every | gener|ation.

5 He has shown the | strength · of his | arm:
    he has scattered the | proud in | their con|ceit.

6 He has cast down the mighty | from their | thrones:
    and has | lifted | up the | lowly.

7 He has filled the hungry with | good | things:
    and the rich he has | sent a|way | empty.

8 He has come to the help of his | servant | Israel:
    for he has re|membered his | promise · of | mercy,

9 the promise he | made · to our | fathers:
    to Abraham | and his | children · for | ever.

    Glo|ry to | God: Father | Son and | Holy | Spirit;
    As in the be|ginning · so | now: and for | ever | A|men.

    Other suitable hymns and canticles for use at Evening Prayer are
    to be found in the Second Form for Evening Prayer to be found
    on pages 43-91.

11   The Second Reading, from the New Testament.

12   The Song of Simeon, on seeing the infant Christ, or another hymn.

1 Lord now you let your servant | go in | peace:
    your | word has | been ful|filled.

2 My own eyes have | seen the·sal|vation:
  which you have prepared in the | sight of | every | people;
3 a light to re|veal you·to the | nations:
  and the | glory·of your | people | Israel.

  Glo|ry to | God: Father | Son and | Holy | Spirit;
  As in the be|ginning · so | now: and for | ever | A|men.

13   The Apostles' Creed is said or sung by all, standing

I believe in God, the Father Almighty,
maker of heaven and earth;
and in Jesus Christ, his only Son our Lord,
who was conceived by the Holy Spirit,
born of the virgin Mary,
suffered under Pontius Pilate,
was crucified, dead, and buried.
He descended into hell.
The third day he rose again from the dead.
He ascended into heaven,
and is seated at the right hand of God the Father
    almighty;
from there he shall come to judge the living and the dead.
I believe in the Holy Spirit;
the holy catholic church;
the communion of saints;
the forgiveness of sins;
the resurrection of the body,
and the life everlasting.   Amen.

          The Litany (page 98) may be said or sung here.
          When this is done, the remainder of Evening Prayer may be
          omitted.

14   The Prayers follow.
     The minister first says

The Lord be with you.
  And also with you.

31

All kneel, and the minister continues

Let us pray.

If the Lord's Prayer has already been said, this section may continue at **Lord, show us your mercy.**

Lord, have mercy on us.
   Christ, have mercy on us.
Lord, have mercy on us.

Our Father in heaven,
   hallowed be your Name,
   your kingdom come,
   your will be done
      on earth as in heaven.
Give us today our daily bread.
Forgive us our sins
   as we forgive those who sin against us.
Lead us not into temptation,
   but deliver us from evil.
For the kingdom, the power, and the glory are yours
   now and for ever.   Amen.

Lord, show us your mercy,
   and grant us your salvation.

Lord, save the Queen,
   and mercifully hear our prayers.

Clothe your ministers with righteousness,
   and make your chosen people joyful.

Lord, save your people,
   and bless your inheritance.

Give peace in our time, O Lord,
   for you are our help and strength.

Create in us clean hearts, O God,
   and renew us by your Holy Spirit.

15 Then are said the three *Collects*

  The first Collect, of the day

  The second Collect, for peace

Eternal God, from whom all holy desires, all good purposes, and all just works proceed: give to your servants that peace which the world cannot give, that our hearts may be set to obey your commandments, and that free from the fear of our enemies we may pass our time in trust and quietness; through the merits of Jesus Christ our Saviour.

  Amen.

  The third Collect, of the evening

Lighten our darkness, Lord, we pray: and in your great mercy defend us from all perils and dangers of this night; for the love of your only Son our Saviour Jesus Christ.

  Amen.

  Or

Be present, merciful God, and protect us through the hours of this night: that we, who are wearied by the changes and chances of this fleeting world, may rest on your eternal changelessness; through Jesus Christ our Lord.

  Amen.

‡**16** An *Anthem* or hymn may be sung here.

Except on Sundays, when the Prayers on page 34 are to be used, the service may end with the Grace.

33

Prayers

AT MORNING AND EVENING PRAYER

17 Prayer is offered for those in authority, for the church, and for all people, together with any of the Prayers for Various Occasions (page 91).

The minister may use the following prayers, or others authorized.

A prayer for the Queen and all in authority

Almighty God, the fountain of all goodness, we humbly pray you to bless our sovereign lady, Queen Elizabeth, and all who hold public office in this land: that all things may be ordered in wisdom, righteousness, and peace, to the honour of your holy name, and the good of your Church and people; through Jesus Christ our Lord.
Amen.

or this

Lord God almighty, ruler of the nations of the earth, regard with favour our sovereign lady, Queen Elizabeth, that in all things she may be led by your Spirit and protected by your power. Give wisdom to her ministers, especially the Prime Minister of Australia (N) [and the Premier of this State (N)], to the members of Parliament (especially N), and to all who hold office in this land. Grant that all things may be so ordered and settled by their endeavours on the best and surest foundations, that peace and happiness, truth and justice, faithfulness and true religion, may be firmly established among us, and make us a blessing to other nations; through Jesus Christ our Lord.
Amen.

A prayer for the clergy and people

Almighty and eternal God, you alone work great marvels: send down your spirit of saving grace on all christian people, especially our bishops and other pastors and the congregations in their care; and, that they may truly please you, pour upon them the continual dew of your blessing. Grant this, Lord, for the honour of our advocate and mediator, Jesus Christ.

Amen.

The minister may ask the prayers of the congregation for particular persons and needs.

A prayer for all people

O God, creator and preserver of all mankind: we humbly pray for all sorts and conditions of men, that you would be pleased to make your way known to them, your saving power among all nations.

Especially we pray for the welfare of your catholic church, that it may be guided and governed by your good Spirit, so that all who profess and call themselves Christians may be led into the way of truth and hold the faith in unity of spirit, in the bond of peace, and in righteousness of life.

We commend to your fatherly goodness all who are in any way afflicted or distressed [especially those for whom our prayers have been asked], that it may please you to comfort and relieve them according to their needs, giving them patience in their sufferings, and a happy issue out of all their afflictions. All this we ask for the sake of Jesus Christ our Lord.

Amen.

A general thanksgiving, which may be said by the congregation with the minister

Almighty God, Father of all mercies,
we your unworthy servants give humble and hearty
thanks
for all your goodness and loving kindness to us and to all
men;

35

we bless you for our creation, preservation, and all the
    blessings of this life;
but above all for your amazing love
in the redemption of the world by our Lord Jesus Christ;
for the means of grace;
and for the hope of glory.
And, we pray, give us that due sense of all your mercies,
that our hearts may be truly thankful and that we may
    declare your praise
not only with our lips, but in our lives,
by giving up ourselves to your service,
and by walking before you in holiness and righteousness all
    our days;
through Jesus Christ our Lord,
to whom, with you and the Holy Spirit, be all honour and
    glory,
now and for ever.   Amen.

       or this

Most merciful Father, we humbly thank you
for all your gifts so freely bestowed on us.
For life and health and safety,
for power to work and leisure to rest,
and for all that is beautiful in creation and in the lives of
    men,
we praise and glorify your holy name.
But, above all, we thank you
for your spiritual mercies in Christ Jesus our Lord,
for the means of grace,
and for the hope of glory.
Fill our hearts with all joy and peace in believing;
through Jesus Christ our Lord.   Amen.

18   The service ends with one of the following prayers and the Grace.

     A prayer of Saint Chrysostom

Almighty God, you have given us grace to bring before you

with one accord our common supplications, and you promise
that when two or three are gathered together in your name
you will grant their requests; fulfil now, Lord, the desires and
petitions of your servants, as may be most expedient for
them, granting us in this world knowledge of your truth, and
in the world to come life everlasting.

Amen.

Or

Lord our God, fountain of all wisdom, you know our necessities before we ask and our ignorance in asking: have compassion on our infirmities; and those things, which for our
unworthiness we dare not and for our blindness we cannot
ask, graciously give us for the worthiness of your Son, Jesus
Christ our Lord.

Amen.

Or

Almighty God, you have promised to hear the petitions of
those who ask in your Son's name: mercifully accept us who
have now made our prayers to you; and grant us those things
which we have asked in faith according to your will; through
Jesus Christ our Lord.

Amen.

The Grace

**The grace of our Lord Jesus Christ, and the love of God,
and the fellowship of the Holy Spirit, be with us all evermore. Amen.** 2 Corinthians 13.14

NOTES FOR MORNING AND EVENING PRAYER, FIRST FORM

1 The Song of Zechariah may be used at §11 and the Hymn (Te Deum) at §13 at Morning Prayer.

2 When the Hymn (Te Deum) is used at §13 at Morning Prayer, the Apostles' Creed (§14) may be omitted.

3 When The Holy Communion follows Morning Prayer, Morning Prayer may begin at §7 and end at §11, and The Holy Communion may begin with the Collect and the Reading from the New Testament.

4 When The Holy Communion follows Evening Prayer, Evening Prayer may begin at §7 and end at §10; in which case The Holy Communion may begin with the Collect and the Reading from the New Testament.

5 If Baptism is administered during Morning or Evening Prayer, one of the readings and the Apostles' Creed may be omitted.

6 A sermon may be preached during or after Morning and Evening Prayer.

7 The gifts of the congregation may be received and placed on the holy table at Morning and Evening Prayer.

Another Order of Service
for Prayer and the Hearing of
God's Word

1   The minister greets the people and addresses them in this way

We have met together to thank God for . . .
We shall praise him with . . .
We shall hear from his holy word how . . .
And we shall pray for . . .
To prepare ourselves, let us hear from the word of God.

2   An appropriate sentence from the Bible is read.

3   After which the minister shall say

Let us now confess our sins to almighty God.

    The minister and congregation kneel to say together this
    Confession

Most merciful God,
we humbly admit that we need your help.
We confess that we have wandered from your way:
we have done wrong,
and we have failed to do what is right.
You alone can save us.

Have mercy on us:
wipe out our sins and teach us to forgive others.
Bring forth in us the fruit of the Spirit
that we may live as disciples of Christ.
This we ask
in the name of Jesus our Saviour.   Amen.

4   The minister stands to declare God's forgiveness

God wills that all men should be saved
and in response to his call we acknowledge our sins.

He pardons those who humbly repent and truly believe the gospel.
Therefore we have peace with God, through Jesus Christ,
to whom be blessing and honour for ever.
Amen.

5   The people stand. The minister says

Sing to the Lord a new song,

   And the people reply

For he has done marvellous things.

6   A hymn of praise is sung.

7   A psalm may follow.

8   The Readings. Two readings from the Bible are read.
    They may be interspersed with and/or followed by hymns or canticles or other appropriate responses.
    Silence or discussion may be used.
    The sermon is preached here or later.

9   The Apostles' Creed is said, everyone standing.
    In its place Te Deum (page 24) or some other hymn declaring the Christian faith may be used.

I believe in God, the Father Almighty,
maker of heaven and earth;
and in Jesus Christ, his only Son our Lord,
who was conceived by the Holy Spirit,
born of the virgin Mary,
suffered under Pontius Pilate,
was crucified, dead, and buried.
He descended into hell.
The third day he rose again from the dead.
He ascended into heaven,
and is seated at the right hand of God the Father almighty;
from there he shall come to judge the living and the dead.
I believe in the Holy Spirit;
the holy catholic church;

the communion of saints;
the forgiveness of sins;
the resurrection of the body,
and the life everlasting.   Amen.

10   Prayers follow, the minister first saying

Let us pray.

The Lord be with you.
   And also with you.

Let us pray.

> Everyone kneels. The minister says

Lord, teach us to pray.

> All join in saying the Lord's Prayer

Our Father in heaven,
   hallowed be your Name,
   your kingdom come,
   your will be done
      on earth as in heaven.
Give us today our daily bread.
Forgive us our sins
   as we forgive those who sin against us.
Lead us not into temptation,
   but deliver us from evil.
For the kingdom, the power, and the glory, are yours
   now and for ever.   Amen.

> The minister continues

Be exalted, Lord, above the heavens,
   let your glory cover the earth.

Keep our nation under your care,
   and guide us in justice and truth.

Let your way be known on earth,
   your saving power among all nations.

Send out your light and your truth
that we may tell of your saving works.

Hear our prayers, O Lord,
for we put our trust in you.

11   Then shall follow thanksgivings and prayers for the community, for the work of the church, and for the needs of individuals.

12   Concluding prayer

Almighty God, you have given us grace to bring before you with one accord our common supplications, and you promise that when two or three are gathered together in your name you will grant their requests; fulfil now, Lord, the desires and petitions of your servants, as may be most expedient for them, granting us in this world knowledge of your truth, and in the world to come life everlasting.
Amen.

The Grace

The grace of our Lord Jesus Christ, and the love of God, and the fellowship of the Holy Spirit, be with us all evermore. Amen.   2 Corinthians 13.14

Morning and Evening Prayer
for Each Day of the Week

SECOND FORM

The *First Form* for Morning and Evening Prayer may be used on each day of the week, or these forms may be used.

If the following forms are used independently of The Holy Communion in the *public service on Sundays*, the Apostles' Creed must be used in the morning, the Confession must be used at §3, and the statutory prayers (see §§17,18 on pages 34 to 37) said at the Intercessions.

For *family prayers*, selections from the materials in the following forms may prove helpful. For example, the introductory sentence and/or the opening hymn or psalm, a reading, and the canticle may be followed by the Lord's Prayer and other prayers. Selections should be made according to the needs of the particular family.

When the services are used *by one person alone*, it is recommended that the ending to the readings, the lesser litany, and the responses before the blessing be omitted.

Pauses may be observed after each psalm-portion and after the readings, to respond to the psalmists' invitation to prayer, and to ponder God's word with thankfulness; or a single pause may be observed at a point appropriate to the congregation and occasion. The members of the congregation are advised to use the pauses in applying the words read to their own hearts; or the minister may do this in a brief comment.

When only *one service* is used each day, it is recommended that the morning and evening sentences, opening psalms or hymns, and canticles, be read week and week about.

The *Introductory Sentence* may be read either as a sentence or as a versicle (v/) and response (r/). A seasonal sentence may be read either before or in place of the introductory sentence printed.

On Sunday morning and *each Evening,* at §3, a pause for self-examination may precede this *Confession*

Almighty God, our heavenly Father,
we have sinned against you
in thought, and word, and deed,
and in what we have failed to do.
Have mercy on us,
forgive us all that is past,
and grant that we may serve you
and live a new life to your glory;
through Jesus Christ our Lord.   Amen.

The priest says this *Absolution*

Almighty God,
who forgives all who truly repent,
have mercy on you,
pardon and deliver you from all your sins,
confirm and strengthen you in all goodness,
and keep you in life eternal;
through Jesus Christ our Lord.
Amen.

or the minister may say this *Word of Assurance*

If anyone sins, we have an advocate with the Father, Jesus Christ the righteous: and he is the perfect offering for our sins, and not for ours only but also for the sins of the whole world. 1 John 2.1,2

The appointed *Psalms and Readings* are to be found in the Table of Psalms and Readings for Morning and Evening Prayer.

During *Advent,* the Prayer Book collect for Advent Sunday (page 180) may be used at §4 *in the morning;* and the Prayer Book collect for the Sixth Sunday after the Epiphany (page 190) may be used at §5 *in the evening.*

During *Lent,* the Prayer Book collect for Ash Wednesday (page 192) may be used at §4 *in the morning;* and the Prayer Book collect for the Twelfth Sunday after Trinity (page 250) may be used at §5 *in the evening.*

The prayer provided for use *during Eastertide* at this point in the services may be used throughout the year if desired.

After the Readings the reader may say

This is the word of the Lord.

and the congregation respond

Thanks be to God.

or the reader may say

May your word live in us

and the congregation respond

and bear much fruit to your glory.

The *Morning collect* at §9 may be the first of the morning collects provided at §16 of the first form of Morning Prayer, page 28.

SUNDAY MORNING

1   The minister reads this Sentence

v/ This is the day which the Lord has made,
r/ **we will rejoice and be glad in it.**   Psalm 118.34

2   Then Psalm 95 is said or sung

1   O come let us sing | out · to the | Lord:
     let us shout in triumph to the | rock of | our sal|vation.
2   Let us come before his | face with | thanksgiving: ·
     and cry | out to · him | joyfully · in | psalms.
3   For the Lord is a | great | God:
     and a great | king a·bove | all | gods.
4   In his hand are the | depths · of the | earth:
     and the peaks of the | mountains · are | his | also.
†5   The sea is his and | he | made it:
     his hands | moulded | dry | land.
6   Come let us worship and | bow | down:
     and kneel be|fore the | Lord our | maker.
7   For he is the | Lord our | God:
     we are his | people · and the | sheep of · his | pasture.
8   Today if only you would | hear his | voice:
     'Do not harden your hearts as | Is|rael · did in the |
         wilderness;

9 'When your | fathers | tested me:
  put me to proof though | they had | seen my | works.
11 'Of whom I | swore · in my | wrath:
  "They | shall not | enter · my | rest." '

Glo|ry to | God: Father | Son and | Holy | Spirit;
As in the be|ginning · so | now: and for | ever | A|men.

‡3 A pause for self-examination, the Confession and Absolution (see
    page 44) may be used here.

4   The Psalms as appointed are said or sung, and a pause observed
    after each.

‡5 At the end of the (last) pause, there may follow
Glory to God; Father, Son, and Holy Spirit:
as in the beginning, so now, and for ever.   Amen.

  or this Prayer, which may be said here or after the Intercessions at §9

Let us pray.
Lord, we thank you for your holy Word, and for the fellowship of your
Church; may your Word live in us and bear much fruit to your glory
and the salvation of our fellow-men; through Jesus Christ your Son our
Lord.   **Amen.**

  or, in Eastertide

Lord God, whose blessed Son rose in triumph and set us free: grant us
the fulness of spiritual gifts he promised us, that through the Holy Spirit
our hearts may possess him whom our eyes cannot see, the same Jesus
Christ our Lord.   **Amen.**

6   Readings from the Bible as appointed.

    A pause follows the readings.

7   The Canticle, The Song of Zechariah at the naming of John the
    Baptist (Luke 1.68-79) is said or sung

1 Blessed be the Lord the | God of | Israel:
   for he has come to his | people · and | set them | free.
2 He has raised up for us a | mighty | saviour:
   born of the | house · of his | servant | David.
3 Through his holy prophets he | promised · of | old:
   that he would save us from our enemies
     from the | hands of | all that | hate us.

4 He promised to show | mercy · to our | fathers:
and to re|member · his | holy | covenant.

5 This was the oath he swore to our | father | Abraham:
to set us | free · from the | hands of · our | enemies,

6 free to worship him with|out | fear:
holy and righteous in his sight |
    all the | days of · our | life.

7 And you my child shall be called the prophet of ⌣
    the | Most | High:
for you will go before the | Lord · to pre|pare his | way,

8 to give his people knowledge | of sal|vation:
by the for|giveness · of | all their | sins.

9 In the tender compassion | of our | God:
the dawn from on | high shall | break up|on us;

10 to shine upon those who dwell in darkness and ⌣
    the | shadow · of | death:
and to guide our feet | into · the | way of | peace.

Glo|ry to | God: Father | Son and | Holy | Spirit;
As in the be|ginning · so | now: and for | ever | A|men.

‡8   The Apostles' Creed may be said.

I believe in God, the Father Almighty,
maker of heaven and earth;
and in Jesus Christ, his only Son our Lord,
who was conceived by the Holy Spirit,
born of the virgin Mary,
suffered under Pontius Pilate,
was crucified, dead, and buried.
He descended into hell.
The third day he rose again from the dead.
He ascended into heaven,
and is seated at the right hand of God the Father
almighty;
from there he shall come to judge the living and the dead.

I believe in the Holy Spirit;
the holy catholic church;
the communion of saints;
the forgiveness of sins;
the resurrection of the body,
and the life everlasting. Amen.

9   The Prayers

Lord, have mercy on us.
   Christ, have mercy on us.
Lord, have mercy on us.

Our Father in heaven,
   hallowed be your Name,
   your kingdom come,
   your will be done
     on earth as in heaven.
Give us today our daily bread.
Forgive us our sins
   as we forgive those who sin against us.
Lead us not into temptation,
   but deliver us from evil.
For the kingdom, the power, and the glory are yours
   now and for ever. Amen.

Then is said the *Collect* of the day,
and this Morning Collect

Eternal God and Father, by whose power we are created and by whose love we are redeemed: guide and strengthen us by your Spirit, that we may give ourselves to your service, and live this day in love to one another and to you; through Jesus Christ our Lord. **Amen.**

‡10   Intercessions and Thanksgivings may be made according to local custom and need; or the General Thanksgiving and Prayer for all people (pages 35 and 36) may be used.
They may be followed by the prayer at §5 if it has not already been used there.

11   The minister says

The Lord be with you.
And also with you.
Let us praise the Lord.
Thanks be to God.
The grace of the Lord Jesus Christ, and the love of God, and
the fellowship of the Holy Spirit, be with us all evermore.
Amen.   2 Corinthians 13.14

SUNDAY EVENING

1   The minister reads this Sentence

v/ Grace, mercy, and peace,
r/ **from God our Father and Jesus Christ our Lord.**
                                                          2 Timothy 1.2

2   The Psalm 134 is said or sung

1 Come bless the Lord   all you ǀ servants · of the ǀ Lord:
   you that by night ǀ stand · in the ǀ house of · our ǀ God.
2 Lift up your hands towards the holy place ⌣
      and ǀ bless the ǀ Lord:
   may the Lord bless you from Zion
      the ǀ Lord who · made ǀ heaven · and ǀ earth.

   Gloǀry to ǀ God: Father ǀ Son and ǀ Holy ǀ Spirit;
   As in the beǀginning · so ǀ now: and for ǀ ever ǀ   Aǀmen.

‡3 A pause for self-examination, the Confession and Absolution (see
    page 44) may be used here.

4 The Psalms as appointed are said or sung, and a pause observed
    after each.

‡5 At the end of the (last) pause, there may follow
Glory to God; Father, Son, and Holy Spirit:
as in the beginning, so now, and for ever.   Amen.

or this Prayer, which may be said here or after the Intercessions at §9.

Let us pray.

Lord Christ, eternal Word and Light of the Father's glory: send your light and your truth that we may both know and proclaim your word of life, to the glory of God the Father; for you now live and reign, God for all eternity. **Amen.**

or, in Eastertide

Lord of all life, you bring us from darkness to light, from death to life, and from bondage to freedom, by the resurrection of your only begotten Son: enlighten us likewise by the splendour of your Holy Spirit, and sanctify us wholly; through the same Jesus Christ your Son our Lord. **Amen.**

6 Readings from the Bible as appointed.

A pause follows the readings.

7 The Canticle, The Song of Mary, extolling God's plan of salvation (Luke 1.46-55) is said or sung

1 My soul proclaims the | greatness · of the | Lord:
my spirit re|joices · in | God my | Saviour;

2 for he has looked with favour on his | lowly | servant:
from this day all gener|ations · will | call me | bless-ed;

†3 the Almighty has done | great things | for me:
and | holy | is his | name.

4 He has mercy on | those who | fear him:
. in | every | gener|ation.

5 He has shown the | strength · of his | arm:
he has scattered the | proud in | their con|ceit.

6 He has cast down the mighty | from their | thrones:
and has | lifted | up the | lowly.

7 He has filled the hungry with | good | things:
and the rich he has | sent a|way | empty.

8 He has come to the help of his | servant | Israel:
for he has re|membered his | promise · of | mercy,

9 the promise he | made · to our | fathers:
to Abraham | and his | children · for | ever.

Glo|ry to | God: Father | Son and | Holy | Spirit;
As in the be|ginning · so | now: and for | ever | A|men.

8   The Prayers

Lord, have mercy on us.
Christ, have mercy on us.
Lord, have mercy on us.

Our Father in heaven,
hallowed be your Name,
your kingdom come,
your will be done
on earth as in heaven.
Give us today our daily bread.
Forgive us our sins
as we forgive those who sin against us.
Lead us not into temptation,
but deliver us from evil.
For the kingdom, the power, and the glory are yours
now and for ever.   Amen.

> Then is said the Collect of the day,
> and this Evening Collect

Be present, merciful God, and protect us through the hours
of this night: that we, who are wearied by the changes and
chances of this fleeting world, may rest on your eternal
changelessness; through Jesus Christ our Lord.   **Amen.**

‡9   Intercessions and Thanksgivings may be made according to local
custom and need; or the General Thanksgiving and Prayer for all
people (pages 35 and 36) may be used. They may be followed by
the prayer at §5 if it has not already been used there.

10   The minister says

The Lord be with you.
And also with you.
Let us praise the Lord.
Thanks be to God.

To God who is able to do far more abundantly than all we
ask or think, to him be glory in the Church and in Christ Jesus
to all generations for ever and ever.   **Amen.**   Ephesians 3.21

MONDAY MORNING

1   The minister reads this Sentence

v/ Arise, shine, for your light has come.
r/ **And the glory of the Lord is risen upon us.**   Isaiah 60.1

2   Then Judith 16.13-15 is said or sung

1 I will sing a new | hymn · to my | God:
   O Lord you are great and marvellous
   you are marvellous | in your | strength * in|vincible.
2 Let the whole cre|ation | serve you:
   for you spoke and | all things | came to | be;
3 You sent out your Spirit | and it | formed them:
   no one | can re|sist your | voice.
4 Mountains and seas are | stirred · to their | depths:
   rocks melt like | wax | at your | presence;
5 But to those | who re|vere you:
   you | still | show | mercy.

   Glo|ry to | God: Father | Son and | Holy | Spirit;
   As in the be|ginning · so | now: and for | ever | A|men.

3   The *Psalms* as appointed are said or sung, and a pause observed
     after each.

‡4   At the end of the (last) pause there may follow
Glory to God; Father, Son, and Holy Spirit:
   as in the beginning, so now, and for ever.   Amen.

        or this Prayer, which may be said here or after the Intercessions
        at §9.

Let us pray.
Lord our God, we pray you to drive away the darkness of our hearts; that
we and all men may know you, the one eternal light and the one true God,
blessed for evermore.   **Amen.**

52

or, in Eastertide

Lord, our refuge and hope: help us to consecrate ourselves untiringly to your service with a deep love for you and for our brothers, until the day comes when we shall see the vision of your face in the kingdom of Jesus Christ your Son our Lord. **Amen.**

5   Readings from the Bible as appointed.

A pause follows the readings.

6   The Canticle Te Deum is said or sung

1   We praise | you O | God:
    we acknowledge | you to | be the | Lord.

2   All creation | worships | you:
    the | Father | ever|lasting.

3   To you all angels | cry a|loud:
    with | all the | powers · of | heaven,

4   Cherubim and | Sera|phim:
    ever | sing in | endless | praise,

5   Holy holy holy   Lord God of | power and | might:
    heaven and | earth are | full of · your | glory.

6   The glorious company of a|postles | praise you:
    the goodly | fellowship · of | prophets | praise you.

7   The noble army of | martyrs | praise you:
    through all the world your | holy | church ac|claims you,

8   Father of | majesty · un|bounded:
,   your true and only Son
        and the Holy | Spirit | advocate · and | guide.

9   You Lord Christ are the | King of | glory:
    the e|ternal | Son of the | Father.

10 When you became man to | set us | free:
    you did not dis|dain the | virgin's womb.

11 When you overcame the | sting of | death:
    you opened the kingdom of | heaven to | all be|lievers.

12 You are seated at God's right | hand in | glory:
    we believe that you will | come to | be our | judge.

53

13 Come then Lord and | help your | people:
    bought with the | price of | your own | blood;
14 and bring us | with your | saints:
    to | glory | ever|lasting.

> A longer form of this canticle is to be found on page 24.

‡7   The Apostles' Creed (see page 47) may be said.

8   The Prayers

Lord, have mercy on us.
Christ, have mercy on us.
Lord, have mercy on us.

> Then are said the Lord's Prayer,
> the Collect of the day,
> and this Morning Collect

Eternal God and Father, by whose power we are created and
by whose love we are redeemed: guide and strengthen us by
your Spirit, that we may give ourselves to your service, and
live this day in love to one another and to you; through Jesus
Christ our Lord.   **Amen.**

‡9   Intercessions and Thanksgivings may be made according to the
     local custom and need; or the prayers on page 57 below may be
     used. They may be followed by the prayer at §4 if it has not already
     been used there.

10   The minister says

The Lord be with you.
And also with you
Let us praise the Lord.
Thanks be to God.
May the God of hope fill us with all joy and peace in be-
lieving, so that by the power of the Holy Spirit we may
abound in hope.   **Amen.**   Romans 15.13

MONDAY EVENING

1   The minister reads this Sentence

v/ God's love has been poured into our hearts
r/ **through the Holy Spirit who has been given to us.**

Romans 5.5

2   Then Psalm 93 is said or sung

1 The Lord is King * and has put on | robes of | glory:
    the Lord has put on his glory
      he has | girded · him|self with | strength.

2 He has made the | world so | firm:
    that it | cannot | be | moved.

3 Your throne is es|tablished · from of | old:
    you | are from | ever|lasting.

4 The floods have lifted up O Lord
    the floods have lifted | up their | voice:
    the | floods lift | up their | pounding.

5 But mightier than the sound of many waters
    than the mighty waters or the | breakers · of the | sea:
    the | Lord on | high is | mighty.

6 Your decrees are | very | sure:
    and holiness O Lord a|dorns your | house for | ever.

    Glo|ry to | God: Father | Son and | Holy | Spirit;
    As in the be|ginning · so | now: and for | ever | A|men.

‡3   A pause for self-examination, the Confession, and Absolution (see
     page 44) may be used here.

4   The Psalms as appointed are said or sung, and a pause observed
    after each.

‡5   At the end of the (last) pause, there may follow
Glory to God; Father, Son, and Holy Spirit:
  as in the beginning, so now, and for ever. Amen.

or this Prayer, which may be said here or after the Intercessions
at §9.

Let us pray.

Lord our God, receive the prayer and praise we offer you as our evening
sacrifice; make us to be a light for all the world, delivered by your goodness
from all the works of darkness; through Jesus Christ your Son our Lord.
   Amen.

or, in Eastertide

Lord of life, we pray that by the power of your resurrection you will deliver
us from all selfishness and bring us to the fulness of your joy; for you live
and reign with the Father and the Holy Spirit, now and for ever.   **Amen.**

6   Readings from the Bible as appointed.
    A pause follows the readings.

7   The Canticle, the Song of Mary, extolling God's plan of salvation
    (Luke 1.46-55) is said or sung

1   My soul proclaims the | greatness · of the | Lord:
    my spirit re|joices in | God my | Saviour;

2   for he has looked with favour on his | lowly | servant:
    from this day all gener|ations · will | call me | bless-ed;

3   the Almighty has done | great things | for me:
    and | holy | is his | name.

4   He has mercy on | those who | fear him:
    in | every | gener|ation.

5   He has shown the | strength · of his | arm:
    he has scattered the | proud in | their con|ceit.

6   He has cast down the mighty | from their | thrones:
    and has | lifted | up the | lowly.

7   He has filled the hungry with | good | things:
    and the rich he has | sent a|way | empty.

8   He has come to the help of his | servant | Israel:
    for he has re|membered his | promise · of | mercy.

9   the promise he | made · to our | fathers:
    to Abraham | and his | children · for | ever.

Glo|ry to | God: Father | Son and | Holy | Spirit;
As in the be|ginning · so | now: and for | ever | A|men.

8   The Prayers

Lord, have mercy on us.
Christ, have mercy on us.
Lord, have mercy on us.

> Then are said the Lord's Prayer,
> the Collect of the day,
> and this Evening Collect

Lighten our darkness, Lord, we pray: and in your great
mercy defend us from all perils and dangers of this night;
for the love of your only Son our Saviour Jesus Christ.
Amen.

‡9   Intercessions and Thanksgivings may be made according to local
      custom and need; or those below may be used.
      They may be followed by the prayer at §5 if it has not already been
      used there.

10   The minister says

The Lord be with you.
And also with you.
Let us praise the Lord.
Thanks be to God.

May the God of peace himself sanctify us wholly and may
our spirit, soul, and body be kept sound and blameless at the
coming of our Lord Jesus Christ.   **Amen.**

1 Thessalonians 5.23

INTERCESSIONS AND THANKSGIVINGS

Almighty God,
maker of all things and Father of us all,
you have shown us in Christ the purpose of your creation
and called us to responsible service in the world:

We give thanks

for the order of created things
for the resources of the earth
for the gift of human life . . .
for your continuing work of creation
for man's share in your creative purpose
for your gifts of creative vision and inventive skill
for your faithfulness to man in patience and love
for every human response of obedience and humble achievement . . .

We pray for your world

all nations . . .
our own country . . .
those in authority . . .
the peace of the world . . .
racial harmony . . .
and the reconciliation of all who are at enmity . . .

May we delight in your purpose,
and work to bring all things to their true end;
through Jesus Christ our Lord.   **Amen.**

> A selection should be made from the topics listed, which may be
> supplemented at need.

TUESDAY MORNING

1   The minister reads this Sentence

v/ We will proclaim the name of the Lord:
r/ **ascribe greatness to our God.**   Deuteronomy 32.3

2   Then Psalm 96.1-6 is said or sung

1   O sing to the Lord a | new | song:
  sing to the | Lord | all the | earth.
2   Sing to the Lord and bless his | holy | name:
  proclaim the good news of his sal|vation · from | day ‿
    to | day.

3 Declare his glory a|mong the | nations:
   and his | wonders · a|mong all | peoples.

4 For great is the Lord and | greatly · to be | praised:
   he is more to be | feared than | all | gods.

5 As for all the gods of the nations | they are · mere |
      idols:
   it is the | Lord who | made the | heavens.

6 Majesty and | glory · are be|fore him:
   beauty and | power are | in his | sanctuary.

   Glo|ry to | God: Father | Son and | Holy | Spirit;
   As in the be|ginning · so | now: and for | ever | A|men.

3 The Psalms as appointed are said or sung, and a pause observed
   after each.

‡4 At the end of the (last) pause, there may follow
Glory to God; Father, Son, and Holy Spirit:
as in the beginning, so now, and for ever.   Amen.

      or this Prayer, which may be said here or after the Intercessions
      at §9.
Let us pray.
Lord God, we would love you with our whole heart: increase in us the gifts
of your Spirit and strengthen us all to follow our victorious King, Jesus
Christ, your Son our Lord.   **Amen.**

      or, in Eastertide
Creator Lord, who reconciled us to yourself by the death and resurrection
of your Son, and made with us an eternal covenant; grant that we may show
in our lives what we profess with our lips, to your glory; through Jesus Christ
our Lord.   **Amen.**

5 Readings from the Bible as appointed.

   A pause follows the readings.

6 The Canticle, A Song of Creation (Song of the Three Young Men
   35,60-65), is said or sung

1 Bless the Lord all cre|ated | things:
   sing his | praise · and ex|alt him · for | ever.

2 Bless the Lord all | men · on the | earth:
   sing his | praise · and ex|alt him · for | ever.

59

3 O people of God | bless the | Lord:
   bless the | Lord you | priests · of the | Lord;
4 bless the Lord you | servants · of the | Lord:
   sing his | praise · and ex|alt him · for · ever.
5 Bless the Lord all men of | upright | spirit:
   bless the Lord ⌣
      you that are | holy · and | humble · in | heart.
6 Bless the Father the Son and the | Holy | Spirit:
   sing his | praise · and ex|alt him · for | ever.

> A longer form of this Canticle is to be found on page 61.

‡7 The Apostles' Creed (see page 47) may be said.

8 The Prayers

Lord, have mercy on us.
  Christ, have mercy on us.
Lord, have mercy on us.

> Then are said the Lord's Prayer,
> the Collect of the day,
> and this Morning Collect

Eternal God and Father, by whose power we are created and by whose love we are redeemed: guide and strengthen us by your Spirit that we may give ourselves to your service and live this day in love to one another and to you; through Jesus Christ our Lord. **Amen.**

‡9 Intercessions and Thanksgivings may be made according to local custom and need; or the prayers on page 65 may be used. They may be followed by the prayer at §4 if it has not already been used there.

10 The minister says

The Lord be with you.
  And also with you.
Let us praise the Lord.
  Thanks be to God.

May the Lord bless us and keep us; the Lord make his face to shine upon us, and be gracious to us; the Lord lift up his countenance upon us, and give us peace. **Amen.**

Numbers 6.24-26

An alternative form of the Canticle, A Song of Creation (Song of the Three Young Men, 35-65)

1 Bless the Lord all cre|ated | things:
   sing his | praise·and ex|alt him·for | ever.

2 Bless the | Lord you | heavens:
   sing his | praise·and ex|alt him·for | ever.

3 Bless the Lord you | angels·of the | Lord:
   bless the | Lord all | you his | hosts;

4 bless the Lord you waters a|bove the | heavens:
   sing his | praise·and ex|alt him·for | ever.

5 Bless the Lord | sun and | moon:
   bless the | Lord you | powers of | heaven;

6 bless the Lord all | rain and | dew:
   sing his | praise·and ex|alt him·for | ever.

7 Bless the Lord all | winds that | blow:
   bless the Lord you | fire and | heat;

8 bless the Lord scorching wind and | bitter | cold:
   sing his | praise·and ex|alt him·for | ever.

9 Bless the Lord dews and | falling | snows:
   bless the | Lord you | nights and | days;

10 bless the Lord | light and | darkness:
   sing his | praise·and ex|alt him·for | ever.

11 Bless the Lord | frost and | cold:
   bless the | Lord you | ice and | snow;

12 bless the Lord | lightnings·and | clouds:
   sing his | praise·and ex|alt him·for | ever.

13 O let the earth | bless the | Lord:
   bless the | Lord you | mountains·and | hills;

14 bless the Lord all that | grows·in the | ground:
   sing his | praise·and ex|alt him·for | ever.

15 Bless the | Lord you · springs:
   bless the | Lord you | seas and | rivers;
16 bless the Lord you whales and all that | swim · in ⌣
      the | waters:
   sing his | praise · and ex|alt him · for | ever.
17 Bless the Lord all | birds · of the | air:
   bless the | Lord you | beasts and | cattle;
18 bless the Lord all | men · on the | earth:
   sing his | praise · and ex|alt him · for | ever.
19 O people of God | bless the | Lord:
   bless the | Lord you | priests · of the | Lord;
20 bless the Lord you | servants · of the | Lord:
   sing his | praise · and ex|alt him · for | ever.
21 Bless the Lord all men of | upright | spirit:
   bless the Lord ⌣
      you that are | holy · and | humble · in | heart;
22 Bless the Lord Azarias Ana|nias · and | Misael:
   sing his | praise · and ex|alt him · for | ever.
†23 Bless the Father the Son and the | Holy | Spirit:
   sing his | praise · and ex|alt him · for | ever.

TUESDAY EVENING

   1   The minister reads this Sentence

v/ Sing to the Lord, sing praise to him;
r/ **tell all the wonderful things he has done.**   Psalm 105.2

   2   Then Psalm 96.7-13 is said or sung

7 Render to the Lord you families | of the | nations:
   render to the | Lord | glory · and | might.
8 Render to the Lord the honour | due · to his | name:
   bring offerings and | come in|to his | courts.
9 O worship the Lord in the beauty | of his | holiness:
   let the whole earth | stand in | awe of | him.

10 Say among the nations that the | Lord is | king:
 he has made the world so firm that it can never be ⌣
  moved
   and he shall | judge the | peoples · with | equity.

11 Let the heavens rejoice   and let the | earth be | glad:
  let the sea | roar and | all that | fills it;

12 Let the fields rejoice and | every·thing | in them:
  then shall all the trees of the wood ⌣
   shout with | joy be|fore the | Lord;

†13 For he comes   he comes to | judge the | earth:
  he shall judge the world with righteousness
   and the | peoples | with his | truth.

Glo|ry to | God: Father | Son and | Holy | Spirit;
As in the be|ginning · so | now: and for | ever | A|men.

‡3   A pause for self-examination, the Confession, and Absolution (see
   page 44) may be used here.

4   The Psalms as appointed are said or sung, and a pause is observed
   after each.

‡5   At the end of the (last) pause, there may follow
Glory to God; Father, Son, and Holy Spirit:
as in the beginning, so now, and for ever.   Amen.

    or this Prayer, which may be said here or after the Intercessions
    at §9.
Let us pray.
God our Father, you sent Jesus the Saviour into the world of sin, and
delivered him up to death for us: kindle in our hearts the same love with
which Jesus the Lord loved his own to the end; for he now lives and reigns
with you and the Holy Spirit, God, now and for ever.   **Amen.**

    or, in Eastertide
Lord God, through your beloved Son you reconciled all things to yourself,
making peace by the blood of his cross: fill us and those for whom we pray
with your peace and joy; through Jesus Christ our Lord.   **Amen.**

6   Readings from the Bible as appointed.
    A pause follows the readings.

7   The Canticle, The Song of the Three Young Men (28-34), is said
or sung

1 **Bless the Lord | God of·our | fathers:**
bless his | holy·and | glori·ous | name;

2 **bless him in his holy and | glori·ous | temple:**
sing his | praise·and ex|alt him·for | ever.

3 **Bless him who be|holds the | depths:**
bless him who | sits be|tween the | cherubim;

4 **bless him on the | throne of·his | kingdom:**
sing his | praise·and ex|alt him·for | ever.

5 **Bless him in the | heights of | heaven:**
sing his | praise·and ex|alt him·for | ever.

6 **Bless the Father the Son and the | Holy | Spirit:**
sing his | praise·and ex|alt him·for | ever.

8   The Prayers

Lord, have mercy on us.
Christ, have mercy on us.
Lord, have mercy on us.

> Then are said the Lord's Prayer,
> the Collect of the day,
> and this Evening Collect

Be present, merciful God, and protect us through the hours
of this night: that we, who are wearied by the changes and
chances of this fleeting world, may rest on your eternal
changelessness; through Jesus Christ our Lord.   **Amen.**

‡9   Intercessions and Thanksgivings may be made according to local
custom and need; or those on page 65 may be used.
They may be followed by the prayer at §5 if it has not already been
said there.

10   The minister says

The Lord be with you.
And also with you.
Let us praise the Lord.
Thanks be to God.

May the Lord of peace himself give us peace at all times and in all ways. **Amen.**

2 Thessalonians 3.16

INTERCESSIONS AND THANKSGIVINGS

God our Father,
you gave your Son Jesus Christ
to share our common life,
to grow in wisdom,
to work with his hands,
and to make known the ways of your kingdom:

We give thanks

for his revelation of yourself
for his care and acceptance of people
for his joy in obedience . . .
for the value he gave to human work
for the strength he promised us in serving others
for the call to follow in his way . . .
for all opportunities of work and leisure
for all the truth we have learned
for all the discoveries man has made . . .

We pray for our human society

those who work . . .
the unemployed . . .
those who teach and those who learn . . .
research workers . . .

those who work in the press, radio, and television . . .
those who maintain the life of our community . . .

Give us reverence for the truth,
and wisdom to use the knowledge you give us
to the glory of your Name
and the benefit of mankind
through Jesus Christ our Lord. **Amen.**

A selection should be made from the topics listed, which may be supplemented at need.

65

WEDNESDAY MORNING

1   The minister reads this Sentence

v/ Rejoice always; pray without ceasing;
r/ **in everything give thanks; for this is the will of God in
Christ Jesus.**   1 Thessalonians 5.16-18

2   Then Tobit 13.1-4,6 is said or sung

1   Blessed is the God who | lives for | ever:
    and | blessed | is his | kingdom.

2   For he afflicts and | he shows | mercy:
    he leads down to Hades and brings up again
        and there is no one who | can es|cape his | hand.

3   Acknowledge him before the nations O | sons of | Israel:
    for he has | scattered | us a|mong them.

4   Make his | greatness | known there:
    and exalt him in the | presence · of | all the | living;

5   because he is our | Lord and | God:
    he | is our | Father · for | ever.

6   If you turn to him with all your heart‿
        and with | all your | soul:
    to | do · what is | true be|fore him,

7   then he will | turn to | you:
    and will not | hide his | face | from you.

8   But see what | he will | do with you:
    give thanks to | him with | your full | voice.

9   Praise the | Lord of | righteousness:
    and exalt the | King · of the | ages · A|men.

3   The Psalms as appointed are said or sung, and a pause observed
    after each.

‡4   At the end of the (last) pause, there may follow
Glory to God; Father, Son, and Holy Spirit:
as in the beginning, so now, and for ever.   Amen.

66

or this Prayer, which may be said here or after the Intercessions at §9.

Let us pray.

God our Father, we consecrate this day to your service; may all our thoughts, words, and actions be well-pleasing to you and serve the good of our brothers and sisters; through Jesus Christ our Lord. **Amen.**

or, in Eastertide

Lord God, who delivered us from the powers of darkness and brought us into the kingdom of your beloved Son: strengthen us to live in this world without belonging to it; through Jesus Christ our Lord. **Amen.**

5 Readings from the Bible as appointed.

A pause follows the readings.

6 The Canticle, The Song of Zechariah at the naming of John the Baptist (Luke 1.68-79), is said or sung

1 Blessed be the Lord the | God of | Israel:
for he has come to his | people · and | set them | free.

2 He has raised up for us a | mighty | saviour:
born of the | house · of his | servant | David.

3 Through his holy prophets he | promised · of | old:
that he would save us from our enemies
from the | hands of | all that | hate us.

4 He promised to show | mercy · to our | fathers:
and to re|member · his | holy | covenant.

5 This was the oath he swore to our | father | Abraham:
to set us | free · from the | hands of · our | enemies,

6 free to worship him with|out | fear:
holy and righteous⌣
in his sight | all the | days of · our | life.

7 And you my child shall be called the prophet of⌣
the | Most | High:
for you will go before the | Lord · to pre|pare his | way,

8 to give his people knowledge | of sal|vation:
by the for|giveness · of | all their | sins.

9 In the tender compassion | of our | God:
the dawn from on | high shall | break up|on us,

67

10 to shine upon those who dwell in darkness and
the | shadow · of | death:
and to guide our feet | into · the | way of | peace.
Glo|ry to | God: Father | Son and | Holy | Spirit;
As in the be|ginning · so | now: and for | ever | A|men

‡7   The Apostles' Creed (see page 47) may be said.

8   The Prayers

Lord, have mercy on us.
Christ, have mercy on us.
Lord, have mercy on us.

       Then are said the Lord's Prayer,
       the Collect of the day,
       and this Morning Collect

Eternal God and Father, by whose power we are created and
by whose love we are redeemed: guide and strengthen us by
your Spirit, that we may give ourselves to your service, and
live this day in love to one another and to you; through Jesus
Christ our Lord.   **Amen.**

‡9   Intercessions and Thanksgivings may be made according to local
custom and need; or the prayers on page 72 may be used.
They may be followed by the prayer at §4 if it has not already been
used there.

10   The minister says

The Lord be with you.
And also with you.
Let us praise the Lord.
Thanks be to God.

May the God of steadfastness and encouragement grant us
to live in such harmony with one another in accord with
Christ Jesus, that we may with one voice glorify our God and
Father.   **Amen.**   Romans 15.5-6

WEDNESDAY EVENING

1   The minister reads this Sentence

v/   Seek the Lord while he may be found;
r/   **call upon him while he is near.**   Isaiah 55.6

2   Then Psalm 67 is said or sung

1   Let God be gracious to | us and | bless us:
   and make his | face | shine up|on us,

2   That your ways may be | known on | earth:
   your liberating | power · a|mong all | nations.

3   Let the peoples | praise you · O | God:
   let | all the | peoples | praise you.

4   Let the nations be | glad and | sing:
   for you judge the peoples with integrity
     and govern the | nations · up|on | earth.

5   Let the peoples | praise you · O | God:
   let | all the | peoples | praise you.

6   Then the earth will | yield its | fruitfulness:
   and | God our | God will | bless us.

†7   God | shall | bless us:
   and all the | ends · of the | earth will | fear him.

   Glo|ry to | God: Father | Son and | Holy | Spirit;
   As in the be|ginning · so | now: and for | ever | A|men.

‡3   A pause for self-examination, the Confession, and Absolution (see
   page 44) may be used here.

4   The Psalms as appointed are said or sung, and a pause is observed
   after each.

‡5   At the end of the (last) pause there may follow

Glory to God; Father, Son, and Holy Spirit:
   as in the beginning, so now, and for ever.   Amen.

or this Prayer, which may be said here or after the Intercessions at §9.

Let us pray.

Creator Lord, you have driven away the darkness of ignorance by the light of your Word: increase our faith and understanding, and grant that no temptation may stifle the love kindled in us by your Holy Spirit's power; hear us, through Jesus Christ your Son our Lord.   **Amen.**

or, in Eastertide

Lord, who conquered death by the cross, changed your people's sorrow into joy, and gave your apostles commandment to proclaim your resurrection: grant that in the power of the Holy Spirit everyone may come to know the benefits won by that death and resurrection, to the glory of God the Father.   **Amen.**

6   Readings from the Bible as appointed.
     A pause follows the readings.

7   The Canticle, the Hymn to the Word (John 1.1-5,10-14,16), is said or sung.

1 In the beginning | was the | Word:
  and the | Word | was with | God,

2 and the | Word was | God:
  he was | in the · be|ginning · with | God.

3 All things were | made through | him:
  and without him ‿
      was not anything | made that | was| made.

4 In | him was | life:
  and the | life · was the | light of | men.

5 The light shines | in the | darkness:
  and the darkness | has not | over|come it.

6 He was | in the | world:
  and the world was made through him
      yet the | world |knew him | not.

7 He came to his | own | home:
  and his own | people · re|ceived him | not.

8 But to all who received him who be|lieved on · his| name
  he has given power to be|come | children · of | God;

9 who were born not of blood
      nor of the | will of · the | flesh:
  nor of the will of | man | but of | God.

10 And the | Word · became | flesh:
    and dwelt among us | full of | grace and | truth;
11 we have be|held his | glory:
    glory as of the | only | Son · from the | Father.
12 And from his fulness have we | all re|ceived:
    and | grace up|on | grace.

    Glo|ry to | God: Father | Son and | Holy | Spirit;
    As in the be|ginning · so | now: and for | ever | A|men.

> Or The Song of Simeon (page 30) may be used.

8   The Prayers

Lord, have mercy on us.
Christ, have mercy on us.
Lord, have mercy on us.

> Then are said the Lord's Prayer,
> the Collect of the day,
> and this Evening Collect

Lighten our darkness, Lord, we pray: and in your great
mercy defend us from all perils and dangers of this night;
for the love of your only Son our Saviour Jesus Christ.
Amen.

‡9   Intercessions and Thanksgivings may be made according to local
     custom and need; or those on page 72 may be used.
     They may be followed by the prayer at §5 if it has not already been
     said there.

10   The minister says

The Lord be with you.
And also with you.
Let us praise the Lord.
Thanks be to God.

May our Lord Jesus Christ himself, and God our Father,
comfort our hearts and establish them in every good work
and word.   **Amen.**   2 Thessalonians 2.16-17

INTERCESSIONS AND THANKSGIVINGS

Holy Father,
you have reconciled us to yourself in Christ;
and by your Holy Spirit you enable us to be your children:

We give thanks

> for Christ your obedient son
> for his bearing of the sin of the world in his own body on the
> cross
> for his victory over evil and suffering and death . . .
> for the joy and wonder of human love and friendship
> for the lives to which our own are bound
> for the gift of peace with you and with one another . . .
> for the communities in whose life we share
> for all human relationships in which reconciliation is experienced
> . . .

We pray for our families and friends

> home and family life . . .
> children who have no home . . .
> friends and relations . . .
> neighbours . . .
> those we meet in our daily life and work . . .
> those from whom we are estranged . . .

Help us to share in the obedience of your Son,
that we may love and serve one another in your peace;
through Jesus Christ our Lord,
who in the unity of the Holy Spirit,
is one with you for ever.   **Amen.**

> A selection should be made from the topics listed, which may be
> supplemented at need.

72

THURSDAY MORNING

1 The minister reads this Sentence

v/ To him who sits upon the throne and to the Lamb
r/ **be blessing and honour and glory and might for ever
and ever.** Revelation 5.13

2 Then Ephesians 1.3-6 is said or sung

1 Let us give thanks to the God
⠀⠀and Father of our Lord | Jesus | Christ:
⠀⠀for he has blessed us in our union with Christ
⠀⠀⠀⠀by giving us every spiritual | gift · in the | heavenly | world.
2 Before the | world was | made:
⠀⠀God had already chosen us | to be | his in | Christ,
3 so that | we should · be | holy:
⠀⠀and with|out | fault be|fore him.
4 Be|cause · of his | love:
⠀⠀God had already de|cided · that | through Christ | Jesus
5 he would bring us to him|self as | sons:
⠀⠀this was his | pleasure | and his | purpose.
6 Let us praise God for his | glori·ous | grace:
⠀⠀for the free gift he gave | us in | his dear | Son.
⠀⠀Glo|ry to | God:⠀⠀Father | Son and | Holy | Spirit;
⠀⠀As in the be|ginning · so | now:⠀⠀and for | ever |⠀A|men.

3 The Psalms as appointed are said or sung, and a pause observed
⠀⠀after each.

‡4 At the end of the (last) pause, there may follow

Glory to God; Father, Son, and Holy Spirit:
as in the beginning, so now, and for ever.⠀Amen.

⠀⠀⠀⠀or the Prayer which follows, which may be said here or after the
⠀⠀⠀⠀Intercessions at §9.

Let us pray.
Lord God, by your Holy Spirit you enlighten the darkness of ignorance and sin: grant that his light may shine in our hearts and bind us wholly to your service; through Jesus Christ our Lord. **Amen.**

  or, in Eastertide

Lord God, who wonderfully created us and even more wonderfully restored our humanity: strengthen us by your Holy Spirit to triumph over suffering and death, and grant us eternal joy; through Jesus Christ our Lord. **Amen.**

5 Readings from the Bible as appointed.
  A pause follows the readings.

6 The following Canticle, A Song of Isaiah (12.2-6), is said or sung.

1 'Behold God is | my sal|vation:
  I will trust and | will not | be af|raid;
2 for the Lord God is my | strength · and my | song:
  and | he has · be|come my · sal|vation.'
3 With joy you will draw water from the | waters of ·
      sal|vation:
  and | you will | say · in that | day,
4 'Give thanks to the Lord * call up|on his | name:
  make known his deeds among the nations
      proclaim that his | name | is ex|alted.
5 Sing praises to the Lord for he has | done | gloriously:
  let this be | known in | all the | earth.
6 Shout and sing for joy O inhabitants | of Jer|usalem:
  for great in your midst is the | Holy | One of | Israel.'

  Glo|ry to | God: Father | Son and | Holy | Spirit;
  As in the be|ginning · so | now: and for | ever | A|men

‡7 The Apostles' Creed (see page 47) may be said.

8 The Prayers
Lord, have mercy on us.
  Christ, have mercy on us.
Lord, have mercy on us.

Then are said the Lord's Prayer,
the Collect of the day,
and this Morning Collect

Eternal God and Father, by whose power we are created and by whose love we are redeemed: guide and strengthen us by your Spirit, that we may give ourselves to your service, and live this day in love to one another and to you; through Jesus Christ our Lord. **Amen.**

‡9   Intercessions and Thanksgivings may be made according to local custom and need; or the prayers on page 78 may be used.
They may be followed by the prayer at §4 if it has not already been used there.

10   The minister says

The Lord be with you.
And also with you.
Let us praise the Lord.
Thanks be to God.

May the God of peace equip us with everything good so that we may do his will; and may he work in us that which is pleasing in his sight; through Jesus Christ, to whom be glory for ever. **Amen.**   see Hebrews 13.20,21

THURSDAY EVENING

1   The minister reads this Sentence

v/ **The Lord our God the Almighty reigns.**
r/ **Let us rejoice and exult and give him the glory.**
                 Revelation 19.6-7

2   Then Psalm 100 is said or sung

1 O shout to the Lord in triumph | all the | earth:
serve the Lord with gladness
and come before his | face with | songs of | joy.

2 Know that the Lord | he is | God:
  it is he who has made us and we are his
    we are his | people · and the | sheep of · his | pasture.
3 Come into his gates with thanksgiving
    and into his | courts with | praise:
  give thanks to him and | bless his | holy | name.
4 For the Lord is good * his loving mercy | is for | ever:
  his faithfulness through|out all | gener|ations.

  Glo|ry to | God: Fa†her | Son and | Holy | Spirit;
  As in the be|ginning · so | now: and for | ever | A|men.

  ‡3   A pause for self-examination, the Confession, and Absolution (see
        page 44) may be used here.

  4   The Psalms as appointed are said or sung, and a pause is observed
        after each.

  ‡5   At the end of the (last) pause, there may follow

Glory to God; Father, Son, and Holy Spirit:
as in the beginning, so now, and for ever.   Amen.

        or this Prayer, which may be said here or after the Intercessions
        at §9.

Let us pray.
Lord God, we thank you for all your gifts to us: grant us to accept both
pain and joy in faith and hope, and never to fail in love to you and to our
fellow-men; through Jesus Christ your Son our Lord.   **Amen.**

        or, in Eastertide

Holy Spirit, Lord of all life, comfort us and give us peace when we call to
you; turn the anxiety of sin into the joy of forgiveness, and bring every one
to acknowledge Jesus Christ as Lord.   **Amen.**

  6   Readings from the Bible as appointed.

        A pause follows the readings.

  7   The Canticle. A Song of Christ's Glory (Philippians 2.6-11) is said
        or sung

1 Christ Jesus was in the | form of | God:
  but he did not | cling · to e|quality · with | God.
2 He emptied himself * taking the | form of · a | servant:
  and was | born · in the | likeness of | men;

3 and being found in human form ⌣
    he | humbled · him|self:
  and became obedient unto death | even | death · on ⌣
    a | cross.

4 Therefore God has | highly · ex|alted him:
  and bestowed on him the | Name a · bove | every | name,

5 that at the name of Jesus every | knee should | bow:
  in heaven and on | earth and | under · the | earth;

6 and every tongue confess that Jesus | Christ is | Lord:
  to the | glory · of | God the | Father.

Glo|ry to | God: Father | Son and | Holy | Spirit;
As in the be|ginning · so | now: and for | ever | A|men.

8 The Prayers

Lord, have mercy on us.
Christ, have mercy on us.
Lord, have mercy on us.

        Then are said the Lord's Prayer,
        the Collect of the day,
        and this Evening Collect

Be present, merciful God, and protect us through the hours of this night: that we who are wearied by the changes and chances of this fleeting world, may rest on your eternal changelessness; through Jesus Christ our Lord. **Amen.**

‡9 Intercessions and Thanksgivings may be made according to local custom and need; or those on page 78 may be used.
    They may be followed by the prayer at §5 if it has not already been said there.

10 The minister says

The Lord be with you.
And also with you.
Let us praise the Lord.
Thanks be to God.

The grace of our Lord Jesus Christ, and the love of God, and the fellowship of the Holy Spirit, be with us all evermore. **Amen.**

2 Corinthians 13.14

INTERCESSIONS AND THANKSGIVINGS

Eternal God,
you raised Jesus our Lord from death and gave him glory,
and through him you called your church into being
that your people might know you,
and that they might make your Name known:

We give thanks

> for the gospel committed to your church for the whole world
> for the continuing presence and power of the Holy Spirit
> for the ministry of word, sacrament, and prayer . . .
> for the mission you have called us to share
> for the call to unity and its fruit in common action
> for the faithful witness of those who follow our Lord . . .
> for all works of christian compassion
> for every service which proclaims your love . . .

We pray for the church

> universal and local . . .
> the ministries of the church . . .
> the mission of the church . . .
> the renewal of the church . . .
> our fellow-christians in this place . . .

In peace and unity may your people offer you the unfailing
    sacrifice of praise,
that the whole world may know your rule,
and all nations know your salvation and your glory;
through Jesus Christ our Lord.   Amen.

> A selection should be made from the topics listed, which may be
> supplemented at need.

FRIDAY MORNING

1   The minister reads this Sentence

v/ Through Christ let us offer up a sacrifice of praise to
      God,
r/ **the fruit of lips that acknowledge his Name.**

Hebrews 13.15

2   Then Hebrews 10.19-22 is said or sung

1   We have com|plete | freedom:
      to go into the most holy place by | means of · the | death ⌣
          of | Jesus.
2   He opened for us a new way   a | living | way:
      through the curtain | through his | own | body.
3   Since we have a great high priest⌣
          set over the | household · of | God:
      let us come near to God ⌣
          with a sincere | heart and | sure | faith,
4   with hearts that have been made clean⌣
          from a | guilty | conscience:
      and bodies | washed with | pure | water.

      Glo|ry to | God: Father | Son and | Holy | Spirit;
      As in the be|ginning · so | now: and for | ever | A|men.

3   The Psalms as appointed are said or sung, and a silence observed
      after each.

‡4   At the end of the (last) pause, there may follow
Glory to God; Father, Son, and Holy Spirit:
as in the beginning, so now, and for ever.   Amen.

          or this Prayer, which may be said here or after the Intercessions
          at §9.
Let us pray.
We pray for your Church, Lord; deliver it from all evil, perfect it in your
love, and by the power of your Holy Spirit gather us and all men into your
kingdom; through Jesus Christ your Son our Lord.   **Amen.**

or, in Eastertide

Creator Spirit, Advocate promised by our Lord Jesus: increase our faith and help us to walk in the light of your presence, to the glory of God the Father; through Jesus Christ our Lord. **Amen.**

5 Readings from the Bible as appointed.

A pause follows the readings.

6 The Canticle, Saviour of the World (author unknown) is said or sung

1 Jesus Saviour of the world
    come to us | in your | mercy:
  we look to | you to | save and | help us.

2 By your cross and your life laid down
    you set your | people | free:
  we look to | you to | save and | help us.

3 When they were ready to perish⌣
    you | saved · your dis|ciples:
  we look to | you to | come to · our | help.

4 In the greatness of your mercy⌣
    loose us | from our | chains:
  forgive the | sins of | all your | people.

5 Make yourself known as our Saviour⌣
    and | mighty · De|liverer:
  save and | help us · that | we may | praise you.

6 Come now and dwell with us | Lord Christ | Jesus:
  hear our | prayer · and be | with us | always.

7 And when you | come in · your | glory:
    make us to be one with you
    and to | share the | life of · your | kingdom.

‡7 The Apostles' Creed (see page 47) may be said.

8 The Prayers

Lord, have mercy on us.
  Christ, have mercy on us.
Lord, have mercy on us.

Then are said the Lord's Prayer,

the Collect of the day,

and this Morning Collect

Eternal God and Father, by whose power we are created and by whose love we are redeemed: guide and strengthen us by your Spirit, that we may give ourselves to your service, and live this day in love to one another and to you; through Jesus Christ our Lord. **Amen.**

‡9 Intercessions and Thanksgivings may be made according to local custom and need; or the prayers on page 84 may be used.
They may be followed by the prayer at §4 if it has not already been used there.

10 The minister says

The Lord be with you.
And also with you.
Let us praise the Lord.
Thanks be to God.

Peace be to us all, and love with faith, from God the Father and the Lord Jesus Christ. **Amen.** Ephesians 6.23

FRIDAY EVENING

1 The minister reads this Sentence

v/ Peace to those who are far off.
r/ **Peace to those who are near!** Ephesians 2.17

2 Then Ephesians 2.4-7 is said or sung

1 God who is | rich in | mercy:
out of the great | love with | which he | loved us,
2 even when we were dead | through our | trespasses:
made us a|live to|gether · with | Christ,
3 and raised us | up with | him:
and made us sit with him ⌣
in the heavenly | places | in Christ | Jesus,

4 that he might show the immeasurable riches ǀ of his ǀ ⌣
    grace:
 in kindness ǀ towards us ǀ in Christ ǀ Jesus.

 Gloǀry to ǀ God: Father ǀ Son and ǀ Holy ǀ Spirit;
 As in the beǀginning · so ǀ now: and for ǀ ever ǀ   Aǀmen

‡3 A pause for self-examination, the Confession, and Absolution (see
    page 44) may be used here.

 4 The Psalms as appointed are said or sung, and a pause observed
    after each.

‡5 At the end of the (last) pause there may follow
Glory to God; Father, Son, and Holy Spirit:
as in the beginning, so now, and for ever.   Amen.

    or this Prayer, which may be said here or after the Intercessions
    at §9.
Let us pray.
Lord, our God, our Creator, Redeemer, and Sanctifier: we ask you to
cleanse us from all hypocrisy, to unite us to our fellow men and women by
the bonds of peace and love, and to confirm us in holiness; now and for
ever.   **Amen.**

    or, in Eastertide
Saviour God, whose purpose it was from eternity to save mankind: complete
your work in the world; raise up the fallen, give new life to the weary, and
bring all things to harmony and perfection in the kingdom of your Son Jesus
Christ our Lord.   **Amen.**

 6 Readings from the Bible as appointed.
    A pause follows the readings.

 7 The Canticle, A Song to the Lamb (Revelation 4.11; 5.9b-10), is
    said or sung.

1 Glory and ǀ honour · and ǀ power:
   are yours by ǀ right O ǀ Lord our ǀ God:
2 for you creǀated ǀ all things:
   and by your ǀ will they ǀ have their ǀ being.
3 Glory and ǀ honour · and ǀ power:
   are yours by ǀ right O ǀ Lamb who ǀ was slain;

4 for by your blood you ransomed | men for | God:
  from every race and language
    from | every | people · and | nation,
5 to make them a | kingdom · of | priests:
  to stand and | serve be|fore our | God.
6 To him who sits on the throne | and · to the | Lamb:
  be praise and honour   glory and might
    for ever and | ever. | A|men.

8   The Prayers

Lord, have mercy on us.
Christ, have mercy on us.
Lord, have mercy on us.

> Then are said the Lord's Prayer,
> the Collect of the day,
> and this Evening Collect

Lighten our darkness, Lord, we pray; and in your great
mercy defend us from all perils and dangers of this night;
for the love of your only Son our Saviour Jesus Christ.
Amen.

‡9   Intercessions and Thanksgivings may be made according to local
      custom and need; or those on page 84 may be used.
      They may be followed by the prayer at §5 if it has not already been
      used there.

10   The minister says

The Lord be with you.
And also with you.
Let us praise the Lord.
Thanks be to God.

May the God of all grace, who has called us to his eternal
glory in Christ, himself restore, establish, strengthen us. To
him be the dominion for ever and ever. **Amen.**

1 Peter 5.10-11

INTERCESSIONS AND THANKSGIVINGS

Gracious Lord and Father,
you have given us in Christ à merciful Saviour
to present to you the world in all its need:

We give thanks

> for the presence of Christ in our weakness and in our strength
> for the power of Christ to transform our suffering . . .
> for all ministries of healing
> for all agencies of relief
> for everyone who sets men free from fear, pain, distress . . .
> for the assurance that your mercy knows no limit
> for the privilege of sharing your work of renewal through prayer,
>   suffering and joy . . .

We pray for all who suffer

> the hungry, refugees . . .
> prisoners, the persecuted . . .
> the workless, the homeless . . .
> those who bring sin and suffering to others . . .
> all who try to bring relief and care to those in need . . .

In darkness and in light, in trouble and in joy,
help us to trust your love,
to serve your purpose,
and to praise your holy Name;
through Jesus Christ our Lord.   Amen.

> A selection should be made from the topics listed, which may be
> supplemented at need.

SATURDAY MORNING

1   The minister reads this Sentence

v/ **God has shone in our hearts,**
r/ **to give the light of the knowledge of the glory of God**
in the face of Jesus Christ.   2 Corinthians 4.6

2   Then Psalm 150 is said or sung

1 Praise the Lord * O praise | God · in his | sanctuary:
   praise him in the | firma·ment | of his | power.

2 Praise him for his | mighty | acts:
   praise him according to | his a|bundant | goodness.

3 Praise him in the blast of the | ram's | horn:
   praise him up|on the | lute and | harp.

4 Praise him with the | timbrel · and | dances:
   praise him up|on the | strings and | pipe.

5 Praise him on the | high · sounding | cymbals:
   praise him up|on the | loud | cymbals.

6 Let everything that has breath | praise the | Lord:
   O | praise | –the | Lord!

   Glo|ry to | God: Father | Son and | Holy | Spirit;
   As in the be|ginning · so | now: and for | ever | A|men.

3   The Psalms as appointed are said or sung, and a pause observed
    after each.

‡4   At the end of the (last) pause, there may follow
Glory to God; Father, Son, and Holy Spirit:
as in the beginning, so now and for ever.   Amen.

        or this Prayer, which may be said here or after the Intercessions
        at §9.
Let us pray.
Creator God, whose praise and power are proclaimed by the whole creation:
we pray you to receive our morning prayers and to renew us in your service;
through Jesus Christ our Lord.   **Amen.**
        or, in Eastertide
Christ Jesus, triumphant King and our only hope: grant to us and to those
for whom we pray, forgiveness of our sins, deliverance from all that afflicts
us, and entrance into your eternal kingdom; that we may praise you with
the Father and the Holy Spirit now and for ever.   **Amen.**

5   Readings from the Bible as appointed.
    A pause follows the readings.

6   The Canticle, Great and Wonderful (Revelation 15.3-4), is said or
    sung

1   Great and wonderful are your deeds ⌣
     Lord | God · the Al|mighty:
  just and true are your | ways O | king · of the | nations.
2   Who shall not revere and praise your | Name O | Lord?
  for | you a|lone are | holy.
3   All nations shall come and worship | in your | presence:
  for your just | dealings · have | been re|vealed.
4   To him who sits on the throne | and · to the | Lamb:
  be praise and honour glory and might ⌣
     for ever and | ever. | A|men.

  ‡7   The Apostles' Creed (see page 47) may be said.

  8   The Prayers

Lord, have mercy on us.
Christ, have mercy on us.
Lord, have mercy on us.

        Then are said the Lord's Prayer,
        the Collect of the day,
        and this Morning Collect

Eternal God and Father, by whose power we are created and by whose love we are redeemed: guide and strengthen us by your Spirit, that we may give ourselves to your service, and live this day in love to one another and to you; through Jesus Christ our Lord.   **Amen.**

  ‡9   Intercessions and Thanksgivings may be made according to local
      custom and need; or the prayers on page 89 may be used.
      They may be followed by the prayer at §4 if it has not already been
      used there.

  10   The minister says

The Lord be with you.
And also with you.
Let us praise the Lord.
Thanks be to God.

May the peace of God which passes all understanding keep our hearts and minds in Christ Jesus.   **Amen.** Philippians 4.7

SATURDAY EVENING

1   The minister reads this Sentence

v/ Grace to you and peace
r/ **from God our Father and the Lord Jesus Christ.**

Ephesians 1.2

2   Then Psalm 23 is said or sung

1   The Lord | is my | shepherd:
    therefore | can I | lack | nothing.

2   He will make me lie down in | green | pastures:
    and | lead me · be|side still | waters.

3   He will re|fresh my | soul:
    and guide me in right pathways | for his | name's | sake.

4   Though I walk through the valley of the shadow of ⌣
        death
        I will | fear no | evil:
    for you are with me
        your | rod · and your | staff | comfort me.

5   You spread a table before me
        in the face of | those who | trouble me:
    you have anointed my head with oil | and my | cup · will ⌣
        be | full.

6   Surely your goodness and loving-kindness ⌣
        will follow me * all the | days · of my | life:
    and I shall dwell in the | house · of the | Lord for | ever.

    Glo|ry to | God: Father | Son and | Holy | Spirit;
    As in the be|ginning · so | now: and for | ever | A|men.

‡3 A pause for self-examination, the Confession, and Absolution (see
    page 44) may be used here.

4   The Psalms as appointed are said or sung, and a pause is observed
    after each.

‡5   At the end of the (last) pause there may follow

Glory to God; Father, Son, and Holy Spirit:
as in the beginning, so now, and for ever.   Amen.

        or this Prayer, which may be said here or after the Intercessions
        at §9.

Let us pray.
Lord God, grant us your peace, love, and aid: help us to love one another
in the power of the Holy Spirit, and make us one as you are one, through
Jesus Christ your Son our Lord.   **Amen.**

        or, in Eastertide
God of light and glory; we pray that the light of your glory may shine on
us and that we may be truly thankful for all your blessings; through Jesus
Christ your Son our Lord.   **Amen.**

6   Readings from the Bible as appointed.

     A pause follows the readings.

7   The Canticle, The Easter Anthems (1 Corinthians 5.7; Romans
     6.9; 1 Corinthians 15.20), or, in Lent, the Canticle Saviour of the
     World (page 80), is said or sung.

1   Christ our **Passover** has been | sacri·ficed | for us:
    so let us | cele|brate the | feast,

2   not with the old **leaven** of cor|ruption·and | wickedness:
    but with the unleavened | bread of·sin|cerity·and | truth.

3   Christ once **raised** from the dead | dies no | more:
    death has no | more do|minion | over him.

4   In **dying** he died to sin | once for | all:
    in | living·he | lives to | God.

5   See **yourselves** therefore as | dead to | sin:
    and alive to God in | Jesus | Christ our | Lord.

6   Christ has been | raised·from the | dead:
    the | firstfruits·of | those who | sleep.

7   For as by | man came | death:
    by man has come also the resur|rection | of the | dead;

8   for as in | Adam·all | die:
    even so in Christ shall | all be | made a|live.

    Glo|ry to | God: Father | Son and | Holy | Spirit;
    As in the be|ginning · so | now: and for | ever | A|me

8   The Prayers

Lord, have mercy on us.
Christ, have mercy on us.
Lord, have mercy on us.

> Then are said the Lord's Prayer,
> the Collect of the day,
> and this Evening Collect

Be present, merciful God, and protect us through the hours
of this night: that we, who are wearied by the changes
and chances of this fleeting world, may rest on your eternal
changelessness; through Jesus Christ our Lord.   **Amen.**

‡9   Intercessions and Thanksgivings may be made according to local
custom and need; or those below may be used.
They may be followed by the prayer at §5 if it has not already been
used there.

10   The minister says

The Lord be with you.
And also with you.
Let us praise the Lord.
Thanks be to God.

May the God of peace, who brought again from the dead
our Lord Jesus, equip us with everything good that we may
do his will, to whom be glory for ever.
Amen.   see Hebrews 13.20,21

INTERCESSIONS AND THANKSGIVINGS

Eternal God,
who declared in Christ Jesus
the completion of all your purposes of love;

We give thanks

for the triumphs of the gospel that herald your salvation
for the signs of renewal that declare the coming of your kingdom
for the revelation of the work of your grace in human lives . . .
for the unceasing praise of the company of heaven
for the promise to those who mourn that all tears will be wiped away
for the pledge of death destroyed and victory won . . .
for our foretaste of eternal life through baptism and the holy communion
for our hope in the Spirit
for the communion of saints
for all who rest in Christ . . .

We pray for the sick

those in pain . . .
the handicapped, the aged . . .
those who are tempted and despairing . . .
those who minister to them and care for them . . .
those who mourn . . .

May we live by faith, walk in hope, and be renewed in love,
until the whole world reflects your glory,
and you are all in all.
Even so, come Lord Jesus.
Amen.

A selection should be made from the topics listed, which may be supplemented at need.

Prayers for Various Occasions

Prayers for the Sick are to be found on pages 570ff.

1 A Prayer for Parliament

Most gracious God, ruler of all the nations,
we pray for the parliament of this State/Commonwealth
    (now assembled);
direct and prosper all its work
to the advancement of your glory,
and the safety and welfare of this country;
so that peace and happiness, truth and justice,
may be established among us;
through Jesus Christ our Lord. **Amen.**

2 A Prayer for the Spread of the Gospel

We praise you, Lord of all,
for the gifts of Christ our ascended King:
for apostles, prophets, evangelists, pastors and teachers.
Hear our prayer for all who do not know your love
and have not heard the gospel of our Saviour Jesus Christ.
Send out your light and truth
through the messengers of your word;
help us to support them by our prayers and offerings,
and hasten the coming of your kingdom;
through Jesus Christ our Lord. **Amen.**

3 A Prayer for Ordinands for use in the Ember seasons and at other
    times

Almighty God, giver of all that is good,
you have appointed various orders of ministry in your
    Church;
bless those who are to be called to the sacred ministry.
So fill them with your truth and clothe them with holiness,

91

that they may faithfully minister to the glory of your name
and to the benefit of your people.
We ask this through Jesus Christ our Lord.   **Amen.**

4   A Prayer for the Increase of the Sacred Ministry

Almighty God,
look with compassion on the world you have redeemed
by the death of your Son Jesus Christ.
Move the hearts of many
to offer themselves for the sacred ministry of your Church,
so that by their lives and labours
your light may shine in the darkness
and the coming of your kingdom be advanced;
through Jesus Christ our Lord.   **Amen.**

5   A Prayer in Time of Drought, Flood, or Bushfire

All things look to you, O Lord,
to give them their food in due season:
look in mercy on your people,
and hear our prayer for those whose lives and livelihood
are threatened by drought (or flood, or fire).
In your mercy save both man and beast.
Guide and bless the labours of your people,
that we may enjoy the fruits of the earth
and give you thanks with grateful hearts.
We ask this through our Lord Jesus Christ.   **Amen.**

6   A Prayer for the Members of the Armed Forces

Eternal God, the only source of peace;
we pray for all who serve us in the defence forces of this
     land.
Give them courage and comfort in all dangers,
and help us, we pray, to seek for all people
the freedom to serve you and each other in peace and justice.
We ask this through Jesus Christ our Lord.   **Amen.**

7   A General Prayer for Ships at Sea

Eternal Lord God,
you alone spread out the heavens and rule the raging of the
     sea;
we pray for all those who go down to the sea in ships
and follow their trade in great waters.
Grant *them* your strength and protection
as *they* face the dangers of *their* calling,
and keep *them* in the hour of special need;
for Jesus Christ's sake.   **Amen.**

§§8-11 may be used before the blessing at The Holy Communion.

8   A Prayer for God's Help

Assist us mercifully, O Lord,
in these our supplications and prayers;
and so guide your servants
towards the attainment of everlasting salvation
that, among the changes and chances of this mortal life,
we may always be defended
by your gracious and ready help;
through Jesus Christ our Lord.   **Amen.**

9   A Prayer for God's Guidance

Almighty Lord, and everlasting God,
we pray that you will direct, sanctify, and govern
our hearts and bodies in the ways of your laws
and the works of your commandments;
that through your mighty protection, here and ever,
we may be kept safe in body and soul
to give glory to your holy Name;
through our Lord and Saviour Jesus Christ.   **Amen.**

10   A Prayer after hearing Holy Scripture read

Lord,
we pray that the words we have heard today
may be grafted in our hearts

and bring forth in us the fruit of good works
to the honour and praise of your name;
through Jesus Christ our Lord.   **Amen.**

or this

Heavenly Father,
give us faith to receive your word,
understanding to know what it means,
and the will to put it into practice;
through Jesus Christ our Lord.   **Amen.**

11   A Prayer of Dedication

Teach us, O gracious Lord,
to begin our works with reverence,
to go on in obedience,
and finish them with love;
and then to wait patiently in hope,
and with cheerful countenance to look up to you,
whose promises are faithful and rewards infinite;
through Jesus Christ our Lord.   **Amen.**

12   A Prayer of Dedication which may be used at the end of Morning
or Evening Prayer

Almighty God,
we thank you for the gift of your holy word.
May it be a lantern to our feet,
a light to our paths,
and strength to our lives.
Take and use us
to love and serve all people
in the power of the Holy Spirit
and in the name of your Son
Jesus Christ our Lord.   **Amen.**

13   For Unity

God the Father of our Lord Jesus Christ,
our only Saviour, the Prince of Peace;

94

give us grace seriously to lay to heart
the great dangers we are in by our unhappy divisions.
Take away all hatred and prejudice,
and whatever else may hinder us from godly union and
concord:
that, as there is but one body, and one Spirit,
and one hope of our calling,
one Lord, one faith, one baptism,
one God and Father of us all,
so we may be all of one heart, and of one mind,
united in one holy bond of truth and peace,
of faith and charity,
and may with one mind and one mouth glorify you;
through Jesus Christ our Lord.   **Amen.**

14   During the Vacancy of a See or of a Parochial Charge

Lord God,
you are our eternal shepherd and guide.
In your mercy grant your Church in *this diocese*
a shepherd after your own heart
who will walk in your ways
and with loving care watch over your people,
that your name may be glorified;
through Jesus Christ our Lord.   **Amen.**

15   For a Synod

God our Father,
you judge your people with wisdom and rule us with love.
Give a spirit of understanding
to the synod of *this diocese*/to the General Synod of our
Church
that it may make wise decisions
that will give glory to you
and be a blessing to your people.
Grant this through our Lord Jesus Christ.   **Amen.**

16 For Schools, Universities, and other Places of Learning

Almighty Father,
who commanded us to love you with all our mind;
look with your gracious favour, we pray,
on our Universities, Colleges, and Schools.
Bless all who teach and all who learn;
grant that they may seek and love the truth,
grow in wisdom and knowledge,
and in humility of heart ever look to you,
the source of all wisdom and understanding.
We ask this through Jesus Christ our Lord.   **Amen.**

17 For Peace

God of the nations, whose kingdom rules over all,
have mercy on our broken and divided world.
Shed abroad your peace in the hearts of all men
and banish from them the spirit that makes for war;
that all races and people may learn to live
as members of one family
and in obedience to your laws;
through Jesus Christ our Lord.   **Amen.**

18 For Industrial Peace

Almighty and everlasting God,
grant that we may live and work together in brotherhood
    and peace.
Give to all a spirit of respect and trust
and an earnest desire to seek for justice and the common
    good;
through Jesus Christ our Lord.   **Amen.**

19 For Families

Almighty God, our heavenly Father,
whose Son Jesus Christ shared at Nazareth the life of an
    earthly home:

bless our homes, we pray.
Help parents to impart the knowledge of you and your
    love;
and children to respond with love and obedience.
May our homes be blessed with peace and joy;
through Jesus Christ our Lord. **Amen.**

20   For Absent Ones

Lord our God, present in every place;
we pray you to protect with your loving care
those we love and who are now away from us.
Let your fatherly hand direct them;
prosper them in your way;
grant them strength for their needs;
and inspire in them an unwavering faith in you,
that they may live always to your honour and glory;
through Jesus Christ our Lord. **Amen.**

21   For Travellers

Lord, hear our prayer for (these) your servants on their
    journey;
watch over them,
be their companion on the way,
protect them in every danger,
and grant them a greater knowledge of you
in all that they undertake;
we ask this through our Lord Jesus Christ, your Son.
    Amen.

The Litany

1 Prayer of approach to God

God the Father, creator of heaven and earth,
  have mercy on us.
God the Son, redeemer of the world,
  have mercy on us.
God the Holy Spirit, the strengthener,
  have mercy on us.
Holy, blessed, and glorious Trinity, three persons and one God,
  have mercy on us.

2 Prayers for deliverance

Lord, remember not our offences, nor the offences of our forefathers; spare us, good Lord, spare your people whom you have redeemed with your precious blood.
  Spare us, good Lord.
From all evil and mischief; from sin; from the craft and assaults of the devil; from your wrath; and from everlasting damnation,
  good Lord, deliver us.
From all spiritual blindness; from pride, vainglory, and hypocrisy; from envy, hatred, and malice; and from all uncharitableness,
  good Lord, deliver us.
From all deadly sin; and from the deceits of the world, the flesh, and the devil,
  good Lord, deliver us.
From all false doctrine, heresy, and schism; from hardness of heart, and contempt of your word and commandment,
  good Lord, deliver us.
From earthquake and tempest; from drought, fire, and flood; from civil strife and violence; from war and murder; and from dying suddenly and unprepared,
  good Lord, deliver us.

3 Prayer recalling Christ's saving work

By the mystery of your holy incarnation; by your holy birth; by your circumcision and obedience to the law; by your baptism, fasting, and temptation,
good Lord, deliver us.

By your agony and bitter grief; by your cross and passion; by your precious death and burial; by your glorious resurrection and ascension; and by the coming of the Holy Spirit,
good Lord, deliver us.

In our times of trouble; in our times of prosperity; in the hour of death, and on the day of judgment,
good Lord, deliver us.

4 Prayers of intercession

Receive now our prayers, Lord God. May it please you to rule and govern your holy church universal and lead it in the right way.
Hear us, good Lord.

for our country

Strengthen your servant Elizabeth our Queen in true worship and holiness of life; be her defender and keeper, that she may always seek your honour and glory.
Hear us, good Lord.

Bless and defend all who strive for our safety and protection, and shield them in all dangers and adversities.
Hear us, good Lord.

Grant wisdom and insight to those who govern us, and to judges and magistrates the grace to execute justice with mercy.
Hear us, good Lord.

for the church

Enlighten all bishops, priests, and deacons, with true knowledge and understanding of your word, that in their preaching and living they may declare it clearly and show its truth.
Hear us, good Lord.

99

* Bless your servants preparing to be deacons or priests; pour your grace upon them, that they may fulfil their ministry for the building up of your church and the glory of your holy name.

Hear us, good Lord.

Encourage and prosper your servants who spread the gospel in all the world, and send out labourers into the harvest.

Hear us, good Lord.

Bless and keep your people, that all may find and follow their true vocation and ministry.

Hear us, good Lord.

Give us a heart to love and reverence you, that we may diligently live according to your commandments.

Hear us, good Lord.

To all your people give growth in grace to listen to your word, to receive it gladly, and to bring forth the fruit of the Spirit.

Hear us, good Lord.

Bring into the way of truth all who have erred and are deceived.

Hear us, good Lord.

Strengthen those who stand firm in the faith; encourage the fainthearted; raise up those who fall; and finally beat down Satan under our feet.

Hear us, good Lord.

for all people

To all nations grant unity, peace and concord; and to everyone in your world give dignity, food, and shelter.

Hear us, good Lord.

---

* at ordinations

Bless your servant[s] now to be ordained to the ministry of [deacons and priests]; pour . . .

Grant us abundant harvests; strength and skill to conserve the resources of the earth; and wisdom to use them well.

Hear us, good Lord.

Enlighten with your Spirit all places of education and learning.

Hear us, good Lord.

Come to the help of all who are in danger, necessity, and trouble; protect all who travel by land, air, or water; and show your pity on all prisoners and captives.

Hear us, good Lord.

Strengthen and preserve all women who are in childbirth, and all young children; and comfort the aged and lonely.

Hear us, good Lord.

Defend and provide for the widowed and the fatherless, the refugees and the homeless, and all who are desolate and oppressed.

Hear us, good Lord.

Heal those who are sick in body or mind; and give skill and compassion to all who care for them.

Hear us, good Lord.

Forgive our enemies, persecutors, and slanderers; and turn their hearts.

Hear us, good Lord.

Grant us true repentance; forgive our sins, negligences, and ignorances; and strengthen us by your Holy Spirit to amend our lives according to your holy word.

Hear us, good Lord.

> If the service of Holy Communion follows, the Litany may end here.

5   Concluding prayers

Son of God, we ask you to hear us.

Son of God, we ask you to hear us.

Jesus, Lamb of God, you take away the sin of the world,

grant us your peace.

101

Lord, have mercy on us.
Christ, have mercy on us.
Lord, have mercy on us.

Our Father in heaven,
  hallowed be your Name,
  your kingdom come,
  your will be done
    on earth as in heaven.
Give us today our daily bread.
Forgive us our sins
  as we forgive those who sin against us.
Lead us not into temptation,
  but deliver us from evil.
For the kingdom, the power, and the glory are yours
  now and for ever.   Amen.

> The minister may here use other authorized prayers; he may ask
> the prayers of the congregation for particular persons and needs;
> he may read the collect of the day.

A prayer of Saint Chrysostom

Almighty God, you have given us grace to bring before you
with one accord our common supplications, and you promise
that when two or three are gathered together in your name
you will grant their requests; fulfil now, Lord, the desires and
petitions of your servants, as may be most expedient for
them, granting us in this world knowledge of your truth, and
in the world to come life everlasting.   **Amen.**

The grace

**The grace of our Lord Jesus Christ, and the love of God,
and the fellowship of the Holy Spirit, be with us all evermore.   Amen.**

NOTES

1   The Litany may be said or sung as a separate service; or instead of the
last part of Morning or Evening Prayer; or before The Holy Communion.
2   When The Holy Communion follows the Litany, §5 of The Litany and
the Intercession of The Holy Communion may be omitted.

PRAYER
AT THE END OF THE DAY

1   The minister says

The Lord almighty grant us a quiet night and a perfect
end. **Amen.**

‡2   When the Confession is not said at Evening Prayer, it is said
here.

It may be preceded by a pause for self-examination.

The forms provided for Evening Prayer (page 20 or page 44) may
be used, or the following

Lord Jesus, you came to call sinners to repentance,
   have mercy on us.
Lord Jesus, sent to heal those who are burdened in soul,
   have mercy on us.
Lord Jesus, now seated at the Father's right hand to intercede for us,
   have mercy on us.

3   Then the minister says

Our help is in the name of the Lord,
   who made heaven and earth.

and all say together

Glory to God; Father, Son, and Holy Spirit:
as in the beginning, so now, and for ever. Praise the Lord!

‡4   This Hymn, or another, may be sung here

1 Hail, gladdening Light, of his pure glory poured
    Who is the immortal Father, heavenly, blest,
    Holiest of Holies, Jesus Christ, our Lord.
2 Now we are come to the sun's hour of rest,
    The lights of evening round us shine,
    We hymn the Father, Son, and Holy Spirit divine.

3 Worthiest art thou at all times to be sung
   With undefiled tongue,
Son of our God, giver of life, alone!
Therefore in all the world thy glories, Lord, they own.

5   One or more of the Psalms 4, 91, and 134 is said or sung.

Psalm 4

1 Answer me when I call O | God of · my | righteousness:
   when I was hard-pressed you set me free
      be gracious to me | now and | hear my | prayer.
2 Sons of men
      how long will you turn my | glory · to my | shame:
   how long will you love what is worthless
      and | seek | after | lies?
3 Know that the Lord has shown me⌣
      his | wonder·ful | kindness:
   when I call to the | Lord | he will | hear me.
4 Tremble and | do no | sin:
   commune with your own heart up|on⌣
      your | bed · and be | still.
5 Offer the sacrifices | that are | right:
   and | put your | trust · in the | Lord.
6 There are many who say
      'Who will | show us · any | good?:
   the light of your countenance O | Lord has | gone | from us
7 Yet you have given my | heart more | gladness:
   than they have when their corn | wine and | oil in|crease.
8 In peace I will lie | down and | sleep:
   for you alone Lord | make me | dwell in | safety.

   Glo|ry to | God: Father | Son and | Holy | Spirit;
   As in the be|ginning · so | now: and for | ever | A|men

Psalm 91

1 He who dwells in the shelter of the | Most | High:
   who abides under the | shadow | of the · Al|mighty,

2 He will say to the Lord
  'You are my refuge | and my | stronghold:
  my | God in | whom I | trust.'
3 For he will deliver you from the | snare · of the | hunter:
  and | from the · des|troying | curse.
4 He will cover you with his wings
  and you will be safe | under · his | feathers:
  his faithfulness will | be your | shield · and de|fence.
5 You shall not be afraid of any | terror · by | night:
  or of the | arrow · that | flies by | day,
6 Of the pestilence that walks a|bout in | darkness:
  or the | plague · that des|troys at | noonday.
7 A thousand may fall beside you
  and ten thousand at your | right | hand:
  but | you it | shall not | touch;
8 Your own | eyes shall | see:
  and look on the re|ward | of the · un|godly.

9 The Lord him|self · is your | refuge:
  you have | made the · Most | High your | stronghold.
10 Therefore no | harm · will be|fall you:
  nor will any | scourge come | near your | tent.
11 For he will com|mand his | angels:
  to | keep you · in | all your | ways.
12 They will bear you | up · in their | hands:
  lest you dash your | foot a|gainst a | stone.
13 You will tread on the | lion · and the | adder:
  the young lion and the serpent ⌣
    you will | trample | under | foot.
14 'He has set his love upon me
    and therefore I | will de|liver him:
  I will lift him out of danger ⌣
    be|cause · he has | known my | name.
15 'When he calls upon me | I will | answer him:
  I will be with him in trouble
    I will | rescue him · and | bring him · to | honour.

16 'With long | life · I will | satisfy him:
    and | fill him · with | my sal|vation.'

Glo|ry to | God: Father | Son and | Holy | Spirit;
As in the be|ginning · so | now: and for | ever | A|men

Psalm 134

1 Come bless the Lord   all you | servants · of the | Lord:
   you that by night | stand · in the | house of · our | God.
2 Lift up your hands toward the holy place ⌣
      and | bless the | Lord:
   may the Lord bless you from Zion
      the | Lord · who made | heaven · and | earth.

Glo|ry to | God: Father | Son and | Holy | Spirit;
As in the be|ginning · so | now: and for | ever | A|men

The following arrangement of Psalms is also suitable:
Sunday, 91; Monday, 86; Tuesday, 143.1-11; Wednesday, 31.1-6
and 130; Thursday, 16; Friday, 88; and Saturday, 4 and 134.

6 The following, or some other Reading from the Bible

Sunday   **The servants of the Lamb shall see his face, and his
name shall be on their foreheads. And night shall be no more;
they need no light of lamp or sun, for the Lord God will be
their light, and they shall reign for ever and ever.**

Revelation 22.4-5

Monday   **God has not destined us for wrath, but to obtain salvation through our Lord Jesus Christ, who died for us so that
whether we wake or sleep we might live with him.**

1 Thessalonians 5.9-10

Tuesday   **Be sober, be watchful. Your adversary the devil
prowls around like a roaring lion, seeking someone to devour.
Resist him, be firm in your faith, knowing that the same experience of suffering is required of your brotherhood
throughout the world.**   1 Peter 5.8-9

Wednesday   Be angry but do not sin; do not let the sun go down on your anger, and give no opportunity to the devil.

Ephesians 4.26-27

Thursday   May the God of peace himself sanctify you wholly; and may your spirit and soul and body be kept sound and blameless at the coming of our Lord Jesus Christ.

1 Thessalonians 5.23

Friday   You, O Lord, are in the midst of us, and we are called by your name; leave us not.

Jeremiah 14.9

Saturday   Hear O Israel: the Lord our God is one Lord; and you shall love the Lord your God with all your heart, and with all your soul and with all your might. And these words which I command you this day shall be upon your heart; and you shall teach them diligently to your children, and shall talk of them when you sit in your house, and when you walk by the way, and when you lie down, and when you arise.

Deuteronomy 6.4-7

After the Reading the congregation may respond

Thanks be to God.

and/or the following may be said or sung

Into your hands, Lord, I commend my spirit. [Alleluia, alleluia.]
Into your hands, Lord, I commend my spirit. [Alleluia, alleluia.]
You have redeemed us, Lord, God of truth.
I commend my spirit. [Alleluia, alleluia.]
Glory to God; Father, Son, and Holy Spirit.
Into your hands, Lord, I commend my spirit. [Alleluia, alleluia.]

7   Then the Canticle, the Song of Simeon (Luke 2.29ff) is said or sung

Save us, Lord, while we are awake; protect us while we are asleep;
that we may keep watch with Christ and rest with him in peace.

1 Lord, now you let your servant | go in | peace:
  your | word has | been ful|filled.
2 My own eyes have | seen the · sal|vation:
  which you have prepared in the | sight of | ev'ry | people:
3 a light to re|veal you · to the | nations:
  and the | glory · of your | people | Israel.
  Glory to God; Father, Son, and Holy Spirit:
  as in the beginning, so now and for ever.   Amen.

  **[Save us, Lord, while we are awake; protect us while we are asleep;
  that we may keep watch with Christ and rest with him in peace.]**

‡8   Intercessions may follow here according to need and local custom.

9   The service ends with one or more of the following prayers

In your mercy, Lord,
dispel the darkness of this night.
Let your household so sleep in peace
that at the dawn of a new day
they may with joy waken in your name;
through Christ our Lord.   **Amen.**

        This prayer may be used if it has not been used at Evening
        Prayer

Lighten our darkness, Lord, we pray: and in your great
mercy defend us from all perils and dangers of this night;
for the love of your only Son our Saviour Jesus Christ.
Amen.

Lord, be the guest of this *house*;
keep far from it all the deceits of the evil one.
May your holy angels watch over us
as guardians of our peace.
And may your blessing be always upon us,
through Jesus Christ our Lord.   **Amen.**

Lord Jesus Christ, Son of the living God,
who at this evening hour rested in the sepulchre,
and sanctified the grave to be a bed of hope to your people:

make us so to abound in sorrow for our sins,
which were the cause of your passion,
that when our bodies lie in the dust
we may live with you, through the saving merits of your
    cross;
for you live and reign with the Father and the Holy Spirit,
one God, now and for ever. **Amen.**

As watchmen look for the morning
so we wait eagerly for you, O Lord.
Come with the dawning of the day
and make yourself known to us in the breaking of the
    bread,
for you are our God for ever and ever. **Amen.**

Suitable on Sunday

God our Father,
as we have celebrated today the mystery of the Lord's
    resurrection,
grant our humble prayer;
free us from all harm,
that we may sleep in peace and rise in joy to sing your
    praise;
through Christ our Lord. **Amen.**

Suitable on Saturday

Come to visit us, Lord, this night,
so that by your strength we may rise at daybreak
to rejoice in the resurrection of Christ your Son,
who lives and reigns for ever and ever. **Amen.**

10 The minister concludes the service by saying

Let us praise the Father, the Son, and the Holy Spirit;
let us praise and magnify him for ever.

The almighty and merciful God preserve us and give us his
blessing. **Amen.**

The Holy Communion

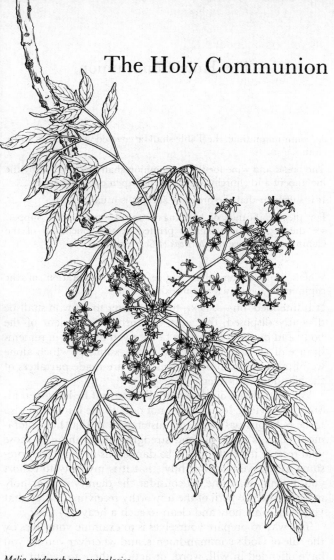

Melia azedarach var. australasica
White cedar

The Holy Communion

At communion time, the Table shall be covered with a clean white cloth.

The bread and wine for the communion shall be provided by the incumbent and churchwardens at the expense of the parish.

It is sufficient that the bread be such as is usually eaten.

For the significance of kneeling to receive the Lord's Supper, see the declaration which is printed at the conclusion of the Communion service in *The Book of Common Prayer.*

When the minister gives notice of the celebration of the communion, he may read this exhortation:

It is intended, on . . . next, to administer to all who shall be devoutly disposed, the most comforting sacrament of the body and blood of Christ, to be received by them in remembrance of his meritorious cross and passion, by which alone we obtain remission of our sins, and are made partakers of the kingdom of heaven.

We must thank our heavenly Father that he has given his Son our Saviour Jesus Christ, not only to die for us, but also to be our spiritual food and sustenance in that holy sacrament. This is so divine and strengthening a thing to those who receive it worthily, and so dangerous to those who presume to receive it unworthily, that it is my duty to exhort you, in the meantime, to consider the dignity of that holy mystery and the peril of the unworthy receiving of it, so that you may come holy and clean to such a heavenly feast.

The way to prepare yourselves is to examine your lives by the rule of God's commandments, and wherever you see you have offended in will, word, or action, there to repent and confess your sin to God, with full purpose of amendment of life. And if you think that you have injured not only God but also your neighbour, then you must ask his forgiveness as well, and make good, to the full extent of your ability, any injury or wrong that he has suffered at your hands. You must likewise forgive others who have injured you, if you desire God to forgive your offences. For if you receive the holy communion without God's forgiveness, you only increase the judgment under which you already stand. So then, should any of you be a blasphemer of God, a hinderer of his word, an adulterer, or be in malice, or envy, or in any other serious offence, repent of your sin, or else do not come to that holy table.

And since no one should come to the Lord's table without a full trust in God's mercy and a quiet conscience, if there is any one of you who cannot quieten his conscience by these means, but needs further help or counsel, let him come to me, or to some other discreet and learned minister of God's word, and open his grief, that by the ministry of God's holy word he may receive the benefit of absolution, together with spiritual counsel and advice, and so be quietened in his conscience, and resolve all scruples and doubts.

The Holy Communion

FIRST ORDER

THE WORD AND THE PRAYERS

‡1   A psalm, hymn, or anthem may be sung when the ministers enter, or after the sentence of scripture(§3).

     The priest may begin the service at the prayer desk, or at some other convenient place.

‡2   The priest may greet the people

The Lord be with you.
  And also with you.

‡3   A Sentence of Scripture appropriate to the day may be read.

‡4   The Litany (page 98) may be said or sung.

     If this is done, §§ 5, 6, and 17 of this Order may be omitted.

5   The people kneeling, this Prayer of Preparation is said by the priest, or the priest and people together

Let us pray.
Almighty God,
to whom all hearts are open,
all desires known,
and from whom no secrets are hidden:
cleanse the thoughts of our hearts
by the inspiration of your Holy Spirit,
that we may perfectly love you,
and worthily magnify your holy name,
through Christ our Lord.   **Amen.**

6   The priest reads aloud the Commandments, Exodus 20.1-17 (or the alternative following, see Mark 12.30-31 and Matthew 22.37-40); and the people ask God's forgiveness for their past transgressions, and grace to keep God's laws in the future. The com-

114

mandments may be read omitting the words in brackets. They may also be read as a continuous whole without the responses except that which follows the tenth commandment.

God spoke these words, and said:
I am the Lord your God. You shall have no other gods but me.

Lord, have mercy on us: and incline our hearts to keep this law.

You shall not make for yourself a graven image, or any likeness of anything that is in heaven above, or on the earth beneath, or in the water under the earth. You shall not bow down to them or worship them. [For I the Lord your God am a jealous God, visiting the iniquity of the fathers upon the children to the third and fourth generation of those who hate me, but showing steadfast love to thousands of those who love me and keep my commandments.]

Lord, have mercy on us: and incline our hearts to keep this law.

You shall not take the name of the Lord your God in vain. [For the Lord will not hold him guiltless who takes his name in vain.]

Lord, have mercy on us: and incline our hearts to keep this law.

Remember the sabbath day, to keep it holy. Six days you shall labour and do all your work; but the seventh day is a sabbath to the Lord your God; in it you shall not do any work, you, or your son, or your daughter, your man-servant, your maid-servant, or your cattle, or the sojourner who is within your gates. [For in six days the Lord made heaven and earth, the sea, and all that is in them, and rested the seventh day; therefore the Lord blessed the seventh day, and hallowed it.]

Lord, have mercy on us: and incline our hearts to keep this law.

Honour your father and your mother, that your days may be long in the land which the Lord your God gives you.

Lord, have mercy on us: and incline our hearts to keep this law.

You shall do no murder.

Lord, have mercy on us: and incline our hearts to keep this law.

You shall not commit adultery.

Lord, have mercy on us: and incline our hearts to keep this law.

You shall not steal.

Lord, have mercy on us: and incline our hearts to keep this law.

You shall not bear false witness against your neighbour.

Lord, have mercy on us: and incline our hearts to keep this law.

You shall not covet your neighbour's house; you shall not covet your neighbour's wife, or his servant, or his maid, or his ox, or his ass, or anything that is his.

Lord, have mercy on us: and write your law in our hearts by your Holy Spirit.

A shorter form of the Commandments is to be found on page 135.

Or this

Our Lord Jesus Christ said:
You shall love the Lord your God with all your heart, and with all your soul, and with all your mind, and with all your strength. This is the great and first commandment. And a second is like it: You shall love your neighbour as yourself. On these two commandments hang all the law and the prophets.

Lord, have mercy on us: and write your law in our hearts by your Holy Spirit.

Or on weekdays

Lord, have mercy on us.
Christ, have mercy on us.
Lord, have mercy on us.

7 The priest says

Let us pray.

He then says the Collect of the day.

‡8 A Reading from the Old Testament (or as appointed) may be read.

It is introduced, **The reading from . . ., chapter . . ., beginning at verse . . .;** and at the end, **Here ends the reading.** Or the reader concludes, **This is the word of the Lord,** and then the people may respond, **Thanks be to God.**

‡9 A psalm, hymn, or canticle may be said or sung between the readings.

10 The Epistle or Reading from the New Testament is read. It is introduced and concluded in the same manner as the Old Testament reading.

11 The people stand for the Gospel, which is introduced

The holy Gospel is written in the . . . chapter of the Gospel according to Saint . . ., beginning at the . . . verse.

The people may respond
Glory to you, Lord Christ.

After the Gospel, the reader may say
This is the gospel of the Lord.
Praise to you, Lord Christ.

12 The Sermon may be preached here, or after the creed.

13 The Nicene Creed is said or sung, all standing. It may be omitted on weekdays.

We believe in one God,
the Father, the Almighty,
maker of heaven and earth,
of all that is, seen and unseen.

We believe in one Lord, Jesus Christ,
the only Son of God,
eternally begotten of the Father,
God from God, Light from Light,
true God from true God,
begotten, not made,

of one Being with the Father.
Through him all things were made.
For us men and for our salvation
he came down from heaven:
by the power of the Holy Spirit
he was incarnate of the Virgin Mary, and became
man.
For our sake he was crucified under Pontius Pilate;
he suffered death and was buried.
On the third day he rose again
in accordance with the Scriptures;
he ascended into heaven
and is seated at the right hand of the Father.
He will come again in glory to judge the living and the
dead,
and his kingdom will have no end.

We believe in the Holy Spirit, the Lord, the giver of life,
who proceeds from the Father and the Son.
With the Father and the Son he is worshipped and
glorified.
He has spoken through the Prophets.
We believe in one holy catholic and apostolic Church.
We acknowledge one baptism for the forgiveness of
sins.
We look for the resurrection of the dead,
and the life of the world to come. Amen.

14 The Sermon is preached here if it has not been preached earlier.

15 The priest begins the Offertory, saying one or more of these verses

Let your light so shine before men, that they may see your
good works and give glory to your Father who is in
heaven. Matthew 5.16

Not every one who says to me, 'Lord, Lord,' shall enter the
kingdom of heaven, but he who does the will of my Father
who is in heaven. Matthew 7.21

118

As we have opportunity, let us do good to all men, and especially to those who are of the household of faith.

Galatians 6.10

Do not neglect to do good and to share what you have, for such sacrifices are pleasing to God.　　　Hebrews 13.16

He who sows sparingly will also reap sparingly, and he who sows bountifully will also reap bountifully. Each one must do as he has made up his mind, not reluctantly or under compulsion, for God loves a cheerful giver.　　　2 Corinthians 9.6,7

If any one has the world's goods and sees his brother in need, yet closes his heart against him, how does God's love abide in him?　　　1 John 3.17

Let him who is taught the word share all good things with him who teaches.　　　Galatians 6.6

Offer to God a sacrifice of thanksgiving, and pay your vows to the Most High.　　　Psalm 50.14

Call upon me in the day of trouble, says the Lord; I will deliver you, and you shall glorify me.　　　Psalm 50.15

Through Jesus let us continually offer up a sacrifice of praise to God, that is, the fruit of lips that acknowledge his name.

Hebrews 13.15

He who brings thanksgiving as his sacrifice honours me, says the Lord.　　　Psalm 50.23

16　While these sentences are being read, the alms and other offerings of the people are collected and brought to the priest who reverently presents and places them on the holy table.

A hymn may also be sung during the collection.

And when there is a communion, the priest then places sufficient bread and wine on the table; or he may do so at §20.

17　The priest may bid special prayers and thanksgivings.

He then says the Intercession.

If there are no alms or oblations, the words in italics in the first paragraph of this prayer are omitted.

Let us pray for all people, and for the Church throughout the world.

Almighty and everliving God, we are taught by your holy word to make prayers and supplications and to give thanks for all people: we ask you in your mercy *to accept our alms and oblations and* to receive our prayers which we offer to your divine majesty.

We pray that you will lead the nations of the world in the ways of righteousness and peace, and guide their rulers in wisdom and justice for the tranquillity and good of all. Bless especially your servant Elizabeth our Queen, her representatives and ministers, her parliaments, and all who exercise authority in this land. Grant that they may impartially administer justice, restrain wickedness and vice, and uphold integrity and truth. And we ask you of your goodness, Lord, to comfort and sustain all who in this transitory life are in trouble, sorrow, need, sickness, or any other adversity.

We beseech you to inspire continually the universal Church with the spirit of truth, unity, and concord; and grant that all who confess your holy name may agree in the truth of your holy word, and live in unity and godly love.

Give grace, heavenly Father, to all bishops and other ministers [especially N our bishop and . . .], that, by their life and teaching, they may set forth your true, life-giving word, and rightly and duly administer your holy sacraments. And to all your people give your heavenly grace, and especially to this congregation here present, that they may receive your word with reverent and obedient hearts, and serve you in holiness and righteousness all the days of their life.

And we also bless your holy name for all your servants who have died in the faith of Christ. Give us grace to follow their good examples, that with them we may be partakers of your eternal kingdom.

Grant this, Father, for Jesus Christ's sake, our only

mediator and advocate, who lives and reigns with you in the unity of the Holy Spirit, now and for ever.

Amen.

‡18   If there is no communion, the service concludes here with the Lord's Prayer, other authorized prayers at the discretion of the minister, and the Grace or the Blessing.

‡19   A hymn may be sung here.

THE LORD'S SUPPER

(An alternative order of §§ 20 to 27 is set out on pages 131 to 133)

20   The priest places on the holy Table sufficient bread and wine for the communion (if he has not already done so) and reads this Exhortation, or at least the final paragraph (omitting 'then')

Brothers and sisters in Christ, we who come to receive the holy communion of the body and blood of our Saviour Christ can come only because of his great love for us. For, although we are completely undeserving of his love, yet in order to raise us from the darkness of death to everlasting life as God's sons and daughters, our Saviour Christ humbled himself to share our life and to die for us on the cross. In remembrance of his death, and as a pledge of his love, he has instituted this holy sacrament which we are now to share.

But those who would eat the bread and drink the cup of the Lord must examine themselves, and amend their lives. They must come with a penitent heart and steadfast faith. Above all they must give thanks to God for his love towards us in Christ Jesus.

You, then, who truly and earnestly repent of your sins, and are in love and charity with your neighbours, and intend to lead a new life, following the commandments of God and

121

walking in his holy ways, draw near with faith, and take this holy sacrament to strengthen and comfort you. But first, let us make a humble confession of our sins to Almighty God.

21   A pause for self-examination may be observed.
      All then say this General Confession, kneeling

**Almighty God, Father of our Lord Jesus Christ,
maker of all things, judge of all men,
we acknowledge with shame the sins we have committed,
by thought, word, and deed, against your divine majesty,
provoking most justly your wrath and indignation against
    us.
We earnestly repent, and are heartily sorry for all our mis-
    doings.
Have mercy on us, most merciful Father.
For your Son our Lord Jesus Christ's sake
forgive us all that is past,
and grant that from this time forward
we may serve and please you in newness of life,
to the honour and glory of your name,
through Jesus Christ our Lord.   Amen.**

22   The priest, or the bishop if he is present, stands and pronounces
      this Absolution

Almighty God our heavenly Father, who of his great mercy has promised forgiveness of sins to all who with hearty repentance and true faith turn to him: have mercy on you; pardon and deliver you from all your sins; confirm and strengthen you in all goodness; and keep you in eternal life; through Jesus Christ our Lord. **Amen.**

23   The Words of Assurance.
      The priest says one or more of these sentences

Hear the words of assurance for those who truly turn to Christ:

Jesus said: Come to me, all who labour and are heavy laden, and I will give you rest. *Matthew 11.28*

God so loved the world that he gave his only Son, that whoever believes in him should not perish but have eternal life. *John 3.16*

The saying is sure and worthy of full acceptance, that Christ Jesus came into the world to save sinners. *1 Timothy 1.15*

If any one sins, we have an advocate with the Father, Jesus Christ the righteous; and he is the perfect offering for our sins. *1 John 2.1,2*

24　The priest begins the Thanksgiving and Communion

Lift up your hearts.
We lift them to the Lord.
Let us give thanks to the Lord our God.
It is right to give him thanks and praise.

It is indeed right, and our bounden duty, that we should at all times and in all places give thanks to you, Lord, holy Father, mighty Creator, and eternal God.

On certain days a special preface (see §25 below) is said here: otherwise the priest, or the priest and people together, continue

Therefore with angels and archangels, and with the whole company of heaven, we proclaim your great and glorious name, evermore praising you, and saying:

**Holy, holy, holy, Lord God of hosts,
heaven and earth are full of your glory.
Glory to you, O Lord most high.**

‡25　Special prefaces

Christmas, Presentation, Annunciation
And now we praise you because you gave your only Son Jesus Christ to be born for us. By the power of the Holy Spirit he was made man and was born of the virgin Mary his mother; being himself without sin, to make us clean from all sin.

[Lent

And now we praise you for the love of your only Son our Lord Jesus Christ who, though he is one with you and the Holy Spirit, humbled himself and was obedient to death, even death on a cross, that we might have life through him.]

Easter

But chiefly are we bound to praise you for the glorious resurrection of your Son Jesus Christ our Lord. He is the true passover lamb who was offered for us and has taken away the sin of the world. By his death he has destroyed death; by his rising to life again he has restored to us eternal life.

Ascension

We praise you through our Lord Jesus Christ, who was seen by his disciples after his resurrection and in their sight ascended into heaven to sit at your right hand and to prepare a place for us, that where he is we might also be and reign with him in glory.

Whitsun

We praise you through our Lord Jesus Christ and in the strength of the Holy Spirit. For, as our Lord promised, the Holy Spirit came down from heaven upon the apostles, to teach them and to lead them into all truth; giving them boldness with fervent zeal to preach the gospel to all nations, by which we have been brought out of darkness into the true knowledge of you and of your Son Jesus Christ.

Trinity

Whom we worship with our Saviour Jesus Christ and the Holy Spirit the Sanctifier, three persons in one God. For all that we believe of your glory, Father, we believe also of the glory of your Son and of the Holy Spirit. We worship you, one God in Trinity and Trinity in unity.

[Dedication festival and other occasions
We praise you through Jesus Christ our Lord, the true high priest who has cleansed us from sin and made us a royal priesthood called to serve you for ever.]

[Saints' days
We praise you for the example and encouragement of your saints; for their witness to the truth of your gospel; and for the hope of glory which we share with them in Jesus Christ our Lord.]

‡26 After each of these prefaces the priest, or the priest and people together, continues

Therefore with angels and archangels, and with the whole company of heaven, we proclaim your great and glorious name, evermore praising you, and saying:

Holy, holy, holy, Lord God of hosts,
heaven and earth are full of your glory.
Glory to you, O Lord most high.

27 Then the priest, kneeling down at the Lord's table, says this prayer in the name of all who are to receive the communion (or all may join with him in the prayer)

We do not presume
to come to your table, merciful Lord,
trusting in our own righteousness,
but in your manifold and great mercies.
We are not worthy
so much as to gather up the crumbs under your table.
But you are the same Lord
whose nature is always to have mercy.
Grant us, therefore, gracious Lord,
so to eat the flesh of your dear Son Jesus Christ,
and to drink his blood,
that we may evermore dwell in him,
and he in us.
  Amen.

28 When the priest has so arranged the bread and wine that he may more conveniently and appropriately take and break the bread before the people and take the cup into his hands, he says this Prayer of Consecration

All glory to you, our heavenly Father, for in your tender mercy you gave your only Son Jesus Christ to suffer death on the cross for our redemption; who made there, by his one oblation of himself once offered, a full, perfect, and sufficient sacrifice for the sins of the whole world; and who instituted, and in his holy gospel commanded us to continue, a perpetual memory of his precious death until his coming again.

Hear us, merciful Father, and grant that we who receive these gifts of your creation, this bread and this wine, according to your Son our Saviour Jesus Christ's holy institution, in remembrance of his death and passion, may be partakers of his most blessed body and blood; who on the night he was betrayed *Here the priest takes the paten in his hands* took bread, and when he had given you thanks, *He breaks the bread* he broke it, and gave it to his disciples, saying, 'Take, eat; *He lays his hand on all the bread* this is my body which is given for you; do this in remembrance of me.' Likewise after supper *He takes the cup in his hands* he took the cup, and when he had given you thanks, he gave it to them saying, 'Drink from this, all of you; for *He lays his hand on the vessels in which is wine to be consecrated* this is my blood of the new covenant, which is shed for you and for many for the remission of sins; do this, as often as you drink it, in remembrance of me.'

All answer

Amen.

29 The priest receives the communion in both kinds himself, and then distributes it similarly to the other communicants; first to any bishops, priests, and deacons, who are present, and then to the other communicants; into their hands, all kneeling.

When the minister gives the bread he says

The body of our Lord Jesus Christ, which was given for you,
preserve your body and soul to everlasting life; take and eat
this in remembrance that Christ died for you, and feed on
him in your heart by faith with thanksgiving.

When the minister gives the cup he says

The blood of our Lord Jesus Christ, which was shed for you,
preserve your body and soul to everlasting life; drink this in
remembrance that Christ's blood was shed for you, and be
thankful.

Instead of these words, the invitation together with the alternative
words of distribution on page 149 may be used; and the communicant may answer   **Amen**

During the Communion hymns or anthems (see page 153) may be
sung.

30   If the consecrated bread or wine prove insufficient for the communion, the priest is to consecrate more, beginning at **Our Saviour
Christ on the night** . . . for the blessing of the bread; and at **Likewise after supper** . . . for the blessing of the cup.

31   When all have communicated, the minister reverently places on
the table what remains of the consecrated elements.
If he does not then consume them (see §36) he covers them with
a clean white cloth.

A Sentence of Scripture may be said here or during the Communion.

32   The priest says

Let us pray. [As our Saviour Christ has taught us, we are
confident to say,]

Our Father in heaven,
hallowed be your Name,
your kingdom come,
your will be done
on earth as in heaven.

Give us today our daily bread.
Forgive us our sins
  as we forgive those who sin against us.
Lead us not into temptation,
  but deliver us from evil.
For the kingdom, the power, and the glory are yours
  now and for ever.   Amen.

33   Then is said one or both of the prayers following

Lord and heavenly Father, we your servants entirely desire your fatherly goodness mercifully to accept this our sacrifice of praise and thanksgiving, and to grant that, by the merits and death of your Son Jesus Christ, and through faith in his blood, we and your whole Church may receive forgiveness of our sins and all other benefits of his passion.

And here we offer and present to you, O Lord, ourselves, our souls and bodies, to be a reasonable, holy, and living sacrifice, humbly beseeching you that all we who are partakers of this holy communion may be fulfilled with your grace and heavenly benediction.

And although we are unworthy, through our many sins, to offer you any sacrifice, yet we pray that you will accept this, the duty and service we owe, not weighing our merits but pardoning our offences, through Jesus Christ our Lord; by whom and with whom, in the unity of the Holy Spirit, all honour and glory are yours, Father Almighty, now and for ever.
  Amen.

Almighty and everliving God, we heartily thank you that you graciously feed us, who have duly received these holy mysteries, with the spiritual food of the most precious body and blood of your Son our Saviour Jesus Christ, and assure us thereby of your favour and goodness towards us and that

we are true members of the mystical body of your Son, the blessed company of all faithful people, and are also heirs, through hope, of your eternal kingdom, by the merits of the most precious death and passion of your dear Son. And we humbly beseech you, heavenly Father, so to assist us with your grace, that we may continue in that holy fellowship, and do all such good works as you have prepared for us to walk in; through Jesus Christ our Lord, to whom with you and the Holy Spirit be all honour and glory, now and for ever.
Amen.

34   This Hymn of Praise (Gloria in excelsis) is said or sung.

Glory to God in the highest
   and peace to his people on earth.
Lord God, heavenly King,
almighty God and Father,
   we worship you, we give you thanks,
   we praise you for your glory.

Lord Jesus Christ, only Son of the Father,
Lord God, Lamb of God,
you take away the sin of the world:
   have mercy on us;
you are seated at the right hand of the Father:
   receive our prayer.

For you alone are the Holy One;
you alone are the Lord;
you alone are the Most High,
Jesus Christ,
with the Holy Spirit,
in the glory of God the Father.   Amen.

35 The priest, or the bishop if he is present, lets the people depart with this Blessing

The peace of God which passes all understanding, keep your hearts and minds in the knowledge and love of God, and of his Son Jesus Christ our Lord; and the blessing of God Almighty, the Father, the Son, and the Holy Spirit, be amongst you, and remain with you always.

Amen.

36 If any of the consecrated bread and wine remain it shall not be carried out of the church, but the priest and such other of the communicants as he shall request shall consume it after the Communion or immediately after the Blessing (see also §31).

NOTES

1 The reader may preface the announcement of the Gospel with the salutation, 'The Lord be with you', to which the people respond, **'And also with you'.**

2 The sermon may be omitted on weekdays.

3 Formal notices may be given before the service begins, before the sermon, after the Nicene Creed, or after the Intercession.

4 Another version of 'Holy, holy, holy, . . .' is to be found on page 146.

ALTERNATIVE ORDER FOR §§ 20-27
THE LORD'S SUPPER

20 The priest places on the holy Table sufficient bread and wine for
the communion (if he has not already done so), and says one or
more of these sentences

Hear the words of assurance for those who truly turn to
Christ:

Jesus said: Come to me, all who labour and are heavy laden,
and I will give you rest. Matthew 11.28

God so loved the world that he gave his only Son, that whoever believes in him should not perish but have eternal life.
John 3.16

The saying is sure and worthy of full acceptance, that Christ
Jesus came into the world to save sinners. 1 Timothy 1.15

If any one sins, we have an advocate with the Father, Jesus
Christ the righteous; and he is the perfect offering for our
sins. 1 John 2.1,2

21 The priest continues

You who truly and earnestly repent of your sins, and are in
love and charity with your neighbours, and intend to lead
a new life, following the commandments of God and walking
in his holy ways, draw near with faith, and take this holy
sacrament to strengthen and comfort you. But first, let us
make a humble confession of our sins to Almighty God.

22 A pause for self-examination may be observed.

All then say this General Confession, kneeling.

**Almighty God, Father of our Lord Jesus Christ,
maker of all things, judge of all men,**

we acknowledge with shame the sins we have committed,
by thought, word, and deed, against your divine majesty,
provoking most justly your wrath and indignation against
    us.
We earnestly repent, and are heartily sorry for all our mis-
    doings.
Have mercy on us, most merciful Father.
For your Son our Lord Jesus Christ's sake
forgive us all that is past,
and grant that from this time forward
we may serve and please you in newness of life,
to the honour and glory of your name,
through Jesus Christ our Lord.   Amen.

23   The priest, or the bishop if he is present, stands and pronounces
       this Absolution

Almighty God our heavenly Father, who of his great mercy
has promised forgiveness of sins to all who with hearty repentance and true faith turn to him; have mercy on you;
pardon and deliver you from all your sins; confirm and
strengthen you in all goodness; and keep you in eternal life;
through Jesus Christ our Lord.   **Amen.**

‡24   Then this prayer may be said by the priest, kneeling down at the
       Lord's table, in the name of all who are to receive the communion
       (or all may join with him in the prayer)

We do not presume
to come to your table, merciful Lord,
trusting in our own righteousness,
but in your manifold and great mercies.
We are not worthy
so much as to gather up the crumbs under your table.
But you are the same Lord
whose nature is always to have mercy.

Grant us, therefore, gracious Lord,
so to eat the flesh of your dear Son Jesus Christ,
and to drink his blood,
that we may evermore dwell in him,
and he in us.   Amen.

‡25   All standing, the priest may give this Greeting of Peace

The peace of the Lord be always with you.
And also with you.

26   When the priest has so arranged the bread and wine that he may
more conveniently and appropriately take and break the bread before the people and take the cup into his hands, he begins the
Thanksgiving and Communion

[The Lord be with you.
And also with you.]

Lift up your hearts.
We lift them to the Lord.
Let us give thanks to the Lord our God.
It is right to give him thanks and praise.

It is indeed right, and our bounden duty, that we should at
all times and in all places give thanks to you, Lord, holy
Father, mighty Creator, and eternal God.

On certain days a special preface is said here: otherwise the priest,
or the priest and people together, continue

Therefore with angels and archangels, and with the whole
company of heaven, we proclaim your great and glorious
name, evermore praising you, and saying:

Holy, holy, holy is the Lord of hosts.
Heaven and earth are full of his glory.
Glory to you, Lord God most high.

27   For the special prefaces see §§ 25 and 26 on page 123ff.
28   The priest continues with the Prayer of Consecration on page
126.

The Holy Communion

SECOND ORDER

The parts of the service are set out for three different ministers: the presiding priest or bishop; the deacon or assisting priest; and other ministers or authorized assistants. The parts assigned to the deacon or assisting priest may be read by the priest, or all three parts may be read by the priest. When there is no communion, all three parts may be read by a deacon or authorized layman; save that a deacon or authorized layman says 1 John 2.1,2 in place of the Absolution:

Hear these words of assurance from Saint John: If anyone sins, we have an advocate with the Father, Jesus Christ the righteous; and he is the perfect offering for our sins, and not for ours only but also for the sins of the whole world.

THE WORD AND THE PRAYERS

‡1   A Psalm, Hymn, or Anthem may be sung when the ministers enter or after the Greeting (§2).

  2   The priest greets the congregation

> **The Lord be with you.**
> **And also with you.**

[During the Easter season he may add

> **Christ is risen.**
> **He is risen indeed.**]

‡3   A Sentence of Scripture appropriate to the day may be read.

134

4 This Prayer of Preparation is said

[Let us pray.]

**Almighty God,
to whom all hearts are open,
all desires known,
and from whom no secrets are hidden:
cleanse the thoughts of our hearts
by the inspiration of your Holy Spirit,
that we may perfectly love you,
and worthily magnify your holy name,
through Christ our Lord.   Amen.**

5. The Ten Commandments or one of the forms below is used, and the people ask God's forgiveness and the grace to keep his word.

a *The Ten Commandments* (see Exodus 20.1-17)
The commandments may be read as a continuous passage, or after each commandment except the last the people may answer

Lord, have mercy on us: and incline our hearts to keep this law.

The full form of the commandments on page 115 may be used.

Hear the commandments which God gave his people Israel.

1 I am the Lord your God who brought you out of the land of slavery; you shall have no other gods but me.

2 You shall not make for yourself a graven image, or any likeness of anything that is in heaven above, or that is on the earth beneath, or that is in the water under the earth; you shall not bow down to them or serve them.

3 You shall not take the name of the Lord your God in vain.

4 Remember the sabbath day to keep it holy. Six days shall you labour and do all you have to do, but the seventh day is the sabbath of the Lord your God.

135

5 Honour your father and your mother.

6 You shall do no murder.

7 You shall not commit adultery.

8 You shall not steal.

9 You shall not bear false witness against your neighbour.

10 You shall not covet anything that is your neighbour's.

Lord, have mercy on us: and write your law in our hearts by your Holy Spirit.

> b *The Two Great Commandments* (see Matthew 22.37-40 and Mark 12.30-31)

Our Lord Jesus Christ said:
You shall love the Lord your God with all your heart, and with all your soul, and with all your mind, and with all your strength. This is the great and first commandment. And a second is like it: You shall love your neighbour as yourself. On these two commandments hang all the law and the prophets.

Lord, have mercy on us: and write your law in our hearts by your Holy Spirit.

> c *Kyrie eleison*
> These forms may be used together with either of the preceding forms, or they may be used by themselves.

Lord, have mercy on us. or	**Lord, have mercy.**
Christ, have mercy on us.	**Christ, have mercy.**
Lord, have mercy on us.	**Lord, have mercy.**

and/or

Holy God, holy and mighty, holy and immortal, have mercy on us.

> Kyrie eleison ('Lord, have mercy') may be repeated according to local custom or the musical setting used for it.

‡6 The Confession may be said here (instead of at §16). The deacon says

In penitence and faith let us confess our sins to almighty God.

All kneel. A pause for self-examination may be observed.

Merciful God,
our maker and our judge,
we have sinned against you in thought, word, and deed:
we have not loved you with our whole heart,
we have not loved our neighbours as ourselves;
we repent, and are sorry for all our sins.
Father, forgive us.
Strengthen us to love and obey you in newness of life;
through Jesus Christ our Lord. Amen.

The priest, or bishop if present, stands and pronounces this Absolution

Almighty God,
who has promised forgiveness to all who turn to him in faith,
pardon you and set you free from all your sins,
strengthen you to do his will,
and keep you in eternal life;
through Jesus Christ our Lord. **Amen.**

‡7 This Hymn of Praise (Gloria in excelsis) may be sung or said, all standing

Glory to God in the highest
and peace to his people on earth.
Lord God, heavenly King,
almighty God and Father,
we worship you, we give you thanks,
we praise you for your glory.

Lord Jesus Christ, only Son of the Father,
Lord God, Lamb of God,
you take away the sin of the world:
have mercy on us;
you are seated at the right hand of the Father:
receive our prayer.

**For you alone are the Holy One;
you alone are the Lord;
you alone are the Most High,
Jesus Christ,
with the Holy Spirit,
in the glory of God the Father.   Amen.**

8   The priest says

Let us pray.

He then says the Collect of the Day.

‡9   All sit for the Reading from the Old Testament or as appointed.

After each reading the reader may say

This is the word of the Lord.
Thanks be to God.

A Psalm may be sung or said.

10   The Reading from the New Testament (other than from the Gospels)

A Hymn or Anthem may be sung.

11   All stand for the Gospel Reading.

The Gospel is announced

**The gospel of our Lord Jesus Christ according to . . ., chapter
. . ., beginning at verse . . .**

and there may be said
Glory to you, Lord Christ.

After the Gospel, the reader may say
This is the gospel of the Lord.
Praise to you, Lord Christ.

12   The Sermon is preached here, or after the Creed.

13   All stand for the Nicene Creed which is said or sung.
It may be omitted on weekdays.

We believe in one God,
   the Father, the Almighty,
   maker of heaven and earth,
   of all that is, seen and unseen.

We believe in one Lord, Jesus Christ,
   the only Son of God,
   eternally begotten of the Father,
   God from God, Light from Light,
   true God from true God,
   begotten, not made,
   of one Being with the Father.
   Through him all things were made.
For us men and for our salvation
   he came down from heaven:
by the power of the Holy Spirit
   he was incarnate of the Virgin Mary, and became
      man.
For our sake he was crucified under Pontius Pilate;
   he suffered death and was buried.
   On the third day he rose again
     in accordance with the Scriptures;
   he ascended into heaven
     and is seated at the right hand of the Father.
He will come again in glory to judge the living and the
     dead,
   and his kingdom will have no end.

We believe in the Holy Spirit, the Lord, the giver of life,
   who proceeds from the Father and the Son.
   With the Father and the Son he is worshipped and
     glorified.
He has spoken through the Prophets.
We believe in one holy catholic and apostolic Church.
We acknowledge one baptism for the forgiveness of sins.
We look for the resurrection of the dead,
   and the life of the world to come.   Amen.

14   The Prayers are offered by one or more persons.

They may follow the form printed below or one of the forms given on pages 156-158.

Pauses may be allowed for silent prayer and thanksgiving.

The response

> Lord, in your mercy
> **hear our prayer**

may be used after the detailed additions instead of the response printed after each section.

For the use of the following form see also Note 9 on page 154.

The priest says

Let us pray for all people and for the Church throughout the world.

The minister says

Almighty God, your Son Jesus Christ has promised that you will hear us when we ask in faith: receive the prayers we offer.

For the church

We give thanks for . . .   We pray for . . .
the church in other countries; the church in Australia;
this diocese; N our Bishop; this *parish*; . . .

Strengthen your people for their witness and work in the world, and empower your ministers faithfully to proclaim the gospel and to administer your holy sacraments. Unite in the truth all who confess your name, that we may live together in love and proclaim your glory in all the world.

> Father, hear our prayer,
> **through Jesus Christ our Lord.**

For all peoples

We give thanks for . . .   We pray for . . .
the peoples of the world; their leaders; Elizabeth our Queen; Australia, and those who make and administer our laws; all who have responsibility; all men and women in their daily work . . .

Give wisdom to those in authority in every land, and guide all peoples in the way of righteousness and peace, so that they may share with justice the resources of the earth, work together in trust, and seek the common good.

      Father, hear our prayer,
      through Jesus Christ our Lord.

For our community

We give thanks for . . .   We pray for . . .
one another; our local community; people known to us (especially . . .); . . .

We commend to your keeping, Father, ourselves and each other, our families, our neighbours, and our friends. Enable us by your Spirit to live in love for you and for one another.

      Father, hear our prayer,
      through Jesus Christ our Lord.

For those in need

We pray for . . .
those who suffer; the sick; the poor; the distressed; the lonely; the outcast; the persecuted; those who mourn; those who care for them; . . .

We give thanks for . . .

Comfort and heal, merciful Lord, all who are in sorrow, need, sickness, or any other trouble. Give them a firm trust in your goodness; help those who minister to them; and bring us all into the joy of your salvation.

      Father, hear our prayer,
      through Jesus Christ our Lord.

Thanksgiving for the faithful departed

We give thanks for the life and work of . . .

We praise you, Lord God, for your faithful servants in every age, and we pray that we, with all who have died in the faith of Christ, may be brought to a joyful resurrection and the fulfilment of your eternal kingdom.

The priest says

EITHER

Hear us, Father,
through Jesus Christ our Lord,
who lives and reigns with you
in the unity of the Holy Spirit,
one God, now and for ever.   Amen.

OR

Accept our prayers through Jesus Christ our Lord, who
taught us to pray,

Our Father in heaven,
   hallowed be your Name,
   your kingdom come,
   your will be done
      on earth as in heaven.
Give us today our daily bread.
Forgive us our sins
   as we forgive those who sin against us.
Lead us not into temptation,
   but deliver us from evil.
For the kingdom, the power, and the glory are yours
   now and for ever.   Amen.

When there is no Communion, the Lord's Prayer should be used
here and the Confession at §6, and the service ends with [a hymn,
during which the gifts of the people may be received and
presented] the General Thanksgiving (page 35), and the Grace.

PREPARATION FOR THE LORD'S SUPPER

‡15   One or more of these (or other suitable verses of Scripture) may
       be read

Jesus said: Come to me all who labour and are heavy laden,
and I will give you rest. Take my yoke upon you, and learn

142

from me; for I am gentle and lowly of heart, and you will find rest for your souls. For my yoke is easy and my burden is light.
Matthew 11.28-30

Jesus said: I am the bread of life; he who comes to me shall not hunger, and he who believes in me shall never thirst.
John 6.35

Jesus said: A new commandment I give to you, that you love one another, even as I have loved you.
John 13.34

Whenever you stand praying, forgive, if you have anything against any one; so that your Father also who is in heaven may forgive you your trespasses.
Mark 11.25

God so loved the world that he gave his only Son, that whoever believes in him should not perish but have eternal life.
John 3.16

Saint Paul said: As often as you eat the bread and drink the cup of the Lord, you proclaim the Lord's death until he comes. Whoever, therefore, eats the bread or drinks the cup in an unworthy manner will be guilty of profaning the body and blood of the Lord. Let a man examine himself, and so eat of the bread and drink of the cup.
I Corinthians 11.26-28

> The Exhortation on page 121 may be read here. If the Confession is not to follow immediately, this Exhortation should end with the words . . . to strengthen and comfort you.

‡16 This Prayer may be said, all kneeling

[Let us pray.]

**We do not presume
to come to your table, merciful Lord,
trusting in our own righteousness,
but in your manifold and great mercies.
We are not worthy
so much as to gather up the crumbs under your table.
But you are the same Lord
whose nature is always to have mercy.**

Grant us, therefore, gracious Lord,
so to eat the flesh of your dear Son Jesus Christ,
and to drink his blood,
that we may evermore dwell in him,
and he in us.   Amen.

17   The Confession is said here, if it has not been said at §6.

The deacon says

In penitence and faith let us confess our sins to almighty
God.

All kneel. A pause for self-examination may be observed.

Merciful God,
our maker and our judge,
we have sinned against you in thought, word, and deed:
we have not loved you with our whole heart;
we have not loved our neighbours as ourselves;
we repent, and are sorry for all our sins.
Father, forgive us.
Strengthen us to love and obey you in newness of life;
through Jesus Christ our Lord.   Amen.

The priest, or bishop if present, stands and pronounces this ·
Absolution

Almighty God,
who has promised forgiveness to all who turn to him in
    faith,
pardon you and set you free from all your sins,
strengthen you to do his will,
and keep you in eternal life;
through Jesus Christ our Lord.
Amen.

18   All stand, and the Greeting of Peace is given by the priest (see also
Note 10 on page 154)

We are the body of Christ.
His Spirit is with us.
The peace of the Lord be always with you.
And also with you.

A hymn may be sung.

19 The gifts of the people are brought to the Lord's Table. They may
be presented in silence, or the following prayer may be used

Blessed are you, Lord God our Father;
through your goodness we have these gifts to share.
Accept and use our offerings for your glory
and for the service of your kingdom.
Blessed be God for ever.

THE THANKSGIVING

20 The priest takes the bread and wine for the communion, places
them upon the Lord's Table, and says this Prayer of Thanksgiving
and Consecration (or one of the forms on pages 159-166). On certain days special additions may be made to this Prayer, and these
are to be found on pages 167-171.

[The Lord be with you.
And also with you.]

Lift up your hearts.
We lift them to the Lord.

Let us give thanks to the Lord our God.
It is right to give him thanks and praise.

All glory and honour, thanks and praise
be given to you at all times and in all places,
Lord, holy Father, true and living God,
through Jesus Christ our Lord.

145

For he is your eternal Word
through whom you have created all things from the
      beginning
and formed us in your own image.

In your great love you gave him
to be made man for us and to share our common life.

In obedience to your will
your Son our Saviour offered himself as a perfect sacrifice,
and died upon the cross for our redemption.
Through him you have freed us from the slavery of sin
and reconciled us to yourself,
our God and Father.

He is our great high priest
whom you raised from death
and exalted to your right hand on high
where he ever lives to intercede for us.

Through him you have sent upon us
your holy and life-giving Spirit
and made us a royal priesthood
called to serve you for ever.

Therefore with angels and archangels
and with all the company of heaven
we proclaim your great and glorious name,
for ever praising you and saying:

Holy, holy, holy Lord, God of power and might,
heaven and earth are full of your glory.
Hosanna in the highest.

Merciful Father, we thank you
for these gifts of your creation, this bread and this wine,
and we pray that we who eat and drink them
in the fellowship of the Holy Spirit
in obedience to our Saviour Christ
in remembrance of his death and passion
may be partakers of his body and his blood,

He takes the bread into his hands and says

who on the night he was betrayed took bread;
and when he had given you thanks
he broke it, and gave it to his disciples, saying,
'Take, eat. This is my body which is given for you.
Do this in remembrance of me.'

He takes the cup into his hands and says

After supper, he took the cup,
and again giving you thanks
he gave it to his disciples, saying,
'Drink from this, all of you.
This is my blood of the new covenant
which is shed for you and for many
for the forgiveness of sins.
Do this, as often as you drink it, in remembrance of me.'

Christ has died;
Christ is risen;
Christ will come again.

Father, with this bread and this cup,
we do as our Saviour has commanded;
we celebrate the redemption he has won for us;
we proclaim his perfect sacrifice
made once for all upon the cross,
his mighty resurrection and glorious ascension;
and we look for his coming
to fulfil all things according to your will.

Renew us by your Holy Spirit,
unite us in the body of your Son,
and bring us with all your people
into the joy of your eternal kingdom;
through Jesus Christ our Lord,
with whom and in whom,
by the power of the Holy Spirit,
we worship you, Father almighty,
in songs of never-ending praise:

**Blessing and honour and glory and power
are yours for ever and ever.   Amen.**

‡21   If the Lord's Prayer has not already been said, it is said here or
after the Communion

As our Saviour Christ has taught us, we are confident
to say,

**Our Father in heaven,
   hallowed be your Name,
   your kingdom come,
   your will be done
      on earth as in heaven.
Give us today our daily bread.
Forgive us our sins
   as we forgive those who sin against us.
Lead us not into temptation,
   but deliver us from evil.
For the kingdom, the power, and the glory are yours
   now and for ever.   Amen.**

THE COMMUNION

22   The priest breaks the bread before the people.
He may do so in silence, or he may say

[We who are many are one body in Christ,
for we all share in the one bread.]

23   [The priest may say

Come let us take this holy sacrament of the body and blood of Christ in remembrance that he died for us, and feed on him in our hearts by faith with thanksgiving.]

The priest and the other communicants receive the holy communion.

When the minister gives the bread he says

The body of our Lord Jesus Christ, which was given for you, preserve your body and soul to everlasting life; take and eat this in remembrance that Christ died for you, and feed on him in your heart by faith with thanksgiving.

or

The body of Christ keep you in eternal life.

or

Take and eat this in remembrance that Christ died for you, and be thankful.

The communicant may answer

Amen.

When the minister gives the cup he says

The blood of our Lord Jesus Christ, which was shed for you, preserve your body and soul to everlasting life; drink this in remembrance that Christ's blood was shed for you, and be thankful.

or

The blood of Christ keep you in eternal life.

or

Drink this in remembrance that Christ's blood was shed for you, and be thankful.

The communicant may answer

Amen.

During the Communion, hymns or anthems (see Note 1 on page 153) may be sung.

AFTER COMMUNION

‡24   A Sentence of Scripture may be said.

‡25   If the Lord's Prayer has not been said earlier, it is used here.

The priest says

Let us pray.
As our Saviour Christ has taught us, we are confident to say,

Our Father in heaven,
  hallowed be your Name,
  your kingdom come,
  your will be done
    on earth as in heaven.
Give us today our daily bread.
Forgive us our sins
  as we forgive those who sin against us.
Lead us not into temptation,
  but deliver us from evil.
For the kingdom, the power, and the glory are yours
  now and for ever.   Amen.

‡26   The priest may say this or another suitable prayer (see page 172).

[Let us pray.]
Father, we thank you
that you feed us who have received these holy mysteries
with the spiritual food of the body and blood of our Saviour,
      Jesus Christ.
We thank you for this assurance of your goodness and
      love,
and that we are living members of his body
and heirs of his eternal kingdom.
Accept this our sacrifice of praise and thanksgiving,
and help us to grow in love and obedience,
that with all your saints we may worship you for ever.

27 All say together

**Father, we offer ourselves to you
as a living sacrifice
through Jesus Christ our Lord.
Send us out in the power of your Spirit
to live and work to your praise and glory.   Amen.**

28 A hymn may be sung, which may be Gloria in excelsis (see page 137) if it has not already been used at §7.

29 The priest, or bishop if present, says this or the appropriate seasonal Blessing (see below)

The peace of God which passes all understanding keep your hearts and minds in the knowledge and love of God, and of his Son, Jesus Christ our Lord;
and the blessing of God almighty, the Father, the Son, and the Holy Spirit, be amongst you and remain with you always. **Amen.**

30 The deacon may say

Go in peace to love and serve the Lord:
   In the name of Christ.   Amen.

Seasonal Blessings which may be used at §29

Advent   Christ, the Sun of righteousness shine upon you and make you ready to meet him when he comes in glory;
and the blessing . . .

Christmas   May Christ the Son of God gladden your hearts by his coming to dwell among us, and bring you his peace;
and the blessing . . .

Epiphany and Transfiguration   May Christ the Son of God be manifest to you, that your lives may be a light to the world;
and the blessing . . .

Lent   Christ give you strength to overcome all temptation, to deny yourself, and to take up your cross and follow him; and the blessing . . .

or   Christ our crucified Saviour draw you to himself, that you may find in him a sure hope and the assurance of sins forgiven;
and the blessing . . .

Easter   The God of peace, who brought again from the dead our Lord Jesus, the great shepherd of the sheep, through the blood of the everlasting covenant, make you perfect in every good work to do his will, working in you what is pleasing in his sight;
and the blessing . . .

Ascension   Christ our exalted king pour upon you his abundant gifts and bring you to reign with him in glory;
and the blessing . . .

Whitsun   God stir up within you the gift of his Spirit that you may confess Jesus Christ as Lord and proclaim the joy of the everlasting gospel wherever you may be;
and the blessing . . .

Trinity Sunday   God the Holy Trinity bring you to a knowledge of him as Creator, Redeemer, and Sanctifier,
and the blessing . . .

Saints' days   God give you grace to follow the saints in faith and hope and love, and to know the fruit of his Spirit in your lives;
and the blessing . . .

> Other suitable sentences, such as those at the end of the services in Morning and Evening Prayer Second Form (pages 43-90) may also be used when appropriate before the words
>
> and the blessing . . .

NOTES

1   The following *canticles and anthems* are suitable:

When the ministers enter or after the Greeting
Psalm 95 (page 22)
Judith 16.13-15 (page 52)
Tobit 13.1-4,6 (page 66)
Hebrews 10.19-22 (page 79)
Psalms 23; 43; 93; 96.1-6; 96.7-13; 100; and 150.

Before the Gospel Reading
The Song of Zechariah (page 46)
The Song of Mary (page 50)
The Song of Creation (page 59 or 61)
Ephesians 2.4-7 (page 81)
Great and wonderful (page 86)
Psalm 23

During the Communion
Psalm 67
A Song of Christ's Glory (page 76)
Saviour of the World (page 80)
The Easter Anthems (page 88)
Gloria in excelsis (page 129)

Blessed is he who comes in the name of the Lord;
Hosanna in the highest.

Jesus, Lamb of God, have mercy on us.
Jesus, bearer of our sins, have mercy on us.
Jesus, redeemer of the world, grant us your peace.

Lamb of God, you take away the sin of the world:
    have mercy on us.
Lamb of God, you take away the sin of the world:
    have mercy on us.
Lamb of God, you take away the sin of the world:
    grant us your peace.

Before the Blessing
Te Deum (page 53)
The Song of Simeon (page 30)
The Hymn to the Word (page 70)

153

Ephesians 1.3-6 (page 73)
A Song to the Lamb (page 82)
A Song of Christ's Glory (page 76)

2   When Baptism or Confirmation is to be administered, or Holy Matrimony is to be solemnized, during this service, or when there is no communion, it is appropriate that the *Confession* be at §6.

3   The optional *Sentence of Scripture* permitted at §3 may be sung as an anthem by the choir at §3, or before the opening Greeting; or it may be used immediately before the Collect at §8.

4   *Gloria in excelsis* may be used wherever a hymn is permitted instead of at §7; it may be omitted during Advent and Lent and on weekdays.

5   A *pause for reflection* may be observed at any of the following: before the Collect; after any of the Readings; before the Confession; and after all have received the holy communion.

6   The reader may preface the *announcement of the Gospel reading* with the salutation, 'The Lord be with you', to which the people respond **'And also with you.'**

7   Although the recommended position for the *Sermon* is after the Gospel Reading, it may be after the creed, or before or after any of the readings. A sermon should normally be preached at this service.

8   The plural 'we believe' is original to the *Nicene Creed*, which was a corporate declaration of faith; while the singular is appropriate to the Apostles' Creed which is an act of personal commitment at baptism. Nevertheless, in this service, the Nicene Creed may be used in the singular.

9   The form of *Intercession* on page 140 may be offered as a single prayer without the detailed additions suggested or responses.
The minister need not use all the detailed suggestions on each occasion, nor need he use the precise form, 'We give thanks for . . . We pray for . . .' Any forms should be clearly addressed to God, and not biddings to the congregation. The congregation may join in saying the invariable paragraphs of the prayer.

10   The priest exchanges the *Greeting of Peace*, §18, with the congregation by using the versicle and response. When circumstances permit, all may then exchange the greeting, saying, for example, 'Peace be with you', which they may accompany with a handclasp or other similar action.

11   It is appropriate for all to remain standing during the *Thanksgiving and Consecration* (§20) and the *Breaking of the Bread* (§22). However, it may be considered desirable, at the discretion of the local congregation, for the people to kneel.

12   The consecrated elements may be distributed immediately after the words of institution. In this case, the bread is to be broken at the words 'he broke it', and 'Amen' or one of the acclamations (e.g. 'Christ has died, . . .') is said after '. . . in remembrance of me.'
After the Communion, the service resumes at §25 or §26.

13   If the consecrated bread and/or wine are insufficient for the communion, the priest is to take more bread and/or wine saying the appropriate portions of §20, beginning, 'Merciful Father' and ending 'in remembrance of me'.

14   If any of the consecrated bread and wine remain it shall not be carried out of the church, but the priest and such other of the communicants as he shall request shall reverently consume it after the Communion or immediately after the Blessing.

15   *Notices* may be given before the Prayers (§14) or before the final Blessing (§29).

16   The *Readings from the Old and New Testaments* (§§8 and 10) are introduced, 'A reading from . . ., chapter . . ., beginning at verse . . .'

ALTERNATIVE FORMS FOR §14

THE PRAYERS

14a The Intercession (§17) from The Holy Communion, First Order (page 120) or the Prayer for all people (page 35) may be used.

When it is desired to say the Lord's Prayer after the Prayer of Intercession, the priest introduces it with the words

Accept our prayers through Jesus Christ our Lord, who taught us to pray . . .

14b The Litany (page 98) may be used; it may begin with §4 Receive now our prayers and end with the Lord's Prayer; on weekdays selected petitions from the Litany may be used.

14c The priest says

Let us pray for all people and for the Church throughout the world.

When the following form is used, the minister may add the names of particular persons or needs to the several petitions; he may add other similar petitions.

Almighty God, whose Son Jesus Christ has promised that you will hear us when we ask in faith: receive the prayers we offer.

We pray for the peace of the world and the welfare of your holy Church.
Lord, in your mercy,
hear our prayer.

We pray for our Bishop N, and for all the clergy and people.
Lord, in your mercy,
hear our prayer.

We pray for Elizabeth our Queen, for the leaders of the nations, and for all in authority.
Lord, in your mercy,
hear our prayer.

[We pray for seasonable weather, and for an abundance of the fruits of the earth.
Lord, in your mercy,
hear our prayer.]

[We pray that we may share with justice the resources of the earth, and live in trust and goodwill with one another.
Lord, in your mercy,
hear our prayer.]

We pray for the aged and the infirm, for widows and orphans, and for the sick and suffering.
Lord, in your mercy,
hear our prayer.

We pray for the poor and oppressed, for prisoners and captives, and for all who care for them.
Lord, in your mercy,
hear our prayer.

We pray for ourselves and for each other.
Lord, in your mercy,
hear our prayer.

We praise you, Lord God, for the communion of saints, and for the glorious hope of the resurrection to eternal life.

The priest says
EITHER

Hear us, Father,
through Jesus Christ our Lord,
**who lives and reigns with you
in the unity of the Holy Spirit,
one God, now and for ever.   Amen.**

OR

Accept our prayers through Jesus Christ our Lord,
who taught us to pray,
Our Father in heaven ... now and for ever.   Amen.

157

14d The priest says

Let us pray for all people and for the Church throughout the world.

The minister says

Father, we pray for your holy catholic Church;
that we all may be one in Christ.

Grant that every member of the Church may truly and humbly serve you;
that your Name may be glorified by everyone.

We pray for all bishops, priests, and deacons;
that they may be faithful ministers of your word and sacraments.

We pray for all who govern and exercise authority in the nations of the world;
that there may be peace and justice among all.

Give us strength to do your will in all that we undertake;
that we may be blessed in all our works.

Have compassion on those who suffer or are in grief or trouble;
that they may be delivered from their distress.

We praise you for all your saints who have entered into joy;
may we also share in your heavenly kingdom.

The priest says

EITHER

Hear us, Father,
through Jesus Christ our Lord,
who lives and reigns with you
in the unity of the Holy Spirit,
one God, now and for ever. Amen.

OR

Accept our prayers through Jesus Christ our Lord,
who taught us to pray,
Our Father in heaven ... now and for ever. Amen.

ALTERNATIVE FORMS FOR §§ 20-30

A SECOND FORM OF THE THANKSGIVING

20a The priest takes the bread and wine for the Communion, places
them upon the Lord's table, and says this Prayer of Thanksgiving
and Consecration.

[The Lord be with you.
  And also with you.]

Lift up your hearts.
  We lift them to the Lord.

Let us give thanks to the Lord our God.
  It is right to give him thanks and praise.

All thanks and praise, glory and honour,
be yours at all times, in every place,
creator Lord, holy Father, true and living God.

We praise you that through your eternal Word
you brought the universe into being
and made man in your own image.
You have given us this earth to care for and delight in,
and with its bounty you preserve our life.

We thank you that you bound yourself to mankind
with the promises of a gracious covenant
and called us to serve you in love and peace.

Above all, we give you thanks for your Son,
our Saviour Jesus Christ;
by the power of the Holy Spirit
he was born a man and lived our common life;
to you he offered his life in perfect obedience and trust;
he has delivered us from our sins, brought us new life,
and reconciled us to you, Father, and to one another.

Therefore we join with angels and all created things,
with patriarchs, prophets, and apostles,
and the whole church in heaven and earth,
in their unending song:

Holy, holy, holy Lord, God of power and might,
heaven and earth are full of your glory.
Hosanna in the highest.

And now, Father, we thank you
for these gifts of your creation, this bread and this wine,
and we pray that we who eat and drink them
in the fellowship of the Holy Spirit
in obedience to our Saviour Christ
may be partakers of his body and blood,
and be made one with him and with each other
in peace and love.

The priest takes the bread into his hands and says
For on the night he was betrayed he took bread;
and when he had given you thanks
he broke it, and gave it to his disciples, saying,
'Take, eat. This is my body which is given for you.
Do this in remembrance of me.'

He takes the cup into his hands and says
After supper, he took the cup
and again giving you thanks
he gave it to his disciples, saying,
'Drink from this, all of you.
This is my blood of the new covenant
which is shed for you and for many
for the remission of sins.
Do this, as often as you drink it, in remembrance of me.'

160

**With this bread and this cup
we show forth Christ's death
until he comes in glory.**

With thanksgiving, Father, for the gift of your Son,
we proclaim his passion and death,
his resurrection and ascension,
the outpouring of his Spirit,
and his presence with his people.

Renew us by your Holy Spirit
that we may be united in the body of your Son
and serve you as a royal priesthood
in the joy of your eternal kingdom.

Receive our praises, Father almighty,
through Jesus Christ our Lord,
with whom and in whom,
by the power of the Holy Spirit,
we worship you in songs of never-ending praise:

**Blessing and honour and glory and power
are yours for ever and ever.   Amen.**

21   Please turn to page 171.

A THIRD FORM OF THE THANKSGIVING

20b   The priest takes the bread and wine for the Communion, places
them on the Lord's table, and says this Prayer of Thanksgiving and
Consecration.

[The Lord be with you.
    And also with you.]

Lift up your hearts.
    We lift them to the Lord.

Let us give thanks to the Lord our God.
    It is right to give him thanks and praise.

All thanks and praise, glory and honour,
be yours at all times and in all places,
creator Lord, holy Father, true and living God.

We praise you for your only-begotten Son
through whom you brought the universe into being
and made man in your own image.
You have given us this earth
that we might care for it and delight in it,
and through its bounty you preserve our life.

Above all we thank you
that you sent your Son, our Saviour Jesus Christ:
he is your eternal Word and the clear image of your glory.
By the power of the Holy Spirit
he was made man of the flesh of Mary, his virgin mother;
he took the form of a servant
and, with perfect trust in you,
he lived our common life.
He obeyed you in all things,
even to death on the cross.

He is the true passover Lamb
who was offered for us.
By his death he has destroyed death,
has taken away our sin and the sin of all the world,
and has reconciled us to you, Father,
and to one another.
By his rising to life again
he has brought us into new and everlasting life.

We thank you because you have bound yourself to us
and all mankind
by the promises of the new testament in his blood,
calling us into the fellowship of your saints
to serve you in love and peace,
to witness to the gospel,
and to show forth the fruit of the Spirit in our lives.

Therefore with angels and archangels,
and with all the company of heaven,
we proclaim your great and glorious name,
for ever praising you and saying:

Holy, holy, holy Lord, God of power and might,
heaven and earth are full of your glory.
Hosanna in the highest.

Hear us, merciful Father,
and grant that we who receive these gifts of your creation,
this bread and this wine,
in obedience to our Saviour Christ,
may be partakers of his body and blood,
and be made one with him and with each other
in peace and love.

The priest takes the bread into his hands and says

For on the night he was betrayed he took bread;
and when he had given thanks
he broke it, and gave it to his disciples, saying,
'Take, eat. This is my body which is given for you.
Do this in remembrance of me.'

He takes the cup into his hands and says

After supper, he took the cup
and again giving you thanks
he gave it to his disciples, saying,
'Drink from this, all of you.
This is my blood of the new covenant
which is shed for you and for many
for the remission of sins.
Do this, as often as you drink of it, in remembrance of me.'

163

With this bread and this cup or **Christ has died;**
we show forth Christ's death **Christ is risen;**
until he comes in glory. **Christ will come again.**

We give thanks to you, Father,
for your gift to us of Christ your Son,
our great high priest;
we celebrate and proclaim his perfect sacrifice
made once for all upon the cross,
his resurrection from the dead,
and his ascension into heaven to reign with you in glory.

We thank you for the outpouring of the Spirit upon your
    saints;
renew us, we pray, by the same Holy Spirit,
as we offer ourselves to you through Christ our Saviour
to serve you as a royal priesthood;
and grant that, when he returns to the earth
in power and majesty to judge the living and the dead,
we with all your pilgrim people
may be ready to meet him,
and may worship you for ever.

Receive our prayer and praise, Father,
through Jesus Christ our Lord,
with whom and in whom,
by the power of the Holy Spirit,
we worship you, Father almighty,
in songs of never-ending praise:

Blessing and honour and glory and power
are yours for ever and ever.   Amen.

21   Please turn to page 171.

A FOURTH FORM OF THE THANKSGIVING

20c The priest takes the bread and wine for the Communion, places
them upon the Lord's table, and says this Prayer of Thanksgiving
and Consecration

[The Lord be with you.
  And also with you.]

Lift up your hearts.
  We lift them to the Lord.

Let us give thanks to the Lord our God.
  It is right to give him thanks and praise.

All glory and honour, thanks and praise,
be yours now and always,
Lord, holy Father, mighty Creator, everliving God.
We give thanks and praise for your Son, our Saviour Jesus
  Christ,
who by his death on the cross
and rising to new life
offered the one true sacrifice for sin
and obtained an eternal deliverance for his people.

Therefore with the whole company of heaven
we proclaim your great and glorious name,
for ever praising you and saying:

Holy, holy, holy Lord, God of power and might,
heaven and earth are full of your glory.
Hosanna in the highest.

And now, Father, we pray
that we who receive these your gifts of bread and wine
according to our Saviour's word
may be partakers of his body and blood.

165

The priest takes the bread into his hands and says:

For on the night he was betrayed he took bread;
and when he had given thanks to you, his almighty Father,
he broke it, and gave it to his disciples, saying,
'Take, eat. This is my body which is given for you.
Do this in remembrance of me.'

He takes the cup into his hands and says:

After supper, he took the cup
and again giving you thanks
he gave it to his disciples, saying,
'Drink from this, all of you.
This is my blood of the new covenant
which is shed for you and for many
for the remission of sins.
Do this, as often as you drink it, in remembrance of me.'

With this bread and this cup   or   **Christ has died;**
we show forth Christ's death   **Christ is risen;**
until he comes in glory.   **Christ will come again.**

We offer our prayer and praise, Father,
in the fellowship of the Holy Spirit,
through Jesus Christ our Lord:
Blessing and honour and glory and power
are yours for ever and ever.   **Amen.**

21   Please turn to page 171.

THE PRAYER OF THANKSGIVING AND CONSECRATION WITH SEASONAL ADDITIONS

20d The priest takes the bread and wine for the Communion, places them upon the Lord's table, and says this Prayer of Thanksgiving and Consecration.

[The Lord be with you.
And also with you.]

Lift up your hearts.
We lift them to the Lord.

Let us give thanks to the Lord our God.
It is right to give him thanks and praise.

All glory and honour, thanks and praise
be given to you at all times and in all places,
Lord, holy Father, true and living God,
through Jesus Christ our Lord.
For he is your eternal Word
through whom you have created all things from the
     beginning
and formed us in your own image.

In Advent

In him the day of our deliverance has dawned.
We rejoice that through him you make all things new
and we look for his coming in power and majesty to
     judge the world.

In your great love you gave him
to be made man for us and to share our common life.

At Christmas, Presentation, Annunciation

By the power of the Holy Spirit
he was born of the virgin Mary his mother,
and we have seen his glory,
glory as of the only Son from the Father.

At Epiphany and on the Transfiguration

You have revealed in him your eternal plan of
salvation
and showed him to be the light of all the nations.
His glory has shone among us,
glory as of the only Son from the Father.

In Lent

He was tempted in every way as we are,
yet he did not sin;
and he gives us strength to control our desires,
and to walk in his way of love.

In obedience to your will
your Son our Saviour offered himself as a perfect sacrifice,
and died upon the cross for our redemption.
Through him you have freed us from the slavery of sin
and reconciled us to yourself,
our God and Father.

In the week before Easter and in Eastertide

For he is the true passover Lamb
who was offered for us
and has taken away the sin of the world.

In Eastertide he adds

By his death he has destroyed death
and by his rising to life
he has restored to us eternal life.

He is our great high priest
whom you raised from death
and exalted to your right hand on high
where he ever lives to intercede for us.

In Ascensiontide

He has passed beyond our sight,
not to abandon us but to be our hope,

that where he is we might also be
and reign with him in glory.

Through him you have sent upon us
your holy and life-giving Spirit
and made us a royal priesthood
called to serve you for ever.

In Whitsuntide

By the same Spirit
we are led into all truth
and given power to proclaim with boldness
the glorious gospel to all the world.

On Trinity Sunday

You have revealed to us your glory and love
in the glory and love of the Son and of the Holy
    Spirit;
three persons, one God,
ever to be worshipped and adored.

On saints' days

You have called us into the fellowship of [N and] all
    your saints,
and set before us the example of their witness
and of the fruit of your Spirit in their lives.

Therefore with angels and archangels,
and with all the company of heaven,
we proclaim your great and glorious name,
for ever praising you and saying:

**Holy, holy, holy Lord, God of power and might,
heaven and earth are full of your glory.
Hosanna in the highest.**

Merciful Father, we thank you
for these gifts of your creation, this bread and this wine,
and we pray that we who eat and drink them
in the fellowship of the Holy Spirit
in obedience to our Saviour Christ
in remembrance of his death and passion
may be partakers of his body and his blood,

He takes the bread into his hands and says

who on the night he was betrayed took bread;
and when he had given you thanks
he broke it, and gave it to his disciples, saying,
'Take, eat. This is my body which is given for you.
Do this in remembrance of me.'

He takes the cup into his hands and says

After supper, he took the cup,
and again giving you thanks
he gave it to his disciples, saying,
'Drink from this, all of you.
This is my blood of the new covenant
which is shed for you and for many
for the forgiveness of sins.
Do this, as often as you drink it, in remembrance of me.'

Christ has died;
Christ is risen;
Christ will come again.

Father, with this bread and this cup,
we do as our Saviour has commanded:
we celebrate the redemption he has won for us;
we proclaim his perfect sacrifice
made once for all upon the cross,
his mighty resurrection and glorious ascension;
and we look for his coming
to fulfil all things according to your will.

170

Renew us by your Holy Spirit,
unite us in the body of your Son,
and bring us with all your people
into the joy of your eternal kingdom;
through Jesus Christ our Lord,
with whom and in whom,
by the power of the Holy Spirit,
we worship you, Father almighty,
in songs of never-ending praise:

**Blessing and honour and glory and power
are yours for ever and ever.   Amen.**

‡21   If the Lord's Prayer has not already been said, it is said here or
after the Communion.
The priest says

As our Saviour Christ has taught us we are confident to
say,
**Our Father in heaven,
hallowed be your Name,
your kingdom come,
your will be done
on earth as in heaven.
Give us today our daily bread.
Forgive us our sins
as we forgive those who sin against us.
Lead us not into temptation,
but deliver us from evil.
For the kingdom, the power, and glory are yours
now and for ever.   Amen.**

22   The priest breaks the bread before the people.
He may do so in silence, or he may say

[We who are many are one body in Christ,
For we all share in the one bread.]

171

THE COMMUNION

23   [The priest may say

Come, let us take this holy sacrament of the body and blood
of Christ in remembrance that he died for us, and feed on
him in our hearts by faith with thanksgiving.]

> The priest and the other communicants receive the holy
> communion.
> When the minister gives the bread and the cup he uses one of the
> forms on page 149. The communicant may answer   **Amen.**
> During the Communion, hymns or anthems (see Note 1 on page
> 153) may be sung.

AFTER COMMUNION

‡24   A Sentence of Scripture may be said.

‡25   If the Lord's Prayer (page 171) has not been said earlier, it is used
here. The priest says

Let us pray. As our Saviour Christ has taught us,
    we are confident to say,
Our Father in heaven . . . now and for ever.   Amen.

‡26   The priest may say one of the following prayers, and the congregation responds with the prayer at §27.

[Let us pray.]
Father, we thank you
that you feed us who have received these holy mysteries
with the spiritual food of the body and blood of our Saviour
    Jesus Christ.
We thank you for this assurance of your goodness and love;
that we are living members of his body
and heirs of his eternal kingdom.
Accept this our sacrifice of praise and thanksgiving,
and help us to grow in love and obedience,
that with all your saints we may worship you for ever.

or this

Father of all,
we give you thanks and praise
that when we were still far off
you met us in your Son and brought us home.
Dying and living, he declared your love,
gave us grace, and opened the gate of glory.
May we who share Christ's body live his risen life;
we who drink his cup bring life to others;
we whom the Spirit lights give light to the world.
Keep us in this hope that we have grasped;
so we and all your children shall be free,
and the whole earth live to praise your Name.

or this

Father, you graciously feed us
who have received these holy mysteries
with the bread of life and the cup of eternal salvation.
May we who have reached out our hands to receive this
    sacrament
be strengthened in your service;
we who have sung your praises
tell of your glory and your truth in our lives;
we who have seen the greatness of your love
see you face to face in your kingdom.
For you have made us your own people
by the death and resurrection of your Son our Lord
and by the life-giving power of the Spirit.

or this

Father,
we who believe in your Son Jesus Christ
and have received these pledges of his love,
thank you because you graciously feed us
with the spiritual food of his body and his blood.
By this you assure us of your love and forgiveness,
and that we and all your faithful people

are true members of his body and of each other in him.

Remember your church which you have purchased by his blood,

and gather it in holiness into the kingdom you have prepared for it.

Make us faithful witnesses of the Lord Jesus and his resurrection,

that at his coming we may go out with great joy to meet him,

and be found worthy to worship you

with all your saints for ever.

or either of the prayers at §33 of The Holy Communion, First Order (page 128) may be used, and one of the prayers from §§8-11 of the Prayers for Various Occasions (pages 93-94) may be added.

27   All say together

Father, we offer ourselves to you
as a living sacrifice
through Jesus Christ our Lord.
send us out in the power of your Spirit
to live and work to your praise and glory.   Amen.

‡28   A Hymn may be sung, which may be Gloria in excelsis (page 137) if it has not been used at §7.

29   The priest, or bishop if present, says this or the appropriate seasonal Blessing (see page 151)

The peace of God which passes all understanding keep your hearts and minds in the knowledge and love of God, and of his Son, Jesus Christ our Lord;

and the blessing of God almighty, the Father, the Son, and the Holy Spirit, be amongst you and remain with you always.   **Amen.**

30   The deacon may say

Go in peace to love and serve the Lord:

In the name of Christ.   Amen.

Collects, Readings, and Calendar

Grevillea robusta
Silky oak

Collects and Readings
at the Holy Communion

Two series of collects and readings may be used with the services in this book.

The *One Year Series*, based on the collects, epistles, and Gospels provided in The Book of Common Prayer of 1662, is given in reference form only.*

The *Three Year Series* contains a wider selection of Scripture readings and collects and is given in greater detail. In this series three sets of readings are given to be used on each Sunday; for Christmas day and Easter day two sets are provided either of which may be used at the discretion of the minister. The Sundays after Epiphany, Septuagesima, Sexagesima, Quinquagesima, and the Sundays after Trinity are called *Ordinary Sundays*. The number of them falling before Lent and after Trinity Sunday varies according to the date of Easter. The Table of Sundays and Movable Feasts* shows how this applies in any particular year. The three sets of readings are referred to as *Year A, B, and C*; Year C is a year whose number is divisible by three. Thus 1978 is Year A, 1979 is Year B, 1980 is Year C and so on; see further the Table of Sundays and Movable Feasts.

The *references* are to the Revised Standard Version of the Bible and the version of the Psalter in this Book (but see note below). When other versions are used, some adaptations will be necessary.

Themes are indicated at the head of each day in the Three Year Series. They are offered only as suggestions, and are in no way intended to limit the application of the readings or to bind the preacher to the stated theme.

A *Sentence* is provided for use at §3 of The Holy Communion service. This is intended to do two things: to lead into worship, and to indicate something of the content of the readings for the day.

The *Collects* are given in full in the Three Year Series only. The first is a revised form of a 1662 Prayer Book collect (BCP). All the 1662 Prayer Book collects for Sundays and Holy Days are used, though not always on the days to which they were originally assigned. A Table of Prayer Book collects is to be found on page 178. The alternative collect may be introduced by the bidding printed in square brackets. Where this is done, a pause to allow the congregation to pray silently is appropriate before their personal prayers are collected in the set prayer.

In the *Readings*, verses are stated inclusively. The letter *a* after the number of a verse signifies the first part of that verse, and the letter *b* the second part. A brief indication of the content of each reading is given in the form of a sub-title; this is not intended to be read aloud.

A *Psalm* or psalm-portion is provided as a devotional response following the first reading. This may be sung or read in a manner appropriate to the congregation. It may also be used at §1. The Psalms are referred to in two ways. The first reference is to the Psalter to be found in this Book. The reference in brackets described as 'Grail' is to *The Psalms Singing Version*, published by Collins, London, 1963. A congregational *response* is given with the psalm-references. This provides a brief guide to the general theme of the psalm. It can be used as a congregational antiphon or refrain after each verse or stanza (in the 'Grail' version) of the psalm. When it is used in this way, the reader first reads the response, and the congregation repeat it after him; the congregation also repeat it after the reader has read each verse or stanza of the psalm.

In view of the relation between the psalms and the first readings set in these tables, it is recommended that the Gloria ('Glory to God; Father, . . .') be not used after the psalm.

A sentence from the Bible is provided for use *after Communion* at §31 of the First Order of Service and at §24 of the Second Order of Service. This recalls the readings for the day, and is designed to be used after all have received the holy communion. It may introduce a short pause for reflection and personal prayer. It may also be used as an anthem during the Communion.

---

* The One Year Series and Table of Sundays and Movable Feasts is printed in the large edition with Tables only.

A Table of Prayer Book Collects

The Prayer Book Collects for red-letter days are to be found on pages 268ff, except that for the Epiphany of our Lord (January 6) which is to be found on page 191.

The Collects and Readings
for the Holy Communion

(THREE YEAR SERIES)

THE FIRST SUNDAY IN ADVENT
Your redemption is near at hand

Sentence

To you, O Lord, I lift up my soul, O my God, in you I trust, let
me not be put to shame; let not my enemies exult over me; let none
that wait for you be put to shame. Psalm 25.1-3a

or

Come, let us go up to the mountain of the Lord, to the house of
the God of Jacob; that he may teach us his ways and that we may
walk in his paths. Isaiah 2.3

Collect

Almighty God, give us grace that we may cast away the works of
darkness and put on the armour of light, now in the time of this
mortal life in which your Son Jesus Christ came among us in great
humility; that on the last day, when he comes again in his glorious
majesty to judge the living and the dead, we may rise to the life
immortal; through him who lives and reigns with you and the Holy
Spirit, now and for ever. **Amen.** BCP, Advent 1

or

Let us pray [that we may be ready for Christ's coming.]
All-powerful God,
increase our strength of will for doing good
that Christ may find an eager welcome at his coming
and call us to his side in the kingdom of heaven,
where he lives and reigns with you and the Holy Spirit,
one God, for ever and ever. **Amen.**

Readings

Year A

Isaiah 2.1-5   God's Kingdom of peace
Psalm 122 (Grail 121.1-2,3-4,8-9)
I rejoiced when I heard them say:
let us go to the house of the Lord.
Romans 13.11-14   Our salvation is near
Matthew 24.37-44   Watch!

Year B

Isaiah 63.15 - 64.12 or 63.16b-17; 64.1,3b-8   Longing for God's presence
Psalm 80.1-7 (Grail, 79.2-3a,15,18-19)
Lord, make us turn to you,
let us see your face and we shall be saved.
1 Corinthians 1.3-9   Longing for Christ's return
Mark 13.33-37   Watch!

Year C

Jeremiah 33.14-16   The righteous Branch for David
Psalm 25.1-9 (Grail, 24.4-5,8-9,10&14)
To you, O Lord, I lift my soul.
1 Thessalonians 3.12 - 4.2   Waiting for Christ's return
Luke 21.25-36 or 25-28,34-36   Your liberation is near

After Communion

Righteousness shall go before the Lord, and prepare the path for
him.   Psalm 85.13 TEV

THE SECOND SUNDAY IN ADVENT
The salvation of God

Sentence

[Hear the words of the prophet Isaiah:]
Shake yourself from the dust, says the Lord, arise, O captive
Jerusalem; loose the bonds from your neck, O captive daughter of
Zion.   Isaiah 52.2

Collect

Blessed Lord, you have caused all holy scriptures to be written for
our learning: grant us so to hear them, read, mark, learn, and inwardly digest them, that, encouraged and supported by your holy

181

Word, we may embrace and always hold fast the joyful hope of
everlasting life, which you have given us in our Saviour Jesus
Christ. **Amen.** BCP, Advent 2

or

Let us pray [that nothing may hinder us from receiving Christ with
   joy.]
God of power and mercy,
open our hearts in welcome.
Remove the things that hinder us from receiving Christ with joy,
so that we may share his wisdom
and become one with him
when he comes in glory,
for he lives and reigns with you and the Holy Spirit,
one God for ever and ever. **Amen.**

Readings

Year A

Isaiah 11.1-10   The longed-for Messiah
Psalm 72.12-21 (Grail, 71.1-2,7-8,12-13,17)
   Justice shall flourish in his time,
   and fulness of peace for ever.
Romans 15.4-13 or 4-9   Christ our hope
Matthew 3.1-12   The Kingdom of heaven is at hand!

Year B

Isaiah 40.1-11 or 1-5,9-11   Prepare the way of the Lord
Psalm 85.8-13 (Grail, 84.9-10,11-12,13-14)
   Lord, let us see your kindness,
   and grant us your salvation.
2 Peter 3.8-14   The day of the Lord
Mark 1.1-8   The Forerunner

Year C

Baruch 5.1-9   Rejoice, Jerusalem shall be restored
   or
Isaiah 40.1-11   Prepare the way of the Lord
Psalm 126 (Grail, 125)
   The Lord has done great things for us;
   we are filled with joy.
Philippians 1.3-11 or 3-6,8-11   Be ready for the Day of Christ
Luke 3.1-6   All mankind shall see the salvation of our God

After Communion

Save us by your might, Lord; answer our prayer, so that the people
you love may be rescued. Psalm 60.5 TEV

THE THIRD SUNDAY IN ADVENT
Rejoice! The Lord is near!

Sentence

O people in Zion who dwell at Jerusalem; you shall weep no more.
The Lord will surely be gracious to you at the sound of your cry;
he will cause his majestic voice to be heard. Isaiah 30.19a,30b

Collect

Almighty God, we pray that the course of this world may be so
peaceably ordered through your guidance that your church may
joyfully serve you in all godly quietness; through Jesus Christ our
Lord. **Amen.** BCP, Trinity 5

or

Let us pray [that God will fill us with joy at the coming of
    Christ.]
Lord God,
may we, your people,
who look forward to the birthday of Christ
experience the joy of salvation
and celebrate that feast with love and thanksgiving.
We ask this through our Lord Jesus Christ, your Son,
who lives and reigns with you and the Holy Spirit,
one God, for ever and ever. **Amen.**

Readings

Year A

Isaiah 35.1-10 or 1-6a,10   God himself will come to save us
Psalm 146.5-10 (Grail, 145.6b-7,8-9,8c9c10)
    Lord, come and save us. or   *Alleluia!*
James 5.7-10   Do not lose heart
Matthew 11.2-11   The one to come is here!

Year B

Isaiah 61.1-7 or 1-2a,10-11   I will greatly rejoice in the Lord

183

For the Psalm, The Magnificat (p. 56)   *My soul rejoices in my God.*
1 Thessalonians 5.16-24   Ready for the coming of our Lord
John 1.6-8,19-28   He who comes after me stands among you

Year C

Zephaniah 3.14-18a   The Lord will renew us by his love
For the Psalm, Isaiah 12.2-6 (2-3,4,5-6) or Benedictus (p. 46)
   Cry out with joy and gladness:
   for among you is the great and Holy One of Israel.
Philippians 4.4-7   The Lord is near
Luke 3.10-18   What must we do?

After Communion

[Hear the word of the Lord:] Strengthen the weak hands, and make firm the feeble knees. Say to those who are of a fearful heart, 'Be strong, fear not.'   Isaiah 35.3,4a

THE FOURTH SUNDAY IN ADVENT

The promised Saviour

Sentence

Shower, O heaven, from above,
and let the skies rain down righteousnesss;
let the earth open, and bring forth salvation.   Isaiah 45.8
   or
Thus says the Lord: Turn to me and be saved,
all the ends of the earth!
From my mouth has gone forth in righteousness
a word that shall not return:
'To me every knee shall bow, every tongue shall swear.'
                                                    Isaiah 45.22,23

Collect

We beseech you, Lord, pour your grace into our hearts; that, as we have known the incarnation of your Son Jesus Christ by the message of an angel, so by his cross and passion we may be brought to the glory of his resurrection, who lives and reigns with you and the Holy Spirit, one God, for ever and ever.   **Amen.**

                                      BCP, Annunciation of the BVM

184

or

Let us pray [that Christ will truly come into our hearts]
Lord,
fill our hearts with your love,
and as you revealed to us by an angel
the coming of your Son as man,
so lead us through his suffering and death
to the glory of his resurrection,
for he lives and reigns with you and the Holy Spirit,
one God, for ever and ever.   **Amen.**

Readings

Year A

Isaiah 7.10-14   A virgin shall conceive
Psalm 24 (Grail, 23.1-2,3-4,5-6)
  Let the Lord enter;
  he is king of glory.
Romans 1.1-7   Jesus, son of David, Son of God
Matthew 1.18-25   God's call to Joseph

Year B

2 Samuel 7.1-12, or 1-5,8b-12,14a,16
  God's promise to the house of David
Psalm 89.19-29 (Grail, 88.2-3,4-5,27&29)
  For ever I will sing the goodness of the Lord.
Romans 16.25-27   God reveals his age-long purpose in Jesus
Luke 1.26-38   God's call to Mary

Year C

Micah 5.2-5a   The shepherd of the Lord
Psalm 80.8-19 (Grail, 79.2-3,15,18-19)
  Lord, make us turn to you,
  let us see your face and we shall be saved.
Hebrews 10.5-10   Christ came to do God's will
Luke 1.39-45   Mary visits Elizabeth

After Communion

Behold, a young woman shall conceive and bear a son, and shall
call his name Immanuel.   Isaiah 7.14

185

CHRISTMAS DAY AT MIDNIGHT

A Son is born

Sentence

While gentle silence enveloped all things, and night in its swift course was now half gone, your all-powerful Word leapt from heaven, from the royal throne, into the midst of the land that was doomed.   Wisdom 18.14-15

or

This is our God; we have waited for him, that he might save us.
This is the Lord; we have waited for him; let us be glad and rejoice in his salvation.   Isaiah 25.9

Collect

Loving Father, who sent your only Son into the world that we might have life through faith in him: grant that we who celebrate his birth on this most holy night may come at last to the fulness of life in your heavenly kingdom; where he now lives and reigns with you and the Holy Spirit, now and for ever.   **Amen.**

or

Let us pray [that our joy in the birth of Christ will last for ever.]
Father,
you make this holy night radiant
with the splendour of Jesus Christ our light.
We welcome him as Lord, the true light of the world.
Bring us to eternal joy in the kingdom of heaven,
where he lives and reigns with you and the Holy Spirit,
one God, for ever and ever.   **Amen.**

Readings

Isaiah 9.2-7 or 2-4,6-7   A son is given to us
Psalm 96.7-13 (Grail, 95.1-2a,2b-3,11-12,13)
   Today a saviour has been born to us;
   he is Christ the Lord.
Titus 2.11-14   The grace of God has appeared
Luke 2.1-14   Today the Saviour is born

After Communion

Blessed be the Lord God of Israel, for he has visited and redeemed his people, and has raised up a horn of salvation for us in the house of his servant David.   Luke 1.68,69

186

CHRISTMAS DAY – DURING THE DAY
(First Service)
The shepherds at the manger

Sentence

The people that walked in darkness have seen a great light; for to us a child is born, to us a son is given.   Isaiah 9.2

Collect

Almighty God, you have given us your only Son to take our nature upon him and as at this time to be born of a pure virgin: grant that we, being born again and made your children by adoption and grace, may daily be renewed by your Holy Spirit; through our Lord Jesus Christ, who lives and reigns with you and the Holy Spirit, one God, for ever and ever.   **Amen.**   BCP, Christmas Day

or

Let us pray [that the love of Christ will be a light to the world.]
Father,
we are filled with the new light
by the coming of your Word among us.
May the light of faith
shine in our words and actions.
Grant this through our Lord Jesus Christ, your Son,
who lives and reigns with you and the Holy Spirit,
one God, for ever and ever.   **Amen.**

Readings

Isaiah 62.11-12   Your saviour comes
Psalm 97 (Grail, 96.1-2,11-12)
   A light will shine on us this day:
   the Lord is born for us.
Titus 3.4-7   Saved by his love
Luke 2.15-20   The shepherds visit the infant Jesus

After Communion

Sing for joy to the Lord, all the earth; praise him with songs and shouts of joy. All people everywhere have seen the victory of our God.   Psalm 98.4,3b TEV

CHRISTMAS DAY – DURING THE DAY
(Second Service)
Word made flesh

Sentence

To us a child is born, to us a son is given;
and the government will be upon his shoulder,
and his name will be called 'Wonderful, Counsellor, Mighty
God.'   Isaiah 9.6

Collect

Almighty God, you have given us your only Son to take our nature
upon him and as at this time to be born of a pure virgin: grant
that we, being born again and made your children by adoption and
grace, may daily be renewed by your Holy Spirit; through our Lord
Jesus Christ, who lives and reigns with you and the Holy Spirit,
one God, for ever and ever.   **Amen.**   BCP, Christmas Day
   or
Let us pray [for the glory promised by the birth of Christ.]
Lord God,
we praise you for creating man,
and still more for restoring him in Christ.
Your Son shared our weakness,
and we share his glory,
for he lives and reigns with you and the Holy Spirit,
one God, for ever and ever.   **Amen.**

Readings

Isaiah 52.7-10   The salvation of our God
Psalm 98 (Grail, 97.1,2-3a,3b-4,5-6)
   All the ends of the earth have seen the saving power of God.
Hebrews 1.1-6   God speaks to us through his Son
John 1.1-18 or 1-5,9-14   The Word was made flesh

After Communion

The Word became flesh and dwelt among us, full of grace and
truth; we have beheld his glory, glory as of the only Son from the
Father.   John 1.14

THE SUNDAY AFTER CHRISTMAS
The family

Sentence

The shepherds went in haste and found Mary and Joseph, and the baby lying in a manger.   Luke 2.16

Collect

Lord our God, you have given us as our example the life of Jesus in his home: grant that all Christian families may be so bound together in love and service that we may rejoice together in your heavenly home; through Jesus Christ our Lord, who lives and reigns with you and the Holy Spirit, now and for ever.   **Amen.**

or

Let us pray [for peace in our families.]
Father,
help us to live as the holy family,
united in respect and love.
Bring us to the joy and peace of your eternal home.
Grant this through our Lord Jesus Christ, your Son,
who lives and reigns with you and the Holy Spirit,
one God, for ever and ever.   **Amen.**

Readings

Sirach 3.2-14 or 2-6,12-14 or Genesis 1.26-31   The honour due to parents
Psalm 128 (Grail, 127.1-2,3,4-5)
Happy are those who fear the Lord and walk in his ways.
Colossians 3.12-21   Christian life in the world
  Year A
Matthew 2.13-23 or 13-15,19-23   The escape to Egypt
  Year B
Luke 2.22-40   Jesus grew in wisdom and stature
  Year C
Luke 2.41-52   The boy Jesus in the temple

After Communion

Jesus went down with Mary and Joseph and came to Nazareth, and was obedient to them; and Jesus increased in wisdom and in stature, and in favour with God and man.   Luke 2.51,52

189

THE SECOND SUNDAY AFTER CHRISTMAS
God with us

Sentence

The people that walked in darkness
have seen a great light.
For to us a child is born,
to us a son is given;
and his name will be called
'Everlasting Father, Prince of Peace.' Isaiah 9.2a, 6ad

Collect

Almighty Father, whose blessed Son was revealed so that he might
destroy the works of the devil and make us the children of God and
heirs of eternal life: grant that having this hope we may purify ourselves as he is pure; that, when he shall appear again with power
and great glory, we may be made like him in his eternal and glorious kingdom, where with you, Father, and with the Holy Spirit,
he lives and reigns, one God, for evermore. **Amen.**

BCP, Epiphany 6

or

Almighty God, who wonderfully created man in your own image,
and yet more wonderfully restored him: grant, we pray, that as
your Son our Lord Jesus Christ was made in our likeness, so we
may share his divine nature; we ask this through Jesus Christ, your
Son, who lives and reigns with you and the Holy Spirit, one God,
now and for ever. **Amen.**

or

Let us pray [that all mankind may be enlightened by the
Gospel.]
God of power and life,
glory of all who believe in you,
fill the world with your splendour,
and show the nations the light of your truth.
We ask this through our Lord Jesus Christ, your Son,
who lives and reigns with you and the Holy Spirit,
one God, for ever and ever. **Amen.**

190

Readings

Proverbs 8.22-31 or Sirach 24.1-12 or 1-2,8-12
   The wisdom of God lives in his people
Psalm 147.12-20 (Grail, 147.12-13,14-15,19-20)
   The Word of God became man, and lived among us.   or   *Alleluia!*
Ephesians 1.3-6,15-18   Spiritual blessings
John 1.1-18   We saw his glory

After Communion

To all who received him, who believed in his name, Christ gave
power to become children of God.   John 1.12

THE EPIPHANY OF OUR LORD (January 6)
The nations see God's salvation

Sentence

The Lord whom you seek will suddenly come to his temple; the
messenger of the covenant in whom you delight, behold, he is
coming, says the Lord of hosts.   Malachi 3.1b

Collect

O God, who by the leading of a star manifested your beloved Son
to the gentiles: mercifully grant that we, who know you now by
faith, may after this life enjoy the splendour of your glorious Godhead; through Jesus Christ our Lord.   **Amen.**   BCP, Epiphany
   or
Let us pray [that we will be guided by the light of faith.]
Father,
you revealed your Son to the nations
by the guidance of a star.
Lead us to your glory in heaven
by the light of faith.
We ask this through our Lord Jesus Christ, your Son,
who lives and reigns with you and the Holy Spirit,
one God, for ever and ever.   **Amen.**

Readings

Isaiah 60.1-6   The glory of the Lord
Psalm 72.1-11 (Grail, 71.1-2,7-8,10-11,12-13)
   Lord, every nation on earth will adore you.

191

Ephesians 3.1-6 or 2-3a,5-6   God reveals his age-long purpose
Matthew 2.1-12   Wise men worship Christ the King

After Communion

We have seen his star in the East, and have come to worship him.

Matthew 2.2b

NOTE: The collects and readings for the Ordinary Sundays (see pages 222ff and the Table of Sundays and Movable Feasts) are used between the Epiphany of our Lord and Ash Wednesday.

THE FIRST DAY OF LENT (Ash Wednesday)
Penitence and discipline

Sentence

The Lord is merciful to all, for he can do all things; and he overlooks men's sins, that they may repent. He spares all things, for they are his, and he is the Lord who loves the living.

Wisdom 11.23,26

or

The Lord is merciful and gracious,
he does not deal with us according to our sins,
nor requite us according to our iniquities.   Psalm 103.8a,10

Collect

Almighty and everlasting God, you hate nothing that you have made, and you forgive the sins of all who are penitent: create and make in us new and contrite hearts, that we, lamenting our sins and acknowledging our wretchedness, may obtain from you, the God of all mercy, perfect remission and forgiveness; through Jesus Christ our Lord.   **Amen.**   BCP, Ash Wednesday

or

Let us pray [that we may keep a true fast.]
Lord,
protect us in our struggle against evil.
Help us to honour you by our self-denial
and make this season holy.
Grant this through our Lord Jesus Christ, your Son,
who lives and reigns with you and the Holy Spirit,
one God, for ever and ever.   **Amen.**

Readings

Joel 2.12-18   Call to repentance and fasting
Psalm 51.1-13 (Grail, 50.3-4,5-6a,12-13,14-15)
   Be merciful, O Lord, for we have sinned.
2 Corinthians 5.16 - 6.2 or 5.20 - 6.2   Be reconciled to God
Matthew 6.1-21 or 1-6,16-18   Almsgiving, prayer, and fasting

After Communion

Happy is the man who enjoys reading the law of the Lord, and
studying it day and night.   Psalm 1.2 TEV

THE FIRST SUNDAY IN LENT

Worship God. Serve only him

Sentence

When you call to me, says the Lord, I will answer you; I will be
with you in trouble, I will rescue you and honour you.

See Psalm 91.15,16

Collect

Lord Jesus Christ, for our sake you fasted forty days and forty
nights: give us grace to use such abstinence that, our flesh being
subdued to the spirit, we may always obey your will in righteousness and true holiness, to your honour and glory; for you live and
reign with the Father and the Holy Spirit, one God, for evermore.
Amen.   BCP, Lent 1

or

Let us pray [that we may grow in the self-sacrificing love of
   Christ.]
Father,
help us to understand the meaning
of your Son's death and resurrection,
and teach us to reflect it in our lives.
Grant this through our Lord Jesus Christ, your Son,
who lives and reigns with you and the Holy Spirit,
one God, for ever and ever.   **Amen.**

Readings

Year A

Genesis 2.7-9; 3.1-7   Creation and fall

193

Psalm 51.1-13 (Grail, 50.3-4,5-6,12-13,14-15)
Be merciful, O Lord, for we have sinned.
Romans 5.12-19 or 17-19   Sin and forgiveness
Matthew 4.1-11   Jesus tempted

Year B

Genesis 9.8-15   God makes a covenant with Noah
Psalm 25.1-9 (Grail, 24.4-5,6-7,8-9)
Your ways, O Lord, are love and truth, to those who keep your covenant.
1 Peter 3.18-22   The baptismal covenant
Mark 1.12-15   Jesus tempted

Year C

Deuteronomy 26.[1-]4-10   The Old Testament confession of faith
Psalm 91.1-12 (Grail, 90.1-2,10-11,12-13,14-15)
Be with me, Lord, when I am in trouble.
Romans 10.5-13 or 8-13   The christian confession of faith
Luke 4.1-13   Jesus tempted

After Communion

The Most High will cover you with his wings; you will be safe
under his care; his faithfulness will protect and defend you.

Psalm 91.4 TEV

THE SECOND SUNDAY IN LENT
Transfiguration

Sentence

[We pray with the psalmist:]
My heart says to the Lord, 'Your face, Lord, do I seek.' Hide not
your face from me. Turn not your servant away in anger, for you
have been my help.   Psalm 27.8-9

Collect

We beseech you, almighty God, look on the heartfelt desires of your
servants, and stretch forth the right hand of your power to be our
defence against all our enemies; through Jesus Christ our Lord.
Amen.   BCP, Lent 3

or
Let us pray [that we may respond to the Word of God.]
God our Father,
help us to hear your Son.
Enlighten us with your word,
that we may find the way to your glory.
We ask this through our Lord Jesus Christ, your Son,
who lives and reigns with you and the Holy Spirit,
one God, for ever and ever. **Amen.**

Readings

Year A

Genesis 12.1-4a   The call of Abraham
Psalm 33.13-21 (Grail, 32.4-5,18-19,20-21)
Lord, let your mercy be on us, as we place our trust in you.
2 Timothy 1.8b-10   The call to holiness
Matthew 17.1-9   Jesus transfigured

Year B

Genesis 22.1-18 or 1-2,9a,10-13,15-18   Abraham offers his son
Psalm 116.11-16 (Grail, 115.10-11,16-17,18-19)
I will walk in the presence of the Lord, in the land of the living.
Romans 8.31b-34   God did not spare his own Son
Mark 9.2-10   Jesus transfigured

Year C

Genesis 15.5-18 or 5-12,17-18   God's covenant with Abraham
Psalm 27.9-17 (Grail, 26.1,7-8a,8b-9,13-14)
The Lord is my light and my salvation.
Philippians 3.17 - 4.1 or 3.20 - 4.1   Our transfiguration
Luke 9.28b-36   Jesus transfigured

After Communion

This is my beloved Son, with whom I am well pleased; listen to
him.   Matthew 17.5

THE THIRD SUNDAY IN LENT
Turn to God, the Source of Life

Sentence

My eyes are ever toward the Lord, for he will pluck my feet out of the net. Turn to me, and be gracious to me; for I am lonely and afflicted.   Psalm 25.15-16

or

The Lord says: I will sprinkle clean water upon you, and you shall be clean from all your uncleanness. A new heart I will give you, and a new spirit I will put within you.   Ezekiel 36.25-26

Collect

Almighty God, we confess that we have no power of ourselves to help ourselves: keep us outwardly in our bodies and inwardly in our souls, that we may be defended from all adversities that may happen to the body, and from all evil thoughts that may assault and hurt the soul; through Jesus Christ our Lord.   **Amen.**

BCP, Lent 2

or

Let us pray [for confidence in the love and strength of God to over-
    come all our weakness.]
Father,
you have taught us to express our love for you
by prayer, denial of self, and works of mercy.
When we are discouraged by our weakness,
give us confidence in your love.
We ask this through our Lord Jesus Christ, your Son,
who lives and reigns with you and the Holy Spirit,
one God, for ever and ever.   **Amen.**

Readings

NOTE: The readings for Year A may be used every year.

Year A

Exodus 17.3-7   Water from the rock
Psalm 95 (Grail, 94.1-2,6-7,8-9)
    If today you hear his voice, harden not your hearts.
Romans 5.1-8 or 1-2,5-8   God's love poured into our hearts
John 4.5-42 or 4.4-15,19b-26,39a,40-42   The water of life

196

After Communion

Jesus said: Whoever drinks of the water that I shall give him will never thirst; the water that I shall give him will become in him a spring of water welling up to eternal life.   John 4.14

Year B

Exodus 20.1-17 or 1-3,7-8,12-17   The Ten Commandments
Psalm 19.7-14 (Grail, 18.8,9,10,11)
   Lord, you have the words of everlasting life.
1 Corinthians 1.22-25   We preach Christ crucified
John 2.13-25   Destroy this temple, and I will build it again

After Communion

Even the sparrow finds a home, and a swallow a nest for herself, where she may lay her young, at your altars, O Lord of hosts. Blessed are those who dwell in your house, ever singing your praise.   Psalm 84.3,4

Year C

Exodus 3.1-15 or 1-8a,13,15   Moses at the burning bush
Psalm 103.8-18 (Grail, 102.1-2,3-4,6-7,8&11)
   The Lord is kind and merciful.
1 Corinthians 10.1-13 or 1-6,10-12   Learn from the old Israel's experience
Luke 13.1-9   We all stand under God's judgments

After Communion

Even the sparrow finds a home, and a swallow a nest for herself, where she may lay her young, at your altars, O Lord of hosts. Blessed are those who dwell in your house, ever singing your praise.   Psalm 84.3,4

THE FOURTH SUNDAY IN LENT

New life

Sentence

Rejoice with Jerusalem and be glad for her, all you who love her; rejoice in her joy, all you who mourn over her, that you may drink deeply with delight from the abundance of her glory.

Isaiah 66.10-11

Collect

Almighty God, grant that we, who justly deserve to be punished for our sinful deeds, may in your mercy and kindness be pardoned and restored; through our Lord and Saviour Jesus Christ.   **Amen.**

BCP Lent 4

197

or

Let us pray [for a greater faith and love.]
Father of peace,
we are joyful in your Word,
your Son Jesus Christ,
who reconciles us to you.
With our eyes fixed on him,
let us run the race that is set before us
with the eagerness of faith and love.
We ask this through our Lord Jesus Christ, your Son,
who lives and reigns with you and the Holy Spirit,
one God, for ever and ever. **Amen.**

Readings

NOTE: The readings for Year A may be used every year

Year A

1 Samuel 16.1-13 or 1,6-7,10-13a   David, God's chosen instrument
Psalm 23 (Grail, 22)
  The Lord is my shepherd;
    there is nothing I shall want.
Ephesians 5.8-14   What pleases the Lord
John 9.1-41 or 1,6-9,13-17,34-38   That God might be glorified (The blind man's sight restored)
  After Communion

One thing I know, though I was blind, now I see.   John 9.25b

Year B

2 Chronicles 36.15-21 or 14-16,19-23   The prophets' rejection brought wrath
Psalm 137.1-6 (Grail, 136.1-2,3,4-5,6)
  Let my tongue be silenced, if I ever forget you!
Ephesians 2.4-10   God gave us new life in Christ
John 3.14-21 Man's rejection of Jesus brought life
  After Communion

God so loved the world that he gave his only Son, that whoever believes in him should not perish but have eternal life.   John 3.16

Year C

Joshua 5.2-12 or 9a,10-12   The joy of Passover
Psalm 34.1-10 (Grail, 33.2-3,4-5,6-7)
  Taste and see the goodness of the Lord.
2 Corinthians 5.14-21 or 17-21   Reconciliation

Luke 15.1-3, 11-32 or 11-32   From death, life (The lost son)
  After Communion
Son, it was fitting to make merry and be glad, for this your brother
was dead, and is alive; he was lost, and is found.   Luke 15.32

THE FIFTH SUNDAY IN LENT
The resurrection and the life

Sentence
[In the name of Christ, the psalmist prays:] Vindicate me, O God,
and defend my cause against an ungodly people; from deceitful
and unjust men deliver me, for you are the God in whom I take
refuge.   Psalm 43.1,2a

Collect
We beseech you, almighty God, to look in mercy on your people:
that by your great goodness they may be governed and preserved
evermore; through Jesus Christ our Lord.   **Amen.**   BCP, Lent 5
  or
Let us pray [for the zeal to follow Christ.]
Father,
help us to be like Christ your Son,
who loved the world and died for our salvation.
Inspire us by his love,
guide us by his example,
who lives and reigns with you and the Holy Spirit,
one God, for ever and ever.   **Amen.**

Readings
NOTE: The readings for Year A may be used every year
  Year A
Ezekiel 37.12-14   I will put my Spirit within you
Psalm 130 (Grail, 129.1-2,3-4,5-7,7b-8)
  With the Lord there is mercy, and fulness of redemption.
Romans 8.1-11 or 8-11   The life-giving Spirit
John 11.1-45 or 3-7,17,20-27,33b-45   I am the resurrection and the life

199

I am the resurrection and the life, says the Lord; he who believes in me, though he die, yet shall he live.   John 11.25

Year B

Jeremiah 31.31-34   The new covenant

Psalm 51.1-10 (Grail, 50.3-4,12-13,14-15)

Create a clean heart in me, O God.

Hebrews 5.7-9   The source of eternal salvation

John 12.20-33   Unless a grain of wheat falls to the ground

After Communion

Unless a grain of wheat falls into the earth and dies, it remains alone; but if it dies, it bears much fruit.   John 12.24

Year C

Isaiah 43.16-21   The mighty salvation of God

Psalm 126 (Grail, 125.1-2a,2b-3,4-5,6)

The Lord has done great things for us; we are filled with joy.

Philippians 3.2-14 or 8-14   The prize

John 8.1-11   Neither do I condemn you

After Communion

Jesus said: Woman, where are they? Has no one condemned you? She said, No one, Lord. And Jesus said, Neither do I condemn you; go, and do not sin again.   John 8.10,11

THE SUNDAY BEFORE EASTER (Palm Sunday)
The crucified King

Sentence

Lift up your heads, O gates! and be lifted up, O ancient doors! that the king of glory may come in. Who is this King of glory? The Lord of hosts, he is the King of glory!   Psalm 24.9,10

Collect

Almighty and everlasting God, in tender love towards mankind you sent your Son, our Saviour Jesus Christ, to take our nature upon him and to suffer death on the cross, that all mankind should follow the example of his great humility: grant that we may follow the example of his suffering, and also be made partakers of his resurrection; through him who lives and reigns with you and the Holy Spirit, now and for ever.   **Amen.**

BCP, Sunday next before Easter

or

Let us pray [for a closer union with Christ in his passion.]
Almighty, ever-living God,
you have given the human race Jesus Christ our Saviour
as a model of humility.
He fulfilled your will
by becoming man and giving his life on the cross.
Help us to bear witness to you
by following his example of suffering,
and make us worthy to share in his resurrection.
We ask this through our Lord Jesus Christ, your Son,
who lives and reigns with you and the Holy Spirit,
one God, for ever and ever.   **Amen.**

Readings

Isaiah 50.4-7   The suffering servant
Psalm 22.6-22 (Grail, 21.8-9,17-18,19-20,23-24)
   My God, my God, why have you abandoned me?
Philippians 2.5-11   Christ became obedient

Year A

Matthew 26.14 - 27.66 or 27.11-54   The passion of Christ

Year B

Mark 14.1 - 15.47 or 15.1-39   The passion of Christ

Year C

Luke 22.14 - 23.56 or 23.1-49   The passion of Christ

After Communion

Christ became obedient to death, even death on a cross.

Philippians 2.8

MONDAY BEFORE EASTER
Christ crucified

Sentence

[In the name of Christ, the psalmist prays:]
Contend, O Lord, with those who contend with me;
fight against those who fight against me,
and rise for my help!

Psalm 35.1-2

201

Collect as on Sunday, or

All-powerful God,
by the suffering and death of your Son,
strengthen and protect us in our weakness.
We ask this through our Lord Jesus Christ, your Son,
who lives and reigns with you and the Holy Spirit,
one God, for ever and ever. **Amen.**

Readings

Isaiah 42.1-7   The servant of God
Psalm 27.1-7 or Isaiah 42.1-7 (1,2-3,4,5,6-7)
The Lord is my light and my salvation.
John 12.1-11   Mary anoints Jesus for his burial

After Communion

My servant will not fail or be discouraged till he has established
justice in the earth; and the coastlands wait for his law.

Isaiah 42.4

TUESDAY BEFORE EASTER

Christ crucified

Sentence

[In the name of Christ, the psalmist prays:]
Give me not up to the will of my adversaries;
for false witnesses have risen against me,
and they breathe out violence.   Psalm 27.12

Collect as on Sunday or

Father,
may we receive your forgiveness and mercy
as we celebrate the passion and death of the Lord,
who lives and reigns with you and the Holy Spirit,
one God, for ever and ever. **Amen.**

Readings

Isaiah 49.1-6   The light to the nations
Psalm 71.1-8 (Grail, 70.1-2,3-4,5-6,14-15&17)
I will sing of your salvation.
John 13.21-38 or 21-33 (36-38)   One of you will betray me

After Communion

God did not spare his own Son but gave him up for us all.

Romans 8.32

WEDNESDAY BEFORE EASTER
Christ crucified

Sentence

At the name of Jesus every knee should bow, in heaven and on earth and under the earth. Because God has highly exalted him and bestowed on him the name which is above every name, let every tongue confess that Jesus Christ is Lord, to the glory of God the Father.

Philippians 2.9-11

Collect as on Sunday, or

Father,
in your plan of salvation
your Son Jesus Christ accepted the cross
and freed us from the power of the enemy.
May we come to share the glory of his resurrection,
for he lives and reigns with you and the Holy Spirit,
one God, for ever and ever.   **Amen.**

Readings

Isaiah 50.4-9a   The suffering servant
Psalm 69.17-22 (Grail, 68.8-10,20-21,31-34)
   Lord, in your great love, answer me.
Matthew 26.14-25   Jesus betrayed

After Communion

The Son of man came not to be served but to serve, and to give his life as a ransom for many.

Matthew 20.28

THURSDAY BEFORE EASTER (Maundy Thursday)
The Lord's Supper

Sentence

We are to glory in the cross of our Lord Jesus Christ, by which the world has been crucified to us, and we to the world.

see Galatians 6.14

Collect

Almighty Father, look graciously upon this your family, for which
our Lord Jesus Christ was willing to be betrayed and given up into
the hands of wicked men, and to suffer death upon the cross; who
now lives and reigns with you and the Holy Spirit, one God, for
ever and ever. **Amen.**   BCP, Good Friday

or

God our Father,
we are gathered here to share in the supper
which your Son left to his Church to reveal his love.
He gave it to us when he was about to die
and commanded us to celebrate it in remembrance of him.
We pray that sharing this sacrament
we may find the fulness of love and life.
Grant this through our Lord Jesus Christ, your Son,
who lives and reigns with you and the Holy Spirit,
one God, for ever and ever. **Amen.**

or, at Morning and Evening Prayer

Father,
by the power of the Holy Spirit,
you anointed your only Son Messiah and Lord of creation;
and you have given us a share in his suffering and his kingdom.
Help us to be faithful witnesses in the world
to the salvation Christ won for all mankind.
We ask this through our Lord Jesus Christ, your Son,
who lives and reigns with you and the Holy Spirit,
one God, for ever and ever. **Amen.**

Readings

Exodus 12.1-14 or 1-8, 11-14   The passover meal
Psalm 116.11-16 (Grail, 115.12-13,15-16,17-18)
   Our blessing-cup is a communion with the blood of Christ.
1 Corinthians 11.23-26   The last supper
John 13.1-15   Perfect love – Jesus washes the disciples' feet

After Communion

Christ, our paschal lamb, has been sacrificed.   1 Corinthians 5.7

GOOD FRIDAY

Christ crucified

Sentence

Jesus said: Now is the judgment of this world, now shall the ruler of this world be cast out; and I, when I am lifted up from the earth, will draw all men to myself.   John 12.31

or

[In Christ's name, the prophet Micah asks:]
O my people, what have I done to you? In what have I wearied you? Answer me! Remember how I brought you up from the land of Egypt, that you may know the saving acts of the Lord.

Micah 6.3-5

Collect

Almighty Father, look graciously upon this your family, for which our Lord Jesus Christ was willing to be betrayed and given up into the hands of wicked men, and to suffer death upon the cross; who now lives and reigns with you and the Holy Spirit, one God, for ever and ever. **Amen.**   BCP, Good Friday

or

Father,
your Son, Jesus Christ,
wrought our redemption
by shedding his blood for us.
Watch over us always
and keep us in your love.
We ask this through Christ our Lord.   **Amen.**

[The following two collects may be added.

Almighty and eternal God, by whose Spirit the whole body of the church is governed and sanctified: receive our prayer which we offer before you for the many different members of your holy church; that every one of them in his vocation and ministry may truly and devoutly serve you; through our Lord and Saviour Jesus Christ. **Amen.**   BCP, Good Friday

Merciful God, you have made all men and hate nothing that you have made, nor do you desire the death of a sinner but rather that he should be converted and live: have mercy on your ancient

205

people the Jews, and all who do not know you, or who deny the faith of Christ crucified. Take from them all ignorance, hardness of heart, and contempt of your word; and bring them home to your fold, blessed Lord, so that they may become one flock under one shepherd, Jesus Christ our Lord; who lives and reigns with you and the Holy Spirit, one God, for ever and ever. **Amen.**

BCP, Good Friday]

Readings

Isaiah 52.13 - 53.12   The suffering servant
Psalm 31.11-18 (Grail, 30.2-3, 12a,12b-13,15-16,17-18)
   Father, I put my life in your hands.
Hebrews 4.14 - 5.10 or 4.14-16 and 5.7-9   Jesus our high priest
John 18.1 - 19.42   The passion of Christ

After Communion

If while we were sinners we were reconciled to God by the death of his Son, much more, now that we are reconciled, shall we be saved by his life.   Romans 5.10

EASTER EVE

Collect for use at Morning and Evening Prayer

Grant, Lord, that as we have been baptized into the death of your dear Son our Saviour Jesus Christ, so by continually putting to death our sinful desires we may die to sin and be buried with him, and that through the grave and gate of death we may pass to our joyful resurrection; for his sake who died and was buried and rose again for us, your Son Jesus Christ our Lord. **Amen.**

BCP, Easter Eve

EASTER DAY

(At midnight or early morning)

The resurrection of Christ

Sentence

Christ, our paschal Lamb, has been sacrificed; let us therefore celebrate the festival.   1 Corinthians 5.7-8

Collect

Almighty God, you have conquered death through your dearly beloved Son Jesus Christ and opened to us the gate of everlasting life: grant us by your grace to set our mind on things above, so that by your continual help our whole life may be transformed; through Jesus Christ our Lord, who is alive and reigns with you and the Holy Spirit in everlasting glory.   **Amen.**   BCP, Easter Day

or, if at night

Let us pray [that the risen Christ will raise us up and renew our lives.]

Lord God,
you have brightened this night
with the radiance of the risen Christ.
Quicken the spirit of sonship in your Church;
renew us in mind and body
to give you whole-hearted service.
Grant this through our Lord Jesus Christ, your Son,
who lives and reigns with you and the Holy Spirit,
one God, for ever and ever.   **Amen.**

Readings

Exodus 14.15 - 15.1a   God saves his people
Psalm 18.27-31 or Exodus 15.1b-3,4-8,9-10,11-12,13-18
   Let us sing to the Lord;
   he has covered himself in glory.

NOTE: on Easter morning a longer series of readings may be read. They are to be found on page 208*.

Romans 6.1-11 or 3-11   Christ will never die again
Psalm 118.14-24 (Grail, 117.11-12,15c-16,22-23)
   Alleluia, alleluia, alleluia!

Year A
Matthew 28.1-10   Christ is risen!

Year B
Mark 16.1-8   Christ is risen!

Year C
Luke 24.1-12   Christ is risen!

After Communion

Christ, our paschal Lamb, has been sacrificed; let us therefore celebrate the festival.   1 Corinthians 5.7-8

* On Easter morning a series of readings from the Old Testament may be used before the reading from the New Testament and the Gospel. These readings tell of God's preparation for his great salvation in Jesus Christ. A selection from the following may be used, though the reading printed above should always be one of those chosen.

   i Genesis 1.1 - 2.3 or 1.1,26-31a   Creation
     Psalm 104.11-25 (Grail, 103.1-2,5-6,10-12,13-14,24)
         Lord, send out your Spirit,
         and renew the face of the earth.
     or
     Psalm 33.1-12 (Grail, 32.4-5,6-7,12-13)
         The earth is full of the goodness of the Lord.
  ii Genesis 22.1-18 or 1-2,9-13,15-18   The sacrifice of Isaac
     Psalm 16.7-11 (Grail, 15.5-6,9-10,11)
         Keep me safe, O God; you are my hope.
 iii Exodus 14.15 - 15.1a   God saves his people
     For the Psalm, Exodus 15.1b-3,4-8,9-10,11-12,13-18
         Let us sing to the Lord;
         he has covered himself in glory.
  iv Isaiah 54.4-14   God is our redeemer
     Psalm 30 (Grail, 29.2&4,5-6,11-13)
         I will praise you, Lord, for you have rescued me.
   v Isaiah 55.1-11   The promise of a new covenant
     For the Psalm, Isaiah 12.2,3-4,5-6
         You will draw water joyfully from the springs of salvation.
  vi Baruch 3.9-15,32 - 4.4   Walk in God's way
     Psalm 19.7-14 (Grail, 18.8,9,10,11)
         Lord, you have the words of everlasting life.

vii Ezekiel 36.16-28   Washed in pure water
   Psalm 42 (Grail, 41.3,5; 42.3,4)
      Like a deer that longs for running streams, my soul longs for you, my God.
   or
   Psalm 51.10-17 (Grail, 50.12-13,14-15,18-19)
      Create a clean heart in me, O God.

EASTER DAY

(During the day)

The resurrection of Christ

Sentence

The Lord is risen indeed, alleluia; to him be glory and dominion
for ever and ever. [This is the day which the Lord has made; let
us rejoice and be glad in it.]   Luke 24.34;
                                                     Revelation 1.6;
                                                    [Psalm 118.24]

Collect

Almighty God, you have conquered death through your dearly
beloved Son Jesus Christ and opened to us the gate of everlasting
life: grant us by your grace to set our mind on things above, so that
by your continual help our whole life may be transformed; through
Jesus Christ our Lord, who is alive and reigns with you and the
Holy Spirit in everlasting glory.   **Amen.**   BCP, Easter Day

   or

Let us pray [that we may know the risen Christ.]
God our Father,
by raising Christ your Son,
you conquered the power of death
and opened for us the way to eternal life.
In our celebration today
raise us up and renew our lives
by the Spirit that is within us.
Grant this through our Lord Jesus Christ, your Son,
who lives and reigns with you and the Holy Spirit,
one God, for ever and ever.   **Amen.**

Readings

Acts 10.34-43 or 34a,37-43   God has raised Jesus
Psalm 118.19-29 (Grail, 117.1-2,15b-17,22-23)
   Alleluia, alleluia, alleluia!
Colossians 3.1-4   Where Christ is
or   1 Corinthians 5.6b-8   Christ our Passover
John 20.1-9   The empty tomb
or   The appropriate Gospel from Easter Day at Midnight
or   Luke 24.13-35   The walk to Emmaus

After Communion

Christ, our paschal Lamb, has been sacrificed; let us, therefore,
celebrate the festival.   1 Corinthians 5.7-8

THE SUNDAY AFTER EASTER

Life and peace in Christ

Sentence

The stone which the builders rejected has become the head of the
corner. This is the Lord's doing; it is marvellous in our eyes.

Psalm 118.24-25

Collect

Almighty Father, you have given your only Son Jesus Christ to die
for our sins and to rise again for our justification: grant that we
may put away the old leaven of corruption and wickedness, and
always serve you in sincerity and truth; through the merits of Jesus
Christ our Lord.   **Amen.**   BCP, Easter 1
or

Let us pray [for a deeper awareness of God's blessings to us in
   baptism.]
God of mercy,
you wash away our sins,
you give us new birth in the Spirit,
and you redeem us in the blood of Christ.
As we celebrate Christ's resurrection
increase our awareness of these blessings,
and renew your gift of life within us.
We ask this through our Lord Jesus Christ, your Son,
who lives and reigns with you and the Holy Spirit,
one God, for ever and ever.   **Amen.**

210

Readings

Year A

Acts 2.42-47   The life of the early Christians
Psalm 118.19-29 (Grail, 117.2-4,13-15a,22-24)
  Give thanks to the Lord for he is good, his love is everlasting.   or   *Alleluia!*
1 Peter 1.3-9   New birth
John 20.19-31   Jesus appears to his disciples

Year B

Acts 4.32-35   The life of the early christians
Psalm 118.19-29 (Grail, 117.2-4,13-15a,22-24)
  Give thanks to the Lord for he is good, his love is everlasting.   or   *Alleluia!*
1 John 5.1-6   Begotten by God
John 20.19-31   Jesus appears to his disciples

Year C

Acts 5.12-16   The life of the early christians
Psalm 118.19-29 (Grail, 117.2-4,13-15a,22-24)
  Give thanks to the Lord for he is good, his love is everlasting.   or   *Alleluia!*
Revelation 1.9-19 or 9-13,17-19   The Risen Christ
John 20.19-31   Jesus appears to his disciples

After Communion

Jesus said to Thomas, Put your finger here, and see my hands; and
put out your hand, and place it in my side; do not be faithless, but
believing.   John 20.27

THE SECOND SUNDAY AFTER EASTER

Witnesses to the resurrection

Sentence

Make a joyful noise to God, all the earth; sing to the glory of his
name; give to him glorious praise. [Saviour God, 'How terrible are
your deeds! Great is your power.']   Psalm 66.1-3

Collect

Almighty God, you have given your only Son to be for us both a
sacrifice for sin and also an example of godly life; give us grace that
we may always thankfully receive the immeasurable benefit of his
sacrifice, and also daily endeavour to follow in the blessed steps
of his most holy life; who now lives and reigns with you and the
Holy Spirit, one God, for evermore.   **Amen.**   BCP, Easter 2

211

or

Let us pray [that Christ will give us a share in his glory.]
God our Father,
may we look forward with hope to our resurrection,
for you have made us your sons and daughters,
and restored the joy of our youth.
We ask this through our Lord Jesus Christ, your Son,
who lives and reigns with you and the Holy Spirit,
one God, for ever and ever. **Amen.**

Readings

Year A

Acts 2.(14,)22-28   The pangs of death could not hold Christ
Psalm 16 (Grail, 15.1&5,7-8,9-10,11)
 Lord, you will show us the path of life.   or   *Alleluia!*
1 Peter 1.17-21   Set free by the sacrifice of Christ
Luke 24.13-35   Jesus known in the breaking of the bread
 After Communion

Jesus was made known to the disciples in the breaking of the
bread.   Luke 24.35

Year B

Acts 3.13-19 or 13-15,17-19   He whom you crucified, him God has raised
Psalm 4 (Grail, 4.2,4,7,9)
 Lord, let your face shine on us.   or   *Alleluia!*
1 John 2.1-6   Our advocate
Luke 24.35-48   Christ has fulfilled the Scriptures
 After Communion

Thus it is written, that the Christ should suffer and on the third
day rise from the dead, and that repentance and forgiveness of sins
should be preached in his name to all nations.   Luke 24.46-47

Year C

Acts 5.27b-41 or 27b-32,40-41   We are witnesses
Psalm 30 (Grail, 29.2&4,5-6,11&13)
 I will praise you, Lord, for you have rescued me.   or   *Alleluia!*
Revelation 5.11-14   Worthy is the Lamb that was slain
John 21.1-19 or 1-14   The risen Jesus by the Lake of Galilee
 After Communion

Jesus was made known to the disciples in the breaking of the
bread.   Luke 24.35

212

THE THIRD SUNDAY AFTER EASTER
The Good Shepherd

Sentence

The Lord is my shepherd, I shall not want; the earth is full of the
steadfast love of the Lord. By the word of the Lord the heavens
were made, and all their host by the breath of his mouth.

Psalm 23.1 and 33.5-6

Collect

Almighty God, you alone can order the unruly wills and passions
of sinful men: grant to your people that they may love what you
command and desire what you promise, that so, among the many
and varied changes of the world, our hearts may surely there be
fixed where true joys are to be found; through Jesus Christ our
Lord. **Amen.** BCP, Easter 4

or

Let us pray [that Christ our shepherd will lead us.]
Almighty and ever-living God,
you give us new strength
from the courage of Christ our shepherd.
May he lead us to join the saints in heaven,
where he lives and reigns with you and the Holy Spirit,
one God, for ever and ever. **Amen.**

Readings

Year A

Acts.2.[14,],36-41 Jesus both Lord and Christ
Psalm 23 (Grail, 22.1-3a,3b-4,5,6)
The Lord is my shepherd; there is nothing I shall want. or *Alleluia!*
1 Peter 2.20b-25 The shepherd and bishop of our souls
John 10.1-10 The good shepherd

Year B

Acts 4.8-12 The power of his name
Psalm 118.1-9 (Grail, 117.1&8-9,21-23,26-29)
The stone rejected by the builders has become the corner stone. or *Alleluia!*
1 John 3.1-2 The love of God
John 10.11-18 The good shepherd

213

After Communion

I am the good shepherd, says the Lord, the good shepherd lays
down his life for the sheep.   John 10.11

THE FOURTH SUNDAY AFTER EASTER
The Good News

Sentence

[O sing to the Lord a new song, for he has done marvellous things.]
The Lord has made known his victory, and he has revealed his vindication in the sight of the nations.   Psalm 98.[1-]2

Collect

Almighty God, you show to those who are in error the light of your
truth so that they may return into the way of righteousness: grant
to all who are admitted into the fellowship of Christ's service that
they may renounce those things that are contrary to their profession and follow all such things as are agreeable to it; through
our Lord Jesus Christ.   **Amen.**   BCP, Easter 3

or

Let us pray [that we may enjoy true freedom.]
God our Father,
look upon us with love.
You redeem us and make us your children in Christ.
Give us true freedom
and bring us to the inheritance you promised.
We ask this through our Lord Jesus Christ, your Son,
who lives and reigns with you and the Holy Spirit,
one God, for ever and ever.   **Amen.**

214

Readings

Year A

Acts 6.1-7   The spirit of the Gospel
Psalm 33.1-5 or 1-12 (Grail, 32.1-2,4-5,18-19)
  Lord, let your mercy be on us, as we place our trust in you.   or   *Alleluia!*
1 Peter 2.4-9[-10]   Set apart to sing God's praises
John 14.1-12   The way, the truth, and the life

Year B

Acts 9.26-31   Paul preaches fearlessly in the name of the Lord
Psalm 22.23-32 (Grail, 21.26b-27,28-30,31-32)
  I will praise you, Lord, in the assembly of your people.   or   *Alleluia!*
1 John 3.18-24   Living the Good News
John 15.1-8   The true vine

Year C

Acts 14.21b-27   God opens the door for the Gospel
Psalm 145.8-21 (Grail, 144.8-9,10-12,13)
  I will praise your name for ever, my king and my God.   or   *Alleluia!*
Revelation 21.1-5   God will wipe away all tears
John 13.31-35   The new commandment

After Communion

Jesus said, I am the vine, you are the branches. He who abides in
me, and I in him, he it is that bears much fruit, for apart from me
you can do nothing.   John 15.5

THE FIFTH SUNDAY AFTER EASTER

The Holy Spirit, the Teacher

Sentence

Declare this with a shout of joy, proclaim it, send it forth to the
end of the earth: say, 'The Lord has set his people free.'

                                                    Isaiah 48.20

Collect

Heavenly Father, the giver of all good things, fill our hearts with
thankfulness, and grant that by your holy inspiration we may think
those things that are good, and by your merciful guidance may perform them; through our Lord Jesus Christ.   **Amen.** BCP, Easter 5

or

Let us pray [that we may practise the faith we profess.]
Ever-living God,
help us to celebrate joyfully
the resurrection of the Lord
and to express in our lives
the love we celebrate.
Grant this through our Lord Jesus Christ, your Son,
who lives and reigns with you and the Holy Spirit,
one God, for ever and ever. **Amen.**

Readings

Year A

Acts 8.5-17 or 5-8,14-17 They received the Holy Spirit
Psalm 66.1-8 (Grail, 65.1-3a,4-5,6-7,16&20)
   Let all the earth cry out to God with joy. or *Alleluia!*
1 Peter 3.15-22 or 15-18 Raised to life
John 14.15-21 The Spirit of truth

Year B

Acts 10.25-48 or 25-26,34-35,44-48 The Holy Spirit came upon them
Psalm 98 (Grail, 97.1,2-3a,3b-4)
   The Lord has revealed to the nations his saving power. or *Alleluia!*
1 John 4.7-10 God is love
John 15.9-17 You are my friends

Year C

Acts 15.1-2,22-29 It seems good to the Holy Spirit and to us
Psalm 67. (Grail, 66.2-3,5,6&8a)
   O God, let all the nations praise you! or *Alleluia!*
Revelation 21.10-23 or 10-14,22-23 The holy city
John 14.23-29 The Holy Spirit will teach you everything

After Communion

Jesus said, If you love me, you will keep my commandments, and
I will pray to the Father, and he will give you another Counsellor
to be with you for ever.   John 14.15,16

THE ASCENSION DAY

Christ, risen, ascended, glorified

Sentence

[As the apostles were looking on, Jesus was lifted up, and a cloud took him out of their sight. Two angels said to the disciples:]
Men of Galilee, why do you stand looking into heaven? This Jesus will come in the same way as you saw him go into heaven.

Acts 1.[9,]11

Collect

Grant, we pray, almighty God, that as we believe your only begotten Son to have ascended into heaven, so we may also in heart and mind there ascend, and with him continually dwell; who lives and reigns with you and the Holy Spirit, one God, for ever and ever.
Amen BCP, Ascension Day

or

Let us pray [that Christ will lead us to eternal life.]
God our Father,
make us joyful in the ascension of your Son Jesus Christ.
May we follow him into the new creation,
for his ascension is our glory and our hope.
We ask this through our Lord Jesus Christ, your Son,
who lives and reigns with you and the Holy Spirit,
one God, for ever and ever. **Amen.**

Readings

Acts 1.1-11 The Ascension
Psalm 47 (Grail, 46.2-3,6-7,8-9)
God ascends to his throne with shouts of joy. or *Alleluia!*
Ephesians 1.15-23 or 17-23 All things are under his feet

Year A

Matthew 28.16-20 All authority belongs to Jesus

Year B

Mark 16.15-20 or Luke 24.46-53 The Ascension

Year C

Luke 24.46-53 The Ascension

After Communion

Jesus said, Lo, I am with you always, to the close of the age.

Matthew 28.20

217

THE SUNDAY AFTER THE ASCENSION
Waiting on God

Sentence

Lord, you have said, 'Seek my face.' My heart says to you, 'Your face, Lord, do I seek.' Do not hide your face from me.

or

The Lord God said, 'Seek my face.' Our heart replies, 'You, Lord, do I seek; do not hide your face from us.'   Psalm 27.8-9

Collect

O God, the king of glory, you have exalted your only Son Jesus Christ with great triumph to your kingdom in heaven: leave us not desolate, but send your Holy Spirit to strengthen us, and exalt us to where our Saviour Christ has gone before, who lives and reigns with you and the Holy Spirit, one God, for evermore. **Amen.**
                                        BCP, Sunday after Ascension

or

Let us pray [That we may recognise the presence of Christ.]
Father,
help us to keep in mind that Christ our Saviour
lives with you in glory
and promised to remain with us until the end of time.
We ask this through our Lord Jesus Christ, your Son,
who lives and reigns with you and the Holy Spirit,
one God, for ever and ever. **Amen.**

Readings

Year A
Acts 1.12-14   Devoted to prayer
Psalm 27.1-8 (Grail, 26.1,4,7-8)
   God is king of all the earth.   or   *Alleluia!*
1 Peter 4.13-16   Sharing Christ's sufferings
John 17.1-11   Disciples in the world

Year B
Acts 1.15-26 or 15-17,20-26   Witnesses to the resurrection

218

Psalm 103.19-22 (Grail, 102.1-2,11-12,19-20)
The Lord has set his throne in heaven. or *Alleluia!*
1 John 4.11-16   If we love one another, God abides in us
John 17.11b-19   One with the Father and the Son

Year C

Acts 7.55-60   The Son of man standing at God's right hand
Psalm 97 (Grail, 96.1-2,6-7,9)
The Lord is king, the most high over all the earth. or *Alleluia!*
Revelation 22.12-20 or 12-14,17-20   Come, Lord Jesus!
John 17.20-26   One with the Father and the Son

After Communion

Jesus prayed for his disciples, I pray that they may all be one, even as you, Father, are in me, and I in you, that they also may be in us, so that the world may believe that you have sent me.

John 17.21

or

How wonderful it is, how pleasant, for God's people to live together like brothers!   Psalm 133.1 TEV

WHIT SUNDAY
(PENTECOST)
The Holy Spirit

Sentence

God's love has been poured into our hearts through the Holy Spirit who has been given to us.   Romans 5.5

or

The Spirit of the Lord has filled the world, and that which holds all things together knows what he said.   Wisdom 1.7

Collect

Almighty God, who taught the hearts of your faithful people by sending to them the light of your Holy Spirit: grant to us by the same Spirit to have a right judgment in all things and always to rejoice in his holy comfort; through the merits of Christ Jesus our Saviour, who lives and reigns with you and the Holy Spirit, one God, now and for ever. **Amen.**   BCP, Whit Sunday

or

Let us pray [that the Spirit will work through us to bring Christ
to the world.]
God our Father,
let the Spirit you sent on your Church
to begin the teaching of the gospel
continue to work in the world
through the hearts of all who believe.
We ask this through our Lord Jesus Christ, your Son,
who lives and reigns with you and the Holy Spirit,
one God, for ever and ever. **Amen.**

Readings
Acts 2.1-11   Filled with the Holy Spirit
Psalm 104.26-32 (Grail, 103.1 & 24,29 & 30,31 & 34)
   Lord, send out your Spirit, and renew the face of the earth. or *Alleluia!*
1 Corinthians 12.1-13 or 3-7,12-13   The unity of the Spirit
John 20.19-23   Receive the Holy Spirit

After Communion
They were all filled with the Holy Spirit and began to tell the
mighty works of God.   Acts 2.4,11

TRINITY SUNDAY
God the Holy Trinity

Sentence
Blessed be God the Father and his only begotten Son and the Holy
Spirit; for he has shown that he loves us.

or

Christ Jesus came and preached peace to you who were far off, and
peace to those who were near; for through him we have access in
the one Spirit to the Father.   Ephesians 2.17-18

Collect
Almighty and everlasting God, you have given us your servants
grace by the confession of a true faith to acknowledge the glory of
the eternal Trinity, and by your divine power to worship you as
One: we humbly pray that you would keep us steadfast in this faith
and evermore defend us from all adversities; through Christ our
Lord. **Amen.**   BCP, Trinity Sunday

220

or

Let us pray [to the one God, Father, Son, and Spirit, that our lives
    may bear witness to our faith.]
Father,
you sent your Word to bring us truth
and your Spirit to make us holy.
Through them we come to know the mystery of your life.
Help us to worship you, one God in three Persons,
by proclaiming and living our faith in you.
Grant this through our Lord Jesus Christ, your Son,
who lives and reigns with you and the Holy Spirit,
one God, for ever and ever. **Amen.**

Readings

Year A

Exodus 34.4-9 or 4-6,8-9   The Lord God
For the Psalm, Song of the Three Young Men 29-34
  Glory and praise for ever!
2 Corinthians 13.11-14   The grace of God
John 3.16-18   God sent his Son to bring us his life

Year B

Deuteronomy 4.32-40 or 32-34,39-40   The Lord is God
Psalm 33.13-21 (Grail, 32.4-5,6-7,18-19,20&22)
  Happy are the people the Lord has chosen to be his own.
Romans 8.14-17   The christian experience of the Trinity
Matthew 28.16-20   In the name of the Trinity

Year C

Proverbs 8.22-31   The wisdom of God
Psalm 8 (Grail, 8.4-5,6-7,8-9)
  O Lord, our God, how wonderful is your name in all the earth.
Romans 5.1-5   The christian experience of the Trinity
John 16.12-15   Jesus speaks of his Father and the Spirit

After Communion

God has sent the Spirit of his Son into our hearts, crying, 'Abba!
Father!'   Galatians 4.6

NOTE: The collects and readings for the *Ordinary Sundays* which follow are
      used on the Sundays after Epiphany and the Sundays after Trinity.
      See note on page 176.

221

THE FIRST ORDINARY SUNDAY

The baptism of Jesus

For the Sunday

Sentence

When Jesus was baptized, he went up immediately from the water, and behold, the heavens were opened and he saw the Spirit of God descending upon him like a dove, and alighting on him; and lo, a voice from heaven, saying, 'This is my beloved Son, in whom I am well pleased.'

Matthew 3.16-17

Collect

Eternal Father, who declared Jesus our Lord to be your beloved Son at his baptism: grant that we and all who have become his members through baptism may rejoice to be your children and the servants of all men; through Jesus Christ our Lord, who lives and reigns with you and the Holy Spirit, one God, for ever and ever. **Amen.**

or

Let us pray [that we will be faithful to our baptismal calling.]

Almighty, eternal God,

when the Spirit descended upon Jesus

at his baptism in the Jordan,

you revealed him as your own beloved Son.

Keep us, your children born of water and the Spirit,

faithful to our calling.

We ask this through our Lord Jesus Christ, your Son,

who lives and reigns with you and the Holy Spirit,

one God, for ever and ever. **Amen.**

For the weekdays

Sentence

Worthy are you, our Lord and God, to receive glory and honour and power, for you created all things, and by your will they existed and were created.

Revelation 4.11

Collect

Lord, mercifully receive the prayers of your people who call upon you; and grant that we may perceive and know what things we ought to do, and also may have grace and power faithfully to perform them; through Jesus Christ our Lord. **Amen.**

BCP, Epiphany 1

or

Let us pray [that we may know and do what God wills.]
Father of love,
hear our prayer.
Help us to know your will
and to do it with courage and faith.
Grant this through our Lord Jesus Christ, your Son,
who lives and reigns with you and the Holy Spirit,
one God, for ever and ever. **Amen.**

Readings

Isaiah 42.1-7 or 1-4,6-7   The servant of the Lord
Psalm 29 (Grail, 28.1-2,3-4,3b&10)
The Lord will bless his people with peace.
Acts 10.34-38   Jesus anointed with the Holy Spirit and with power

Year A

Matthew 3.13-17   The baptism of Jesus

Year B

Mark 1.7-11   The baptism of Jesus

Year C

Luke 3.15-22 or 15-16,21-22   The baptism of Jesus

After Communion

The Spirit of the Lord God is upon me, because the Lord has
anointed me to bring good tidings to the afflicted.   Isaiah 61.1

THE SECOND ORDINARY SUNDAY

The Lord is here!

Sentence

All the earth worships you, O Lord most high;
sings praises to you, and worships your holy Name. see Psalm 66.4

Collect

Almighty and everlasting God, ruler of all things in heaven and
earth, mercifully hear the supplications of your people, and grant
us your peace all the days of our life; through Jesus Christ our Lord.
Amen.   BCP, Epiphany 2

223

or

Let us pray [for the gift of God's peace.]
Father of heaven and earth, hear our prayers,
and show us the way to peace in the world.
Grant this through our Lord Jesus Christ, your Son,
who lives and reigns with you and the Holy Spirit,
one God, for ever and ever.   **Amen.**

Readings

Year A

Isaiah 49.3-6 or 3,5-6   A light to the nations
Psalm 40.8-13 (Grail, 39.2&4a,7-8a,8b-9,10)
   Here am I, Lord; I come to do your will.
1 Corinthians 1.1-3   Grace and peace from God
John 1.29-34   The Lamb of God

Year B

1 Samuel 3.2-19 or 3-10,19   Speak, Lord
Psalm 40.8-13 (Grail, 39.2&4a,7-8a,8b-9,10)
   Here am I, Lord; I come to do your will.
1 Corinthians 6.12-20 or 13-15,17-20   The temple of the Holy Spirit
John 1.35-42   We have found the Messiah

Year C

Isaiah 62.1-5   God will rejoice in Zion
Psalm 96.7-13 (Grail,95.1-2a,2b-3,7-8a,8b-9)
   Proclaim his marvellous deeds to all the nations.
1 Corinthians 12.4-11   The gifts of the Spirit
John 2.1-12   The wedding at Cana

After Communion

We know and believe the love God has for us, and this commandment we have from him, that he who loves God should love his
brother also.   1 John 4.16,21

THE THIRD ORDINARY SUNDAY

Repent and believe the Good News

Sentence

O sing to the Lord a new song; sing to the Lord, all the earth.
Honour and majesty are before him; strength and beauty are in
his sanctuary.   Psalm 96.1,6

Collect

Lord God, the strength of all who put their trust in you:
mercifully accept our prayers, and because through the weakness
of our mortal nature we can do nothing good without you, grant
us the help of your grace, that in keeping your commandments we
may please you both in will and deed; through Jesus Christ our
Lord. **Amen.**   BCP, Trinity 1

or

Let us pray [for unity and peace.]
All powerful and ever-living God,
help us to respond to your love that is within us,
that what we do in the name of your Son
may lead mankind to unity and peace.
We ask this through our Lord Jesus Christ, your Son,
who lives and reigns with you and the Holy Spirit,
one God, for ever and ever. **Amen.**

Readings

Year A

Isaiah 9.1b-4(-7)   The peace of God
Psalm 27.9-17 (Grail, 26.1,4,13-14)
   The Lord is my light and my salvation.
1 Corinthians 1.10-17 or 10-13,17   Be united!
Matthew 4.12-23 or 12-17   Light has dawned

Year B

Jonah 3.1-10 or 1-5,10   The penitence of Nineveh
Psalm 25.1-9 (Grail, 24.4-5,6-7,8-9)
   Teach me your ways, O Lord.
1 Corinthians 7.29-31   Living in the last times
Mark 1.14-20   Repent, and believe the good news

Year C

Nehemiah 8.2-10 or 2-4a,5-6,8-10   Joy in repentance
Psalm 19.7-14 (Grail, 18.8,9,10,15)
   Your words, Lord, are spirit and life.
1 Corinthians 12.12-30 or 12-14,27   You are the body of Christ
Luke 1.1-4; 4.14-21   Good news to the poor

225

After Communion

Look to the Lord, and be radiant; so your faces shall never be
ashamed. Psalm 34.5
or

Jesus said, I am the light of the world; he who follows me will not
walk in darkness, but will have the light of life. John 8.12

THE FOURTH ORDINARY SUNDAY

Faith, hope, and love

Sentence

We have thought on your steadfast love, O Lord, in the midst of
your temple. As your Name, O God, so your praise reaches to the
ends of the earth. Psalm 48.9-10

Collect

Lord, you have taught us that whatever we do without love is
worth nothing: send your Holy Spirit and pour into our hearts that
most excellent gift of love, the true bond of peace and of all virtues,
without which whoever lives is counted dead before you; grant this,
for your only Son Jesus Christ's sake. **Amen.** BCP, Quinquagesima
or

Let us pray [for a greater love of God and of our fellows.]
Lord our God,
help us to love you with all our hearts
and to love all men as you love them.
Grant this through our Lord Jesus Christ, your Son,
who lives and reigns with you and the Holy Spirit,
one God, for ever and ever. **Amen.**

Readings

Year A

Zephaniah 3.11-13 or 2.3; 3.12-13   A humble and lowly people
Psalm 146 (Grail, 145.6b-7,8-9,8c-10)
   Happy are the poor in spirit; the kingdom of heaven is theirs.   or   *Alleluia!*
1 Corinthians 1.26-31   God chooses the weak
Matthew 5.1-12   True happiness

After Communion

Blessed are the poor in spirit, for theirs is the kingdom of heaven.
Blessed are the meek, for they shall inherit the earth.
Matthew 5.3,5

Year B

Deuteronomy 18.15-20   The prophet of God
Psalm 95 (Grail, 94.1-2,6-7a,7b-9)
  If today you hear his voice,
  harden not your hearts.
1 Corinthians 7.32-35   Undivided devotion to the Lord
Mark 1.21-28   The new teaching with authority
  After Communion

Let your face shine on your servants, Lord; save us in your steadfast
love. Let us not be put to shame, O Lord, for we call on you.

Psalm 31.16,17

Year C

Jeremiah 1.4-5,17-19   Prophet to the nations
Psalm 71.1-13 (Grail, 70.1-2,3-4,5-6,8&17)
  I will sing of your salvation.
1 Corinthians 12.31 - 13.13 or 13.4-13   Love
Luke 4.21-30   God's love is universal
  After Communion

Faith, hope, and love abide, but the greatest of these is love.

1 Corinthians 13.13

THE FIFTH ORDINARY SUNDAY

The gospel proclaimed

Sentence

O come, let us worship and bow down, let us kneel before the Lord,
our Maker. For he is our God, and we are the people of his pasture,
and the sheep of his hand.   Psalm 95.6-7

Collect

God, our refuge and strength, the author of all godliness, hear the
devout prayers of your Church: and grant that what we ask in faith
we may surely obtain; through Jesus Christ our Lord.   **Amen.**

BCP, Trinity 23

or

Let us pray [for God's protection.]
Father,
watch over your family
and keep us safe in your care,
for all our hope is in you.

227

Grant this through our Lord Jesus Christ, your Son,
who lives and reigns with you and the Holy Spirit,
one God, for ever and ever. **Amen.**

Readings

Year A

Isaiah 58.7-10 Your light will shine like the dawn
Psalm 112 (Grail, 111.4-5,6-7,8-9)
The just man is a light in darkness to the upright.
1 Corinthians 2.1-5 Christ crucified
Matthew 5.13-16 The light of the world

Year B

Job 7.1-7 or 1-4,6-7 The desolation of alienation from God
Psalm 146 (Grail, 145.1,2-4,5-6)
Praise the Lord who heals the broken-hearted. or *Alleluia!*
1 Corinthians 9.16-23 or 16-19,22-23 Proclaiming the good news
Mark 1.29-39 Jesus brings release

Year C

Isaiah 6.1-8(-13) Here am I, send me!
Psalm 138.1-6 (Grail, 137.1-2a,2b-3,4-5,7b)
In the sight of the angels I will sing your praises, Lord.
1 Corinthians 15.1-11 or 3-8,11 The faith once delivered to the saints
Luke 5.1-11 They left all and followed him

After Communion

Let us thank the Lord for his steadfast love, for his wonderful works
to the sons of men; for he satisfies him who is thirsty, and the
hungry he fills with good things.   Psalm 107.8,9

or

Blessed are those who mourn, for they shall be comforted. Blessed
are those who hunger and thirst for righteousness, for they shall
be satisfied.   Matthew 5.4,6

THE SIXTH ORDINARY SUNDAY

Trust and obey

Lord, be a rock of refuge for me, a strong fortress to save me; for your Name's sake lead me and guide me. Psalm 31.2-3

or

God so loved the world that he gave his only Son, that whoever believes in him should not perish but have eternal life. John 3.16

Collect

Let your merciful ears, Lord God, be open to the prayers of your people; and so that they may obtain their petitions, make them to ask such things as will please you; through Jesus Christ our Lord. **Amen.** BCP, Trinity 10

or

Let us pray [that everything we do will be guided by God's law of love.]
God our Father,
you have promised to remain for ever
with those who do what is just and right.
Help us to live in your presence.
We ask this through our Lord Jesus Christ, your Son,
who lives and reigns with you and the Holy Spirit,
one God, for ever and ever. **Amen.**

Readings

Year A

Deuteronomy 10.12-22 Choose obedience
or Sirach 15.15-20 Choose obedience
Psalm 119.1-8 (Grail, 118.1-2,4-5,17-18,33-34)
Happy are they who follow the Law of the Lord.
1 Corinthians 2.6-10 The hidden wisdom of God
Matthew 5.17-37 or 20-22,27-28,33-34,37
Jesus' teaching about the Law

Year B

Leviticus 13.1-2,45-46 The law concerning lepers
Psalm 32.1-8 (Grail, 31.1-2,5,11)
*I turn to you, Lord, in the time of trouble,
and you fill me with the joy of salvation.*

1 Corinthians 10.31 - 11.1   Imitators of Christ
Mark 1.40-45   Jesus cleanses the leper

Year C

Jeremiah 17.5-8   Happiness
Psalm 1 (Grail, 1.1-2,3,4-6)   *Happy are they who hope in the Lord.*
1 Corinthians 15.12-20 or 12,16-20
   Christ's resurrection, source of our hope
Luke 6.17-26 or 17,20-26   The happiness of Christ's disciples

After Communion

God so loved the world that he gave his only Son, that whoever believes in him should not perish but have eternal life.   John 3.16

THE SEVENTH ORDINARY SUNDAY
Love and forgiveness

Sentence

We put our trust in the steadfast love of the Lord; our heart shall rejoice in his salvation. We will sing to the Lord, because he has dealt bountifully with us.   Psalm 13.5,6

Collect

Grant us, Lord, we pray, the spirit to think and do always such things as are right, that we who cannot do anything that is good without you, may in your strength be able to live according to your will; through Jesus Christ our Lord.   **Amen.**   BCP, Trinity 9

or

Let us pray [that God will make us more like Christ, his Son.]
Father,
keep before us the wisdom and love
you have revealed in your Son.
Help us to be like him
in word and deed,
for he lives and reigns with you and the Holy Spirit,
one God, for ever and ever.   **Amen.**

Readings

Year A

Leviticus 19.1-2,17-18   Love of neighbour

230

Psalm 103.1-5 (Grail, 102.1-2,3-4,8-10,12-13)
The Lord is kind and merciful.
1 Corinthians 3.16-23 Belonging to Christ
Matthew 5.38-48 Love for enemies

Year B

Isaiah 43.18-25 or 18-19,21-22,24-25 The forgiveness of God
Psalm 41.1-[3,10-]13 (Grail, 40.2-3,4-5,13-14)
Lord, heal my soul, for I have sinned against you.
2 Corinthians 1.18-22 Jesus, the fulfilment of all God's promises
Mark 2.1-12 Authority to forgive sins

Year C

1 Samuel 26.2-23 or 2,7-9,12-13,22-23 Saul and David reconciled
Psalm 103.1-5 (Grail, 102.1-2,3-4,8-10,12-13)
The Lord is kind and merciful.
1 Corinthians 15.42-50 or 45-49 Made like Christ
Luke 6.27-38 Love for enemies

After Communion

We will praise you, Lord, with all our heart, we will tell all the
things you have done. We will sing with joy because of you. We
will sing praise to you, Most High. Psalm 91.1,2 TEV

or

If you forgive men their trespasses, your heavenly Father also will
forgive you; but if you do not forgive men their trespasses, neither
will your Father forgive your trespasses. Matthew 6.14,15

THE EIGHTH ORDINARY SUNDAY

Years A and B: *The loving-kindness of the Lord*
Year C: *Whence comes goodness?*

Sentence

Jesus promised: I am with you always, to the close of the age.
Matthew 28.20

or

The Lord was my strength; he brought me forth into a broad place;
he delivered me, because he delighted in me. Psalm 18.18,19

231

Collect

Keep your Church, Lord God, with your continual mercy, and because the frailty of man without you cannot but fall, keep us always under your protection, and lead us to everything that makes for our salvation; through Jesus Christ our Lord. **Amen.**

or   BCP, Trinity 15

Let us pray [that God will bring peace to the world and freedom to his Church.]

Lord,
guide the course of world events
and give your Church the joy and peace
of serving you in freedom.
We ask this through our Lord Jesus Christ, your Son,
who lives and reigns with you and the Holy Spirit,
one God, for ever and ever. **Amen.**

Readings
Year A

Isaiah 49.14-18 or 14-15   God's eternal love
Psalm 62.1-8 (Grail, 61.2-3,6-7,8)
  Rest in God alone, my soul.
1 Corinthians 4.1-5   Stewards of God's mysteries
Matthew 6.24-34   The heavenly Father's care

Year B

Hosea 2.16-22 or 16-17,21-22   The heavenly bridegroom
Psalm 103.6-18 (Grail, 102.1-2,3-4,8-10,12-13)
  The Lord is kind and merciful.
2 Corinthians 3.1-6   Servants of the new covenant
Mark 2.18-22   Our response to God

Year C

Ecclesiastes 10.12-14   A man's words betray him
or   Sirach 27.4-7   A man's words betray him
Psalm 92.5-15 (Grail, 91.2-3,13,14-16)
  Lord, it is good to give thanks to you.
1 Corinthians 15.54-58   Victory is through Jesus Christ
Luke 6.39-45   A tree and its fruit

After Communion

We rely on your constant love, O Lord; we will be glad, because you will save us. We will sing to the Lord, because he has been good to us.   Psalm 13.5,6 TEV

THE NINTH ORDINARY SUNDAY
Faith

Sentence

Jesus said: I tell you, whatever you ask in prayer, believe that you receive it, and you will.   Mark 11.24

or

Turn to me, and be gracious to me; for I am lonely and afflicted. Consider my affliction and my trouble, and forgive all my sins.

Psalm 25.16,18

Collect

Almighty God, whose never-failing providence governs all things in heaven and earth: we humbly ask you to put away from us all hurtful things, and to give us whatever may be profitable for us; through Jesus Christ our Lord.   **Amen.**   BCP, Trinity 8

or

Let us pray [for God's care and protection.]
Father,
your love never fails.
Hear our call.
Keep us from danger
and provide for all our needs.
Grant this through our Lord Jesus Christ, your Son,
who lives and reigns with you and the Holy Spirit,
one God, for ever and ever.   **Amen.**

Readings

Year A

Deuteronomy 11.18-28 or 18,26-28   A blessing and curse
Psalm 31.1-8 (Grail, 30.2-3a,3b-4,17&25)
   Lord, be my rock of safety.
Romans 3.21-31 or 21-25[,28]   Justified by faith
Matthew 7.21-27   The two house builders

Year B

Deuteronomy 5.12-15   Do unto others
Psalm 81.1-7 (Grail, 80.3-4,5-6a,6b-8a,10-11)
   Sing with joy to God our help.
2 Corinthians 4.6-11[-12]   Jesus seen in us
Mark 2.23 - 3.6 or 2.23-28   Lord of the sabbath

Year C

1 Kings 8.41-43   Solomon's prayer for the stranger
Psalm 117 (Grail, 116)
   Go out to all the world, and tell the good news.   or   *Alleluia!*
Galatians 1.1-10 or 1-2,6-10   A servant of Christ
Luke 7.1-10   The Roman officer's faith

After Communion

Jesus said, Whatever you ask in prayer, believe that you receive it, and you will.   Mark 11.24

THE TENTH ORDINARY SUNDAY
New life in Christ

Sentence

The Lord is my light and my salvation;
whom shall I fear?
The Lord is the stronghold of my life;
of whom shall I be afraid?   Psalm 27.1

Collect

Lord God, without you we are not able to please you; mercifully grant that your Holy Spirit may in all things direct and rule our hearts; through Jesus Christ our Lord.   **Amen.**   BCP, Trinity 19
   or
Let us pray [for the guidance of the Holy Spirit.]
God of wisdom and love,
source of all good,
send your Spirit to teach us your truth
and guide our actions
in your way of peace.
We ask this through our Lord Jesus Christ, your Son,
who lives and reigns with you and the Holy Spirit,
one God, for ever and ever.   **Amen.**

Readings

Year A

Hosea 6.3-6   God's demand for love
Psalm 50.7-15 (Grail, 49.1-2&8,12-13,14-15)
   To the upright I will show the saving power of God.

234

Romans 4.18-25   God's promise received by faith
Matthew 9.9-13   Jesus calls Matthew

Year B

Genesis 3.8-15   Temptation and fall
Psalm 130 (Grail, 129.1-2,3-4,5-6,7b-8)
With the Lord there is mercy, and fulness of redemption.
2 Corinthians 4.13 - 5.5 or 4.13 - 5.1   Living by faith
Mark 3.20-35   Satan defeated

Year C

1 Kings 17.17-24   A dead child restored to life
Psalm 30.4-12 (Grail, 29.2&4,5-6,11-13)
I will praise you, Lord, for you have rescued me.
Galatians 1.11-19   Paul's call
Luke 7.11-17   Jesus raises the widow's son

After Communion

God is love, and he who abides in love abides in God, and God
abides in him.   1 John 4.16

THE ELEVENTH ORDINARY SUNDAY
The kingdom of God and his forgiveness

Sentence

Hear, O Lord, when I cry aloud, be gracious to me and answer me.
Cast me not off, forsake me not, God of my salvation. Psalm 27.7,9

Collect

Lord, we pray that your grace may always uphold and encourage
us, and make us continually to be given to all good works; through
Jesus Christ our Lord.   **Amen.**   BCP, Trinity 17

or

Let us pray [for the grace to follow Christ more closely.]
Almighty God,
our hope and our strength,
without you we falter.
Help us to follow Christ
and to live according to your will.
We ask this through our Lord Jesus Christ, your Son,
who lives and reigns with you and the Holy Spirit,
one God, for ever and ever.   **Amen.**

Readings

Year A

Exodus 19.2-6   A kingdom of priests, a holy nation
Psalm 100 (Grail, 99.2,3,5)
   We are his people: the sheep of his flock.
Romans 5.6-11   Saved by Christ's life
Matthew 9.36 - 10.8   The kingdom of heaven is near!

Year B

Ezekiel 17.22-24   The Lord makes the small great
Psalm 92.1-5 (Grail, 91.2-3,13,14-16)
   Lord, it is good to give thanks to you.
2 Corinthians 5.6-10   Living by faith
Mark 4.26-34   The parables of the growing seed and the
   mustard seed

Year C

2 Samuel 12.7-13 or 7-10,13   God's forgiveness brings life
Psalm 32.1-8 (Grail, 31.1-2,5,7,11)
   Lord, forgive the wrong I have done.
Galatians 2.16-21 or 16,19-21   Saved by faith
Luke 7.36 - 8.3 or 7.36-50   Faith saves

After Communion

Jesus prayed for his disciples: Holy Father, keep them in your name
which you have given me, that they may be one, even as we are
one.   John 17.11

THE TWELFTH ORDINARY SUNDAY

The love of God supports us

Sentence

The Lord is the strength of his people, he is the saving refuge of
his anointed. O save your people, and bless your heritage; be their
shepherd and carry them for ever.   Psalm 28.8-9

Collect

Lord God, the unfailing helper and guide of those whom you bring
up in your steadfast fear and love, keep us, we pray, under the protection of your good providence, and give us a continual reverence
and love for your holy name; through Jesus Christ our Lord.
Amen.   BCP, Trinity 2

or

Let us pray [that we may grow in the love of God.]
Father,
guide and protector of your people,
grant us an unfailing respect for your name,
and keep us always in your love.
Grant this through our Lord Jesus Christ, your Son,
who lives and reigns with you and the Holy Spirit,
one God, for ever and ever.   **Amen.**

Readings

Year A

Jeremiah 20.10-13   The Lord is the deliverer
Psalm 69.7-13 (Grail, 68.8-10,14-15a,33-35)
   Lord, in your great love, answer me.
Romans 5.12-17 or 12-15   God's gift: Jesus Christ
Matthew 10.26-33   Whom to fear

Year B

Job 38.1-11 or 1,8-11   The might of the Creator
Psalm 107.23-32 (Grail, 106.23-24,25-26,28-29,30-31)
   Give thanks to the Lord, his love is everlasting.   or   *Alleluia!*
2 Corinthians 5.14-21 or 14-17   Ruled by Christ's love
Mark 4.35-41   Jesus calms the storm

Year C

Zechariah 12.10-11   Him whom they have pierced
Psalm 63.1-9 (Grail, 62.2,3-4,5-6,8-9)
   My soul is thirsting for you, O Lord my God.
Galatians 3.26-29   Belonging to Christ
Luke 9.18-24   The Son of man must suffer

After Communion

The Lord is near to all who call to him, who call to him with sincerity. He supplies the needs of all who fear him; he hears their cry and saves them.   Psalm 145.18,19 TEV

or

Jesus said, I am the good shepherd, the good shepherd lays down his life for the sheep.   John 10.11

THE THIRTEENTH ORDINARY SUNDAY
Following Christ

Sentence

Clap your hands, O peoples. Shout out with loud songs of joy.

Psalm 47.1

Collect

Heavenly Father, keep your household the Church continually in your true religion; that those who lean only on the hope of your heavenly grace may always be defended by your mighty power; through Jesus Christ our Lord. **Amen.** BCP, Epiphany 5

or

Let us pray [that Christ will be our light.]
Father,
you call your children
to walk in the light of Christ.
Free us from darkness
and keep us in the radiance of your truth.
We ask this through our Lord Jesus Christ, your Son,
who lives and reigns with you and the Holy Spirit,
one God, for ever and ever. **Amen.**

Readings

Year A

2 Kings 4.8-16 or 8-11,14-16   Welcoming the man of God
Psalm 89.1-9 (Grail, 88.2-3,16-17,18-19)
   For ever I will sing the goodness of the Lord.
Romans 6.3-11 or 3-4,8,11   Buried and raised with Christ
Matthew 10.37-42   Take up your cross

Year B

Genesis 3.8-19   The cause of death
or Wisdom 1.13-15; 2.23-24   The cause of death
Psalm 30.4-12 (Grail, 29.2&4,5-6,11-13)
   I will praise you, Lord, for you have rescued me.
2 Corinthians 8.7-15 or 7,9,13-15   The generosity of Christ
Mark 5.21-43 or 21-24,35-43   Jairus' daughter and the woman with
   the haemorrhage healed

Year C

1 Kings 19.15-21 or 16b,19-21   The call of Elisha

238

Psalm 16 (Grail, 15.1-2,7-8,9-10,11)
You are my inheritance, O Lord.
Galatians 5.(1,)13-18   For freedom Christ has set us free
Luke 9.51-62   The call of Jesus

After Communion

Jesus said, He who finds his life will lose it, and he who loses his life for my sake will find it.   Matthew 10.39

THE FOURTEENTH ORDINARY SUNDAY

The King and the Kingdom

Sentence

We have thought on your steadfast love, O God,
in the midst of your temple.
As your Name, so your praise reaches to the end of the earth.
Your right hand is filled with victory.   Psalm 48.9-10

Collect

Lord, give your people grace to withstand the temptations of the
world, the flesh, and the devil, and with pure hearts and minds
to follow you the only God; through Jesus Christ our Lord.
Amen.   BCP, Trinity 18

or

Let us pray [for forgiveness through the grace of Jesus Christ.]
Father,
through the obedience of Jesus,
your Servant and your Son,
you raised a fallen world.
Free us from sin
and bring us the joy that lasts for ever.
We ask this through our Lord Jesus Christ, your Son,
who lives and reigns with you and the Holy Spirit,
one God, for ever and ever.   **Amen.**

Readings

Year A

Zechariah 9.9-10   The humble king
Psalm 145.1-7 (Grail, 144.1-2,8-9,10-11,13b-14)
I will praise your Name for ever, my King and my God.   or   *Alleluia!*

Romans 8.9-13 or 9,11-13   Living by the Spirit
Matthew 11.25-30   Come to me!

Year B
Ezekiel 2.2-5   A prophet among them
Psalm 123 (Grail, 122.1-2a,2b-3,4-5)
   Our eyes are fixed on the Lord, pleading for his mercy.
2 Corinthians 12.7-10   Paul's humiliation
Mark 6.1-6   Jesus despised

Year C
Isaiah 66.10-14   Zion's future hope
Psalm 66.1-8 (Grail, 65.1-3a,4-5,6-7a,16-17)
   Let all the earth cry out to God with joy.
Galatians 6.14-18   Being a new creature
Luke 10.1-20 or 1-12,17-20 or 1-9   Proclaiming the gospel of the
   Kingdom

After Communion
O taste and see that the Lord is good. Happy is the man who takes
refuge in him.   Psalm 34.8
   or
Jesus said, Come to me, all who labour and are heavy laden, and
I will give you rest.   Matthew 11.28

THE FIFTEENTH ORDINARY SUNDAY

Faithfulness

Sentence
The Lord shows us the path of life;
in his presence there is fulness of joy,
in his right hand are pleasures for evermore.   see Psalm 16.11

Collect
Lord of all power and might, the author and giver of all good
things, graft in our hearts the love of your Name, increase in us
true religion, nourish us with all goodness, and so by your mercy
keep us; through Jesus Christ our Lord. **Amen.**   BCP, Trinity 7
   or
Let us pray [that the gospel may be our rule of life.]
God our Father,
your light of truth
guides us in the way of Christ.

May all who follow him
reject what is contrary to the gospel.
We ask this through our Lord Jesus Christ, your Son,
who lives and reigns with you and the Holy Spirit,
one God, for ever and ever.   **Amen.**

Readings

Year A

Isaiah 55.6-11 or 10-11   The God who acts
Psalm 65.9-14 (Grail, 64.10,11,12-13a,13b-14)
   The seed that falls on good ground will yield a fruitful harvest.
Romans 8.18-23(-25)   The future glory
Matthew 13.1-23 or 1-9   The parable of the sower

Year B

Amos 7.12-15   The call to prophecy
Psalm 85.8-13 (Grail, 84.9-10,11-12,13-14)
   Lord, let us see your kindness, and grant us your salvation.
Ephesians 1.3-14 or 3-10   Spiritual blessings in Christ
Mark 6.7-13   Jesus sends out the Twelve disciples

Year C

Deuteronomy 30.10-14   Obedience to God
Psalm 69.31-38 (Grail, 68.14-15,31-32,33-34,36-37)
   Turn to the Lord in your need, and you will live.
Colossians 1.15-20   The person and work of Christ
Luke 10.25-37   Who is my neighbour?

After Communion

Sing praise to the Lord, his faithful people; remember what the
Holy One has done and give him thanks.   Psalm 30.4 TEV

THE SIXTEENTH ORDINARY SUNDAY

Ministers and stewards of the gospel

Sentence

Behold, God is our helper; the Lord is the upholder of our life. With
a free-will offering let us sacrifice to him; give thanks to the name
of the Lord, for it is good.   see Psalm 54.4,6

Collect

Lord Jesus Christ, at your first coming you sent your messenger
to prepare the way before you: grant that the ministers and stewards of your mysteries may likewise make ready your way, by turning the hearts of the disobedient to the ways of the righteous, that
at your second coming to judge the world we may be found an acceptable people in your sight; for you live and reign with the Father
and the Holy Spirit, now and for ever. **Amen.**   BCP, Advent 3

or

Let us pray [to be kept faithful in the service of God.]
Lord,
be merciful to your people.
Fill us with your gifts
and make us always eager to serve you
in faith, hope, and love.
Grant this through our Lord Jesus Christ, your Son,
who lives and reigns with you and the Holy Spirit,
one God, for ever and ever. **Amen.**

Readings

Year A

Deuteronomy 32.36-41   The patience and mercy of God
   or Wisdom 12.13-19 or 13,16-19   The patience and mercy of God
Psalm 86.4-13 (Grail, 85.5-6,9-10,15-16a)
   Lord, you are good and forgiving.
Romans 8.26-30 or 26-27   The Spirit pleads for us
Matthew 13.24-43 or 24-30   The parable of the weeds

Year B

Jeremiah 23.1-6   The Lord will gather his people
Psalm 23 (Grail, 22.1-3a,3b-4,5,6)
   The Lord is my shepherd; there is nothing I shall want.
Ephesians 2.13-18   Christ is our peace
Mark 6.30-34   Sheep without a shepherd

Year C

Genesis 18.1-10a   Abraham is promised a son
Psalm 15 (Grail, 14.1-3a,3b-4a,4b-5)
   He who does justice will live in the presence of the Lord.
Colossians 1.24-28   Paul's ministry to the church
Luke 10.38-42   Jesus visits Martha and Mary

242

After Communion

The Lord says, Behold, I stand at the door and knock; if anyone hears my voice and opens the door, I will come in to him and eat with him, and he with me.   Revelation 3.20

THE SEVENTEENTH ORDINARY SUNDAY
Living for God now and for ever

Sentence

God is in his holy habitation. God gives the desolate a home to dwell in; he gives power and strength to his people.

see Psalm 68.5-6,35

Collect

Almighty God, the protector of all who put their trust in you, without whom nothing is strong, nothing is holy: increase and multiply upon us your mercy, so that with you as our ruler and guide, we may so pass through things temporal that we finally lose not the things eternal; grant this, heavenly Father, for our Lord Jesus Christ's sake.   **Amen.**   BCP, Trinity 4

or

Let us pray [that we will make good use of the gifts that God has given us.]

God our Father and protector,
without you nothing is holy,
nothing has value.
Guide us to everlasting life
by helping us to use wisely
the blessings you have given to the world.
We ask this through our Lord Jesus Christ, your Son,
who lives and reigns with you and the Holy Spirit,
one God, for ever and ever.   **Amen.**

Readings

Year A

1 Kings 3.5-12 or 5, 7-12   Solomon's prayer for understanding
Psalm 119.57-64 (Grail, 118.57&72,76-77,127-128,129-130)
   Lord, I love your commands.
Romans 8.28-30   The future glory
Matthew 13.44-52   Parables of the Kingdom

243

Year B

2 Kings 4.42-44   Elisha feeds a hundred men
Psalm 145.8-21 (Grail, 144.10-11,15-16,17-18)
   The hand of the Lord feeds us; he answers all our needs.
Ephesians 4.1-6   The unity of the Spirit
John 6.1-15   Jesus feeds the five thousand

Year C

Genesis 18.20-32   Abraham intercedes for Sodom
Psalm 138 (Grail, 137.1-2a,2b-3,6-7a,7b-8)
   Lord, on the day I called for help, you answered me.
Colossians 2.11-14   Fulness of life in Christ
Luke 11.1-13   Jesus's teaching on prayer

After Communion

Be imitators of God, as beloved children; and walk in love, as
Christ loved us and gave himself up for us.   Ephesians 5.1,2

THE EIGHTEENTH ORDINARY SUNDAY

God's generosity and our response

Sentence

Jesus says: I am the bread of life; he who comes to me shall not
hunger, and he who believes in me shall never thirst.   John 6.35
   or

Be pleased, O God, to deliver me; I am poor and needy, hasten
to me, O God, you are my helper and deliverer, O Lord, do not
tarry.   Psalm 70.1,5

Collect

Raise up your great power, Lord, and come among us to save us;
that, although through our sins we are grievously hindered in running the race that is set before us, your plentiful grace and mercy
may speedily help and deliver us; through the sufficiency of your
Son our Lord, to whom with you and the Holy Spirit be honour
and glory, now and for ever.   **Amen.**   BCP, Advent 4
   or

Let us pray [for the gift of God's forgiveness and love.]
Father of everlasting goodness,
our creator and guide,
be close to us
and hear the prayers of all who praise you.

244

Forgive our sins and restore us to life.
Keep us safe in your love.
Grant this through our Lord Jesus Christ, your Son,
who lives and reigns with you and the Holy Spirit,
one God, for ever and ever.   **Amen.**

Readings

Year A

Isaiah 55.1-3   Come to the waters
Psalm 145.14-21 (Grail, 144.8-9,15-16,17-18)
The hand of the Lord feeds us; he answers all our needs.
Romans 8.35-39 or 35,37-39   The love of God
Matthew 14.13-21   Jesus feeds the five thousand

Year B

Exodus 16.2-15 or 2-4,12-15   Bread from heaven
Psalm 78.16-30 (Grail, 77.3-4a,23-24,25-26)
The Lord gave them bread from heaven.
Ephesians 4.17-24 or 17, 20-24   The new man
John 6.24-35   Bread from heaven

Year C

Ecclesiastes 2.18-23 or 1.2; 2.20-23   Human ineffectiveness
Psalm 95 (Grail 94.1-2,6-7a,7b-9)
If today you hear his voice, harden not your hearts.
Colossians 3.1-11 or 1-5,9-11   Real life in Christ
Luke 12.13-21   The parable of the rich fool

After Communion

Jesus said: Truly, truly I say to you, it was not Moses who gave
you the bread from heaven; my Father gives you true bread from
heaven. For the bread of God is that which comes down from
heaven, and gives life to the world.   John 6.32,33
   or

Jesus said: A man's life does not consist in the abundance of his
possessions.   Luke 12.15

THE NINETEENTH ORDINARY SUNDAY

Faithfulness to God's call

Sentence

Praise the Lord, his people; he fills you with the finest of the wheat. see Psalm 148.12,14

or

Have regard for your covenant, Lord; let the poor and needy praise your Name. Arise, O God, plead your cause; remember how the ungodly scoff at you all the day. Psalm 74.20-22

Collect

Lord God, you know that we cannot put our trust in anything that we do: help us to have faith in you alone, and mercifully defend us by your power against all adversity; through Jesus Christ our Lord. **Amen.** BCP, Sexagesima

or

Let us pray [that we may grow in the love of God.]
Almighty and ever-living God,
your Spirit made us your children,
confident to call you Father.
Increase your Spirit within us
and bring us to our promised inheritance.
Grant this through our Lord Jesus Christ, your Son,
who lives and reigns with you and the Holy Spirit,
one God, for ever and ever. **Amen.**

Readings

Year A

1 Kings 19.9-13 or 9,11-13 The still small voice
Psalm 85.8-13 (Grail, 84.9-10,11-12,13-14)
   Lord, let us see your kindness, and grant us your salvation.
Romans 9.1-5 Prayer for one's own
Matthew 14.22-33 Jesus walks on the water
After Communion

Jesus said to his fearful disciples: Take heart, it is I; have no fear.
Matthew 14.27

Year B

1 Kings 19.4-8 Elijah fed by God

Psalm 34.1-10 (Grail, 33.2-3,4-5,6-7,8-9)
O taste and see the goodness of the Lord.
Ephesians 4.30 - 5.2   Walk in love
John 6.41-51   The living bread

After Communion

Jesus said, I am the living bread which came down from heaven;
if anyone eats of this bread, he will live for ever; and the bread
which I shall give for the life of the world is my flesh.   John 6.51

Year C

Isaiah 63.7-9   God the saviour
or Wisdom 18.5-9   God the saviour
Psalm 33.13-21 (Grail, 32.1&12,18-19,20&22)
Happy the people the Lord has chosen to be his own.
Hebrews 11.1-19 or 1-2,8-19 or 1-2,8-12   Faith
Luke 12.32-48 or 35-40   Be prepared

After Communion

Those who trust in the Lord are like Mount Zion which can never
be shaken, never be moved. As the mountains surround Jerusalem,
so the Lord surrounds his people, from now on and for ever.

Psalm 125.1,2 TEV

THE TWENTIETH ORDINARY SUNDAY

The will and call of God

Sentence

O Lord God of hosts, hear our prayer; give ear, O God of Jacob.
For a day in your courts is better than a thousand elsewhere.

Psalm 84.8,10

Collect

God our Father, you have prepared for those who love you such
good things as pass man's understanding: pour into our hearts such
love towards you, that we, loving you above all things, may obtain
your promises which exceed all that we can desire; through Jesus
Christ our Lord.   **Amen.**   BCP, Trinity 6

or

Let us pray [that the love of God may raise us beyond what we
    see to the unseen glory of his kingdom.]
God our Father,
may we love you in all things and above all things
and reach the joy you have prepared for us
beyond all our imagining.
We ask this through our Lord Jesus Christ, your Son,
who lives and reigns with you and the Holy Spirit,
one God, for ever and ever.   **Amen.**

Readings

Year A
Isaiah 56.1-7 or 1,6-7   Called to be servants
Psalm 67 (Grail, 66.2-3,5,6&8a)
    O God, let all the nations praise you.
Romans 11.13-32 or 13-15,29-32   The salvation of the gentiles
Matthew 15.21-28   A woman's faith

Year B
Proverbs 9.1-6   The invitation of God
Psalm 34.11-18 (Grail, 33.2-3,10-11,12-13,14-15)
    O taste and see the goodness of the Lord.
Ephesians 5.15-20   Living in the light
John 6.51-58   The flesh and blood of the Son of man

Year C
Jeremiah 38.2-10 or 4-6,8-10   Not peace but a sword
Psalm 40.1-7 (Grail, 39.2,3,4,18)
    Lord, come to my aid!
Hebrews 12.1-4   Looking to Jesus
Luke 12.49-53   Jesus the cause of division

After Communion

With the Lord there is steadfast love, and with him is plenteous
redemption.   Psalm 130.7

THE TWENTY-FIRST ORDINARY SUNDAY

God's sons and daughters

Sentence

Incline your ear, O Lord, and answer us. Save your servants who trust in you. Be gracious to us, O Lord, for to you do we cry all the day long.   Psalm 86.1-3

or

The Lord says: He who eats my flesh and drinks my blood has eternal life, and I will raise him up at the last day.   John 6.54

Collect

Lord God, you know us to be set in the midst of so many great dangers that by reason of the frailty of our nature we cannot always stand upright: grant us such strength and protection as may support us in all dangers and carry us through all temptations; through Jesus Christ our Lord. **Amen.**   BCP, Epiphany 4

or

Let us pray [that God will make us one in mind and heart.]
Father,
help us to seek the values
that will bring us lasting joy in this changing world.
In our desire for what you promised
make us one in mind and heart.
Grant this through our Lord Jesus Christ, your Son,
who lives and reigns with you and the Holy Spirit,
one God, for ever and ever. **Amen.**

Readings

Year A

Isaiah 22.19-23   God's steward
Psalm 138 (Grail, 137.1-2a,2b-3,6-7)
  Lord, your love is eternal; do not forsake the work of your hands.
Romans 11.33-36   Praise to God
Matthew 16.13-20   The keys of the Kingdom of heaven

Year B

Joshua 24.1-18 or 1-2,15-18   We will serve the Lord
Psalm 34.11-18 (Grail, 33.2-3,16-17,18-19,20-21,22-23)
  O taste and see the goodness of the Lord.
Ephesians 5.21-32(-33)   The mystery of marriage and of the church

John 6.60-69   The words of eternal life
    Year C
Isaiah 66.18b-21   Brothers from all nations
Psalm 117 (Grail, 116)
    Go out to all the world and tell the good news.   or   *Alleluia!*
Hebrews 12.5-13 or 5-7,11-13   God our Father
Luke 13.22-30   The narrow door

    After Communion
To all who received him, who believed in his name, he gave power
to become children of God.   John 1.12

THE TWENTY-SECOND ORDINARY SUNDAY
Finding favour with God

    Sentence
Be gracious to me, O Lord, for to you do I cry all the day long.
You, O Lord, are good and forgiving, abounding in steadfast love
to all who call on you.   Psalm 86.3,5
    or
The Lord is good and forgiving,
abounding in steadfast love to all who call on him.   see Psalm 86.5

    Collect
Almighty and everlasting God, you are always more ready to hear
than we to pray, and constantly give more than either we desire
or deserve: pour down on us the abundance of your mercy, forgiving us those things of which our conscience is afraid, and giving
us those good things which we are not worthy to ask, except
through the merits and mediation of Jesus Christ, your Son our
Lord. **Amen.**   BCP, Trinity 12
    or
Let us pray [that God will increase our faith and bring to perfection
    the gifts he has given us.]
Almighty God,
every good thing comes from you.
Fill our hearts with love for you,
increase our faith,
and by your constant care
preserve in us the good you have given us.

We ask this through our Lord Jesus Christ, your Son,
who lives and reigns with you and the Holy Spirit,
one God, for ever and ever.   **Amen.**

Readings

Year A

Jeremiah 20.7-9
   The word of the Lord is for me a reproach and derision.
Psalm 63 (Grail, 62.2,3-4,5-6,8-9)
   My soul is thirsting for you, O Lord my God.
Romans 12.1-12 or 1-8   Life in God's service
Matthew 16.21-27   Following the crucified Lord

Year B

Deuteronomy 4.1-8 or 1-2,6-8   Keep the commands of the Lord
Psalm 15 (Grail, 14.1-2,3-4a,4b-5)
   He who does justice will live in the presence of the Lord.
James 1.17-27 or 17-18,21-22   Be doers of the word
Mark 7.1-23 or 1-8,14-15,21-23
   The commandments of God and the traditions of men

Year C

Proverbs 2.1-15   Finding favour with the Lord
or Sirach 3.17-29 or 17-18,20,28-29   Finding favour with the Lord
Psalm 68.1-8 (Grail, 67.4-5,6-7,10-11)
   God, in your goodness you have made a home for the poor.
Hebrews 12.18-24 or 18-19,22-24a   Mount Zion
Luke 14.7-14   Hospitality and humility

After Communion

Teach us, O Lord, the way of your statutes; and we will keep it
to the end. Give us understanding, that we may keep your Law
and observe it with our whole heart.   see Psalm 119.33-34

THE TWENTY-THIRD ORDINARY SUNDAY

Christian freedom

Sentence

You are righteous, Lord, and right are your judgments. Deal with
your servant according to your steadfast love.   Psalm 119.137,154

or

Jesus said: I am the light of the world; he who follows me will not walk in darkness, but will have the light of life.　　　John 8.12

Collect

Lord, we pray, absolve your people from their offences; that through your bountiful goodness we may be set free from the chains of those sins which in our frailty we have committed: grant this, heavenly Father, for the sake of Jesus Christ, our Lord and Saviour.　**Amen.**　　　　　　　　　　BCP, Trinity 24

or

Let us pray [that we may realize the freedom God has given us in making us his sons and daughters.]

God our Father,
you redeem us
and make us your children in Christ.
Look on us,
give us true freedom
and bring us to the inheritance you promised.
Grant this through our Lord Jesus Christ, your Son,
who lives and reigns with you and the Holy Spirit,
one God, for ever and ever.　**Amen.**

Readings

Year A

Ezekiel 33.7-9　Responsibility
Psalm 95 (Grail, 94.1-2,6-7a,7b-9)
　If today you hear his voice, harden not your hearts.
Romans 13.8-14 or 8-10　Duties toward one another
Matthew 18.15-20　A brother who sins

Year B

Isaiah 35.(3-)4-7　The salvation of our God
Psalm 146 (Grail, 145.6b-7,8-9,8c&9c&10)
　Praise the Lord, my soul! or　*Alleluia!*
James 2.1-5　God has chosen the poor
Mark 7.31-37　Jesus heals a deaf and dumb man

Year C

Exodus 15.1-12　The salvation of God
or Wisdom 9.13-18　The salvation of God

Psalm 90.1-12 (Grail, 89.3-4,5-6,12-13,14-15)
In every age, O Lord, you have been our refuge.
Philemon or Philemon 9-10, 12-17   A very dear brother
Luke 14.25-33   The cost of being a disciple

After Communion
We will live in complete freedom, because we have tried to obey
your teachings, O Lord.   Psalm 119.45 TEV

THE TWENTY-FOURTH ORDINARY SUNDAY
Salvation and forgiveness

Sentence
May the Lord give peace to those who wait for him and may his
prophets proclaim his name. His ears are open to the prayer of his
servants.   see Sirach 36.15,16

Collect
Merciful Lord, grant to your faithful people pardon and peace,
that they may be cleansed from all their sins, and serve you with
a quiet mind; through Jesus Christ our Lord.   **Amen.**
                                         BCP, Trinity 21

or

Let us pray [that God will keep us faithful in his service.]
Almighty God,
our creator and guide,
may we serve you with all our heart
and know your forgiveness in our lives.
We ask this through our Lord Jesus Christ, your Son,
who lives and reigns with you and the Holy Spirit,
one God, for ever and ever.   **Amen.**

Readings

Year A

Exodus 34.5-9   Forgiveness and being forgiven
or Sirach 27.30 - 28.7   Forgiveness and being forgiven
Psalm 103.6-14 (Grail, 102.1-2,3-4,9-10,11-12)
   The Lord is kind and merciful; slow to anger, and rich in compassion.
Romans 14.7-12 or 7-9   None of us lives for himself
Matthew 18.21-35   The parable of the unforgiving servant

Year B

Isaiah 50.4-9   The obedient servant of the Lord
Psalm 116.1-9 (Grail, 114.1-2,3-4,5-6&9)
   I will walk in the presence of the Lord in the land of the living.
   or   *Alleluia!*
James 2.14-26 or 14-18   Faith and actions
Mark 8.27-35   The cost of being a disciple

Year C

Exodus 32.7-14 or 7-11,13-14   The Lord relented
Psalm 51.10-19 (Grail, 50.2-3,12-13,17&19)
   I will rise and go to my father.
1 Timothy 1.12-17   Gratitude for God's mercy
Luke 15.1-32 or 1-10   The lost sheep

After Communion

How precious, O God, is your constant love. Men find protection
under the shadow of your wings.   Psalm 36.7 TEV

THE TWENTY-FIFTH ORDINARY SUNDAY

Duty to neighbour

Sentence

Thus says the Lord: There is no other god besides me, a righteous
God and Saviour, turn to me and be saved, all the ends of the earth.
                                                  Isaiah 45.21,22

Collect

Almighty and eternal God, by whose Spirit the whole body of the
church is governed and sanctified: receive our prayer which we offer before you for the many different members of your holy church;
that every one of them in his vocation and ministry may truly and
devoutly serve you; through our Lord and Saviour Jesus Christ.
Amen.   BCP, Good Friday 2

or

Lord, let your continual pity cleanse and defend your church, and
because it cannot continue in safety without your aid, keep it evermore by your help and goodness; through Jesus Christ our Lord.
Amen.   BCP, Trinity 16

or

Let us pray [that we will grow in the love of God and of one
   another.]

254

Father,
guide us, as you guide creation
according to your law of love.
May we love one another
and come to perfection
in the eternal life prepared for us.
We ask this through our Lord Jesus Christ, your Son,
who lives and reigns with you and the Holy Spirit,
one God, for ever and ever. **Amen.**

Readings

Year A

Isaiah 55.6-9 My thoughts are not your thoughts
Psalm 145.14-21 (Grail, 144.2-3,8-9,17-18)
 The Lord is near to all who call him.
Philippians 1.19-26 or 20-24,27 To live is Christ
Matthew 20.1-16 The workers in the vineyard

Year B

Hosea 4.1-6 The Lord's controversy with his people
or Wisdom 2.12-20 or 12,17-20 The thoughts of the ungodly
Psalm 54 (Grail, 53.3-4,5,6&8)
 The Lord upholds my life.
James 3.16 - 4.3 or 3.13-18 Peacemakers
Mark 9.30-37 Servant of all

Year C

Amos 8.4-7(-10) Social sins
Psalm 113 (Grail, 112.1-2,4-6,7-8)
 Praise the Lord who lifts up the poor. or *Alleluia!*
1 Timothy 2.1-8 Prayer for all
Luke 16.1-13 The shrewd manager
or Luke 16.10-13 God and mammon

After Communion

The Lord has showed you, O man, what is good; and what does
the Lord require of you but to do justice, and to love kindness, and
to walk humbly with your God? Micah 6.8

THE TWENTY-SIXTH ORDINARY SUNDAY

True repentance

Sentence

All that you have done to us, Lord, you have done in true judgment; for we have sinned in all things and have not obeyed your commandments; give glory to your Name, O Lord, and deal with us in your forbearance.   Song of the Three Young Men 8,17,20,19

Collect

Lord God, you declare your almighty power chiefly in showing mercy and pity: grant us such a measure of your grace that, running in the way of your commandments, we may obtain your promises, and share in your heavenly treasure; through Jesus Christ our Lord. **Amen.**   BCP, Trinity 11

or

Let us pray [for God's forgiveness and for the happiness it
    brings.]
Father,
you show your almighty power
in your mercy and forgiveness.
Continue to fill us with your gifts of love.
Help us to hurry towards the eternal life you promised
and to come to share in the joys of your kingdom.
Grant this through our Lord Jesus Christ, your Son,
who lives and reigns with you and the Holy Spirit,
one God, for ever and ever. **Amen.**

Readings

Year A

Ezekiel 18.25-28(-32)   Repentance
Psalm 25.1-9 (Grail, 24.4-5,6-7,8-9)
    Remember your mercies, O Lord.
Philippians 2.1-11   Christ's humility and greatness
Matthew 21.28-32   Jesus's authority

Year B

Numbers 11.25-29   The Lord's people
Psalm 19.7-14 (Grail, 18.8,10,12-13,14)
    The precepts of the Lord give joy to the heart.
James 5.1-6   Warning to the rich
Mark 9.38-48 or 38-43,45,47-48   Temptations to sin

Year C
Amos 6.1-7 or 1a,4-7   Luxury condemned
Psalm 146 (Grail, 145.6b-7,8-9,8c&9c&10)
  Praise the Lord, my soul!   or   *Alleluia!*
1 Timothy 6.11-16   The personal life of the man of God
Luke 16.19-31   The rich man and Lazarus

After Communion

By this we know love, that Christ lays down his life for us; and
we ought to lay down our lives for the brethren.   1 John 3.16
  or

Create a pure heart in us, O God, and put a new and loyal spirit
in us.   Psalm 51.10 TEV

THE TWENTY-SEVENTH ORDINARY SUNDAY
The righteous shall live by faith

Sentence

The Lord is the king who rules over all things, the universe is in
his power and there is no one who can oppose him. He has made
heaven and earth and he is Lord of all.   see Esther 13.9-11

Collect

Almighty God, creator of all things and giver of every good and
perfect gift, hear with favour the prayers of your people, that we
who are justly punished for our offences may mercifully be
delivered by your goodness, for the glory of your name; through
Jesus Christ our Saviour, who lives and reigns with you and the
Holy Spirit, one God, now and for ever.   **Amen.**

                                              BCP, Septuagesima
  or

Let us pray [that God will forgive our failings and bring us
  peace.]
Father,
your love for us
surpasses all our hopes and desires.
Forgive our failings,
keep us in your peace,
and lead us in the way of salvation.
We ask this through our Lord Jesus Christ, your Son,
who lives and reigns with you and the Holy Spirit,
one God, for ever and ever.   **Amen.**

Readings

Year A

Isaiah 5.1-7   The parable of the vineyard
Psalm 80.8-19 (Grail, 79.9-10,13-14,15-16,19-20)
   The vineyard of the Lord is the house of Israel.
Philippians 4.(4-)6-9   A christian approach to life
Matthew 21.33-43   The parable of the tenants in the vineyard

Year B

Genesis 2.18-24   Partners who complete each other's being
Psalm 128 (Grail, 127.1-2,3,4-6)
   May the Lord bless us all the days of our lives.
Hebrews 2.9-11   Made perfect through suffering
Mark 10.2-16 or 2-12   Marriage and divorce

Year C

Habakkuk 1.2-3; 2.2-4 or 2.1-4   The righteous will live by faith
Psalm 95.1-9 (Grail, 94.1-2,6-7a,7b-9)
   If today you hear his voice, harden not your hearts.
2 Timothy 1.6-14 or 6-8,13-14   Good things entrusted to us
Luke 17.5-10   Faith and duty

After Communion

Behold, he whose soul is not upright in him shall fail, but the
righteous shall live by his faith.   Habakkuk 2.4

THE TWENTY-EIGHTH ORDINARY SUNDAY

What does the Lord require of you?

Sentence

If you, O Lord, should mark iniquity, Lord, who could stand? But
there is forgiveness with you, God of Israel.   Psalm 130.3-4

Collect

Graciously hear us, Lord God; and grant that we, to whom you
have given the desire to pray, may by your mighty aid be defended
and strengthened in all dangers and adversities; through Jesus
Christ our Lord.   **Amen.**   BCP, Trinity 3
   or

Let us pray [that God will help us to love one another.]
Lord,
our help and guide,

make your love the foundation of our lives.
May our love for you express itself
in our eagerness to do good for others.
Grant this through our Lord Jesus Christ, your Son,
who lives and reigns with you and the Holy Spirit,
one God, for ever and ever.   **Amen.**

Readings

Year A

Isaiah 25.6-9   Be glad in the salvation of God
Psalm 23 (Grail, 22.1-3a,3b-4,5,6)
I shall live in the house of the Lord all the days of my life.
Philippians 4.12-20 or 12-14,19-20   The power that Christ gives
Matthew 22.1-14 or 1-10   The parable of the wedding feast

Year B

1 Kings 3.3-14   Solomon's prayer for wisdom
or Wisdom 7.7-11   Prayer for wisdom
Psalm 90.11-17 (Grail, 89.12-13,14-15,16-17)
Fill us with your love, O Lord, and we will sing for joy.
Hebrews 4.12-13   The word of God
Mark 10.17-30 or 17-27   The rich man

Year C

2 Kings 5.(10-)14-17   Humility
Psalm 98 (Grail, 97.1,2-3a,3b-4)
The Lord has revealed to the nations his saving power.
2 Timothy 2.8-13   Hold firm
Luke 17.11-19   Jesus makes ten lepers clean

After Communion

Religion that is pure and undefiled before God and the Father is
this: to visit orphans and widows in their affliction, and to keep
oneself unstained from the world.   James 1.27

THE TWENTY-NINTH ORDINARY SUNDAY
Prayer and service

Sentence

We call upon you, Lord, for you answer us; incline your ear to us,
hear our words. Keep us as the apple of the eye; hide us in the
shadow of your wings.   Psalm 17.6,8

Collect

Almighty and everlasting God, mercifully look on our infirmities; and in all our dangers and necessities stretch out your right hand to help and defend us; through Jesus Christ our Lord.   **Amen.**

BCP, Epiphany 3

or

Let us pray [for the gift of joy in our service of God and man.]
Almighty and ever-living God,
our source of power and inspiration,
give us strength and joy
in serving you as followers of Christ,
who lives and reigns with you and the Holy Spirit,
one God, for ever and ever.   **Amen.**

Readings

Year A

Isaiah 45.1-6 or 1,4-6   None like the Lord
Psalm 96 (Grail, 95.2-3,4-5,7-8,9-10)
   Give the Lord glory and honour.
1 Thessalonians 1.1-5   Faith, hope, and love
Matthew 22.15-21   The question about paying taxes

Year B

Isaiah 53.7-12 or 10-11   The servant of the Lord
Psalm 33.13-21 (Grail, 32.4-5,18-19,20-21)
   Lord, let your mercy be on us, as we place our trust in you.
Hebrews 4.14-16   Jesus the great high priest
Mark 10.35-45 or 42-45   The example of Jesus

Year C

Exodus 17.8-13   The intercession of Moses
Psalm 121 (Grail, 120.1-2,3-4,5-6,7-8)
   Our help is from the Lord who made heaven and earth.
2 Timothy 3.14 - 4.2   The man of God
Luke 18.1-8   The parable of the widow and the judge

After Communion

The Son of man came not to be served but to serve, and to give his life as a ransom for many.   Mark 10.45

260

THE THIRTIETH ORDINARY SUNDAY
The prayer of the humble

Sentence

Let the hearts of those who seek the Lord rejoice. Seek the Lord
and his strength, seek his presence continually.   Psalm 105.3-4

Collect

Almighty and eternal God, grant that we may grow in faith, hope,
and love; and that we may obtain what you promised, make us
love what you command; through Jesus Christ our Lord.   **Amen.**
                                                          BCP, Trinity 14

or

Let us pray [for the strength to do God's will.]
Almighty and ever-living God,
strengthen our faith, hope, and love.
May we do with loving hearts
what you ask of us
and enter more fully the life you promise.
We ask this through our Lord Jesus Christ, your Son,
who lives and reigns with you and the Holy Spirit,
one God, for ever and ever.   **Amen.**

Readings

Year A

Exodus 22.21-27   Be merciful as the Father is merciful
Psalm 18.48-52 (Grail, 17.1-4,47-48)
  I love you, Lord, my strength.
1 Thessalonians 1.5b-10   Christian life and faith
Matthew 22.34-40   The great commandment

Year B

Jeremiah 31.7-9   The Lord has saved his people
Psalm 126 (Grail, 125.1-2a,2b-3,4-5,6)
  The Lord has done great things for us; we are filled with joy.
Hebrews 5.1-6(-10)   Jesus the great high priest
Mark 10.46-52   Jesus heals blind Bartimaeus

Year C

Exodus 12.12-22   What God requires
or Sirach 35.12b-18a or 12b-14,16-18a   The prayer of the humble
Psalm 34.11-22 (Grail, 33.2-3,16-17,19&23)
  The Lord hears the cry of the poor.

261

2 Timothy 4.6-18 or 6-9,16-18   A good servant of Christ Jesus
Luke 18.9-14   The parable of the Pharisee and the tax collector

After Communion

Behold, the eye of the Lord is on those who fear him, on those who hope in his steadfast love, that he may deliver their souls from death, and keep them alive in famine.   Psalm 33.18,19

THE THIRTY-FIRST ORDINARY SUNDAY
God's saving love

Sentence

The sinner cries to God: Do not forsake me, O Lord.
O my God, be not far from me,
make haste to help me, O Lord, my salvation.   Psalm 38.21-22

Collect

Merciful God, it is by your gift alone that your faithful people offer you true and acceptable service; grant that we may so faithfully serve you in this life that we fail not finally to obtain your heavenly promises; through the merits of Jesus Christ our Lord.   **Amen.**
                                                    BCP, Trinity 13

or

Let us pray [that our lives may reflect our faith.]
God of power and mercy,
only with your help
can we offer you fitting service and praise.
May we live the faith we profess
and trust your promise of eternal life.
Grant this through our Lord Jesus Christ, your Son,
who lives and reigns with you and the Holy Spirit,
one God, for ever and ever.   **Amen.**

Readings

Year A

Malachi 1.14 - 2.10 or 1.14 - 2.2,8-10   Priestly ministry
Psalm 131 (Grail, 130.1,2,3)
   In you, Lord, I have found my peace.
1 Thessalonians 2.7-13 or 7-9,13   The ministry of the gospel

262

Matthew 23.1-12   Jesus warns against false teachers

Year B
Deuteronomy 6.1-6   Love the Lord
Psalm 18.48-52 (Grail, 17.2-4,47,48)
I love you, Lord, my strength.
Hebrews 7.23-28   Christ's priesthood
Mark 12.28-34   The great commandment

Year C
Hosea 14.1-7   God's mercy and love
or   Wisdom 11.22 - 12.2   God's mercy and love
Psalm 145 (Grail, 144.1-2,8-9,10-11,13b-14)
I will praise your name for ever, my King and my God.
2 Thessalonians 1.11 - 2.2   Worthy of his call
Luke 19.1-10   Jesus and Zacchaeus

After Communion
Lord, you show us the path that leads to life; your presence fills
us with joy, and your help brings pleasure for ever.

Psalm 16.11 TEV

THE THIRTY-SECOND ORDINARY SUNDAY
Life eternal

Sentence
Let our prayer come before you, O Lord,
incline your ear to our cry.   Psalm 88.2
    or
The Lord is my shepherd, I shall not want;
he makes me lie down in green pastures.   Psalm 23.1-2

Collect
Almighty and merciful God, of your bountiful goodness keep us
from everything that may hurt us, that we may be ready in body
and soul cheerfully to accomplish whatever you want us to do;
through Jesus Christ our Lord.   **Amen.**   BCP, Trinity 20
    or
Let us pray [for health of mind and body.]
God of power and mercy,
protect us from all harm.

263

Give us freedom of spirit
and health in mind and body
to do your work on earth.
We ask this through our Lord Jesus Christ, your Son,
who lives and reigns with you and the Holy Spirit,
one God, for ever and ever. **Amen.**

Readings

Year A

Proverbs 3.21-26   Life-giving wisdom
or   Wisdom 6.12-16   Life-giving wisdom
Psalm 63.1-9 (Grail, 62 2 3-4,5-6,7-8)
My soul is thirsting for you, O Lord my God.
1 Thessalonians 4.13-18 or 13-14   The Lord's coming
Matthew 25.1-13   The bridegroom comes!

Year B

1 Kings 17.10-16   Elijah and the famine
Psalm 146 (Grail, 145.6b-7,8-9,8c&9c&10)
Praise the Lord, my soul!   or   *Alleluia!*
Hebrews 9.24-28   Christ's sacrifice takes away sins
Mark 12.38-44 or 41-44   The widow's offering

Year C

Malachi 3.16-18   The one who serves God
or 2 Maccabees 7.1-14 or 1-2,9-14   Life eternal
Psalm 17.6-12 (Grail, 16.1-2,5-6,8&15)
Lord, when your glory appears,
my joy will be full.
2 Thessalonians 2.16 - 3.5   Pray for us
Luke 20.27-38 or 34-38   The question about rising from death

After Communion

This is eternal life, that men may know the only true God, and
Jesus Christ whom he has sent.   John 17.3

THE THIRTY-THIRD ORDINARY SUNDAY

Living between the Cross and Christ's return

Sentence

Thus says the Lord, I know the plans I have for you, plans for your
welfare and not for evil, to give you a future and a hope.

Jeremiah 29.11

Collect

Father in heaven, keep your household the church steadfast in faith and love, that through your protection it may be free from all adversities, and may devoutly serve you in good works to the glory of your name; through Jesus Christ our Lord.   **Amen.**

BCP, Trinity 22

or

Let us pray [that God will help us to be faithful.]
Father of all that is good,
keep us faithful in serving you,
for to serve you is our lasting joy.
We ask this through our Lord Jesus Christ, your Son,
who lives and reigns with you and the Holy Spirit,
one God, for ever and ever.   **Amen.**

Readings

Year A

Proverbs 31.10-31 or 10-13,19-20,30-31   The good wife
Psalm 128 (Grail, 127.1-2,3,4-5)
Happy are those who fear the Lord.
1 Thessalonians 5.1-6(-11)   Be ready for the Lord's coming
Matthew 25.14-30 or 14-15,19-20   The parable of the three servants

Year B

Daniel 12.1-3   Michael our prince
Psalm 16 (Grail, 15.5-6,9-10,11)
Keep me safe, O God; you are my hope.
Hebrews 10.11-18 or 11-14,18   Christ's single offering
Mark 13.24-32   The coming of the Son of man

Year C

Malachi 4.1-2a   The sun of righteousness
Psalm 98 (Grail, 97.5-6,6,7-8,9)
The Lord comes to rule the earth with justice.
2 Thessalonians 3.6-13   The obligation to work
Luke 21.5-19   Troubles and persecution

After Communion

At Emmaus, the disciples said to Jesus, Stay with us, for it is towards evening and the day is now far spent.   Luke 24.29

265

THE THIRTY-FOURTH ORDINARY SUNDAY
Christ the King

Sentence

Worthy is the Lamb who was slain to receive power and wealth and wisdom and might and honour and glory and blessing. To him be glory and dominion for ever and ever.   Revelation 5.12;1.6

For the Sunday

Collect

God our Father, whose will is to bring all things to order and unity in our Lord Jesus Christ; grant that all the peoples of the world, now divided and torn apart by sin, may be brought together in his kingdom of love; through Jesus Christ our Lord. **Amen.**

or

Let us pray [that all men will acclaim Jesus as Lord.]
Almighty and merciful God,
you break the power of evil
and make all things new
in your Son Jesus Christ, the King of the universe.
May all in heaven and earth acclaim your glory
and never cease to praise you.
We ask this through our Lord Jesus Christ, your Son,
who lives and reigns with you and the Holy Spirit,
one God, for ever and ever. **Amen.**

For the weekdays

Collect

Stir up, Lord, the wills of your faithful people, that they may produce abundantly the fruit of good works, and receive your abundant reward; through Jesus Christ our Lord. **Amen.**

BCP, Trinity 25

or

Let us pray [that the Spirit of God will renew our lives.]
Lord,
increase our eagerness to do your will
and help us to know the saving power of your love.
Grant this through our Lord Jesus Christ, your Son,
who lives and reigns with you and the Holy Spirit,
one God, for ever and ever. **Amen.**

266

Readings

Year A

Ezekiel 34.11-16 or 11-12,15-17   The Lord is the shepherd of his sheep
Psalm 23 (Grail, 22.1-2a,2b-3,5-6)   *The Lord is my shepherd;*
there is nothing I shall want.
1 Corinthians 15.20-28 or 20-26,28   Christ's rule
Matthew 25.31-46   The parable of the supreme court

Year B

Daniel 7.13-14   The one like a son of man
Psalm 93 (Grail, 92.1a,1b-2,5)
The Lord is king; he is robed in majesty.
Revelation 1.4-8   John's vision of Christ the King
John 18.33-37   The King

Year C

2 Samuel 5.1-3   David anointed as king
Psalm 122 (Grail, 121.1-2,3-4a,4b-5)
I rejoiced when I heard them say:
Let us go to the house of the Lord.
Colossians 1.11-20 or 15-20   The person and work of Christ
Luke 23.35-43   The King of the Jews

After Communion

Let all the house of Israel know assuredly that God has made this
Jesus whom you crucified both Lord and Christ.   Acts 2.36

THE COLLECTS AND READINGS
FOR SAINTS' DAYS
January-December

THE NAMING AND CIRCUMCISION OF
OUR LORD JESUS CHRIST
(January 1)

Born of a woman, born under the Law

Sentence

To us a child is born, to us a son is given;
and his name will be called 'Everlasting Father, Prince of Peace.'

Isaiah 9.6,7

Collect

Almighty God, whose blessed Son was circumcised and for man's
sake became obedient to the Law: purify our hearts and all our
members, so that we may die to all sinful desires and in all things
obey your holy will; through Jesus Christ our Lord.   **Amen.**

BCP, Circumcision

or

God our Father,
you gave to your incarnate Son the name of Jesus
to be a sign of our salvation.
May every tongue confess that Jesus Christ is Lord
to your eternal glory;
for he now lives and reigns with you and the Holy Spirit,
one God, for ever and ever.   **Amen.**

Readings

Numbers 6.22-27   Blessing through God's name
Psalm 67 (Grail, 66.2-3,5,6&8)
May God bless us in his mercy.
Galatians 4.4-7   Born of a woman
Luke 2.15-21   Named Jesus

After Communion

When the time had fully come, God sent forth his Son, born of a
woman, born under the Law, to redeem those who were under the
law.

Galatians 4.4,5a

268

NOTE: for the Epiphany of our Lord see page 191.

THE CONVERSION OF SAINT PAUL

(January 25)

The apostle to the Gentiles

Sentence

I am not ashamed, for I know whom I have believed, and I am sure that he is able to guard until that day what he has entrusted to me.   2 Timothy 1.12

Collect

Almighty God, we thank you that through the preaching of the apostle Saint Paul you have caused the light of the gospel to shine throughout the world: grant that, as we remember his wonderful conversion, we may show our thankfulness for it by following the holy doctrine which he taught; through our Lord Jesus Christ. **Amen.**   BCP, Conversion

or

God our Father,
you taught the gospel to all the world
through the preaching of Paul your apostle.
May we who celebrate his conversion to the faith
follow him in bearing witness to your truth.
We ask this through our Lord Jesus Christ, your Son,
who lives and reigns with you and the Holy Spirit,
one God, for ever and ever.   **Amen.**

Readings

Acts 22.3-16 or 9.1-22   Paul's conversion and baptism
Psalm 117 (Grail, 116)
   Go out to all the world, and tell the good news.
Galatians 1.11-24   How Paul became an apostle
Mark 16.15-18   The commission to preach the gospel

After Communion

Saint Paul wrote, I have been crucified with Christ; it is no longer I who live, but Christ who lives in me; and the life I now live in the flesh I live by faith in the Son of God, who loved me and gave himself for me.   Galatians 2.20

THE PRESENTATION OF CHRIST IN THE TEMPLE
or the Purification of Saint Mary
(February 2)
Christ Jesus our Sacrifice

Sentence

We have thought upon your steadfast love, O Lord, in the midst of your temple. As your Name, O God, so your praise reaches to the ends of the earth. Psalm 48.9-10

Collect

Almighty and everliving God, we humbly pray that, as your only Son was presented in the temple as a child in accordance with the Law, so may we be dedicated to you with pure and clean hearts, through him, our Saviour and Redeemer Jesus Christ our Lord. **Amen.** BCP, Purification

or

All-powerful Father,
Christ your Son became man for us
and was presented in the temple.
May he free our hearts from sin
and bring us into your presence.
We ask this through our Lord Jesus Christ, your Son,
who lives and reigns with you and the Holy Spirit,
one God, for ever and ever. **Amen.**

Readings

Malachi 3.1-4   The Lord will come to his temple
Psalm 24 (Grail, 23.7,8,9,10)
  Who is this king of glory?
  It is the Lord.
Hebrews 2.14-18   Made like us in all things
Luke 2.22-40   My eyes have seen your salvation

After Communion

My eyes have seen your salvation which you have prepared in the presence of all peoples. Luke 2.30,31

270

SAINT MATTHIAS'S DAY
(February 24)
Friends of God

Sentence

You did not choose me, but I chose you and appointed you, that you should go and bear fruit, and that your fruit should abide, said the Lord Jesus.   John 15.16

Collect

Almighty God, you chose your faithful servant Matthias to be numbered among the twelve apostles in the place of Judas: grant that your church may always be preserved from false apostles, and may be guided by true and faithful pastors; through Jesus Christ our Lord. **Amen.**   BCP, Matthias

or

Father,
you called Saint Matthias
to share in the mission of the apostles.
May we receive with joy the love you share with us
and be counted among those you have chosen.
We ask this through our Lord Jesus Christ, your Son,
who lives and reigns with you and the Holy Spirit,
one God, for ever and ever. **Amen.**

Readings

Acts 1.15-17,20-26   Matthias chosen
Psalm 113 (Grail, 112.1-2,3-4,5-6,7-8)
   The Lord will give him a seat
   with the leaders of his people.
Philippians 3.13-21   Running toward the goal
John 15.9-17   Not servants, but friends

After Communion

Jesus said: You are my friends if you do what I command you.
                                                   John 15.14

271

THE ANNUNCIATION OF THE BLESSED VIRGIN MARY
(March 25)
The Word was made flesh

Sentence

When Christ came into the world he said, Sacrifice and offerings you have not desired, but you have prepared a body for me. Then I said, 'Lo, I have come to do your will, O God, as it is written of me in the roll of the book.'   Hebrews 10.5,7

Collect

We beseech you, Lord, pour your grace into our hearts; that, as we have known the incarnation of your Son Jesus Christ by the message of an angel, so by his cross and passion we may be brought to the glory of his resurrection, who lives and reigns with you and the Holy Spirit, one God, for ever and ever.   **Amen.**

BCP, Annunciation

or

God our Father,
your Word became man and was born of the virgin Mary.
May we become more like Jesus Christ
whom we acknowledge as our redeemer, both God and man.
We ask this through our Lord Jesus Christ, your Son,
who lives and reigns with you and the Holy Spirit,
one God, for ever and ever.   **Amen.**

Readings

Isaiah 7.10-14   A virgin shall conceive
Psalm 40.8-13 (Grail 39.7-8a,8b-9,10,11)
   Here am I, Lord;
   I come to do your will.
Hebrews 10.4-10   I am coming to obey your will
Luke 1.26-38   You are to conceive and bear a son

After Communion

Mary said, Behold, I am the handmaid of the Lord; let it be to me according to your word.   Luke 1.38

SAINT MARK'S DAY
(April 25)

Proclaiming the gospel in word and deed

Sentence

Go into all the world and preach the gospel to the whole creation. He who believes and is baptized will be saved; but he who does not believe will be condemned.   Mark 16.14-15

Collect

Almighty God, we thank you for the gospel of your Son Jesus Christ committed to us by the hand of your evangelist Saint Mark: grant that we may not be carried away with every changing wind of teaching, but may be firmly established in the truth of your word; through Jesus Christ our Lord.   **Amen.**   BCP, Mark
   or

Father,
you gave Saint Mark
the privilege of proclaiming your gospel.
May we profit by his wisdom
and follow Christ more faithfully.
Grant this through our Lord Jesus Christ, your Son,
who lives and reigns with you and the Holy Spirit,
one God, for ever and ever.   **Amen.**

Readings

Isaiah 62.6-12   The watchmen of the Lord
Psalm 89.1-9 (Grail, 88.2-3,6-7,16-17)
   For ever I will sing
   the goodness of the Lord.
Ephesians 4.7-16   Christ's gifts
or 1 Peter 5.5b-14   Be firm in your faith
Mark 16.15-20   The commission to preach the gospel

After Communion

These things are written that you may believe that Jesus is the Christ, the Son of God, and that believing you may have life in his name.   John 20.31

SAINT PHILIP AND SAINT JAMES'S DAY
(May 1 or 3)
Jesus is Lord

Sentence

'Lord, show us the Father and we shall be satisfied.' 'Have I been with you so long, and you still do not know me? He who has seen me has seen the Father.'   John 14.8-9

Collect

Almighty God, whom truly to know is eternal life: grant us perfectly to know your Son Jesus Christ to be the way, the truth, and the life, that, following in the steps of your holy apostles Saint Philip and Saint James, we may steadfastly walk in the way that leads to eternal life; through Jesus Christ your Son our Lord. **Amen.**   BCP, Philip and James
   or

God our Father,
every year you give us joy
on the festival of the apostles Philip and James.
May we with them
share in the suffering, death, and resurrection
of your only Son
and come to the eternal vision of your glory.
We ask this through our Lord Jesus Christ, your Son,
who lives and reigns with you and the Holy Spirit,
one God, for ever and ever.   **Amen.**

Readings

Isaiah 30.18-21   This is the Way
Psalm 19.1-6 (Grail, 18.2-3,4-5)
   Their message goes out through all the earth.
   or   *Alleluia!*
1 Corinthians 15.1-8   The Lord appeared to James
John 14.6-14   Jesus answers Philip's request

After Communion

Jesus said to Philip, He who has seen me has seen the Father.
                                                 John 14.9

274

SAINT BARNABAS THE APOSTLE

(June 11)

Proclaiming the gospel in word and life

Sentence

Today we celebrate the festival of Saint Barnabas, who was a good man, full of the Holy Spirit and of faith.   see Acts 11.24

Collect

Lord God Almighty, who endowed your apostle Barnabas with faith and the Holy Spirit for the work to which he was called: do not leave us destitute of your abundant gifts, or of grace to use them always for your honour and glory; through Jesus Christ our Lord. **Amen.**   BCP, Barnabas

or

God our Father,
you filled Saint Barnabas with faith and the Holy Spirit,
and sent him to convert the nations.
Help us to proclaim the gospel by word and deed.
We ask this through our Lord Jesus Christ, your Son,
who lives and reigns with you and the Holy Spirit,
one God, for ever and ever.   **Amen.**

Readings

Job 29.11-16   A gracious man
Psalm 98 (Grail, 97.1,2-3a,3b-4,5-6)
   *The Lord has revealed to the nations
   his saving power.*
Acts 11.19-26 or 21b-26; 13.1-3   A good man
Matthew 10.7-13   The apostolic message

After Communion

Jesus said, No longer do I call you servants, for the servant does not know what his master is doing; but I have called you friends, for all that I have heard from my Father I have made known to you.   John 15.15

275

SAINT JOHN BAPTIST'S DAY
(June 24)
The Lord's forerunner

Sentence

There was a man sent from God whose name was John. He came for a testimony, to bear witness to the light, to make ready for the Lord a people prepared.   John 1.6-7; Luke 1.16-17

Collect

Almighty God, by whose providence your servant John the Baptist was wonderfully born, and sent to prepare the way for your Son our Saviour by preaching repentance: grant that we may truly repent according to his teaching, and following his example may constantly speak the truth, boldly rebuke vice, and patiently suffer for the truth's sake; through Jesus Christ our Lord.   **Amen.**

                                                          BCP, John Baptist

or

God our Father,
you raised up John the Baptist
to prepare a perfect people for Christ the Lord.
Give your Church joy in spirit
and guide those who believe in you
into the way of salvation and peace.
We ask this through our Lord Jesus Christ, your Son,
who lives and reigns with you and the Holy Spirit,
one God, for ever and ever.   **Amen.**

Readings

Isaiah 49.1-6   A light to the nations
Psalm 139.1-11 (Grail, 138.1-3,13-14a,14b-15)
   I praise you for I am wonderfully made.
Acts 13.(16-)22-26   The witness of John
Luke 1.57-66,80   The birth and naming of John

After Communion

Jesus said, Truly I say to you, among those born of woman there has risen no one greater than John the Baptist; yet he who is least in the kingdom of heaven is greater than he.   Matthew 11.11

SAINT PETER'S DAY
(June 29)
Simon the rock

Sentence

Jesus said to Peter, 'Blessed are you, Simon bar Jona! Flesh and blood have not revealed to you who I am, but my Father who is in heaven.'   Matthew 16.17

Collect

Almighty God, who by your Son Jesus Christ gave your apostle Peter many excellent gifts, and commanded him earnestly to feed your flock: enable, we pray, all bishops and pastors diligently to preach your holy word, and your people obediently to follow it, that they may receive the crown of everlasting glory; through Jesus Christ our Lord.   **Amen.**   BCP, Peter

or

Almighty God, who inspired Simon Peter to confess Jesus as the Christ and Son of the living God: keep your Church firm in this faith, that in unity and peace it may proclaim one truth and follow one Lord, your Son our Saviour Jesus Christ, who lives and reigns with you and the Holy Spirit, now and always.   **Amen.**

or

Praise to you,
the God and Father of our Lord Jesus Christ.
In your great mercy
you have given us new birth and hope
through the power of Christ's resurrection.
Through Saint Peter and your apostles
your Church first received the faith.
Keep us true to their teaching.
Grant this through our Lord Jesus Christ, your Son,
who lives and reigns with you and the Holy Spirit,
one God, for ever and ever.   **Amen.**

Readings

Acts 12.1-11   Peter delivered from prison
Psalm 34.1-10 (Grail, 33.2-3,4-5,6-7,8-9)
   The angel of the Lord will rescue those who fear him.

277

2 Timothy 4.6-18 or 6-8,17-18   The apostolic boast
Matthew 16.13-19   Peter's confession

After Communion

Jesus said to Peter, Feed my sheep. Truly, truly, I say to you, when
you were young, you girded yourself and walked where you would;
but when you are old, you will stretch out your hands and another
will gird you and carry you where you do not wish to go.

John 21.17,18

SAINT MARY MAGDALEN
(July 22)
Witness to Christ's resurrection

Sentence

Jesus said to Mary Magdalen, Go to my brethren and say to them,
I am ascending to my Father and your Father, to my God and your
God.   John 20.17

Collect

Merciful God, whose Son Jesus Christ called Mary Magdalen to
be a witness to his resurrection: mercifully grant that by your grace
we may serve you in the power of his risen life; through Jesus Christ
our Lord.   **Amen.**

or

Father,
your Son first entrusted to Mary Magdalen
the joyful news of his resurrection.
By her example
may we proclaim Christ as our living Lord
and one day see him in glory,
for he lives and reigns with you and the Holy Spirit,
one God, for ever and ever.   **Amen.**

Readings

Song of Songs 3.1-4a   Him whom my heart loves
Psalm 63 (Grail, 62.2,3-4,5-6,8-9)
My soul is thirsting for you, O Lord my God.
2 Corinthians 5.14-17(-21)   The love of Christ

278

John 20.1-18 or 1-2,11-18   Witness to the resurrection

The love of Christ controls us, because we are convinced that one
has died for all; therefore all have died.   2 Corinthians 5.14

SAINT JAMES THE APOSTLE
(July 25)
The seed of the gospel

Sentence
As Jesus walked by the Sea of Galilee, he saw two brothers, James
the son of Zebedee, and John his brother, mending their nets, and
he called them.   Matthew 4.18-22

Collect
Merciful God, whose apostle James left his father, and all that he
had, and without delay obeyed the call of your Son Jesus Christ
and followed him: grant that no worldly affections may draw us
away from steadfast devotion to your service, but that we may be
always ready to do what you command; through Jesus Christ our
Lord. **Amen.**   BCP, James

or

Almighty Father,
by the martyrdom of Saint James
you blessed the work of the early church.
May his profession of faith give us courage
and his example bring us strength.
We ask this through our Lord Jesus Christ, your Son,
who lives and reigns with you and the Holy Spirit,
one God, for ever and ever. **Amen.**

Readings
Jeremiah 45   God's protection
Psalm 126 (Grail, 125.1-2a,2b-3,4-5,6)
    Those who sow in tears, shall reap with shouts of joy.
2 Corinthians 4.7-15   Jesus seen in his followers
Matthew 20.20-28   Sharing Christ's suffering and death

279

After Communion

Jesus said, To sit at my right hand and at my left is not mine to grant, but it is for those for whom it has been prepared by my Father.   Matthew 20.23

THE TRANSFIGURATION OF OUR LORD

(August 6)

We shall be like him

Sentence

On the mountain top a bright cloud overshadowed Jesus, and a Voice from the cloud said, This is my beloved Son, with whom I am well pleased; listen to him.   Matthew 17.5

Collect

Eternal God, our glorious King, whose Son Jesus Christ was seen in splendour by his chosen witnesses: give us, your servants, faith to see in him the true light and to walk in his way, that we may be transformed into his likeness and live with him in glory; where he lives and reigns with you and the Holy Spirit, one God, for ever and ever. **Amen.**

or

God our Father,
in the transfigured glory of Christ your Son
you strengthen our faith
by confirming the witness of your prophets,
and show us the splendour
you have prepared for your beloved sons and daughters.
As we listen to the voice of your Son,
help us to become heirs to eternal life with him
who lives and reigns with you and the Holy Spirit,
one God, for ever and ever. **Amen.**

Readings

Daniel 7.9-14 or 9-10,13-14   The one like a son of man
Psalm 97 (Grail, 96.1-2,5-6,9)
The Lord is king, the most high over all the earth.
2 Peter 1.16-19(-21)   The Voice from heaven

Year A

Matthew 17.1-9   The transfiguration of Christ

280

Year B

Mark 9.2-10   The transfiguration of Christ

Year C

Luke 9.28b-36   The transfiguration of Christ

After Communion

Beloved, we are God's children now; it does not yet appear what we shall be, but we know that when he appears we shall be like him, for we shall see him as he is.   1 John 3.2

SAINT BARTHOLOMEW THE APOSTLE

(August 24)

Loyal to Christ

Sentence

Tell of the salvation of the Lord from day to day. Declare his glory among the nations.   Psalm 96.2,3

Collect

Almighty and eternal God, who gave your apostle Bartholomew grace truly to believe and to preach your word: grant that your Church may love that word, and both preach and receive it; through Jesus Christ our Lord.   **Amen.**   BCP, Bartholomew

or

Lord,
sustain within us the faith
which made Saint Bartholomew ever loyal to Christ.
Let your people be the sign of salvation
for all the nations of the world.
We ask this through our Lord Jesus Christ, your Son,
who lives and reigns with you and the Holy Spirit,
one God, for ever and ever.   **Amen.**

Readings

Deuteronomy 18.15-18   I will put my words in his mouth
Psalm 145.10-18 (Grail, 144.10-11,12-13,17-18)
   Your friends tell the glory of your kingship, Lord.
Revelation 21.9b-14   The Twelve
John 1.45-51   A true Israelite

After Communion

Jesus said, Anyone who leaves home or wife or brothers or parents or children for the sake of the Kingdom of God will receive much more in the present age, and eternal life in the age to come.

Luke 18.29,30 TEV

SAINT MATTHEW THE APOSTLE

(September 21)

The message goes out

Sentence

Go and make disciples of all nations, baptising them, and teaching them to observe all that I have commanded you, says the Lord.

Matthew 28.19-20

Collect

Almighty God, whose beloved Son called Matthew from his place of business to be an apostle and evangelist: set us free from all greed and selfish love of money, to follow our Master Jesus Christ; who lives and reigns with you and the Holy Spirit, now and for ever. **Amen.**   BCP, Matthew

or

God of mercy,
you chose a tax-collector, Saint Matthew,
to share the high calling of the apostles.
By his example
help us to follow Christ
and to remain faithful in your service.
We ask this through our Lord Jesus Christ, your Son,
who lives and reigns with you and the Holy Spirit,
one God, for ever and ever.   **Amen.**

Readings

Proverbs 3.1-6   Trust in the Lord
Psalm 19.1-6 (Grail, 18.2-3,4-5)
Their message goes out through all the earth.
Ephesians 4.1-14 or 1-7,11-13   Christ's gifts to his church
Matthew 9.9-13   The call of Matthew

After Communion

Jesus said, Go and learn what this means, I desire mercy, and not sacrifice. For I came not to call the righteous, but sinners.

Matthew 9.13

282

SAINT MICHAEL AND ALL ANGELS
(September 29)

Ministries of angels and men

Sentence

Bless the Lord, all you his angels,
you mighty ones who do his will,
hearkening to the voice of his word.   Psalm 103.20

Collect

Eternal God, by whom the ministries of angels and men have been
ordained and constituted in a wonderful order: grant that as your
holy angels always serve you in heaven, so by your appointment
they may help and defend us on earth; through our Lord and
Saviour Jesus Christ, who lives and reigns with you and the Holy
Spirit, one God, for evermore.   **Amen.**

BCP, Michael and all Angels

or

God our Father,
in a wonderful way you guide the work of angels and men.
May those who serve you constantly in heaven
keep our lives safe from all harm on earth.
Grant this through our Lord Jesus Christ, your Son,
who lives and reigns with you and the Holy Spirit,
one God, for ever and ever.   **Amen.**

Readings

Daniel 7.9-14 or 9-10,13-14   The host of the Lord
Psalm 138.1-6 (Grail, 137.1-2a,2b-3,4-5)
   In the sight of the angels I will sing your praises, Lord.
Revelation 12.7-12a   Michael and his angels
John 1.45-51   The angels witness to the Son of man

After Communion

The angels worship God and say, Amen. Blessing and glory and
wisdom and thanksgiving and honour and power and might be to
our God for ever and ever.   **Amen.**   Revelation 7.12

283

SAINT LUKE THE EVANGELIST
(October 18)
Bringer of good tidings

Sentence

How beautiful upon the mountains are the feet of him who brings
good tidings, who publishes peace, who brings good tidings.

Isaiah 52.7

Collect

Almighty God, who called Luke the physician to be an evangelist
and physician of the soul: grant that through his teaching we may
know the certainty of the things which belong to your kingdom,
and that all the diseases of our souls may be healed; through the
merits of your Son Jesus Christ our Lord. **Amen.** BCP, Luke

or

Father,
you chose Luke the evangelist to reveal
by preaching and writing
the mystery of your love for the poor.
Unite in one heart and spirit
all who glory in your name,
and let all nations come to seek your salvation.
Grant this through our Lord Jesus Christ, your Son,
who lives and reigns with you and the Holy Spirit,
one God, for ever and ever. **Amen.**

Readings

Jeremiah 8.22 - 9.3   Prayer for consolation
Psalm 145.10-18 (Grail, 144.10-11,12-13,17-18)
    Your friends tell the glory of your kingship, Lord.
2 Timothy 4.9-17a   Only Luke is with me
Luke 10.1-9   The harvest is plentiful

After Communion

The harvest is plentiful, but the labourers are few; pray therefore
the Lord of the harvest to send out labourers into his harvest. Go
your way; behold I send you out as lambs in the midst of wolves,
says the Lord.   Luke 10.2,3

SAINT SIMON AND SAINT JUDE, APOSTLES
(October 28)
Building the church

Sentence

Jesus said to his disciples: You did not choose me, but I chose you
and appointed you, that you should go and bear fruit, and that
your fruit should abide. John 15.16

Collect

Almighty God, you have built your Church on the foundation of
the apostles and prophets, with Jesus Christ himself as the chief
corner-stone: grant us to be so joined together in unity of spirit by
their doctrine, that we may grow into a holy temple, acceptable
to you; through Jesus Christ our Lord. **Amen.**

BCP, Simon and Jude

or

Father,
you revealed yourself to us
through the preaching of your apostles Simon and Jude.
Give your Church continued growth
and increase the number of those who believe in you.
Grant this through our Lord Jesus Christ, your Son,
who lives and reigns with you and the Holy Spirit,
one God, for ever and ever. **Amen.**

Readings

Deuteronomy 32.1-4 The good news of God
Psalm 19.1-6 (Grail, 18.2-3,4-5)
Their message goes out through all the earth.
Ephesians 2.(11-)19-22 The foundation of the apostles and prophets
Luke 6.12-16 Jesus chooses the twelve apostles

After Communion

Jesus said, If a man loves me, he will keep my word and my Father
will love him, and we will come to him and make our home with
him. John 14.23

ALL SAINTS' DAY
(November 1)
The saints of God

Sentence

These are they who have come out of the great tribulation; they have washed their robes and made them white in the blood of the Lamb.   Revelation 7.14

Collect

We praise you, heavenly Father, that you have knit together your elect in one communion and fellowship in the mystical body of your Son Christ our Lord; give us grace so to follow your blessed saints in all virtuous and godly living, that we may come to those inexpressible joys that you have prepared for those who love you; through Jesus Christ our Lord.   **Amen.**   BCP, All Saints'

or

Father,
all-powerful and ever-living God,
today we rejoice in the holy men and women
of every time and place.
May we with them know your forgiveness and love.
We ask this through our Lord Jesus Christ, your Son,
who lives and reigns with you and the Holy Spirit,
one God, for ever and ever.   **Amen.**

Readings

Revelation 7.2-14 or 2-4,9-14   The great crowd of witnesses
Psalm 24.1-6 (Grail, 23.1-2,3-4,5-6)
   Lord, this is the people
   that longs to see your face.
1 John 3.1-3   We shall see and be like God
Matthew 5.1-12a   Your reward

After Communion

Blessed are the pure in heart, for they shall see God. Blessed are the peacemakers, for they shall be called sons of God. Blessed are those who are persecuted for righteousness' sake, for theirs is the kingdom of heaven.   Matthew 5.8-10

286

SAINT ANDREW'S DAY

(November 30)

The call of God

Sentence

As Jesus walked by the Sea of Galilee, he saw Simon who is called Peter and Andrew his brother, casting a net into the sea, and he said to them, Follow me, and I will make you fishers of men.

Matthew 4.18-19

Collect

Almighty God, who gave such grace to your apostle Andrew that he readily obeyed the call of your Son Jesus Christ and followed him without delay: grant that we who are called by your holy word may give ourselves at once to do what you command; through Jesus Christ our Lord. **Amen.**   BCP, Saint Andrew

or

Lord,
in your kindness hear our prayers.
You called Andrew the apostle to preach the gospel
and to guide your church in faith.
Sharing in Christ's suffering
may we live with him for ever in glory,
for he is Lord for ever and ever. **Amen.**

Readings

Deuteronomy 30.11-14   The word is very near
Psalm 19.1-6 (Grail, 18.2-3,4-5)
    Their message goes out through all the earth.
Romans 10.8-18   The preaching of Christ
Matthew 4.18-22   Andrew called

After Communion

Andrew first found his brother Simon, and said to him, We have found the Messiah. He brought him to Jesus.   John 1.41,42

287

SAINT THOMAS THE APOSTLE
(December 21 or July 3)
Doubt and faith

You are my God, and I will give thanks to you; you are my God, I will extol you. Psalm 118.28

Eternal God, who strengthened Thomas your apostle, when he was in doubt, with sure and certain faith in the resurrection of your Son our Lord Jesus Christ: grant that we may be not faithless but believing, until we come to see our Saviour in his glory face to face; who lives and reigns with you and the Holy Spirit, one God, now and for ever. **Amen.** BCP, Saint Thomas

or

Almighty Father,
as we honour Thomas the apostle,
free us from all doubt and strengthen us to believe in Jesus
whom he acknowledged as Lord,
and who now lives and reigns with you and the Holy Spirit,
one God, for ever and ever. **Amen.**

Habakkuk 2.1-4 The righteous shall live by faith
Psalm 117 (Grail, 116)
Go out to all the world
and tell the good news.
Ephesians 2.19-22 God's household
John 20.24-29 My Lord and my God!

Jesus said to Thomas, Put your finger here, and see my hands; and put out your hand, and place it in my side; do not be faithless, but believing. John 20.27

or

Blessed are those who have not seen and yet believe. John 20.29

SAINT STEPHEN'S DAY
(December 26 or August 3)
Faithful to death

Sentence
Stephen saw the heavens open, and the Son of man standing at
the right hand of God. Acts 7.56

Collect

Lord Jesus Christ, grant that, in all our sufferings in witness to your
truth, we may learn to look steadfastly to heaven and see by faith
the glory that is to be revealed, and filled with the Holy Spirit may
learn to pray for our persecutors, as Stephen your first martyr
prayed for his murderers to you, blessed Jesus, where you stand at
the right hand of God to aid all who suffer for you, our only
mediator and advocate. **Amen.** BCP, Stephen

or

Lord,
today we celebrate the entrance of Saint Stephen
into eternal glory.
He died praying for those who killed him.
Help us like him to forgive our persecutors
and to love our enemies.
We ask this through our Lord Jesus Christ, your Son,
who lives and reigns with you and the Holy Spirit,
one God, for ever and ever. **Amen.**

Readings
2 Chronicles 24.17-22 A prophet rejected
Psalm 31.1-8 (Grail, 30.3b-4,6&8,17-18a)
Into your hands, O Lord, I entrust my spirit.
Acts 6.8-10; 7.54-60 Heaven opened to receive Stephen
Matthew 10.17-22 The Spirit will speak through you

After Communion

As they were stoning Stephen, he prayed, Lord Jesus, receive my
spirit. Acts 7.59

SAINT JOHN THE EVANGELIST'S DAY
(December 27 or May 6)
Witness to Christ's resurrection

Sentence

The Lord opened his mouth in the midst of the assembly. He found gladness and a crown of rejoicing, and acquired an everlasting name.   Sirach 15.5,6

or

How beautiful upon the mountains are the feet of him who brings good tidings, who publishes peace, who brings good tidings.

Isaiah 52.7

Collect

Merciful Lord, let your glory shine upon your Church; that, enlightened by the teaching of your blessed apostle and evangelist Saint John, we may walk in the light of your truth and come at last to the splendour of eternal life; through Jesus Christ our Lord. **Amen.**   BCP, John

or

God our Father,
you have revealed the mysteries of your Word
through John the apostle.
By prayer and reflection
may we come to understand the wisdom he taught.
Grant this through our Lord Jesus Christ, your Son,
who lives and reigns with you and the Holy Spirit,
one God, for ever and ever. **Amen.**

Readings

Proverbs 8.22-31   In the beginning
Psalm 97 (Grail, 96.1-2,5-6,11-12)
   Let good men rejoice in the Lord.
1 John 1.1-5   Revelation
John 20.2-8   He saw and believed

After Communion

The Word became flesh and dwelt among us, and from his fulness have we all received, grace upon grace.   John 1.14,16

THE INNOCENTS' DAY
(December 28 or February 17)
Innocence

Sentence

O Lord, our Lord, how majestic is your Name in all the earth.
Your glory above the heavens is chanted
by the mouths of babes and infants.   Psalm 8.1,2

or

God chose what is weak in the world to shame the strong; God
chose what is low and despised, even things that are not, to bring
to nothing the things that are.   1 Corinthians 1.27,28

Collect

Almighty God, whose loving purposes cannot be frustrated by the
wickedness of men, so that even infants may glorify you by their
deaths: strengthen us by your grace, that by the innocency of our
lives and the constancy of our faith even to death, we may glorify
your holy Name; through Jesus Christ our Lord. **Amen.**

BCP, Innocents

or

Father,
the holy Innocents offered you praise
by the death they suffered for Christ.
May our lives bear witness
to the faith we profess with our lips.
We ask this through our Lord Jesus Christ, your Son,
who lives and reigns with you and the Holy Spirit,
one God, for ever and ever. **Amen.**

Readings

Jeremiah 31.15-20   Rachel weeping for her children
Psalm 124 (Grail, 123.1&3,4-5,7b-8)
Our soul is escaped like a bird from the hunter's net.
1 John 1.5-2.2   The blood of Jesus cleanses us from all sin
Matthew 2.13-18   Herod slays the children

After Communion

These are they who follow the Lamb wherever he goes; these have
been redeemed from mankind as first fruits for God and the
Lamb.   Revelation 14.4

291

AT A MARRIAGE

Sentence

May the Lord send you help from the holy place,
and give you support from Zion.
May he grant you your heart's desire,
and fulfil all your plans.   Psalm 20.2,4

Collect

Almighty Father, giver of life and love, look in favour on all who
are made one in marriage, and especially upon these your servants
as they enter into their new life together. In your love, deepen their
love; strengthen their wills to keep the promises they have made;
that they may live to your glory and to the good of mankind,
through Jesus Christ our Lord.   **Amen.**

or

O God our Father,
you have taught us by your holy apostle
that love is the fulfilling of the Law:
grant to these your servants N and N
and to all who are made one in matrimony
that, loving one another,
they may continue in your love,
until their lives' end;
through Jesus Christ our Lord.   **Amen.**

Readings

Genesis 1.26 - 2.4a   Made in God's image
Genesis 2(4-9,15-)18-24   One flesh
Song of Songs 2.8-14   The lovers

Psalm 128 (Grail, 127)
  Happy are those who fear the Lord.
Psalm 37.3-7 (Grail, 36.3-7)
  The Lord is kind and merciful.
Psalm 67 (Grail, 66)
  The earth is full of the goodness of the Lord.
Psalm 23; 100; 110; 121; 138.

Ephesians 3.14-end   Grounded in love
Ephesians 5.20-end   Husband and wife in Christian marriage
Colossians 3.12-19   Everything in the name of Jesus

1 Peter 3.1-9(,12)   Unity of spirit
1 John 4.7-16   The love of God

Matthew 5.1-12(-16)   True happiness
Matthew 7.21-29   Hearing and doing
John 2.1-11   Wedding at Cana
John 15.9-17   Abiding in Christ's love

After Communion

Jesus said: A new commandment I give you, that you love one another; even as I have loved you, that you also love one another.   John 13.34

The following readings are also suitable
     [Tobit 8.5-9]
     [Sirach 36.1-4,13-16]
      Romans 8.31b-39
      Romans 12.9-18
      1 Corinthians 6.12-20
      1 Corinthians 12.31-13.13
      1 John 3.18-24
      Revelation 19.6-9

AT AN ORDINATION

Sentence

If any one serves me, says the Lord, he must follow me; and where I am, there my servant shall be also; if any one serves me, the Father will honour him.   John 12.26

   or

The Spirit of the Lord is upon me, because he has anointed me to preach good news to the poor.   Luke 4.18

   or

Jesus said: The Son of man came not to be served but to serve, and to give his life a ransom for many.   Matthew 20.28

In the following list of readings, those selected for the Making of Deacons are marked '**D**', for the Ordering of Priests '**P**', and for the Consecration of a Bishop '**B**'.

Readings

Genesis 14.18-20   Melchizedek, the priest-king of Zion   PB

Numbers 11.16-17,24-25   Bearing the burden of the people   DP

Isaiah 6.1-8   Here am I! Send me   DP

Isaiah 52.7-10   The salvation of our God   B

Isaiah 61.1-3a   To bring good news to the afflicted   DPB

Jeremiah 1.4-9   At the Lord's disposal   DP

Psalm 23 (Grail, 22)
The Lord is my shepherd there is nothing I shall want.

Psalm 84.1-7 (Grail, 83.3-4,5-6,8&11)
Blessed is the man who trusts in you, my God.

Psalm 96.1-5 (Grail, 95.1-2a,2b-3,4-5a,5b-6)
Go out to all the world and tell the good news.

Psalm 96.6-13 (Grail, 95.7-8a,8b-9,10,11-12,13)
For ever I will sing the goodness of the Lord.

Psalm 100 (Grail, 99)
The Lord who made the heavens has called us his friends.

Psalm 117 (Grail, 116)   *Go out to all the world and tell the good news.*

Acts 6.1-7a   Seven men of good repute   D

Acts 6.8-15   The deacon, Stephen   D

Acts 8.26-40   Telling the good news of Jesus   D

Acts 10.36-43   To preach the Gospel   P

Acts 20.17-35   Guardian of the flock   B

Acts 20.28-35   Guardian of the flock   P

Romans 10.9-15   Those who preach good news   P

Romans 12.1-8   Use the gifts God has given   D

Romans 12.4-12   Use the gifts God has given   DP

2 Corinthians 4.1-2,5-7   We preach Jesus Christ as Lord   PB

2 Corinthians 5.14-20   Ambassadors for Christ   PB

Ephesians 4.1-13   The calling to which you have been called   B

Ephesians 4.7-13   The gifts of the ascended Christ to his Church   P

1 Timothy 3.1-7   Qualifications of a bishop   B

1 Timothy 3.8-13   Qualifications of a deacon   D

1 Peter 4.7b-11   Good stewards of God's varied grace   PB

1 Peter 5.1-4   Tend the flock of God   B

294

Matthew 9.35-38   The Lord of the harvest   P
Matthew 10.1-7   The call of the Twelve   B
Matthew 20.25-28   Whoever would be great among you   DP
Matthew 28.18-20   Make disciples   B
Mark 10.35-45   Whoever would be great among you   DP
Luke 10.1-9   The Lord of the harvest   P
Luke 12.35-40   Vigilant servants   DP
Luke 22.14-[20,24-]30   One who serves   DPB
John 10.11-16   The good shepherd   PB
John 12.24-26   Following Christ Jesus   P
John 15.9-17[or, 15b-20]   Messiah's men   PB
John 20.19-23   The commission to declare God's forgiveness   PB
John 21.15-17   Feed my lambs   B

After Communion

Jesus prayed for his disciples: Father, sanctify them in the truth; your word is truth. As you sent me into the world, so have I sent them into the world.   John 17.17,18

or

Saint Paul told the elders of the church at Ephesus: Take heed to yourselves and to all the flock, in which the Holy Spirit has made you guardians, to feed the church of the Lord which he obtained with his own blood.   Acts 20.28

or

Saint Peter wrote to the elders of the churches: Tend the flock of God that is in your charge; not by constraint but willingly, not for shameful gain but eagerly, not as domineering over those in your charge but being examples to the flock. And when the chief Shepherd is manifested you will obtain the unfading crown of glory.   1 Peter 5.2-4

ON THE DAY OF A FUNERAL

Sentence

We believe that Jesus died and rose again. Even so, through Jesus, God will bring with him those who have fallen asleep.

1 Thessalonians 4.14

or

God himself will wipe away every tear from their eyes, and death shall be no more, neither shall there be mourning nor crying nor pain any more, for former things have passed away. Revelation 21.4

or

God so loved the world that he gave his only Son, that whoever believes in him should not perish but have eternal life. John 3.16

Collect

Grant, Lord, that as we have been baptized into the death of your dear Son our Saviour Jesus Christ, so by continually putting to death our sinful desires we may die to sin and be buried with him, and that through the grave and the gate of death we may pass to our joyful resurrection; for his sake who died and was buried and rose again for us, your Son Jesus Christ our Lord. **Amen.**

or

Merciful God, Father of our Lord Jesus Christ,
who is the resurrection and the life of all the faithful;
raise us from the death of sin to the life of righteousness,
that at the last we, with our *brother* N and all who have died in Christ,
may share your eternal joy;
through Jesus Christ our Lord,
who is alive and reigns with you and the Holy Spirit,
for ever and ever. **Amen.**

or

Almighty God,
whose Son our Lord Jesus Christ taught us to pray
for the coming of your kingdom:
grant that when that kingdom comes
we, with your servant N,
and all who have died in the faith of your holy Name,
may enjoy true perfection and happiness
in your eternal and everlasting glory;
through Jesus Christ our Lord. **Amen.**

At the time of a funeral of a child

God our Father,
you know how much our hearts are saddened
by the death of this child.

As we mourn *his* death,
strengthen us in our faith
that *he* is at peace in your eternal kingdom.
We ask this through our Lord Jesus Christ, your Son,
who lives and reigns with you and the Holy Spirit,
one God, for ever and ever. **Amen.**

Readings

Isaiah 25.6-9   The Lord will swallow up death for ever
Isaiah 61.1-3   Good tidings to the afflicted
Lamentations 3.17-26   The mourner's prayer of faith
Daniel 12.1-3   At the resurrection

Psalm 90 (Grail, 89.12-17) *The Lord is my light and my salvation.*
Psalm 23 (Grail, 22) *Though I walk in the valley of darkness, I fear no evil, for you are with me.*
Psalm 122 (Grail, 121) *Let us go rejoicing to the house of the Lord.*
Psalm 130 (Grail, 129) *Out of the depths I cry to you, Lord.*
Acts 10.34-43   God raised Jesus from death
Romans 6.17-21   Set free from death through Christ Jesus
Romans 6.3-9   We shall live with Christ
2 Timothy 2.8-13   A loyal soldier of Christ
  or one of the New Testament readings given at §4 in the Funeral Services.

Matthew 11.25-30   Come to me and rest
Mark 15.33-39   The death of Jesus
Luke 7.11-17   Jesus raises the widow's son
Luke 23.33,39-43   The promise of Jesus
Luke 23.44-49(and 24.1-6a)   The death (and resurrection) of Jesus
  or one of the Gospel readings given at §4 in the Funeral Services

After Communion

Jesus said: I am the bread of life; he who comes to me shall not
hunger, and he who believes in me shall never thirst.   John 6.35
  or

This is the will of my Father, says the Lord, that everyone who
sees the Son and believes in him should have eternal life; and I will
raise him up at the last day.   John 6.40
  or

As the living Father sent me, and I live because of the Father, so
he who eats me will live because of me.   John 6.57

297

The Calendar

JANUARY

1 THE NAMING AND CIRCUMCISION OF OUR LORD JESUS CHRIST
    The first day of the civil year
2 Seraphim of Sarov, spiritual guide, Russia (1759-1833)
6 THE EPIPHANY or THE MANIFESTATION OF CHRIST TO THE GENTILES
10   William Laud, Archbishop of Canterbury, theologian (1573-1645)
13 Hilary of Poitiers, bishop and teacher, France (315-367)
    George Fox, founder of the Society of Friends, England (1624-1681)
14 Sava, founder and first archbishop of the Serbian church (1176-1235)
17 Antony of Egypt, initiator of religious communities (c.251-356)
21 Agnes, Roman martyr and virgin (died 304)
22 Vincent, deacon and martyr, Spain (died 304)
24 Timothy, Titus, and Silas, the companions of Saint Paul
    Francis of Sales, Bishop of Geneva, spiritual writer (1567-1662)
25 THE CONVERSION OF SAINT PAUL
26   Australia Day
27 John Chrysostom, Bishop of Constantinople and teacher (346-407)
28 Thomas Aquinas, theologian (1225-1274)
30   Charles, King of England (1600-1649)

FEBRUARY

2 THE PRESENTATION OF CHRIST IN THE TEMPLE or THE PURIFICATION OF SAINT MARY THE VIRGIN
3 Anskar, Archbishop of Hamburg, missionary to Denmark and Sweden (died 865)
    First Christian service in Australia, conducted by Richard Johnson, Sydney, 1788
6 The Martyrs of Japan, crucified at Nagasaki, 1597
14 Cyril (826-869) and Methodius (815-885) missionaries to the Slavs
20 The Saints and Martyrs of Africa
23 Polycarp, Bishop of Smyrna and martyr (died c.155)
24 SAINT MATTHIAS, APOSTLE AND MARTYR
27   George Herbert, parish priest and poet (1593-1633)

298

MARCH

1 David, Bishop of Menevia (died c.601) and the Saints of Wales

2 Chad, missionary and Bishop of Lichfield (died 672) and the early Saints of England

3 John (1703-1791) and Charles (1707-1788) Wesley, priests, hymnwriters, and founders of Methodism

7 Perpetua and her companions, martyrs at Carthage (died 203)

8 John of God, founder of hospitals and pioneer in the care of the sick and poor, Spain (1495-1550)

12 Gregory I of Rome, bishop, administrator, and teacher (540-604)

17 Patrick, bishop and missionary of Ireland (c.398-461)

18 Cyril of Jerusalem, bishop and teacher (died 386)

19 Joseph of Nazareth, husband of the Blessed Virgin Mary

20 Cuthbert of Lindisfarne, bishop and missionary in Northumbria (died 687)

21 Thomas Cranmer, Archbishop of Canterbury, reformer, liturgist and martyr (1489-1556)

22 Thomas Ken, Bishop of Bath and Wells, non-juror and spiritual teacher (1637-1711)

24 Abbé Paul Couturier, who prayed for Christian unity, France (1881-1953)

25 THE ANNUNCIATION OF THE BLESSED VIRGIN MARY

29 John Keble, priest, poet, initiator of the Oxford movement (1792-1866)

APRIL

3 Richard of Chichester, bishop (1197-1253)

4 Ambrose of Milan, bishop and teacher (c.339-397)

8 The Saints and Martyrs of the Americas

9 Dietrich Bonhoeffer, pastor and theologian, Germany (1906-1945)

11 George Augustus Selwyn, first missionary Bishop of New Zealand (1809-1878)

21 Anselm of Canterbury, archbishop and teacher (1033-1109)

23 George, martyr (died c.303)

25 SAINT MARK, EVANGELIST AND MARTYR

Anzac Day (Gallipoli, 1915)

29 Catherine of Siena, spiritual teacher (1347-1380)

MAY

1 or 3 SAINT PHILIP AND SAINT JAMES, APOSTLES AND MARTYRS

2 Athanasius of Alexandria, bishop and teacher (*c*.296-373)

8 Julian of Norwich, anchoress, mystic, and spiritual writer (1342-1417)

9 Gregory of Nazianzus, bishop and teacher (329-389)

19 Dunstan of Canterbury, archbishop and reformer (909-988)

25 Venerable Bede of Jarrow, priest, scholar, and teacher (*c*.673-745)

26 Augustine of Canterbury, missionary and bishop (died 605)

JUNE

1 Justin, martyr at Rome (*c*.100-165)

3 The young Anglican and Roman Catholic martyrs of Uganda, 1886
John XXIII, inspirer of renewal (1881-1963)

5 Boniface of Mainz, archbishop, missionary to Germany, martyr (died 754)
William Grant Broughton, Bishop of Australia (1788-1853), and the pioneer Christians in Australia.

9 Columba of Iona, abbot and missionary (521-597)

10 Margaret of Scotland, queen, example of lay devotion and charity (1045-1093)

11 SAINT BARNABAS, APOSTLE AND MARTYR

13 Antony of Padua, missionary and preacher (1195-1231)

14 Basil of Caesarea, bishop and teacher (330-397)
Richard Baxter, pastor and author (1615-1691)

22 Alban, first British martyr (died *c*.305)

24 SAINT JOHN THE BAPTIST

27 Cyril of Alexandria, bishop and teacher (died 444)

28 Irenaeus of Lyons, bishop and teacher (130-*c*.200)

29 SAINT PETER, APOSTLE AND MARTYR

JULY

2 Visitation of the Blessed Virgin Mary

6 John Fisher, bishop (1468-1535) and Thomas More (1478-1535), scholars and martyrs for conscience' sake

11 Benedict of Nursia, abbot of Monte Cassino and founder of the Benedictine Order (*c*.480-550)

22 SAINT MARY MAGDALEN
25 SAINT JAMES, APOSTLE AND MARTYR
26 Anne, mother of the Blessed Virgin Mary
28 The Saints and Martyrs of Europe
29 Mary and Martha of Bethany
      William Wilberforce, philanthropist and opponent of the slave trade (1759-1833), and all social reformers
31 Joseph of Arimathea
      Ignatius Loyola, evangelist and founder of the Society of Jesus (1491 or 1495-1556)

AUGUST

4   John Baptist Vianney, parish priest of Ars, France (1786-1859)
5 Oswald, king of Northumbria and martyr (c.605-642)
6 THE TRANSFIGURATION OF OUR LORD JESUS CHRIST
7 The Name of Jesus
8   Dominic, friar and founder of the Order of Preachers (1170-1221)
10 Laurence, deacon and martyr at Rome (died 258)
11 Clare of Assisi, fellow-worker with Francis of Assisi (1194-1253)
      John Henry Newman, cardinal and theologian (1801-1890)
13 Hippolytus, bishop and martyr at Rome (c.170-c.236)
      Florence Nightingale, reformer of nursing (1820-1910)
14   Jeremy Taylor, Bishop of Down, Connor, and Dromore, spiritual writer (1613-1667)
      Maximilien Kolbe, Franciscan priest martyred in Auschwitz, 1940
15 Mary, the Mother of the Lord
20 Bernard of Clairvaux, mystical theologian and poet (1090-1153)
24 SAINT BARTHOLOMEW, APOSTLE AND MARTYR
28 Augustine of Hippo, bishop and teacher (354-430)
31 Aidan of Lindisfarne, bishop and missionary (died 651)
      John Bunyan, Independent preacher and spiritual writer (1628-1688)

SEPTEMBER

2   The martyrs of New Guinea, 1942

8 The birth of Mary, the Mother of the Lord

13 Cyprian of Carthage, bishop and martyr (died 258)

14 Holy Cross day

16 Ninian of Galloway, bishop and missionary (*c.*360-*c.*432), and the Saints of Scotland

20 The Saints and Martyrs of Australia, New Zealand, and the Pacific
John Coleridge Patteson, Bishop of Melanesia, missionary, and martyr (1827-1871)

21 SAINT MATTHEW, APOSTLE, EVANGELIST, AND MARTYR

25 Sergius of Radonezh and Zarov, abbot of Holy Trinity, Moscow, spiritual teacher (1314-1392)
Lancelot Andrewes, Bishop of Winchester, preacher and author (1555-1626)

27 Vincent de Paul, priest, pioneer of the care of the poor (1580-1660)

29 SAINT MICHAEL AND ALL ANGELS

30 Jerome, biblical scholar (*c.*342-420)

OCTOBER

(When the anniversary date of a church's dedication is unknown or falls during Lent, it may be observed on the first Sunday in October.)

4 Francis of Assisi, friar, preacher, and founder of the Franciscan Order (1181-1226)

6 The Saints and Martyrs of Asia

7 William Tyndale, translator of the Bible (1494-1536)

12 Elizabeth Fry, prison reformer, England (1780-1845)

15 Teresa of Avila (1518-1582) and John of the Cross (1542-1591), spiritual teachers in Spain

16 The Reformers and Martyrs of the English Reformation, 1555

17 Ignatius of Antioch, bishop and martyr (*c.*35-*c.*107)

18 SAINT LUKE THE EVANGELIST

19 Henry Martyn, missionary and Bible translator in India and Persia (1781-1812)

23 James of Jerusalem, brother of the Lord, martyr (died *c.*62)

24 United Nations, inaugurated 1945

28 SAINT SIMON AND SAINT JUDE, APOSTLES AND MARTYRS
29   James Hannington, bishop and missionary, martyr in Uganda
        (1847-1885)
30   Martin Luther (1483-1546) and the Continental Reformers

NOVEMBER

1 ALL SAINTS
2   All Souls
3   Richard Hooker, priest, author, apologist of the Church of
        England (c.1554-1600)
8 The Saints, Martyrs, Missionaries, and Teachers of the Anglican
    Communion
10 Leo of Rome, bishop and teacher (died 461)
11 Martin of Tours, evangelist and bishop (died c.387)
12   Charles Simeon of Cambridge, Evangelical teacher and
        promoter of missionary work (1759-1836)
17 Hugh of Lincoln, bishop, pastor, and philanthropist (c.1140-1200)
18 Hilda of Whitby, abbess, controversialist (614-680)
19 Elizabeth of Hungary, princess and philanthropist (1207-1231)
23 Clement of Rome, teacher and martyr (died c.100)
        (Saint Andrew's Eve may be observed as a day of prayer for
        missions)
30 SAINT ANDREW, APOSTLE AND MARTYR

DECEMBER

1   Charles de Foucauld, hermit and servant of the poor
        (1858-1916)
3   Francis Xavier, Portuguese missionary to the Far East
        (1506-1552)
4   Nicholas Ferrar, deacon, man of prayer (1592-1637)
6 Nicholas of Myra, bishop and philanthropist (died c.342)
7 The Patriarchs, Prophets, and Wise Men of the Old Testament
8 Conception of Mary, the Mother of the Lord
21 SAINT THOMAS, APOSTLE AND MARTYR [or, 3 July]
25 CHRISTMAS DAY
26 SAINT STEPHEN, FIRST MARTYR [or, 3 August]

27 SAINT JOHN, APOSTLE AND EVANGELIST [or, 6 May]
28 THE INNOCENTS [or, 17 February]
29 Thomas of Canterbury, bishop and martyr (1118-1170)
30   Josephine Butler, pioneer worker among women in England, France, and India (died 1905)
31   John Wyclif, theologian and reformer, England (*c.*1329-1384)

CONCERNING THE MOVABLE AND IMMOVABLE FEASTS

1 The following days are always to be observed on their due date and not displaced by another observance:
Advent Sunday
Christmas Day (December 25)
The Naming and Circumcision of our Lord Jesus Christ (January 1)
The Epiphany (January 6, or the Sunday following)
The Annunciation (March 25), except as provided below
Ash Wednesday
The Sunday next before Easter
Good Friday
Easter Day
Ascension Day
Whit Sunday
Trinity Sunday.

2 When the Annunciation (March 25) or feast of Saint Mark (April 25) fall between the Sunday next before Easter and the Sunday after Easter, the observance may lapse or be kept on the second Tuesday after Easter.

3 Red-letter days which fall on days listed in 1 above may lapse or be kept on the next available Tuesday.

4 Red-letter days which fall on Sundays other than those listed above in 1 may be observed on the Sunday or on the following Tuesday.

5 The anniversary of a church's dedication and the observance appropriate to the name of the church may be observed as red-letter days; such observance may be kept on the next available Sunday.

6 The following are observed as days of discipline and self-denial: Ash Wednesday and the forty days of Lent, being the forty days which begin with Ash Wednesday excluding Sundays; all the Fridays of the year, unless a red-letter day falls on a Friday; and the Ember days, on which prayers are offered for the clergy and for those who are to be ordained.

The Psalms

Lagunaria patersonii
Pyramid tree or Norfolk Island hibiscus

Devotional headings

In the daily services of the Church, the Psalms form an objective discipline of prayer. Though pre-christian texts, they are nonetheless invitations to christian prayer. After the number of each Psalm a line has been printed to *suggest* a possible christian interpretation of it: this can also be used as a congregational response or refrain. Similar material is provided with each of the series of Collects and Readings at The Holy Communion. At the end of each Psalm a *suggestion* for further prayer arising out of the Psalm is printed.

Notes on the Pointing

1 Breath is to be taken at asterisks, and at the end of lines except when the pointing clearly forbids it, or when the sign ‿ is used to indicate a 'carry-over'. A shorter break or 'mental comma' is indicated by an extra space between words.

2 The dot indicates how the syllables within a bar are to be divided when there are more than two.

3 The sign † indicates use of the second half of a double chant.

4 A double space between verses indicates that a change of chant is appropriate.

5 The final '-ed' is to be pronounced as a separate syllable only when marked with an accent (e.g., blessèd).

6 When psalms are said or sung responsively by alternate verses, it is suggested that verses printed in italics and the *Gloria Patri* be said by all together.

7 The following verses may be omitted in the public service at the discretion of the minister: 17.14; 54.5; 55.16-17; 58; 59.6,14; 68.21-23; 69.24-30; 79.10,12; 83.17; 101.6,9; 109.5-19; 137.7-9; 139.19-22; 140.9-11; 143.12.

8 The *Gloria Patri* is pointed as follows:

Glo|ry to | God:
 Father | Son and | Holy | Spirit;
as in the be|ginning · so | now:
 and for | ever | A|men.

1   *Christ Jesus is our example; help us to follow in his steps.*

1 Blessèd is the man‿
    who has not walked in the counsel | of the · un|godly:
nor followed the way of sinners
    nor taken his | seat a|mongst the | scornful.
2 But his delight is in the | law · of the | Lord:
and on that law will he | ponder | day and | night.
3 He is like a tree planted beside | streams of | water:
that yields its | fruit in | due | season.
4 Its leaves also | shall not | wither:
and look   what|ever · he | does · it shall | prosper.

5 As for the ungodly * it is not | so with | them:
they are like the | chaff · which the | wind | scatters.
6 Therefore the ungodly‿
    shall not stand | up · at the | judgement:
nor sinners in the congre|gation | of the | righteous.
†7 For the Lord cares for the | way · of the | righteous:
but the | way of · the un|godly · shall | perish.

Prayer: for all Christ's followers.

2   *God has given his Christ the nations for his inheritance.*

1 Why are the | nations · in | tumult:
and why do the peoples | cherish · a | vain | dream?
2 The kings of the earth rise up
    and the rulers con|spire to|gether:
against the Lord and a|gainst · his an|ointed | saying,
†3 'Let us break their | bonds a|sunder:
let us throw | off their | chains | from us.'
4 He that dwells in heaven shall | laugh them · to | scorn:
the Lord will | hold them | in de|rision.
5 Then will he speak to them in his wrath
    and terrify them | in his | fury:
'I the Lord have set up my king on | Zion · my | holy | hill.'

6 I will announce the Lord's decree
    that which | he has | spoken:
  'You are my son   this | day have | I be|gotten you.
7 'Ask of me
    and I will give you the nations for | your in|heritance:
  the uttermost parts of the | earth for | your pos|session.
†8 'You shall break them with a | rod of | iron:
  and shatter them in | pieces · like a | potter's | vessel.'
9 Now therefore be | wise O | kings:
  be advised   you that are | judges | of the | earth.
10 Serve the Lord with awe
    and govern yourselves in | fear and | trembling:
  lest he be angry and you | perish | in your | course.
†11 For his wrath is | quickly | kindled:
  blessèd are those that | turn to | him for | refuge.

Prayer: for the nations and their leaders.

3   *Lord, you are close to all who call upon you.*

1 Lord how numerous | are my | enemies:
  many they | are that | rise a|gainst me.
2 Many there are that | talk of me · and | say:
  'There is no | help for · him | in his | God.'

3 But you Lord are about me | as a | shield:
  you are my glory   and the | lifter | up · of my | head.
4 I cry to the Lord with a | loud | voice:
  and he answers me | from his | holy | hill.
5 I lay myself | down and | sleep:
  I wake again be|cause the | Lord sus|tains me.
6 Therefore I will not be afraid ⏝
    of the multitudes | of the | nations:
  who have set themselves a|gainst me · on | every | side.

7 Arise Lord   and deliver me | O my | God:
for you will strike all my enemies upon the cheek
    you will | break the | teeth of·the un|godly.
8 Deliverance be|longs·to the | Lord:
O let your | blessing·be up|on your | people.

Prayer: for the persecuted.

4   *When I call to the Lord he will hear me.*

1 Answer me when I call O | God of·my | righteousness:
when I was hard-pressed you set me free
    be gracious to me | now and | hear my | prayer.
2 Sons of men
    how long will you turn my | glory·to my | shame:
how long will you love what is worthless
    and | seek | after | lies?
3 Know that the Lord has shown me ⌣
    his | wonder·ful | kindness:
when I call to the | Lord | he will | hear me.
4 Tremble and | do no | sin:
commune with your own heart up|on ⌣
    your | bed·and be | still.
5 Offer the sacrifices | that are | right:
and | put your | trust·in the | Lord.
6 There are many who say
    'Who will | show us·any | good?:
the light of your countenance O | Lord has | gone | from us.'
7 Yet you have given my | heart more | gladness:
than they have when their corn | wine and | oil in|crease.
8 In peace I will lie | down and | sleep:
for you alone Lord | make me | dwell in | safety.

Prayer: for the anxious.

5   *Because of your great goodness I will come into your house.*

1 Hear my words O Lord   give | heed · to my | groaning:
   listen to my cry   you that are my | king | and my | God.

2 In the morning when I pray to you
       surely you will | hear my | voice:
   at daybreak I lay my prayers be|fore you · and | look | up.

3 For you are not a God who takes | pleasure · in | wickedness
   nor can any | evil | dwell with | you.

4 The boastful cannot | stand in · your | sight:
   you hate all | those that | work | mischief.

5 Those who speak | lies · you des|troy:
   you abhor the treacherous O Lord
       and | those · that are | stained with | blood.

6 But because of your great goodness ⌣
       I will | come into · your | house:
   I will bow down toward your holy | temple ·
       in | awe and | fear of you.

7 Lead me O Lord in your righteousness
       for my enemies | lie in | wait:
   make | straight your | way be|fore me.

8 For there is no | truth · in their | mouth:
   and within they are | eaten | up by | malice.

9 Their throat is an | open | sepulchre:
   and their tongue speaks | smooth and | flatter·ing | words.

10 Destroy them O God
        let them fall by their | own con|triving:
    cast them out for their many offences
        for | they have · re|belled a|gainst you.

11 But let all who put their trust in | you re|joice:
    let them | shout with | joy for | ever.

12 Be the defender of those who | love your | name:
    let them ex|ult be|cause of | you.

†13 For you will bless O Lord the | man · that is | righteous:
     you will cover him with your | favour | as · with a | shield.

Prayer: for the younger churches.

310

6 *I know that my redeemer lives.*

1 O Lord rebuke me not in your | indig|nation:
 nor chasten me | in your | fierce dis|pleasure.

2 Have mercy upon me O Lord for | I am | weak:
 O Lord heal me for my | very | bones · are a|fraid.

3 My soul also is | greatly | troubled:
 and you Lord how | long will | you de|lay?

4 Turn again O Lord and de|liver · my | soul:
 O save me | for your | mercy's | sake.

5 For in death | no man · re|members you:
 and who can | give you | thanks · from the | grave?

6 I am wearied | with my | groaning:
 every night I drown my bed with weeping
 and | water · my | couch · with my | tears.

†7 My eyes waste a|way for | sorrow:
 they grow dim be|cause of | all my | enemies.

8 Away from me all | you that · do | evil:
 for the Lord has | heard the | voice · of my | weeping.

9 The Lord has heard my | suppli|cation:
 the | Lord · will re|ceive my | prayer.

†10 All my enemies shall be put to shame ⌣
 and | greatly · dis|mayed:
 they shall turn back and be con|founded | in a | moment.

Prayer: for the depressed and the oppressed.

7 *God is our judge and our defender.*

1 O Lord my God   to you have I | come for | shelter:
 save me from all who pursue me
 O | save | and de|liver me,

2 Lest like lions they | tear my | throat:
 lest they carry me | off and | none can | save me.

3 O Lord my God   if I have | done · such a | thing:
 if there is any | wicked·ness | on my | hands,

 4 If I have repaid with evil him that | was my friend:
   or plundered my | enemy · with|out just | cause,

†5 Then let the enemy pursue me and | over|take me:
   let him trample my life to the ground
       and lay my | honour | in the | dust.

 6 Arise O | Lord · in your | anger:
   rise up in | wrath a|gainst my | adversaries.

 7 Awake my God * you that or|dain | justice:
   and let the assembly of the | peoples | gather · a|bout you;

 8 Take your seat | high a|bove them:
   and sit in judgement O | Lord | over · the | nations.

 9 Judge for me O Lord   according | to my | righteousness:
   and | as · my in|tegrity · re|quires.

10 Let the wickedness of the ungodly cease
       but es|tablish · the | righteous:
   for you try the very hearts and minds of | men ⌣
       O | righteous | God.

11 God is my | shield | over me:
   he pre|serves the | true of | heart.

12 God is a | righteous | judge:
   and God condemns | evil | every | day.

13 If a man does not turn he | whets his | sword:
   he bends his | bow and | makes it | ready;

†14 He prepares the | instruments · of | death:
   and makes his | arrows | darts of | fire.

15 See how the ungodly con|ceives | mischief:
   how he swells with wickedness | and gives | birth to | lies.

16 He digs a pit and | hollows · it | out:
   but falls himself into the | trap · he had | made for |
       others.

17 His mischief rebounds upon his | own | head:
   and his violence comes | down · on his | own | pate.

18 I will thank the | Lord · for his | justice:
   I will sing | praises · to the | Lord Most | High.

Prayer: for the victims of injustice.

8   *Your glory is seen in all the world; what is man that you are mindful of him?*

1 O | Lord our | Governor:
  how glorious is your | name in | all the | earth!

2 Your majesty above the heavens is | yet re|counted:
  by the | mouths of | babes and | sucklings.

†3 You have founded a strong defence ‿
   a|gainst your | adversaries:
  to quell the | ene·my | and · the a|venger.

4 When I consider your heavens ‿
   the | work of · your | fingers:
  the moon and the stars which | you have | set in | order,

5 What is man   that you should be | mindful | of him:
  or the son of | man that | you should | care for him?

6 Yet you have made him little | less · than a | god:
  and have | crowned him · with | glory · and | honour.

7 You have made him the | master · of your | handiwork:
  and have put all things in sub|jection · be|neath his | feet,

8 All | sheep and | oxen:
  and all the | creatures | of the | field,

9 The birds of the air and the | fish · of the | sea:
  and everything that moves ‿
   in the pathways | of the | great | waters.

†10 O | Lord our | Governor:
  how glorious is your | name in | all the | earth!

   Prayer: for mankind and the created order.

9 (1)   *The kingdoms of the world become the kingdom of the Lord and of his Christ.*

1 I will give you thanks O Lord with my | whole | heart:
  I will tell of all the | wonders | you have | done.

2 I will re|joice · and be | glad in you:
  I will make my songs to your | name | O Most | High.

3 For my enemies are | driven | back:
   they stumble and | perish | at your | presence.

4 You have maintained my | cause · and my | right:
   you sat en|throned · as a | righteous | judge.

5 You rebuked the heathen nations
     you brought the | wicked · to de|struction:
   you blotted out their | name for | ever · and | ever.

6 The strongholds of the enemy ⌣
     are made a perpetual | deso|lation:
   you plucked up their cities ⌣
   and | even · their | memory · has | perished.

7 The Lord confounds them
     but the Lord en|dures for | ever:
   he has | set up · his | throne for | judgement.

8 He shall judge the | world with | righteousness:
   and deal true | justice | to the | peoples.

9 The Lord is a strong tower to | him that · is op|pressed:
   he is a tower of | strength in | time of | need.

10 All who heed your name will | trust in | you:
   for you have never for|saken | those that | seek you.

   Prayer: for the victims of war.

   (2)   *The Lord sits enthroned for ever; he does not forget the cry of the*
       afflicted.

11 O sing praises to the Lord who | dwells in | Zion:
   tell among the peoples what | great things | he has | done.

12 For he that avenges blood has re|membered · the | poor:
   he has | not for|gotten · their | cry.

13 The Lord has been merciful toward me
     he saw what I | suffered · from my | foes:
   he raised me up a|gain · from the | gates of | death,

14 That I might tell all your praises in the | gates of | Zion:
   that I might re|joice in | your de|liverance.

15 The nations have sunk into the pit ⌣
     they | dug for | others:
   in the very snare they | laid · is their | foot | taken;

16 The Lord has declared himself and up|held the | right:
  the wicked are trapped◡
    in the | work · of their | own | hands.

17 The wicked shall be given | over · to | death:
  and all the nations | that for|get | God.

18 For the needy shall not always | be for|gotten:
  nor shall the hope of the | poor | perish · for | ever.

19 Arise Lord   let not | man pre|vail:
  let the | nations · be | judged be|fore you.

20 Put them in | fear O | Lord:
  and let the nations | know · that they | are but | men.

Prayer: for the poor and the starving.

10   *Blessed are the meek, for they shall inherit the earth.*

1 Why do you stand far | off O | Lord:
  why do you hide your | face in | time of | need?

2 The ungodly in their pride | persecute · the | poor:
  let them be caught in the | schemes they | have de|vised.

3 For the ungodly man boasts of his | heart's de|sire:
  he grasps at profit
    he | spurns · and blas|phemes the | Lord.

4 He says in his arrogance | 'God will · not a|venge':
  'There is no | God' is | all his | thought.

5 He is settled in | all his | ways:
  your statutes O Lord are far above him |◡
    and he | does not | see.

6 He snorts defiance at his enemies
    he says in his heart 'I shall | never · be | shaken:
  I shall walk se|cure from | any · man's | curse.'

†7 His mouth is full of op|pression · and de|ceit:
  mischief and | wickedness · lie | under · his | tongue.

8 He skulks a|bout · in the | villages:
  and | secret·ly | murders · the | innocent.

9 His eyes watch | out · for the | helpless:
  he lurks con|cealed · like a | lion · in a | thicket.

10 He lies in wait to | seize up·on the | poor:
　　he lays hold on the poor man ⏝
　　　　and | drags him | off·in his | net.
11 The upright are crushed and | humbled·be|fore him:
　　and the helpless | fall in|to his | power.
†12 He says in his heart | 'God·has for|gotten:
　　he has covered his | face and | sees | nothing.'

13 Arise O Lord God　lift | up your | hand:
　　for|get·not the | poor for | ever.
14 Why should the wicked man | spurn | God:
　　why should he say in his heart | 'He will | not a|venge'?
15 Surely you see the | trouble·and the | sorrow:
　　you look on　and will take it | into·your | own | hands.
16 The helpless commits him|self to | you:
　　for you are the | helper | of the | fatherless.
†17 Break the | power of·the un|godly:
　　search out his wickedness | till·it is | found no | more.

18 The Lord is king for | ever·and | ever:
　　the heathen have | perished | from his | land.
19 You have heard the longing of the | meek O | Lord:
　　you turned your | ear·to their | hearts' de|sire,
†20 To help the poor and fatherless | to their | right:
　　that men may no more be | terri·fied | from their | land.

Prayer: for the prosperous and powerful.

11　　*We have confidence to enter the sanctuary through the blood of Jesus.*

1 In the Lord I have | found my | refuge:
　　how then can you say to me |
　　　　'Flee·like a | bird·to the | mountains;
2 'Look how the wicked bend their bows
　　　　and notch the arrow up|on the | string:
　　to shoot from the | darkness·at the | true of | heart;

316

3 'If the foundations | are des|troyed:
  what | can the | just man | do?'
4 The Lord is in his holy place
    the Lord is en|throned in | heaven:
  his eyes search out
    his glance | tries the | children · of | men.
5 He tries the | righteous · and the | wicked:
  and him that delights in | violence · his | soul ab|hors.
6 He will rain down coals of fire and brimstone‿
    up|on the | wicked:
  a scorching wind shall | be their | cup to | drink.
7 For the Lord is righteous and loves | righteous | acts:
  the | upright · shall | see his | face.

Prayer: for those tempted to sin.

12 *Blessed are those who hunger and thirst for righteousness.*

1 Help Lord   for there is not one | godly · man | left:
  the faithful have vanished from a|mong the | children
    of | men.
2 Everyone tells | lies · to his | neighbour:
  they flatter with their lips‿
    but | speak · from a | double | heart.
3 If only the Lord would cut off all | flatter·ing | lips:
  and the | tongue that | speaks so | proudly!
4 They say   'By our tongues we | shall pre|vail:
  our lips are our servants | who is | lord | over | us?'
5 Because of the oppression of the poor
    because of the | groaning · of the | needy:
  'I will arise' says the Lord
    'and set them in safety from | those that | snarl | after‿
      them.'
6 The words of the Lord are pure
    as silver re|fined · in a | crucible:
  as gold that is seven times | puri·fied | in the | fire.

7 You will surely | guard us · O | Lord:
and shield us for ever from this | evil | gener|ation,

8 Though the ungodly strut on | every | side:
though the vilest of men have | master·y | of man|kind.

Prayer: for honesty in public life and in ourselves.

13 *Send your Holy Spirit, Lord, that we may abound in hope.*

1 How long O Lord will you so | utterly · for|get me:
how long will you | hide your | face | from me?

2 How long must I suffer anguish in my soul
and be so grieved in my heart | day and | night:
how long shall my | ene·my | triumph | over me?

3 Look upon me O Lord my | God and | answer me:
lighten my | eyes · lest I | sleep in | death;

4 Lest my enemy say   'I have pre|vailed a|gainst him':
lest my foes ex|ult | at my | overthrow.

5 Yet I put my trust in your un|failing | love:
O let my heart re|joice in | your sal|vation.

6 And I will make my | song · to the | Lord:
because he | deals so | bounti·fully | with me.

Prayer: for patience in times of trial.

14 *The word of the cross is folly to those who are perishing, but to those who are being saved it is the power of God.*

1 The fool has said in his heart 'There | is no | God':
they have all become vile and abominable in their doing
there | is not | one that · does | good.

2 The Lord looked down from heaven upon the | children ·
of | men:
to see if there were any who would act | wisely ·
and | seek · after | God.

†3 But they have all turned out of the way
they have all alike be|come cor|rupt:
there is none that does | good | no not | one.

318

4 Are all the evildoers devoid of | under|standing:
   who eat up my people as men eat bread ‿
      and | do not | pray · to the | Lord?
5 They shall be | struck with | terror:
   for God is with the | compa·ny | of the | righteous.
6 Though they frustrate the poor man | in his | hopes:
   surely the | Lord | is his | refuge.
7 O that deliverance for Israel ‿
      might come | forth from | Zion:
   when the Lord turns again the fortunes of his people
      then shall Jacob re|joice and | Israel · be | glad.

   Prayer: for the godless.

15   *Blessed are the pure in heart, for they shall see God.*

1 Lord who may a|bide in · your | tabernacle:
   or who may dwell up|on your | holy | hill?
2 He that leads an uncorrupt life
      and does the | thing · which is | right:
   who speaks the truth from his heart
      and has not | slandered | with his | tongue;
3 He that has done no evil | to his | fellow:
   nor vented a|buse a|gainst his | neighbour;
4 In whose eyes the worthless | have no | honour:
   but he makes much of | those that | fear the | Lord;
5 He that has | sworn · to his | neighbour:
   and will | not go | back · on his | oath;
6 He that has not put his | money · to | usury:
   nor taken a | bribe a|gainst the | innocent.
†7 He that | does these | things:
   shall | never · be | over|thrown.

   Prayer: for grace to show the love of Christ.

16   *The Lord is at my right hand, and I shall not fall.*

1   Preserve | me O | God:
   for in | you · have I | taken | refuge.

2   I have said to the Lord | You are | my lord:
   and all my | good de|pends on | you.

3   As for those who are held | holy · on the | earth:
   the other | gods · in whom | men de|light,

4   Though the idols are many that | men run | after:
   their offerings of blood I will not offer
      nor take their | name up|on my | lips.

5   The Lord is my appointed portion | and my | cup:
   you | hold my | lot · in your | hands.

6   The share that has fallen to me is in | pleasant | places:
   and a fair | land is | my pos|session.

7   I will bless the Lord who has | given · me | counsel:
   at night also | he · has in|structed · my | heart.

8   I have set the Lord | always · be|fore me:
   he is at my right | hand · and I | shall not | fall.

†9 Therefore my heart is glad and my | spirit · re|joices:
   my flesh | also · shall | rest se|cure.

10 For you will not give me over to the | power of | death:
   nor suffer your | faithful one · to | see the | Pit.

11 You will show me the | path of | life:
   in your presence is the fullness of joy
      and from your right hand⌣
      flow de|lights for | ever|more.

   Prayer: for our country.

17   *The Lord alone is my defence.*

1   Hear my just cause O Lord give | heed to · my | cry:
   listen to my prayer that | comes from · no | lying | lips.

2   Let judgement for me
      come | forth from · your | presence:
   and let your | eyes dis|cern the | right.

3 Though you search my heart
  and visit me | in the | night-time:
 though you try me by fire
  you will | find no | wicked·ness | in me.
4 My mouth does not transgress‿
  like the | mouth of | others:
 for I have | kept the | word of·your | lips.
†5 My steps have held firm in the way of | your‿
  com|mands:
 and my feet have not | stumbled | from your | paths.

6 I call upon you O God for you will | surely | answer:
 incline your ear to | me and | hear my | words.
7 Show me the wonders of your steadfast love
  O saviour of those who come to | you for | refuge:
 who by your right hand deliver them‿
  from | those that·rise | up a|gainst them.
8 Keep me as the | apple·of your | eye:
 hide me under the | shadow | of your | wings,
9 From the onslaught | of the | wicked:
 from my enemies that en|circle me·to | take my | life.
10 They have closed their | hearts to | pity:
 and their | mouths speak | proud | things.
11 They advance upon me
  they surround me on | every | side:
 watching how they may | bring me | to the | ground,
†12 Like a lion that is | greedy·for its | prey:
 like a lion's whelp | lurking·in | hidden | places.

13 Arise O Lord
  stand in their way and | cast them | down:
 deliver me from the | wicked | by your | sword.
14 Slay them by your hand O Lord
  slay them so that they | perish·from the | earth:
 de|stroy them·from a|mong the | living.

15 But as for your cherished ones
    let their bellies be filled ⌣
      and let their | sons be | satisfied:
let them pass on their | wealth | to their | children.

16 And I also shall see your face
    because my | cause is | just:
when I awake ⌣
    and see you as you | are I | shall be | satisfied.

Prayer: for Christians suffering for their faith.

18 (1)   *Out of the depths I call to you, O Lord.*

1 I love you O | Lord my | strength:
    O Lord my crag my | fortress · and | my de|liverer,

2 My God   the rock to which I | come for | refuge:
    my shield my mighty saviour | and my | high de|fence.

†3 I called to the Lord with | loud · lamen|tation:
    and I was | rescued | from my | enemies.

4 The waves of | death en|compassed me:
    and the floods of | chaos | over|whelmed me;

5 The cords of the grave | tightened · a|bout me:
    and the snares of | death lay | in my | path.

6 In my anguish I | called · to the | Lord:
    I cried for | help | to my | God.

7 From his temple he | heard my | voice:
    and my cry came | even | to his | ears.

8 The earth heaved and quaked
    the foundations of the | hills were | shaken:
they | trembled · be|cause · he was | angry.

9 Smoke went | out · from his | nostrils:
    and a consuming | fire | from his | mouth.

10 He parted the heavens and | came | down:
    and there was | darkness | under · his | feet.

11 He rode upon the | cherubim · and | flew:
    he came swooping up|on the | wings · of the | wind.

12 He made the | darkness · his | covering:
and his canopy was thick | cloud and | water·y | darkness.

13 Out of his clouds   from the | brightness · be|fore him:
broke | hailstones · and | coals of | fire.

14 The Lord | | thundered · in the | heavens:
the Most | High | uttered · his | voice.

15 He let loose his arrows
he scattered them on | every | side:
he hurled down | lightnings · with the | roar · of the | thunderbolt.

16 The springs of the | sea · were un|covered:
and the found|ations · of the | world laid | bare,

17 At your re|buke O | Lord:
at the blast of the | breath of | your dis|pleasure.

Thanksgiving: for baptism and the new life in Christ.

(2)   *The Lord has raised his Son from death to life.*

18 He reached down from on | high and | took me:
he drew me | out of · the | great | waters.

19 He delivered me from my | strongest | enemy:
from my | foes · that were | mightier · than | I.

20 They confronted me in the | day of · my cal|amity:
but the | Lord was | my up|holder.

21 He brought me out into a | place of | liberty:
and rescued me be|cause · I de|lighted · his | heart.

22 The Lord rewarded me for my | righteous | dealing:
he recompensed me
according to the | cleanness | of my | hands,

23 Because I had kept to the | ways · of the | Lord:
and had not turned from my | God to | do | evil.

24 For I had an eye to | all his | laws:
and did not | put · his com|mandments | from me.

25 I was also | blameless · be|fore him:
and I kept my|self from | wrong|doing.

†26 Therefore the Lord re|warded · my | innocence:
because my hands were | unde|filed · in his | sight.

27 With the faithful you | show your·self | faithful:
   with the | blameless·you | show your·self | blameless;

28 With the | pure·you are | pure:
   but with the | crookèd·you | show yourself·per|verse.

29 For you will save a | humble | people:
   but you bring down the | high looks | of the | proud.

30 You light my lamp O | Lord my | God:
   you make my | darkness | to be | bright.

†31 For with your help I can charge a | troop of | men:
   with the help of my God I can | leap a | city | wall.

Thanksgiving: for Christ's victory over sin and death.

(3)   *If God is for us, who can be against us?*

32 The way of our God is perfect
      the word of the Lord has been | tried·in the | fire:
   he is a shield to | all that | trust in | him.

33 For who is | God·but the | Lord:
   or who is our | rock | but our | God?

34 It is God that | girded me·with | strength:
   that | made my | way | perfect.

35 He made my feet like the | feet·of a | hind:
   and set me sure₁footed·up|on the | mountains.

36 He taught my | hands to | fight:
   and my arms to | aim an | arrow·of | bronze.

37 You gave me the shield of | your sal|vation:
   your right hand upheld me
      and your swift re|sponse has | made me | great.

38 You lengthened my | stride be|neath me:
   and my | ankles | did not | slip.

39 I pursued my enemies and | over|took them:
   nor did I turn again | till·I had | made an | end of them.

40 I smote them till they could | rise no | more:
   and they | fell be|neath my | feet.

41 You girded me with | strength·for the | battle:
   you threw | down my | adver·saries | under me.

42 You caused my enemies to | show their | backs:
and I de|stroyed | those that | hated me.

43 They cried for help
but there was | none to | save them:
they cried to the | Lord · but he | would not | answer.

44 I pounded them fine as dust be|fore the | wind:
I trod them under | like the | mire · of the | streets.

45 You delivered me from the strife of the peoples
you made me the | head · of the | nations:
a people that I had not | known be|came my | servants.

46 As soon as they heard me | they o|beyed me:
and aliens | humbled · them|selves be|fore me.

47 The strength of the aliens | withered · a|way:
they came | falter·ing | from their | strongholds.

48 The Lord lives   and blessèd | be my | rock:
exalted be the | God of | my sal|vation,

49 The God who sees to it that | I am · a|venged:
who sub|dues the | peoples | under me.

50 You set me free from my enemies
you put me out of | reach of · my at|tackers:
you de|livered me · from | vio·lent | men.

51 For this will I give you thanks among the | nations ·
O | Lord:
and sing | praises | to your | name,

†52 To him that gives great triumphs | to his | king:
that deals so faithfully with his anointed
with David and | with his | seed for | ever.

Prayer: for the spread of the gospel.

19   *O praise the Lord, the creator, the sun of righteousness.*

1 The heavens declare the | glory · of | God:
and the | firmament · pro|claims his | handiwork;

2 One day | tells it · to an|other:
and night to | night com|muni·cates | knowledge.

3 There is no | speech or | language:
   nor | are their | voices | heard;

4 Yet their sound has gone out through | all the | world:
   and their | words · to the | ends · of the | earth.

5 There he has pitched a | tent · for the | sun:
   which comes out as a bridegroom from his chamber
      and rejoices like a | strong · man to | run his | course.

6 Its rising is at one end of the heavens
      and its circuit to their | farthest | bound:
   and nothing is | hidden | from its | heat.

7 The law of the Lord is perfect re|viving · the | soul:
   the command of the Lord is true | ‿
      and makes | wise the | simple.

8 The precepts of the Lord are right ‿
      and re|joice the | heart:
   the commandment of the Lord is pure | ‿
      and gives | light · to the | eyes.

9 The fear of the Lord is clean and en|dures for | ever:
   the judgements of the Lord are unchanging ‿
      and | righteous | every | one.

10 More to be desired are they than gold
      even | much fine | gold:
   sweeter also than honey
      than the | honey · that | drips · from the | comb.

11 Moreover by them is your | servant | taught:
   and in keeping them | there is | great re|ward.

12 Who can know his own un|witting | sins?:
   O cleanse me | from my | secret | faults.

13 Keep your servant also from presumptuous sins
      lest they get the | master·y | over me:
   so I shall be clean and | innocent · of | great of|fence.

14 May the words of my mouth ‿
      and the meditation of my heart
      be acceptable | in your | sight:
   O Lord my | strength and | my re|deemer.

Praise: to God for his revelation of himself.

20 *Whoever calls on the name of the Lord will be saved.*

1 May the Lord hear you in the | day of | trouble:
   the God of Jacob | lift you | up to | safety.
2 May he send you his | help · from the | sanctuary:
   and be your | strong sup|port from | Zion.
3 May he remember | all your | offerings:
   and accept with | favour · your | burnt | sacrifices,
4 Grant you your | heart's de|sire:
   and ful|fil | all your | purposes.
†5 May we also rejoice in your victory
      and triumph in the | name of · our | God:
   the Lord per|form all | your pe|titions.

6 Now I know that the Lord will | save · his a|nointed:
   that he will answer him from his holy heaven
      with the victorious | strength · of his | right | hand.
7 Some put their trust in chariots and | some in | horses:
   but we will trust in the | name · of the | Lord our | God.
8 They are brought | down and | fallen:
   but we are made | strong and | stand | upright.
9 O Lord | save the | king:
   and hear us | when we | call up|on you.

   Prayer: for the church in Australia.

21 *You have taken your great power and begun to reign, Lord Christ.*

1 The king shall rejoice in your | strength O | Lord:
   he shall ex|ult in | your sal|vation.
2 You have given him his | heart's de|sire:
   you have not de|nied him · the re|quest · of his | lips.
3 For you came to meet him
      with the | blessings · of suc|cess:
   and placed a crown of | gold up|on his | head.
4 He asked you for | life · and you | gave it him:
   length of | days for | ever · and | ever.

327

5 Great is his glory because of | your sal|vation:
  you have | clothed him · with | honour · and | majesty.

6 You have given him ever|lasting · fe|licity:
  and made him | glad · with the | joy of · your | presence.

†7 For the king puts his | trust · in the | Lord:
  and through the tender mercy of the Most High | ⌣
    he shall | never · be | moved.

8 Your hand shall light up|on your | enemies:
  and your right hand shall | find out | all who | hate you.

9 You will make them like a blazing furnace ⌣
    in the | day of · your | coming:
  the Lord will overwhelm them in his wrath ⌣
    and | fire | shall con|sume them.

10 You will root out their offspring | from the | earth:
  and their seed from a|mong the | children · of | men;

11 Because they have stirred up | evil · a|gainst you:
  and plotted mischief | which they | cannot · per|form.

12 Therefore will you set your | shoulder · to|ward them:
  and draw the string of the | bow to | strike at · their | faces.

13 Arise O Lord in your | great | strength:
  and we will | sing and | praise your | power.

Prayer: that all may know Christ as Lord.

22 (1) *The Lord Jesus is able to help those who are tempted because he himself has suffered.*

1 My God my God why have | you for|saken me:
  why are you so far from helping me
    and from the | words | of my | groaning?

2 My God I cry to you by day but you | do not | answer:
  and by night | also · I | take no | rest.

3 But you con|tinue | holy:
  you that | are the | praise of | Israel.

4 In you our | fathers | trusted:
  they | trusted · and | you de|livered them;

5 To you they cried and | they were | saved:
  they put their trust in you | and were | not con|founded.

328

6 But as for me   I am a worm and | no | man:
the scorn of | men · and de|spised · by the | people.

7 All those that see me | laugh me · to | scorn:
they shoot out their lips at me ‿
   and | wag their | heads | saying,

8 'He trusted in the Lord | let him · de|liver him:
let him de|liver him · if | he de|lights in him.'

9 But you are he that took me | out of · the | womb:
that brought me to lie at | peace · on my | mother's | breast.

10 On you have I been cast | since my | birth:
you are my God | even · from my | mother's | womb.

11 O go not from me   for trouble is | hard at | hand:
and | there is | none to | help.

12 Many | oxen · sur|round me:
fat bulls of Bashan close me | in on | every | side.

13 They gape | wide their | mouths at me:
like | lions · that | roar and | rend.

14 I am poured out like water
   and all my bones are | out of | joint:
my heart within my | breast · is like | melting | wax.

15 My mouth is dried | up · like a | potsherd:
and my | tongue | clings · to my | gums.

16 My hands and my | feet are | withered:
and you | lay me · in the | dust of | death.

17 For many dogs are | come a|bout me:
and a band of evil|doers | hem me | in.

18 I can count | all my | bones:
they stand | staring · and | gazing · up|on me.

19 They part my | garments · a|mong them:
and cast | lots | for my | clothing.

20 O Lord do not | stand far | off:
you are my helper | hasten | to my | aid.

21 Deliver my | body · from the | sword:
my | life · from the | power · of the | dogs;

22 O save me from the | lion's | mouth:
and my afflicted soul from the | horns · of the | wild | oxen.

Meditation: on the passion of Christ.

329

(2) *Thanks be to God who gives us the victory through our Lord Jesus Christ.*

23 I will tell of your | name · to my | brethren:
in the midst of the congre|gation | will I | praise you.

24 O praise the Lord all | you that | fear him:
hold him in honour O seed of Jacob
and let the seed of | Israel | stand in | awe of him.

†25 For he has not despised nor abhorred
the poor man | in his | misery:
nor did he hide his face from him.
but | heard him | when he | cried.

26 From you springs my praise
in the | great · congre|gation:
I will pay my vows in the | sight of | all that | fear you;

27 The meek shall eat of the sacrifice | and be | satisfied:
and those who seek the Lord shall praise him
may their | hearts re|joice for | ever!

28 Let all the ends of the earth remember
and | turn · to the | Lord:
and let all the families of the | nations | worship · be|fore |

29 For the kingdom | is the | Lord's:
and he shall be | ruler | over · the | nations.

30 How can those who sleep
in the earth | do him | homage:
or those that descend
to the | dust bow | down be|fore him?

31 But he has saved my | life · for him|self:
and | my pos|terity · shall | serve him.

†32 This shall be told of my Lord to a future | gener|ation:
and his righteousness declared to a people yet un|born
that | he has | done it.

Thanksgiving: for the resurrection.

23   *Your loving kindness will follow me all the days of my life.*

1 The Lord | is my | shepherd:
therefore | can I | lack | nothing.
2 He will make me lie down in | green | pastures:
and | lead me · be|side still | waters.
3 He will re|fresh my | soul:
and guide me in right pathways | for his | name's | sake.
4 Though I walk through the valley of the shadow of ⌣
death
I will | fear no | evil:
for you are with me
your | rod · and your | staff | comfort me.
5 You spread a table before me
in the face of | those who | trouble me:
you have anointed my head ⌣
with oil | and my | cup · will be | full.
6 Surely your goodness and loving-kindness ⌣
will follow me * all the | days · of my | life:
and I shall dwell in the | house · of the | Lord for | ever.

Praise: to Jesus the Good Shepherd.

24   *You are the King of glory, Lord Christ.*

1 The earth is the Lord's and | all · that is | in it:
the compass of the | world and | those who | dwell therein.
2 For he has founded it up|on the | seas:
and es|tablished it · up|on the | waters.
3 Who shall ascend the | hill · of the | Lord:
or who shall | stand · in his | holy | place?
4 He that has clean hands and a | pure | heart:
who has not set his soul upon idols
nor | sworn his | oath · to a | lie.
5 He shall receive | blessing · from the | Lord:
and recompense from the | God of | his sal|vation.

6 Of such a kind as this are | those who | seek him:
   those who seek your | face O | God of | Jacob.

7 Lift up your heads O you gates
      and be lifted up you ever|lasting | doors:
   and the King of | glory | shall come | in.

8 Who is the | King of | glory?:
   the Lord strong and mighty
      the | Lord | mighty · in | battle.

9 Lift up your heads O you gates
      and be lifted up you ever|lasting | doors:
   and the King of | glory | shall come | in.

10 Who is the | King of | glory?:
   the Lord of hosts | he · is the | King of | glory.

   Praise: to God on behalf of creation.

25   *With the Lord there is mercy and plenteous redemption.*

1 In you O Lord my God have I | put my | hope:
   in you have I trusted   let me not be ashamed
      nor let my | ene·mies | triumph | over me.

2 Let none who wait for you be | put to | shame:
   but let those that break faith ⌣
      be con|founded · and | gain | nothing.

3 Show me your | ways O | Lord:
   and | teach me | your | paths.

4 Lead me in the ways of your | truth and | teach me:
   for you are the | God of | my sal|vation.

5 In you have I hoped | all the · day | long:
   be|cause of · your | goodness · O | Lord.

6 Call to mind your compassion and your | loving-|kindness
   for | they are | from of | old.

7 Remember not the sins of my youth ⌣
      nor | my trans|gressions:
   but according | to your | mercy | think on me.

8 Good and upright | is the | Lord:
   therefore will he direct | sinners | in the | way.

332

†9 The meek he will guide in the | path of | justice:
     and | teach the | humble·his | ways.

10 All the paths of the Lord are | faithful·and | true:
     for those who keep‿
        his | covenant·and | his com|mandments.

11 For your name's | sake O | Lord:
     be merciful to my | sin though | it is | great.

12 Who is he that | fears the | Lord?:
     him will the Lord direct‿
        in the | way that | he should | choose.

13 His soul shall | dwell at | ease:
     and his | children·shall in|herit·the | land.

14 The confidences of God belong to | those that | fear him:
     and his covenant shall | give them | under|standing.

15 My eyes are ever | looking·to the | Lord:
     for he will bring my | feet | out of·the | net.

16 Turn your face toward me | and be | gracious:
     for | I am·a|lone·and in | misery.

17 O free my | heart from | pain:
     and bring me | out of | my dis|tress.

18 Give heed to my af|fliction·and ad|versity:
     and for|give me | all my | sins.

19 Consider my enemies how | many·they | are:
     and they bear a | viol·ent | hate a|gainst me.

20 O keep my | life·and de|liver me:
     put me not to shame   for I | come to | you for | refuge.

21 Let innocence and integrity | be my | guard:
     for in | you | have I | hoped.

†22 O God de|liver | Israel:
     out of | all his | tribu|lation.

Prayer: for sinners.

26   *Worship the Lord in the beauty of holiness.*

1 Give judgement for me O Lord
     for I have walked in | my in|tegrity:
     I have trusted in the | Lord and | not | wavered.

2 Put me to the test O | Lord and | prove me:
   try my | mind | and my | heart.

3 For your steadfast love has been ever be|fore my | eyes:
   and | I have | walked in · your | truth.

4 I have not | sat · with de|ceivers:
   nor con|sorted | with the | hypocrites;

5 I hate the as|sembly · of the | wicked:
   I will not | sit | with the · un|godly.

6 I wash my hands in | innocence · O | Lord:
   that I may | go a|bout your | altar,

†7 And lift up the | voice of | thanksgiving:
   to tell of | all your | marvel·lous | works.

8 Lord I love the house of your | habit|ation:
   and the | place · where your | glory | dwells.

9 Do not sweep me a|way with | sinners:
   nor my | life with | men of | blood,

10 In whose hand is a|bomin|ation:
   and their right | hand is | full of | bribes.

11 As for me   I walk in | my in|tegrity:
   O ransom me | and be | favourable · to|ward me.

†12 My foot stands on an | even | path:
   I will bless the | Lord · in the | great · congre|gation.

Prayer: for the clergy and those who lead in worship.

27   *The Lord is my light; whom shall I fear?*

1 The Lord is my light and my salvation
   whom then | shall I | fear:
   the Lord is the stronghold of my life
   of whom | shall I | be a|fraid?

2 When the wicked   even my enemies and my foes
   come upon me | to de|vour me:
   they shall | stumble | and | fall.

3 If an army encamp against me
   my heart shall | not · be a|fraid:
   and if war should rise a|gainst me | yet · will I | trust.

4 One thing I have asked from the Lord
    which I | will re|quire:
  that I may dwell in the house of the Lord |
    all the | days · of my | life,

†5 To see the fair | beauty · of the | Lord:
  and to | seek his | will · in his | temple.

6 For he will hide me under his shelter
    in the | day of | trouble:
  and conceal me in the shadow of his tent
    and set me | high up|on a | rock.

7 And now he will lift | up my | head:
  above my | ene·mies | round a|bout me.

†8 And I will offer sacrifices in his sanctuary
    with | exul|tation:
  I will sing   I will sing | praises | to the | Lord.

9 O Lord hear my | voice · when I | cry:
  have | mercy · up|on me · and | answer me.

10 My heart has said of you | 'Seek his | face':
  your | face Lord | I will | seek.

11 Do not | hide your | face from me:
  or thrust your | servant · a|side · in dis|pleasure;

12 For you have | been my | helper:
  do not cast me away or forsake me
    O | God of | my sal|vation.

13 Though my father and my | mother · for|sake me:
  the | Lord will | take me | up.

14 Teach me your | way O | Lord:
  and lead me in an even path | for they | lie in | wait for me.

15 Do not give me over to the | will of · my | enemies:
  for false witnesses have risen against me
    and | those who | breathe out | violence.

16 But I believe that I shall surely see
    the | goodness · of the | Lord:
  in the | land | of the | living.

17 O wait for the Lord
　　stand firm and he will | strengthen · your | heart:
　and | wait I | say · for the | Lord.

Prayer: for faithfulness in God's service.

28　*Father, I thank you that you have heard me.*

1 To you will I cry O Lord my Rock
　　be not | deaf · to my | prayer:
　lest if you turn away silent
　　I become like those that go | down | to the | grave.
2 Hear the voice of my supplication
　　when I cry to | you for | help:
　when I lift up my hands⌣
　　toward the | holi·est | place of · your | sanctuary.
3 Do not snatch me away with the ungodly
　　with the | evil|doers:
　who speak peace to their neighbours
　　but nourish | malice | in their | hearts.
4 Repay them ac|cording · to their | deeds:
　and according to the | wickedness · of | their en|deavours;
5 Requite them for the | work · of their | hands:
　and | give them | their de|serts.
6 For they pay no heed to the Lord's acts
　　nor to the operation | of his | hands:
　therefore shall he break them | down · and not | build
　　them | up.

7 Let the Lord's | name be | praised:
　for he has heard the | voice · of my | suppli|cation.
8 The Lord is my strength and my shield
　　in him my heart trusts and | I am | helped:
　therefore my heart dances for joy
　　and in my | song | will I | praise him.
9 The Lord is the | strength · of his | people:
　and a sure refuge for | his a|nointed | king.

10 O save your people
and give your | blessing · to your | own:
be their shepherd and | bear them | up for | ever.

Prayer: for those who harm others.

29 *The Lord sits enthroned as a king for ever.*

1 Ascribe to the Lord you | sons of | heaven:
ascribe to the | Lord | glory · and | might.
2 Ascribe to the Lord the honour | due · to his | name:
O worship the Lord in the | beauty | of his | holiness.
3 The voice of the Lord is up|on the | waters:
the God of glory thunders
the Lord up|on the | great | waters.
4 The voice of the Lord is mighty in | oper|ation:
the voice of the | Lord · is a | glori·ous | voice.
5 The voice of the Lord | breaks the | cedar-trees:
the Lord breaks in | pieces · the | cedars · of | Lebanon.
6 He makes them | skip · like a | calf:
Lebanon and Sirion | like a | young wild | ox.
7 The voice of the Lord di|vides the | lightning-flash:
the voice of the Lord whirls the sands of the desert
the Lord | whirls the | desert · of | Kadesh.
8 The voice of the Lord rends the terebinth trees
and strips | bare the | forests:
in his | temple | all cry | 'Glory'.
9 The Lord sits enthroned a|bove the | water-flood:
the Lord sits en|throned · as a | king for | ever.
10 The Lord will give | strength · to his | people:
the Lord will give to his | people · the | blessing · of | peace.

Praise: for creation.

30 *Lord, you have changed my sorrow into joy.*

1 I will exalt you O Lord
> for you have drawn me | up · from the | depths:
> and · have not suffered my | foes to | triumph | over me.

2 O Lord my | God I | cried to you:
> and | you have | made me | whole.

†3 You brought me back O Lord ‿
> from the | land of | silence:
> you saved my life ‿
> from among | those that · go | down · to the | Pit.

4 Sing praises to the Lord all | you his | faithful ones:
> and give | thanks · to his | holy | name.

5 For if in his anger is havoc
> in his good | favour · is | life:
> heaviness may endure for a night
> but | joy comes | in the | morning.

6 In my prosperity I said   'I shall | never · be | moved:
> your goodness O Lord has | set me · on so | firm a | hill.'

7 Then you | hid your | face from me:
> and | I was | greatly · dis|mayed.

8 I cried to | you O | God:
> and made my petition | humbly | to my | Lord.

9 'What profit is there in my blood
> if I go | down · to the | Pit:
> can the dust give you thanks | ‿
> or de|clare your | faithfulness?

†10 'Hear O | Lord · and be | merciful:
> O | Lord | be my | helper.'

11 You have turned my lamentation | into | dancing:
> you have put off my sackcloth and | girded | me with | joy,

12 That my heart may sing your praise and | never · be |
> silent:
> O Lord my God   I will | give you | thanks for | ever.

Thanksgiving: for deliverance and the promise of deliverance.

31 (1) *Wait for the Lord and keep to his way.*

1 To you Lord have I | come for | shelter:
  let me | never · be | put to | shame.

2 O deliver me | in your | righteousness:
  incline your ear to me | and be | swift to | save me.

3 Be for me a rock of refuge   a fortress | to de|fend me:
  for you are my | high rock | and my | stronghold.

4 Lead me and guide me for your | name's | sake:
  bring me out of the net that they have secretly laid for me
    for | you | are my | strength.

5 Into your hands I com|mit my | spirit:
  you will redeem me | O Lord | God of | truth.

6 I hate those that | clutch vain | idols:
  but my | trust is | in the | Lord.

7 I will rejoice and be glad in your | loving-|kindness:
  for you have looked on my distress
    and | known me | in ad|versity.

8 You have not given me over‿
    to the | power · of the | enemy:
  you have set my feet where | I may | walk at | liberty.

  Prayer: for the unhappy and the depressed.

(2) *O Lord, let your face shine upon your servant.*

9 Have mercy upon me O Lord   for | I am · in | trouble:
  my eye wastes away for grief
    my throat also | and my | inward | parts.

10 For my life wears out in sorrow‿
    and my | years with | sighing:
  my strength fails me in my affliction
    and my | bones | are con|sumed.

11 I am become the scorn of | all my | enemies:
  and my neighbours | wag their | heads · in de|rision.

12 I am a thing of | horror · to my | friends:
  and those that see me in the | street | shrink | from me.

13 I am forgotten like a dead man | out of | mind:
   I have be|come · like a | broken | vessel.

14 For I hear the | whispering · of | many:
   and | fear · is on | every | side;

15 While they plot to|gether · a|gainst me:
   and scheme to | take a|way my | life.

16 But in you Lord have I | put my | trust:
   I have said | 'You | are my | God'.

17 All my days are | in your | hand:
   O deliver me from the power of my | enemies · ⌣
        and | from my | persecutors.

18 Make your face to shine up|on your | servant:
   and save me | for your | mercy's · sake.

19 O Lord let me not be confounded
        for I have | called up|on you:
   but let the wicked be put to shame
        and brought to | silence | in the | grave.

20 Let the lying | lips be | dumb:
   that in pride and contempt ⌣
        speak such | insolence · a|gainst the | just.

21 O how plentiful is your goodness
        stored up for | those that | fear you:
   and prepared in the sight of men
        for all who | come to | you for | refuge.

22 You will hide them in the cover of your presence ⌣
        from the | plots of | men:
   you will shelter them in your refuge|⌣
        from the | strife of | tongues.

23 Blessèd be the | Lord our | God:
   for he has wonderfully shown me his steadfast love
        when I was | as a | city · be|sieged.

24 When I was afraid I | said in · my | haste:
   'I am | cut off | from your | sight'.

25 But you heard the voice of my | supplic|ation:
   when I | cried to | you for | help.

26 Love the Lord all | you his | faithful ones:
   for the Lord guards the true
      but | fully · re|quites the | proud.
†27 Be strong   and let your | heart take | courage:
   all | you that | hope · in the | Lord.

Prayer: for the bereaved.

32   *We are reconciled to God by the death of his Son.*

1 Blessèd is he whose | sin · is for|given:
   whose in|iquity · is | put a|way.
2 Blessèd is the man ‿
      to whom the Lord im|putes no | blame:
   and in whose | spirit · there | is no | guile.
3 For whilst I | held my | tongue:
   my bones wasted a|way · with my | daily · com|plaining.
4 Your hand was heavy upon me | day and | night:
   and my moisture was dried | up · like a |
      drought in | summer.
5 Then I ack|nowledged · my | sin to you:
   and my in|iquity · I | did not | hide;
6 I said   'I will confess my trans|gressions · to the | Lord':
   and so you forgave the | wicked·ness | of my | sin.
7 For this cause shall everyone that is faithful ‿
      make his prayer to you * in the | day of | trouble:
   and in the time of the great water-floods | ‿
      they shall | not come | near him.
8 You are a place to hide me in
      you will pre|serve me · from | trouble:
   you will surround me ‿
      with de|liverance · on | every | side.

9 'I will instruct you
      and direct you in the way that | you should | go:
   I will fasten my eye up|on you · and | give you | counsel.

10 'Be not like horse or mule⌣
    that have no | under|standing:
whose forward course must⌣
    be | curbed with | bit and | bridle.'

11 Great tribulations remain | for the·un|godly:
but whoever puts his trust in the Lord
    mercy em|braces him·on | every | side.

12 Rejoice in the Lord you righteous | and be | glad:
and shout for joy all | you·that are | true of | heart.

Prayer: of confession and thanksgiving for forgiveness.

33 *The earth is filled with the goodness of the Lord.*

1 Rejoice in the | Lord you | righteous:
for it be|fits the | just to | praise him.

2 Give the Lord thanks up|on the | harp:
and sing his praise to the | lute of | ten | strings.

3 O sing him a | new | song:
make sweetest | melody·with | shouts of | praise.

4 For the word of the | Lord is | true:
and | all his | works are | faithful.

5 He loves | righteousness·and | justice:
the earth is filled with the loving-|kindness | of the | Lord

6 By the word of the Lord were the | heavens | made:
and their numberless | stars·by the |
    breath of·his | mouth.

7 He gathered the waters of the sea as | in a | water-skin:
and laid up the | deep | in his | treasuries.

8 Let the whole earth | fear the | Lord:
and let all the inhabitants of the | world |
    stand in | awe of him.

9 For he spoke and | it was | done:
he commanded | and it | stood | fast.

10 The Lord frustrates the | counsels·of the | nations:
he brings to nothing the de|vices | of the | peoples.

11 But the counsels of the Lord shall en|dure for | ever:
   the purposes of his heart from gener|ation · to | gener|ation.

12 Blessèd is that nation whose | God · is the | Lord:
   the people he chose to | be his | own pos|session.

13 The Lord looks down from heaven
      and surveys all the | children · of | men:
   he considers from his dwelling-place⏝
      all the in|habit·ants | of the | earth;

14 He who fashioned the | hearts of · them | all:
   and compre|hends all | that they | do.

15 A king is not saved by a | mighty | army:
   nor is a warrior de|livered · by | much | strength;

16 A horse is a vain hope to | save a | man:
   nor can he rescue | any · by his | great | power.

17 But the eye of the Lord is on | those that | fear him:
   on those that trust in | his un|failing | love,

18 To de|liver them · from | death:
   and to | feed them · in the | time of | dearth.

19 We have waited eagerly | for the | Lord:
   for | he is · our | help · and our | shield.

20 Surely our hearts shall re|joice in | him:
   for we have | trusted · in his | holy | name.

†21 Let your merciful kindness be up|on us · O | Lord:
   even as our | hope | is in | you.

   Prayer: for the leaders of Church and nation.

34 (1)   *O taste and see that the Lord is good.*

1 I will bless the | Lord con|tinually:
   his praise shall be | always | in my | mouth.

2 Let my soul | boast · of the | Lord:
   the humble shall | hear it | and re|joice.

3 O praise the | Lord with | me:
   let us ex|alt his | name to|gether.

343

4 For I sought the Lord's | help · and he | answered:
and he | freed me · from | all my | fears.

5 Look towards him and be | bright with | joy:
your | faces · shall | not · be a|shamed.

6 Here is a wretch who cried and the | Lord | heard him:
and | saved him · from | all his | troubles.

7 The angel of the Lord ⌣
encamps round | those who | fear him:
and de|livers · them | in their | need.

8 O taste and see that the | Lord is | good:
happy the | man who | hides in | him!

9 Fear the Lord all | you his | holy ones:
for those who | fear him | never | lack.

10 Lions may suffer | want · and go | hungry:
but those who seek the | Lord lack | nothing | good.

Thanksgiving: for God's providence and care.

(2) *The fear of the Lord is the beginning of wisdom.*

11 Come my children | listen · to | me:
and I will | teach you · the | fear · of the | Lord.

12 Which of you | relish · es | life:
wants | time · to en|joy good | things?

13 Keep your | tongue from | evil:
and your | lips from | telling | lies.

14 Turn from evil and | do | good:
seek | peace | and pur|sue it.

15 The eyes of God are | on the | righteous:
and his | ears to|wards their | cry.

16 The Lord sets his face against | wrong|doers:
to root out their | memo·ry | from the | earth.

17 The righteous cry   the | Lord | hears it:
and | frees them · from | all · their af|flictions.

18 The Lord is close to those who are | broken-|hearted:
and the | crushed in | spirit · he | saves.

19 The trials of the | righteous · are | many:
but our God de|livers · him | from them | all.

20 He guards | all his | bones:
so | that not | one is | broken.

21 Evil will | slay the | wicked:
and those who hate the | righteous · will | be de|stroyed.

22 The Lord ransoms the | lives · of his | servants:
and none who hide in | him will | be de|stroyed.

Prayer: for a continual sense of God's presence.

35 (1)   *Lord, plead my cause; defend me with your strength.*

1 Contend O Lord with those who con|tend with | me:
fight against | those that | fight a|gainst me.

2 Take up | shield and | buckler:
and a|rise a|rise to | help me.

3 Draw the spear
and bar the way against | those · that pur|sue me:
say to me | 'I am | your de|liverer'.

4 Let those that seek my life
be put to | shame · and dis|graced:
let those that plot my destruction
be | turned | back · and con|founded.

5 Let them be like chaff be|fore the | wind:
with the | angel · of the | Lord | driving them;

6 Let their way be | dark and | slippery:
with the | angel · of the | Lord pur|suing.

7 For without cause
they have secretly | spread a | net for me:
without cause they have | dug a | pit · to en|trap me.

8 Let sudden dis|aster | strike them:
let the net that they have hidden catch them
let them | fall to | their de|struction.

9 Then shall my soul be | joyful · in the | Lord:
and I will | re|joice in | his de|liverance.

10 All my bones shall say | 'Lord · who is | like you?:
for you deliver the poor man
from him that is too strong for him
the poor and needy
from | him that | would de|spoil them.'

11 Malicious witnesses rise | up a|gainst me:
  I am questioned about things of | which I | know | nothing

12 They repay me | evil · for | good:
  I am as | one be|reaved of · his | children.

13 Yet when they were sick I | put on | sackcloth:
  I af|flicted · my|self with | fasting.

14 And if my prayer returned unanswered | to my | bosom:
  I went about mourning
      as though for a |·brother |·or a·· com|panion;

15 I was bowed | down with | grief:
  as | though · for my | own | mother.

16 But when I stumbled   they rejoiced and gathered ‿
      together
      they gathered to|gether · a|gainst me:
  as though they were strangers I never knew
      they | tore at · me | without | ceasing.

†17 When I | slipped they | mocked me:
  and | gnashed · at me | with their | teeth.

Prayer: for the church under persecution.

(2)   *I shall speak of your righteousness all the day long.*

18 Lord how long will | you look | on?:
  take me from the evil they intend
      take me | from a|midst the | lions.

19 And I will give you thanks in the | great · congre|gation:
  I will | praise you · in the | throng · of the | people.

20 Let not those that wrongfully are my enemies |‿
      triumph | over me:
  let not those that hate me without cause |‿
      mock me | with their | eyes.

21 For they speak words that do not | make for | peace:
  they invent lies against those that are | quiet | in
      the | land.

22 They stretch their mouths to | jeer at me · and | say:
  'Aha aha!   We have | seen | all that · we | wish!'.

346

23 And you also have seen O Lord | do not · be | silent:
   O God | go not | far | from me.

24 Bestir yourself   awake to | do me | right:
   to plead my | cause O | Lord my | God.

25 Judge me O Lord my God
     according | to your | righteousness:
   and let them | not re|joice | over me.

26 Let them not say in their hearts   'We | have our | wish':
   let them not | say 'We | have de|stroyed him'.

27 Let those that rejoice at my hurt
     be disgraced and confounded | alto|gether:
   let those that lord it over me⏝
     be | clothed in | shame · and dis|honour.

28 But let those that long for my vindication
     shout for | joy · and re|joice:
   let them say always that the Lord is great
     who takes such de|light · in his | servant's | good.

29 And my tongue shall | speak of · your | righteousness:
   and of your | praise | all the · day | long.

Prayer: for the church in failure and discouragement.

36   *Those who follow Jesus will not walk in darkness, but have the light
of life.*

1 The transgressor speaks⏝
     from the wickedness in his | own | heart:
   there is no fear of | God be|fore his | eyes.

2 For he flatters himself in his | own | sight:
   he hates his in|iquity · to be | found | out.

3 The words of his mouth are wickedness | and de|ceit:
   he has ceased to act | wisely · and | do | good.

4 He plots mischief as he lies up|on his | bed:
   he has set himself on a path that is not good
     he | does not | spurn | evil.

5 Your unfailing kindness O Lord is | in the | heavens:
   and your faithfulness | reaches | to the | clouds.

347

6 Your righteousness is like the | strong | mountains:
  and your justice as the great deep
      you O Lord | save both | man and | beast.

7 How precious O God is your en|during | kindness:
  the children of men shall take refuge ‿
      under the | shadow | of your | wings.

8 They shall be satisfied ‿
      with the good things | of your | house:
  and you will give them drink ‿
      from the | river · of | your de|lights.

9 For with you is the | well of | life:
  and in your | light shall | we see | light.

10 O continue your merciful kindness ‿
      toward | those who | know you:
  and your righteous dealing ‿
      to | those · that are | true of | heart.

11 Let not the foot of the | proud · come a|gainst me:
  nor the hand of the un|godly | drive · me a|way.

12 There are they fallen | those who · do | evil:
  they are thrust down and | shall not | rise a|gain.

Prayer: for Christ's followers in their daily life.

37 (1)   *Commit your life to the Lord and put your trust in him.*

1 Do not | vie · with the | wicked:
  or | envy | those that · do | wrong;

2 For they will soon | wither · like the | grass:
  and fade a|way · like the | green | leaf.

3 Trust in the | Lord and · do | good:
  and you shall dwell in the land ‿
      and | feed in | safe | pastures.

4 Let the Lord be | your de|light:
  and he will | grant you · your | heart's de|sire.

5 Commit your | way · to the | Lord:
  trust | him and | he will | act.

6 He will make your righteousness ‿
    shine as | clear · as the | light:
and your | inno·cence | as the | noonday.

7 Be still before the Lord * and wait | patient·ly | for him:
do not be vexed when a man prospers
    when he puts his | evil | purposes·to | work.

8 Let go of anger and a|bandon | wrath:
let not envy | move you·to | do | evil.

9 For the wicked shall be | cut | down:
but those who wait for the | Lord·shall pos|sess the | land.

10 In a little while the ungodly shall | be no | more:
you will look for him in his place ‿
    but | he will | not be | found.

†11 But the meek shall pos|sess the | land:
and en|joy·the a|bundance·of | peace.

12 The ungodly man plots a|gainst the | righteous:
and | gnashes·at him | with his | teeth.

13 But the Lord shall | laugh him·to | scorn:
for he sees that the | day·for his | overthrow·is | near.

14 The ungodly have drawn the sword and | strung the | bow:
to strike down the poor and needy
    to slaughter | those that | walk in | innocence.

15 Their swords shall pierce their | own | hearts:
and their | bows | shall be | broken.

16 Though the righteous man | has·but a | little:
it is better than the great | wealth of | the un|godly.

17 For the strong arm of the ungodly | shall be | broken:
but the | Lord up|holds the | righteous.

Prayer: for reliance on God in times of danger.

(2)   *The Lord guides those who delight in his way.*

18 The Lord cares for the | lives·of the | innocent:
and their heritage | shall be | theirs for | ever.

19 They shall not be put to shame in the | evil | days:
but in time of famine | they shall | eat their | fill.

349

†20 As for the ungodly they shall perish
    they are the enemies | of the | Lord:
  like fuel in a furnace‿
    they shall | vanish · a|way in | smoke.

21 The ungodly man borrows but does | not re|pay:
  but the | righteous · is | gracious · and | gives.

22 Those who are blessed by God shall pos|sess the | land:
  but those whom he has | cursed · shall be | cut | down.

23 If a man's steps are | guided · by the | Lord:
  and | he de|lights in · his | way,

24 Though he stumble he shall | not fall | headlong:
  for the Lord | holds him | by the | hand.

25 I have been young and | now am | old:
  but I never saw the righteous man forsaken
    or his | children | begging · their | bread.

26 He is ever | gracious · and | lends:
  and his | children | shall be | blessed.

Prayer: for Christ's followers in public life.

(3)   *Wait for the Lord and hold to his way.*

27 Turn from evil and | do | good:
  and you shall | dwell · in the | land for | ever.

28 For the | Lord loves | justice:
  he will | not for|sake his | faithful ones.

29 But the unjust shall be de|stroyed for | ever:
  and the children of the un|godly · shall be | cut | down.

30 The just shall pos|sess the | land:
  and they shall | dwell in | it for | ever.

31 The mouth of the righteous man | utters | wisdom:
  and his | tongue speaks | what is | right.

32 The law of his God is | in his | heart:
  and his | footsteps | will not | slip.

33 The ungodly man watches | out · for the | righteous:
  and | seeks oc|casion · to | slay him.

34 But the Lord will not abandon him | to his | power:
  nor let him be con|demned when | he is | judged.

†35 Wait for the Lord and | hold to · his | way:
  and he will raise you up to possess the land
    to see the un|godly · when | they are · de|stroyed.

36 I have seen the ungodly in | terri·fying | power:
  spreading himself | like a · lux|uri·ant | tree;

37 I passed by again and | he was | gone:
  I searched for him | but · he could | not be | found.

38 Observe the blameless man and con|sider · the | upright:
  for the man of | peace shall | have pos|terity.

39 But transgressors shall be de|stroyed · alto|gether:
  and the posterity of the | wicked · shall be | cut | down.

40 Deliverance for the righteous⌣
    shall | come · from the | Lord:
  he is their | strength in | time of | trouble.

41 The Lord will help them | and de|liver them:
  he will save them from the ungodly and deliver them
    because they | come to | him for | refuge.

Prayer: for Christian people in business.

38   *Do not punish me, O Lord, as I deserve.*

1 O Lord rebuke me not | in your | anger:
  nor chasten me | in your | fierce dis|pleasure.

2 For your arrows have been | aimed a|gainst me:
  and your hand has come | down | heavy · up|on me.

3 There is no health in my flesh
    because of your | indig|nation:
  nor soundness in my bones by | reason |·of my | sin.

4 The tide of my iniquities has gone | over · my | head:
  their weight is a burden too | heavy · for | me to | bear.

5 My wounds | stink and | fester:
  be|cause | of my | foolishness.

6 I am bowed down and | brought so | low:
  that I go | mourning | all the · day | long.

7 For my loins are filled with a | burning | pain:
  and there is no sound | part in | all my | body.

8 I am numbed and | stricken·to the | ground:
  I cry aloud in the | yearning | of my | heart.

9 O Lord   all I long for | is be|fore you:
  and my deep sighing | is not | hidden | from you.

10 My heart is in tumult   my | strength | fails me:
  and even the | light of·my | eyes has | gone from me.

11 My friends and my companions⌣
      hold aloof from | my af|fliction:
  and my | kinsmen | stand far | off.

12 Those who seek my | life | strike at me:
  and those that desire my hurt spread evil tales
      and murmur | slanders | all the | day.

13 But I am like a deaf man and | hear | nothing:
  like one that is dumb who | does not | open·his | mouth.

14 So I have become as one who | cannot | hear:
  in whose | mouth·there is | no re|tort.

15 For in you Lord have I | put my | trust:
  and you will | answer me·O | Lord my | God.

16 For I prayed   'Let them never ex|ult | over me:
  those who turn arrogant | when my | foot | slips.'

17 Truly I am | ready·to | fall:
  and my | pain is | with me·con|tinually.

18 But I ac|knowledge·my | wickedness:
  and I am filled with | sorrow | at my | sin.

19 Those that are my enemies without cause⌣
      are | great in | number:
  and those who hate me | wrongful|ly are | many.

20 Those also who repay evil for good | are a|gainst me:
  because I | seek | after | good.

†21 Forsake me not O Lord
      go not far | from me·my | God:
  hasten to my | help O | Lord·my sal|vation.

Prayer: for the defeated and disappointed.

39 *All my hope is in you, O Lord.*

1 I said 'I will keep watch over my ways
    lest I | sin · with my | tongue:
  I will keep a guard on my mouth
    while the | wicked · are | in my | sight.'

2 I held my tongue and | said | nothing:
  I kept | silent · but | found no | comfort.

3 My pain was increased   my heart grew | hot with|in me:
  while I mused the fire blazed and I | spoke | with my | tongue;

4 'Lord let me | know my | end:
  and the | number | of my | days,

†5 'That I may know how | short my | time is:
  for you have made my days but a handsbreadth
    and my whole | span · is as | nothing · be|fore you.'

6 Surely every man though he stand secure |
    is but | breath:
  man | lives · as a | passing | shadow.

7 The riches he heaps are but a | puff of | wind:
  and he cannot | tell | who will | gather them.

8 And now Lord | what is · my | hope?:
  truly my | hope | is in | you.

9 O deliver me from | all · my trans|gressions:
  do not | make me · the | butt of | fools.

10 I was dumb   I did not | open · my | mouth:
  for surely | it was | your | doing.

11 Take away your | plague | from me:
  I am brought to an | end · by the | blows · of your | hand.

12 When with rebukes you chastise a | man for | sin:
  you cause his fair looks to dissolve in putrefaction
    surely | every · man | is but | breath.

13 Hear my prayer O Lord   and give | ear to · my | cry:
  be not | silent | at my | tears.

14 For I am but a | stranger · with | you:
  a passing guest as | all my | fathers | were.

15 Turn your eye from me   that I may | smile a|gain:
  before I go | hence and | am no | more.

Prayer: for the dying.

40   *I long to do your will, my God, your law delights my heart.*

1 I waited patiently | for the | Lord:
and he in|clined to me · and | heard my | cry.

2 He brought me up from the pit of roaring waters
out of the | mire and | clay:
and set my feet upon a | rock · and made |
firm my | foothold.

3 And he has put a new | song · in my | mouth:
even a song of | thanks·giving | to our | God.

4 Many shall | see it · and | fear:
and shall | put their | trust · in the | Lord.

5 Blessèd is the man who has made the | Lord his | hope:
who has not turned to the proud
or to those who | wander | in de|ceit.

6 O Lord my God
great are the wonderful things which you have done
and your thoughts which | are to|wards us:
there is none to | be com|pared with | you;

†7 Were I to de|clare them · and | speak of them:
they are more than I am | able | to ex|press.

8 Sacrifice and offering you do | not de|sire:
but my | ears · you have | marked · for o|bedience;

9 Burnt-offering and sin-offering you have | not re|quired:
then | said I | Lo I | come.

10 In the scroll of the book it is written of me
that I should | do your | will:
O my God I long to do it
your | law de|lights my | heart.

11 I have declared your righteousness ⌣
in the | great · congre|gation:
I have not restrained my lips O | Lord ⌣
and | that you | know.

12 I have not hidden your righteousness | in my | heart:
I have spoken of your faithfulness |
and of | your sal|vation.

13 I have not kept back␣
    your loving-kindness | and your | truth:
from the | great | congre|gation.

14 O Lord do not withhold your | mercy | from me:
let your loving-kindness␣
    and your | truth | ever · pre|serve me.

15 For innumerable troubles have | come up|on me:
my sins have overtaken me | and I | cannot | see.

16 They are more in number than the | hairs · of my | head:
there|fore my | heart | fails me.

17 Be pleased O | Lord · to de|liver me:
O | Lord make | haste to | help me.

18 Let those who seek my life to | take it · a|way:
be put to shame and con|founded | alto|gether.

19 Let them be turned back and disgraced␣
    who | wish me | evil:
let them be aghast for shame␣
    who | say to me · 'A|ha a|ha!'.

20 Let all who seek you be joyful and | glad be|cause of you:
let those who love your salvation say | always ·
    'The | Lord is | great'.

21 As for me I am | poor and | needy:
but the | Lord will | care | for me.

†22 You are my helper and | my de|liverer:
make no long de|lay O | Lord my | God.

*Prayer: for ordination candidates and others preparing for full-time church
service.*

41   *Though all others forsake me the Lord will take me up.*

1 Blessèd is he that considers the | poor and | helpless:
the Lord will deliver him | in the | day of | trouble.

2 The Lord will guard him and preserve his life
    he shall be counted | happy · in the | land:
you will not give him | over · to the | will · of his |
    enemies.

†3 And if he lies sick on his bed ⌣
      the | Lord · will sus|tain him:
    if illness lays him | low · you will | over|throw it.

 4 I said 'O Lord be | merciful · to|ward me:
    heal me for | I have | sinned a|gainst you.'
 5 My enemies speak evil | of me | saying:
    'When will he die and his | name | perish · for | ever?'
 6 And if one should come to see me
      he mouths | empty | words:
    while his heart gathers mischief
      and | when he · goes | out he | vents it.
 7 All those that hate me whisper to|gether · a|gainst me:
    they de|vise | plots a|gainst me.
 8 They say   'A deadly | thing has · got | hold of him:
    he will not get up a|gain from | where he | lies.'
 9 Even my bosom friend in | whom I | trusted:
    who shared my bread   has | lifted · his | heel a|gainst me.
10 But you O Lord be gracious and | raise me | up:
    and I will repay them | what they | have de|served.
11 By this will I | know that · you | favour me:
    that my enemy | shall not | triumph | over me.
12 Because of my innocence you | hold me | fast:
    you have set me be|fore your | face for | ever.

13 Blessèd be the Lord the | God of | Israel:
    from everlasting to everlasting* | Amen | A—|men.

    Prayer: for those who have been hurt by others.

42   *When shall I come and see God's face?*

 1 As a deer longs for the | running | brooks:
    so longs my | soul for | you O | God.
 2 My soul is thirsty for God * thirsty for the | living | God:
    when shall I | come and | see his | face?

356

3 My tears have been my food | day and | night:
  while they ask me all day long |'Where now | is your | God?'

4 As I pour out my soul by myself I re|member | this:
  how I went to the house of the Mighty One|‿
      into·the | temple·of | God,

†5 To the shouts and | songs of·thanks|giving:
  a multitude | keeping | high | festival.

6 *Why are you so full of | heaviness·my | soul:*
  and | why·so un|quiet·with|in me?

7 *O put your | trust in | God:*
  for I will praise him yet   who is my de|liver·er | and my | God.

8 My soul is | heavy·with|in me:
  therefore I will remember you from the land of Jordan
      from Mizar a|mong the | hills of | Hermon.

9 Deep calls to deep in the | roar of·your | waters:
  all your waves and | breakers | have gone | over me.

10 Surely the Lord will grant his loving mercy |
      in the | daytime:
  and in the night his song will be with me
      a | prayer·to the | God·of my | life.

11 I will say to God my rock
      'Why have | you for|gotten me:
  why must I go like a mourner‿
      be|cause the | enemy·op|presses me?'

†12 Like a sword through my bones‿
      my | enemies·have | mocked me:
  while they ask me all day long |'Where now | is your | God?'

13 *Why are you so full of | heaviness·my | soul:*
  and | why·so un|quiet·with|in me?

14 *O put your | trust in | God:*
  for I will praise him yet   who is my de|liver·er | and my | God.

Prayer: for those in spiritual desolation.

43 *God is my joy and my delight.*

1 Give judgement for me O God
   take up my cause against an un|godly | people:
 deliver me from de|ceitful · and | wicked | men.

2 For you are God my refuge
   why have.you | turned · me a|way:
 why must I go like a mourner‿
   be|cause the | enemy · op|presses me?

3 O send out your light and your truth‿
   and | let them | lead me:
 let them guide me to your holy | hill and | to your | dwelling

4 Then I shall go to the altar of God
   to God my joy and | my de|light:
 and to the harp I shall sing‿
   your | praises · O | God my | God.

5 *Why are you so full of | heaviness · my | soul:*
   and | why · so un|quiet · with|in me?

6 *O put your | trust in | God:*
   for I will praise him yet   who is my de|liver · er | and my | God.

Prayer: for a right approach to holy communion.

44 (1) *Spare us, Lord; do not let your people be put to shame.*

1 We have heard with our ears O God‿
   our | fathers · have | told us:
 what things you did in their | time · ‿
   in the | days of | old;

2 How by your own hand you drove out the nations‿
   and | planted · us | in:
 how you crushed the peoples
   but caused | us to | root and | grow.

3 For it was not by their swords‿
   that our fathers took pos|session · of the | land:
 nor did their own | arm | get them · the | victory,

4 But your right hand your arm⏜
 and the | light of·your | countenance:
 be|cause·you de|lighted·in | them.

5 You are my | king·and my | God:
 who or|dained | victory·for | Jacob.

6 By your power we struck our | ene·mies | through:
 in your name we trod down | those that | rose a|gainst us.

7 For I did not | trust·in my | bow:
 nor | could my | sword | save me;

8 But it was you that delivered us | from our | enemies:
 and put our | adver·saries | to con|fusion.

†9 In God we made our boast | all the·day | long:
 we gave | thanks to·your | name with·out | ceasing.

Prayer: for the church in adversity.

(2) *Lord, come to our help.*

10 [But] now you have cast us off⏜
 and | brought us·to | shame:
 you | go not | out·with our | armies.

11 You have caused us to show our | backs·to the | enemy:
 so that our foes | plunder | us at | will.

12 You have given us like | sheep·to be | butchered:
 you have | scattered us·a|mong the | nations.

13 You have sold your | people·for | nothing:
 and | made a | profit·less | bargain.

14 You have made us a laughing-stock | to our | neighbours:
 mocked and held in de|rision·by | those a|bout us.

15 You have made us a byword a|mong the | nations:
 so that the peoples | toss their | heads in | scorn.

16 My disgrace is before me | all the | day:
 and | shame has | covered·my | face,

17 At the voice of the slanderer | and re|viler:
 at the sight of the | ene·my | and a|venger.

18 All this has come upon us
  though we have | not for|gotten you:
  we have | not be|trayed your | covenant.
19 Our hearts have | not turned | back:
  nor have our steps | strayed | from your | paths.
20 And yet you have crushed us in the | haunt of | jackals:
  and covered us | with the | shadow · of | death.
21 If we had forgotten the | name of · our | God:
  or stretched out our hands ⌣
    in | prayer to · some | strange | god,
22 Would not God | search it | out?:
  for he knows the very | secrets | of the | heart.
23 But for your sake are we killed | all the · day | long:
  we are | counted · as | sheep · for the | slaughter.

24 Rouse yourself O Lord | why · do you | sleep?:
  awake do not | cast us | off for | ever.
25 Why do you | hide your | face:
  and forget our | misery · and | our af|fliction?
26 Our souls are | bowed · to the | dust:
  our | bellies | cleave · to the | ground.
27 Arise O | Lord to | help us:
  and redeem us | for your | mercy's | sake.

  Prayer: for Christian unity.

  45 *Happy are those who are called to the marriage supper of the Lamb.*

1 My heart is astir with fine phrases
  I make my | song · for a | king:
  my tongue is the | pen · of a | ready | writer.
2 You are the fairest of the sons of men
  grace | flows · from your | lips:
  therefore has God | blessed you · for | ever · and | ever.
3 Gird your sword upon your thigh O | mighty | warrior:
  in glory and majesty ⌣
    tread | down your | foes and | triumph!

4 Ride on in the | cause of | truth:
and | for the | sake of | justice.

5 Your right hand shall teach a | terrible·in|struction:
peoples shall fall beneath you
    your arrows shall be sharp‿
    in the | hearts·of·the | king's | enemies.

6 Your throne is the throne of God   it en|dures for | ever:
and the sceptre of your | kingdom·is a | righteous | sceptre.

7 You have loved righteousness and | hated | evil:
therefore God your God * has anointed you‿
    with the oil of | gladness·a|bove your | fellows.

8 All your garments are fragrant‿
    with myrrh | aloes·and | cassia:
music from ivory | pala·ces | makes you | glad.

†9 Kings' daughters are among your | noble | women:
the queen is at your right | hand in | gold of | Ophir.

10 Hear O daughter   consider and in|cline your | ear:
forget your own | people·and your | father's | house.

11 The king de|sires your | beauty:
he is your lord |therefore·bow | down be|fore him.

†12 The richest among the people O | daughter·of | Tyre:
shall en|treat your | favour·with | gifts.

13 The king's daughter is all | glorious·with|in:
her clothing is em|broidered | cloth of | gold.

14 In robes of many colours she is led to | you O | king:
and after her the | virgins | that are | with her.

†15 They are led with | gladness·and re|joicing:
they enter the | palace | of the | king.

16 In place of your fathers | you shall·have | sons:
and make them princes | over | all the | land.

17 And I will make known your‿
    name to every | gener|ation:
therefore the peoples shall | give you | praise for | ever.

Praise: to Christ the King, the Church's bridegroom.

46   *The Lord of hosts is with us, the God of Jacob is our stronghold.*

1 God is our | refuge · and | strength:
a very | present | help in | trouble.

2 Therefore we will not fear ⌣
though the | earth be | moved:
and though the mountains are | shaken · ⌣
in the | midst · of the | sea.

†3 Though the waters | rage and | foam:
and though the mountains quake at the | rising | of the | se

4 There is a river whose streams make glad ⌣
the | city · of | God:
the holy dwelling-place | of the | Most | High.

5 God is in the midst of her
therefore she shall | not be | moved:
God will | help her · and at | break of | day.

6 The nations make uproar and the | kingdoms · are | shake
but God has lifted his | voice ·
and the | earth shall | tremble.

7 *The Lord of | hosts is | with us:*
the God of | Jacob | is our | stronghold.

8 Come then and see what the | Lord has | done:
what destruction he has | brought up|on the | earth.

9 He makes wars to cease in | all the | world:
he breaks the bow and shatters the spear
and burns the | chari·ots | in the | fire.

10 'Be still and know that | I am | God:
I will be exalted among the nations
I will be ex|alted · up|on the | earth.'

11 *The Lord of | hosts is | with us:*
the God of | Jacob | is our | stronghold.

Thanksgiving: for the church and the waters of baptism.

47   *God is king of all the earth.*

1 O clap your hands | all you | peoples:
  and cry aloud to | God with | shouts of | joy.
2 For the Lord Most High | is to · be | feared:
  he is a great | King · over | all the | earth.
3 He cast down | peoples | under us:
  and the | nations · be|neath our | feet.
4 He chose us a land for | our pos|session:
  that was the pride of | Jacob | whom he | loved.

5 God has gone up with the | sound · of re|joicing:
  and the | Lord · to the | blast · of the | horn.
6 O sing praises sing | praises · to | God:
  O sing praises sing | praises | to our | King.
7 For God is the King of | all the | earth:
  O | praise him · in a | well-wrought | psalm.
8 God has become the | King · of the | nations:
  he has taken his seat up|on his | holy | throne.
9 The princes of the peoples are | gathered · to|gether:
  with the | people · of the | God of | Abraham.
10 For the mighty ones of the earth
    are become the | servants · of | God:
  and | he is | greatly · ex|alted.

Praise: to Christ our ascended King.

48   *Throughout the world the holy church acclaims you, Father of majesty unbounded.*

1 Great is the Lord and | greatly · to be | praised:
  in the | city | of our | God.
2 High and beautiful is his | holy | hill:
  it is the | joy of | all the | earth.
3 On Mount Zion where godhead truly dwells
    stands the city of the | Great | King:
  God is well known in her palaces | as a | sure de|fence.

4 For the kings of the | earth as|sembled:
  they gathered to|gether · and | came | on;
5 They saw   they were | struck | dumb:
  they were a|stonished · and | fled in | terror.
6 Trembling took | hold on them · and | anguish:
  as on a | woman | in her | travail;
7 Like the breath of the | east | wind:
  that | shatters · the | ships of | Tarshish.

8 As we have heard   so have we seen ⌣
    in the city of the | Lord of | hosts:
  in the city of our God ⌣
    which | God · has es|tablished · for | ever.
9 We have called to mind your loving-|kindness · O | God:
  in the | midst of | your | temple.
10 As your name is great O God   so also | is your | praise:
  even to the | ends | of the | earth.
11 Your right hand is full of victory
    let Zion's | hill re|joice:
  let the daughters of Judah be | glad ⌣
  be|cause of · your | judgements.
12 Walk about Zion   go round about her ⌣
    and | count · all her | towers:
  consider well her ramparts | pass | through her | palaces;
†13 That you may tell those who come after ⌣
    that | such is | God:
  our God for ever and ever
    and | he will | guide us · e|ternally.

  Thanksgiving: for the church.

49   *Teach us to lay up for ourselves treasures in heaven.*

1 O hear this | all you | peoples:
  give ear all you in|habit · ants | of the | world,
2 All children of men and | sons of | Adam:
  both | rich and | poor a|like.

3 For my mouth shall | speak | wisdom:
and the thoughts of my heart‿
    shall be | full of | under|standing.
4 I will incline my | ear · to a | riddle:
and unfold the mystery to the | sounds | of the | harp.

5 Why should I fear in the | evil | days:
when the wickedness of | my de|ceivers · sur|rounds me,
6 Though they trust to their | great | wealth:
and boast of the a|bundance | of their | riches?
7 No man may | ransom · his | brother:
or give | God a | price | for him,
8 So that he may | live for | ever:
and | never | see the | grave;
9 For to ransom men's | lives · is so | costly:
that he must a|bandon | it for | ever.
10 For we see that | wise men | die:
and perish with the foolish and the ignorant |
    leaving · their | wealth to | others.
11 The tomb is their home for ever
    their dwelling-place throughout | all · gener|ations:
though they called estates | after · their | own | names.
12 A rich man without | under|standing:
is | like the | beasts that | perish.
13 This is the | lot · of the | foolish;
the end of those who are | pleased · with their | own |
    words.
14 They are driven like sheep into the grave‿
    and | death · is their | shepherd:
they slip down | easi·ly | into · the | tomb.
15 Their bright forms shall wear a|way · in the | grave:
and | lose their | former | glory.
†16 But God will | ransom · my | life:
he will take me | from the | power · of the | grave.
17 Do not fear when a | man grows | rich:
when the | wealth · of his | household · in|creases,

18 For he will take nothing a|way · when he | dies:
   nor will his | wealth go | down | after him.

19 Though he counts himself happy | while he | lives:
   and praises you | also | when you | prosper,

20 He will go to the company | of his | fathers:
   who will | never | see the | light.

†21 A rich man without | under|standing:
    is | like the | beasts that | perish.

Prayer: for those held spellbound by 'this world'.

50 (1)   *Teach us, Lord, that you desire steadfast love.*

1 The Lord our God the | Mighty One · has | spoken:
  and summoned the earth
        from the rising of the sun to its | setting | in the | west.

2 From Zion | perfect · in | beauty:
  God has | shone | out in | glory.

3 Our God is coming   he will | not keep | silent:
  before him is devouring fire
        and | tempest | whirls a|bout him.

4 He calls to the | heavens · a|bove:
  and to the earth so | he may | judge his | people.

5 'Gather to | me my | faithful ones:
  those who by sacrifice | made a | coven·ant | with me.'

6 The heavens shall pro|claim his | righteousness:
  for | God him|self is | judge.

7 'Listen my people and | I will | speak:
  O Israel I am God your God
        and | I will | give my | testimony.

8 'It is not for your sacrifices that | I re|prove you:
  for your burnt-|offerings · are | always · be|fore me.

9 'I will take no | bull · from your | farms:
  or | he-goat | from your | pens.

10 'For all the beasts of the forest be|long to | me:
   and so do the | cattle · up|on the | mountains.

366

11 'I know all the | birds · of the | air:
    and the grasshoppers of the | field are | in my | sight.

12 'If I were hungry I | would not | tell you:
    for the whole world is | mine and | all · that is | in it.

13 'Do I eat the | flesh of | bulls:
    or | drink the | blood of | goats?

14 'Offer to God a sacrifice of | thanks|giving:
    and pay your | vows · to the | Most | High.

†15 'Call upon me in the | day of | trouble:
    I will bring you out   and | you shall | glori·fy | me.'

Thanksgiving: for Christ's perfect sacrifice.

(2)   *Let us offer to God a sacrifice of thanks and praise.*

16 [But] God | says · to the | wicked:
    'What have you to do with reciting my laws
        or taking my | coven·ant | on your | lips,

17 'Seeing you | loathe | discipline:
    and have | tossed my | words be|hind you?

18 'When you saw a thief you | went a|long with him:
    and you | threw in · your | lot · with ad|ulterers.

19 'You have loosed your | mouth in | evil:
    and your | tongue strings | lies to|gether.

20 'You sit and speak a|gainst your | brother:
    and slander your | own | mother's | son.

21 'These things you have done   and I | held my | tongue:
    and you thought I was just such an|other | as your|self.

22 'But I | will con|vict you:
    and set before your | eyes what | you have | done.

23 'O consider this   you who for|get | God:
    lest I tear you in pieces
        and | there be | no one · to | save you.

†24 'He honours me who brings sacrifice of | thanks|giving:
    and to him who keeps to my way⌣
        I will | show the · sal|vation · of | God.'

Prayer: that we may be delivered from formalism in worship.

51 *Lord Jesus, remember me when you come in your kingly power.*

1 Have mercy on me O God in your en|during | goodness:
   according to the fullness of your compassion | ‿
      blot out | my of|fences.

2 Wash me thoroughly | from my | wickedness:
   and | cleanse me | from my | sin.

3 For I acknowledge | my re|bellion:
   and my | sin is | ever · be|fore me.

4 Against you only have I sinned
      and done what is evil | in your | eyes:
   so you will be just in your sentence
      and | blameless | in your | judging.

5 Surely in wickedness I was | brought to | birth:
   and in | sin my | mother · con|ceived me.

6 You that desire truth in the | inward | parts:
   O teach me wisdom in the secret | places | of the | heart.

7 Purge me with hyssop and I | shall be | clean:
   wash me and I | shall be | whiter · than | snow.

8 Make me hear of | joy and | gladness:
   let the bones which | you have | broken · re|joice.

9 Hide your | face · from my | sins:
   and | blot out | all · my in|iquities.

10 Create in me a clean | heart O | God:
   and re|new a · right | spirit · with|in me.

11 Do not cast me | out · from your | presence:
   do not take your | holy | spirit | from me.

12 O give me the gladness of your | help a|gain:
   and sup|port me · with a | willing | spirit.

†13 Then will I teach trans|gressors · your | ways:
   and sinners shall | turn to | you a|gain.

14 O Lord God of my salvation
      de|liver me · from | bloodshed:
   and my | tongue shall | sing of · your | righteousness.

15 O Lord | open · my | lips:
   and my | mouth · shall pro|claim your | praise.

16 You take no pleasure in sacrifice or | I would | give it:
   burnt-|offerings · you | do not | want.
17 The sacrifice of God is a | broken | spirit:
   a broken and contrite heart O God | ⌣
      you will | not de|spise.
18 In your graciousness do | good to | Zion:
   re|build the | walls · of Je|rusalem.
19 Then will you delight in right sacrifices
      in burnt-offerings | and ob|lations:
   then will they offer young | bulls up|on your | altar.

Prayer: of sorrow for sin and confidence in God's mercy.

52   *I will trust in the goodness of God for ever.*

1 Why O man of power ⌣
      do you boast | all the · day | long:
   of mischief done to | him · that is | faithful · to | God?
2 You contrive de|stroying | slanders:
   your tongue is like a sharpened | razor · ⌣
      it | cuts de|ceitfully.
3 You have loved evil | and not | good:
   to tell lies | rather · than to | speak the | truth.
4 You love all words that | may do | hurt:
   and | every · de|ceit · of the | tongue.
5 But God will de|stroy you | utterly:
   he will snatch you away and pluck you out of your dwelling
      he will up|root you · from the | land · of the | living.
6 The righteous shall | see it · and | fear:
   they shall | laugh you · to | scorn and | say,
†7 'Behold   this is the man ⌣
      who did not take | God · for his | strength:
   but trusted in the abundance of his riches
      and | found his | strength in | slander.'

8 As for me
    I am like a green olive tree in the | house of | God:
  I will trust in the goodness of | God for | ever · and | ever.
9 I will always give you thanks
    for this was | your | doing:
  I will glorify your name before the faithful
    for | it is | good to | praise you.

Prayer: that we may be delivered from lies and deceit.

53   *All have fallen short of the glory of God.*

1 The fool has said in his heart   'There | is no | God':
  they have all become vile and abominable in their⌣
      wickedness
    there | is not | one that · does | good.
2 God looked down from heaven upon the | children · of | men
  to see if there were any who would act | wisely · ⌣
    and | seek · after | God.
3 But they have all turned aside
    they have all alike be|come cor|rupt:
  there is none that does | good | no not | one.
4 Are all the evildoers devoid of | under|standing:
  who eat up my people as men eat bread
    and | do not | pray to | God?
5 They shall be | struck with | terror:
  for God will scatter the | bones | of the · un|godly.
6 They shall be | put to · con|fusion:
  because | God | has re|jected them.
†7 O that deliverance for Israel⌣
    might come | forth from | Zion:
  when the Lord turns again the fortunes of his people
    then shall Jacob re|joice and | Israel · be | glad.

Prayer: for all mankind alienated from God.

54   *For freedom Christ has set us free.*

1 Save me O God by the | power of · your | name:
  and | vindicate · me | by your | might.

2 Hear my | prayer O | God:
  and | listen · to the | words of · my | mouth.

3 For the insolent have | risen · a|gainst me:
  ruthless men who have not set God be|fore them |◡
  seek my | life.

4 But surely | God is · my | helper:
  The Lord is the up|holder | of my | life.

5 Let evil recoil on those that | would way|lay me:
  O de|stroy them | in your | faithfulness!

6 Then will I offer you sacrifice with a | willing | heart:
  I will praise your name O | Lord for | it is | good.

†7 For you will deliver me from | every | trouble:
  my eyes shall see the | downfall | of my | enemies.

*Prayer: for the Church in places where the name of Christ leads to
persecution.*

55 (1)   *Father, if it be possible, let this cup pass from me.*

1 Hear my | prayer O | God:
  and do not hide your|self from | my pe|tition.

2 Give heed to | me and | answer me:
  I am | restless · in | my com|plaining.

3 I am in turmoil at the | voice · of the | enemy:
  at the | onslaught | of the | wicked.

4 For they bring down dis|aster · up|on me:
  they persecute | me with | bitter | fury.

5 My heart | writhes with|in me:
  and the terrors of | death have | fallen · up|on me.

6 Fear and trembling | come up|on me:
  and | horror | over|whelms me.

7 And I said   'O for the | wings · of a | dove:
  that I might fly a|way and | find | rest.

371

8 'Then I would | flee far | off:
   and make my | lodging | in the | wilderness.

9 'I would hasten to | find me · a | refuge:
   out | of the | blast of | slander,   ·

10 'Out of the tempest of their | calumny · O | Lord:
   and | far · from their | double | tongues.'

11 For I have seen violence and | strife · in the | city:
   day and night they go | round it · up|on its | walls.

12 Evil and wickedness | are with|in it:
   iniquity is within it
       oppression and fraud do | not de|part · from its | streets.

Meditation: on Christ's passion.

(2)   *Not my will, but yours, be done.*

13 It was not an enemy that reviled me
       or I | might have | borne it:
   it was not my foe that dealt so insolently with me
       or I might have | hidden · my|self | from him;

14 But it was you a | man · like my|self:
   my companion | and · my fam|iliar | friend.

†15 Together we en|joyed sweet | fellowship:
   in the | house | of our | God.

16 Let them pass a|way · in con|fusion:
   let death | carry · them | to des|truction;

17 Let them go down a|live to | Sheol:
   for evil is a|mong them | in their | dwellings.

18 But I will | call to | God:
   and the | Lord my | God will | save me.

19 At evening at morning | and at | noon-day:
   I com|plain and | groan a|loud.

20 And he will | hear my | voice:
   and | ransom · my | soul in | peace,

21 From those that bear | down up|on me:
   for | there are | many · a|gainst me.

22 God will hear and | bring them | low:
   he that | is en|throned for | ever.
23 For they do not | keep their | word:
   and they | have no | fear of | God.
24 They lay violent hands⌣
      on those that | are at | peace with them:
   they | break | solemn | covenants.
25 Their mouths are smooth as butter
      but war is | in their | hearts:
   their words are softer than oil
      yet | they are | drawn | swords.
26 Cast your burden on the Lord⌣
      and | he·will sus|tain you:
   he will never suffer the | righteous | man to | stumble.
27 But as for them   you will bring them | down O | God:
   even | to the | depths·of the | Pit.
†28 Bloodthirsty and deceitful men⌣
      shall not live out | half their | days:
   but | I will | trust in | you.

   Prayer: of confidence in the Father's will.

56   *Let me walk before you, Lord, in the light of the living.*

1 Be merciful to me O God
      for men are | treading·me | down:
   all day long my | adver·sary | presses·up|on me.
2 My enemies tread me down | all the | day:
   for there are many that | arrogant·ly | fight a|gainst me.
3 In the | hour of | fear:
   I will | put my | trust in | you.
4 In God whose word I praise
      in God I | trust and | fear not:
   what can | flesh | do to | me?
5 All day long they afflict me | with their | words:
   and every thought is | how to | do me | evil.

6 They stir up hatred | and con|ceal themselves:
   they watch my steps
       while they | lie in | wait for·my | life.

7 Let there be | no es|cape for them:
   bring down the | peoples·in your | wrath O | God.

8 You have counted my anxious tossings
       put my | tears·in your | bottle:
   are not these things | noted | in your | book?

9 In the day that I call to you
       my enemies shall | turn | back:
   this I | know for | God is | with me.

10 In God whose word I praise
       in God I | trust and | fear not:
   what can | man | do to | me?

11 To you O God must I per|form my | vows:
   I will pay the thank-|offer·ing | that is | due.

12 For you will deliver my soul from death‿
       and my | feet from | falling:
   that I may walk before | God·in the | light·of the | living.

Prayer: for opportunity to praise God amid troubles.

57 *You deliver my soul from death, my feet from falling.*

1 Be merciful to me O | God be | merciful:
   for I | come to | you for | shelter;

2 And in the shadow of your wings will | I take | refuge:
   until these | troubles·are | over-|past.

3 I will call to | God Most | High:
   to the God who will ful|fil his | purpose | for me.

4 He will send from | heaven·and | save me:
   he will send forth his faithfulness and his loving-‿
       kindness
       and rebuke | those·that would | trample·me | down.

5 For I lie amidst | raven·ing | lions:
   men whose teeth are spears and arrows
       and their | tongue a | sharpened | sword.

6   *Be exalted O God a|bove the | heavens:*
    and let your glory be | over | all the | earth.

7   They have set a net for my feet
        and I am | brought | low:
    they have dug a pit before me
        but shall | fall · into | it them|selves.

8   My heart is fixed O God my | heart is | fixed:
    I will | sing and | make | melody.

9   Awake my soul   awake | lute and | harp:
    for | I · will a|waken · the | morning.

10 I will give you thanks O Lord a|mong the | peoples:
    I will sing your | praise a|mong the | nations.

11 For the greatness of your mercy |
        reaches · to the | heavens:
    and your | faithful·ness | to the | clouds.

12 *Be exalted O God a|bove the | heavens:*
    and let your glory be | over | all the | earth.

    Meditation: on Christ's prayer in Gethsemane.

58   *Let justice roll down like waters, and righteousness like a mighty stream.*

1   Do you indeed decree what is | just O | rulers:
    do you with uprightness | judge the | children · of | men?

2   No   you work in the land with | evil | heart:
    you look on the violence | that your | hands have | wrought.

3   The wicked are estranged | even · from the | womb:
    they are liars that go a|stray | from their | birth.

4   They are venomous with the | venom · of | serpents:
    like the deaf | asp that | stops its | ears,

†5 And will not heed the | voice · of the | charmers:
    though the | binder · of | spells be | skilful.

6   Break their teeth O | God · in their | mouths:
    shatter the jaws of the | young | lions · O | Lord.

7   Let them dissolve and drain a|way like | water:
    let them be trodden down | let them | wither · like | grass,

375

8 Like a woman's miscarriage that melts ⌣
    and | passes · a|way:
  like an abortive birth that | has not | seen the | sun.
9 Before they know it   let them be cut | down like | thorns:
  like brambles which a | man sweeps | angrily · a|side.
10 The righteous shall rejoice when he | sees the | vengeance:
  he will wash his feet in the | blood of | the un|godly.
11 And men will say
    'There is re|ward · for the | righteous:
  there is indeed a | God who | judges · on | earth.'

    Prayer: for a deep commitment to justice.

    59   *Lord, you are my strength, I will sing praises to you.*

1 Deliver me from my | enemies · O | God:
  lift me to safety from | those that | rise a|gainst me;
2 O deliver me from the | evil|doers:
  and | save me · from | blood·thirsty | men.
3 For they lie in | wait · for my | life:
  savage men | stir up | violence · a|gainst me.
4 Not for my sin or my transgression O Lord
    not for any | evil · I have | done:
  do they run and take | up po|sition · a|gainst me.
5 Arise to | meet me · and | see:
  you that are Lord of | hosts and | God of | Israel.
6 Awake to punish | all the | nations:
  have no mercy on those that so | treacherous·ly | do | wrong.
7 They return every evening   they | howl like | dogs:
  they | prowl a|round the | city.
8 Look how their | mouths | slaver:
  swords strike from their lips
    for they | say | 'Who will | hear it?'
9 But you O Lord will | laugh them · to | scorn:
  you will de|ride | all the | nations.

10 I will look to | you · O my | strength:
   for | God is · my | strong | tower.

11 My God in his steadfastness will | come to | meet me:
   God will show me the | downfall | of my | enemies.

12 Slay them not O Lord   lest my | people · for|get:
   but make them stagger by your | power ⌣
       and | bring them | down.

13 Give them over to punishment * for the sin of their
       mouths ⌣
       for the | words of · their | lips:
   let them be | taken | in their | pride.

14 For the curses and lies that they have uttered
       O consume them | in your | wrath:
   consume them | till they | are no | more;

†15 That men may know that God | rules · over | Jacob:
   even to the | ends | of the | earth.

16 They return every evening   they | howl like | dogs:
   they | prowl a|round the | city.

17 They roam here and there | looking · for | food:
   and | growl · if they | are not | filled.

18 But I will | sing of · your | might:
   I will sing aloud each | morning | of your | goodness.

19 For you have been my | strong | tower:
   and a sure refuge in the | day of | my dis|tress.

†20 I will sing your praises | O my | strength:
   for | God is · my | strong | tower.

Prayer: for deliverance from all who hate us.

60   *By the power of our God we shall do valiantly.*

1 O God you have cast us | off and | broken us:
   you were enraged against us | O re|store us · a|gain!

2 You have caused the land to quake
       you have | rent it | open:
   heal the rifts for the | earth | quivers · and | breaks.

3 You have steeped your people in a | bitter | draught:
   you have given them a | wine to | make them | stagger.

377

4 You have caused those that fear you to | take | flight:
  so that they | run | from the | bow.

†5 O save us by your right | hand and | answer us:
  that those whom you | love may | be de|livered.

6 God has said in his | holy | place:
  'I will exult and divide Shechem
  I will parcel | out the | valley · of | Succoth.

7 'Gilead is mine and Ma|nasseh · is | mine:
  Ephraim is my helmet and | Judah · my | rod · of com|mand

†8 'Moab is my wash-bowl
  over Edom will I | cast my | shoe:
  against Philistia | will I | shout in | triumph.'

9 Who will lead me into the | forti·fied | city:
  who will | bring me | into | Edom?

10 Have you not cast us | off O | God?:
  you | go not | out · with our | armies.

11 Give us your help a|gainst the | enemy:
  for | vain · is the | help of | man.

12 By the power of our God we | shall do | valiantly:
  for it is he that will | tread | down our | enemies.

Prayer: for the triumph of God.

61 *God our eternal refuge, hear our prayer.*

1 Hear my loud | crying · O | God:
  and give | heed | to my | prayer.

2 From the ends of the earth I call to you‿
    when my | heart | faints:
  O set me on the | rock · that is | higher · than | I.

3 For you have | been my | refuge:
  and my strong | tower a|gainst the | enemy.

4 I will dwell in your | tent for | ever:
  and find shelter in the | cover·ing | of your | wings.

5 For you have heard my | vows O | God:
  you have granted the desire‿
    of | those that | fear your | name.

378

6 You will give the | king long | life:
  and his years shall endure through | many | gener|ations.
7 He shall dwell before | God for | ever:
  loving-kindness and | truth shall | be his | guard.
8 So will I ever sing praises | to your | name:
  while I | daily · per|form my | vows.

Prayer: for confidence to pray in the name of Christ.

62 *May the God of hope fill us with all joy and peace.*

1 My soul waits in | silence · for | God:
  for from | him comes | my sal|vation.
2 He only is my rock and | my sal|vation:
  my strong tower   so that | I shall | never · be | moved.
3 How long will you all plot against a | man · to de|stroy him:
  as though he were a leaning | fence · or a | buckling | wall?
4 Their design is to thrust him from his height
      and their de|light · is in | lies:
  they bless with their | lips but | inwardly · they | curse.
5 Nevertheless my soul   wait in | silence · for | God:
  for from | him | comes my | hope.
6 He only is my rock and | my sal|vation:
  my strong tower   so that | I shall | not be | moved.
7 In God is my deliverance | and my | glory:
  God is my strong | rock | and my | shelter.
8 Trust in him at all times | O my | people:
  pour out your hearts before him
      for | God | is our | refuge.
9 The children of men are but breath
      the children of | men · are a | lie:
  place them in the scales and they fly upward
      they | are as | light as | air.
10 Put no trust in extortion
      do not grow | worthless · by | robbery:
  if riches increase | set not · your | heart up|on them.

11 God has spoken once   twice have I | heard him | say:
    that | power be|longs to | God,

12 That to the Lord belongs a | constant | goodness:
    for you reward a man ac|cording | to his | works.

Prayer: for those who do not know God's love.

      63   *Lord my God, for you I long.*

1 O God | you are · my | God:
    eagerly | will I | seek | you.

2 My soul thirsts for you   my | flesh | longs for you:
    as a dry and thirsty | land · where no | water | is.

3 So it was when I beheld you | in the | sanctuary:
    and | saw your | power · and your | glory.

4 For your unchanging goodness is | better · than | life:
    there|fore my | lips shall | praise you.

5 And so I will bless you as | long as · I | live:
    and in your name will I | lift my | hands on | high.

6 My longing shall be satisfied‿
        as with | marrow · and | fatness:
    my mouth shall | praise you · with ex|ultant | lips.

7 When I remember you up|on my | bed:
    when I meditate up|on you · in the | night | watches,

8 How you have | been my | helper:
    then I sing for joy in the | shadow | of your | wings,

†9 Then my | soul | clings to you:
    and | your right | hand up|holds me.

10 Those that seek my life are | marked · for de|struction:
    they shall go down to the deep | places | of the | earth.

11 They shall be de|livered · to the | sword:
    they shall | be a | portion · for | jackals.

†12 The king will rejoice in God
        and all who take oaths on his | name shall | glory:
    but the mouths of | liars | shall be | stopped.

Prayer: for those who devote their lives to prayer.

64   *Father, forgive them; they know not what they do.*

1   Hear my voice O God in | my com|plaining:
    preserve my | life from | fear · of the | enemy.

2   Hide me from the conspiracy | of the | wicked:
    from the | throng of | evil|doers,

3   Who sharpen their | tongues like | swords:
    who string the bow   who take | arrows · of | bitter | words,

4   To shoot from hiding at the | blameless | man:
    to strike at him | sudden·ly | and un|seen.

5   They are confirmed in an | evil | purpose:
    they confide it to one another while they lay the snares|
        saying | 'Who will | see them?'

6   They hatch mischief
        they hide a well-con|sidered | plan:
    for the mind and heart of | man is | very | deep.

7   But God will shoot at them with his | swift | arrows:
    they shall be | sudden·ly | struck | through.

8   The Lord will bring them down ⌣
        for what their | tongues have | spoken:
    and all that see it shall | toss their | heads in | scorn.

9   Then | all men · shall | fear:
    and tell what the Lord has | done ⌣
        and | ponder · his | works.

10 The righteous man shall rejoice in the Lord
        and find in | him his | refuge:
    and all the | upright · in | heart · shall ex|ult.

Prayer: for those suffering because of their race, creed, or colour.

65   *You are the Lord, we acclaim you.*

1   You are to be praised O | God in | Zion:
    to you shall vows be paid | you that | answer | prayer.

2   To you shall all flesh come to con|fess their | sins:
    when our misdeeds prevail against us| ⌣
        you will | purge · them a|way.

†3 Blessèd is the man whom you choose
  and take to yourself to dwell with|in your | courts:
 we shall be filled with the good things of your house|
  of your | holy | temple.

4 You will answer us in your righteousness⌣
  with terrible deeds O | God our | saviour:
 you that are the hope of all the ends of the earth⌣
  and | of the | distant | seas;
5 Who by your strength made | fast the | mountains:
 you | that are | girded · with | power;
6 Who stilled the raging of the seas⌣
  the | roaring · of the | waves:
 and the | tumult | of the | peoples.
7 Those who dwell at the ends of the earth⌣
  are a|fraid at · your | wonders:
 the dawn and the | even · ing | sing your | praises.

8 You tend the | earth and | water it:
 you | make it | rich and | fertile.
9 The river of God is | full of | water:
 and so providing for the earth⌣
  you pro|vide | grain for | men.
10 You drench its furrows
  you level the | ridges · be|tween:
 you soften it with showers and | bless its | early | growth.
11 You crown the | year · with your | goodness:
 and the tracks where you have | passed | drip with | fatness.
12 The pastures of the | wilderness · run | over:
 and the | hills are | girded · with | joy.
13 The meadows are | clothed with | sheep:
 and the valleys stand so thick with corn⌣
  they | shout for | joy and | sing.

Thanksgiving: for the fruits of the earth.

66 *As in Adam all die, so in Christ shall all be made alive.*

1 O shout with joy to God | all the | earth:
   sing to the honour of his name
      and give him | glory | as his | praise.

2 Say to God 'How fearful | are your | works:
   because of your great might⌣
      your | enemies · shall | cower ⌣ be|fore you.'

3 All the | earth shall | worship you:
   and sing to you   and sing | praises | to your | name.

4 Come then and see what | God has | done:
   how terrible are his | dealings · with the | children · of | men.

5 He turned the sea into dry land
      they crossed the | river · on | foot:
   then | were we | joyful · be|cause of him.

6 By his power he rules for ever
      his eyes keep | watch · on the | nations:
   and rebels shall | never | rise a|gainst him.

7 O bless our | God you | peoples:
   and cause his | praises | to re|sound,

8 Who has held our | souls in | life:
   who has not | suffered · our | feet to | slip.

9 For you have | proved us · O | God:
   you have | tried us · as | silver · is | tried.

10 You brought us | into · the | net:
   you laid sharp | torment | on our | loins.

†11 You let men ride over our heads
      we went through | fire and | water:
   but you brought us out | into · a | place of | liberty.

12 I will come into your house with | burnt-|offerings:
   and | I will | pay you · my | vows,

13 The vows that | opened · my | lips:
   that my mouth uttered | when I | was in | trouble.

14 I will offer you burnt-offerings of fattened beasts
      with the sweet | smoke of | rams:
   I will sacrifice a | bull · and the | flesh of | goats.

15 Come then and hear   all | you that · fear | God:
   and I will | tell what | he has | done for me.
16 I called to him | with my | mouth:
   and his | praise was | on my | tongue.
17 If I had cherished wickedness | in my | heart:
   the | Lord would | not have | heard me.
18 But | God has | heard me:
   he has | heeded · the | voice of · my | prayer.
19 Praise | be to | God:
   who has not turned back my prayer
      or his | steadfast | love | from me.

Thanksgiving: for help in time of trial.

67   *Let the peoples praise you, O God, let all the peoples praise you.*

1 Let God be gracious to | us and | bless us:
  and make his | face | shine up|on us,
2 That your ways may be | known on | earth:
  your liberating | power · a|mong all | nations.
3 Let the peoples | praise you · O | God:
  let | all the | peoples | praise you.
4 Let the nations be | glad and | sing:
  for you judge the peoples with integrity
     and govern the | nations · up|on | earth.
5 Let the peoples | praise you · O | God:
  let | all the | peoples | praise you.
6 Then the earth will | yield its | fruitfulness:
  and | God our | God will | bless us.
†7 God | shall | bless us:
  and all the | ends · of the | earth will | fear him.

Prayer: for the conversion of the nations.

384

68 (1) *When Christ ascended on high, he led the enemy captive.*

1 God shall arise   and his enemies | shall be | scattered:
those that hate him shall | flee be|fore his | face.

2 As smoke is dispersed   so shall | they · be dis|persed:
as wax melts before a fire
    so shall the wicked | perish · at the | presence · of | God.

3 But the righteous shall be glad and ex|ult be·fore | God:
they | shall re|joice with | gladness.

4 O sing to God   sing praises | to his | name:
glorify him that rode through the deserts
    him whose name is the Lord |
    and ex|ult be|fore him.

5 He is the father of the fatherless
    he upholds the | cause · of the | widow:
God | in his | holy | dwelling place.

6 He gives the desolate a home to dwell in
    and brings the prisoners out | into · pros|perity:
but rebels must | dwell · in a | barren | land.

7 O God   when you went out be|fore your | people:
when you | marched | through the | wilderness,

8 The earth shook   the heavens | poured down | water:
before the God of Sinai
    before | God the | God of | Israel.

9 You showered down a generous | rain O | God:
you prepared the land of your pos|session · when | it was |
    weary.

10 And there your | people | settled:
in the place that your goodness O God ‿
    had made | ready | for the | poor.

11 The Lord spoke the word   *   and great was the
    company ‿
    of those that | carried · the | tidings:
'Kings with their armies are | fleeing · are | fleeing · a|way.

12 'Even the women at home may | share · in the | spoil:
and will you sit | idly · a|mong the | sheepfolds?

13 'There are images of doves⏝
    whose wings are | covered · with | silver:
and their | pinions · with | shining | gold.'
14 When the Almighty | scattered | kings:
    they were like snow | falling · up|on Mount | Zalmon.

15 The mountain of Bashan is a | mighty | mountain:
    the mountain of Bashan⏝
        is a | mountain · of | many | peaks.
16 O mountains of many peaks   why | look so | enviously:
    at the mountain where God is pleased to dwell
        where the | Lord · will re|main for | ever?
17 The chariots of God are twice ten thousand⏝
        and | thousands up·on | thousands:
    the Lord came from Sinai | into · his | holy | place.
18 When you ascended the heights⏝
        you led the enemy captive * you received | tribute ·
            from | men:
    but rebels shall not | dwell · in the | presence · of | God.

Prayer: for the extension of Christ's kingdom.

(2)   *Sing praises to God, you kingdoms of the earth.*

19 Blessèd be the Lord day by day
        who bears us | as his | burden:
    he is the | God of | our de|liverance.
20 God is to us a | God who | saves:
    by God the Lord do | we es|cape | death.
21 But God shall smite the | heads · of his | enemies:
    the hairy scalp of | those that | walk · in their | sins.
22 The Lord said   'I will bring them | back from | Bashan:
    I will bring them a|gain · from the | deep | sea';
†23 That you may dip your | feet in | blood:
    and the tongues of your | dogs ·
        in the | blood of · your | enemies.

24 Your procession is | seen O | God:
  the procession of my | God and | King · in the | sanctuary.

25 The singers go before   the mu|sicians · come | after:
  and around them the maidens | beating | on the | timbrels.

26 In their choirs they | bless | God:
  those that are sprung from the fount of | Israel | ◡
    bless the | Lord.

27 There is the little tribe of | Benja·min | leading them:
  the throng of the princes of Judah
    the princes of | Zebulun · and the | princes · of | Naphtali.

28 Give the command my God
    in accordance | with your | power:
  that godlike | power where|by you | act for us.

29 Give the command from your temple | at Je|rusalem:
  and | kings shall | bring you | tribute.

30 Rebuke the beast of the reeds
    the herd of bulls amidst the | brutish | peoples:
  tread down those that are greedy for silver
    scatter the | peoples · that | relish | war.

31 Let them bring | bronze from | Egypt:
  let the hands of the Nubians | carry · it | swiftly · to | God.

32 Sing to God you | kingdoms · of the | earth:
  O sing | praises | to the | Lord,

33 To him that rides upon the highest heavens
    that were | from · the be|ginning:
  who utters his voice which | is a | mighty | voice.

34 Ascribe power to God   whose majesty is | over | Israel:
  and his | might is | in the | clouds.

35 Terrible is God who comes from his | holy | place:
  the God of Israel who gives ◡
    power and strength to his people |
    Blessèd | be | God.

Prayer: for the conversion of the nations.

387

69 (1) *I am weary with my crying; Lord, save me.*

1 Save | me O | God:
  for the waters have come up | even | to my | throat.
2 I sink in the deep mire | where no | footing is:
  I have come into deep waters | ⌣
    and the | flood sweeps | over me.
3 I am weary with crying out   my | throat is | parched:
  my eyes fail with | watching·so | long·for my | God.
4 Those that hate me without cause
    are more in number than the | hairs·of my | head:
  those that would destroy me are many
    they oppose me wrongfully
    for I must restore | things·that I | never | took.
5 O God you | know my | foolishness:
  and my | sins·are not | hidden | from you.
6 Let not those who wait for you be shamed ⌣
    because of me   O Lord | God of | hosts:
  let not those who seek you ⌣
    be disgraced on | my account·O | God of | Israel.
7 For your sake have I | suffered·re|proach:
  and | shame has | covered·my | face.
8 I have become a stranger | to my | brothers:
  an alien | to my·own | mother's | sons.
9 Zeal for your house has | eaten·me | up:
  and the taunts of those who taunt | you ⌣
    have | fallen·on | me.
10 I afflicted my|self with | fasting:
  and that was | turned to | my re|proach.
11 I made | sackcloth·my | clothing:
  and I be|came a | byword | to them.
12 Those who sit in the gate | talk of | me:
  and the | drunkards·make | songs a|bout me.
†13 But to you Lord I | make my | prayer:
  at | an ac|cepta·ble | time.

  Prayer: for the lonely and the rejected.

(2)   *When I was thirsty they gave me vinegar to drink.*

14 Answer me O God in your a|bundant | goodness:
    and | with your | sure de|liverance.

15 Bring me out of the mire   so that I | may not | sink:
    let me be delivered from my enemies ⌣
        and | from the | deep | waters.

16 Let not the flood overwhelm me
        or the depths | swallow · me | up:
    let not the | Pit · shut its | mouth up|on me.

17 Hear me O Lord   as your loving-|kindness · is | good:
    turn to me   as | your com|passion · is | great.

18 Do not hide your | face · from your | servant:
    for I am in trouble | O be | swift to | answer me!

19 Draw near to me | and re|deem me:
    O | ransom me · be|cause of · my | enemies!

20 You know | all their | taunts:
    my adversaries are | all | in your | sight.

21 Insults have | broken · my | heart:
    my shame and dis|grace are | past | healing.

Meditation: on the cost to our Lord of our salvation.

(3)   *Seek the Lord, and he will give life to your soul.*

22 I looked for someone to have pity on me
        but | there was | no man:
    for some to | comfort me · but | found | none.

23 They gave me | poison · for | food:
    and when I was thirsty ⌣
        they | gave me | vinegar · to | drink.

24 Let their table be|come a | snare:
    and their sacri|fici·al | feasts a | trap.

25 Let their eyes be darkened   so that they | cannot | see:
    and make their | loins | shake con|tinually.

26 Pour out your | wrath up|on them:
    and let your fierce | anger | over|take them.

27 Let their | camp be | desolate:
   and let | no man | dwell · in their | tents.

28 For they persecute him whom | you have | stricken:
   and multiply the pain⏜
      of | him whom | you have | wounded.

29 Let them have punishment up|on | punishment:
   let them | not re|ceive · your for|giveness.

†30 Let them be blotted out of the | book · of the | living:
   let them not be written | down a|mong the | righteous.

31 As for me I am | poor · and in | misery:
   O God let your de|liver·ance | lift me | up.

32 And I will praise the name of | God · in a | song:
   and | glori·fy | him with | thanksgiving.

33 And that will please the Lord | more · than an | ox:
   more than a bull with | horns and | cloven | hoof.

34 Consider this you that are | meek · and re|joice:
   seek God and | let your | heart be | glad.

35 For the Lord | listens · to the | poor:
   he does not despise his | servants | in cap|tivity.

36 Let the heavens and the | earth | praise him:
   the | seas and | all that | moves in them.

37 For God will | save | Zion:
   he will re|build the | cities · of | Judah.

38 His people shall live there and possess it
      the seed of his servants | shall in|herit it:
   and those who | love his | name shall | dwell in it.

Prayer: for all who hurt others.

70   *Save, Lord: we are perishing!*

1 O God be | pleased · to de|liver me:
   O | Lord make | haste to | help me.

2 Let them be put to shame and confounded⏜
   who | seek my | life:

    let them be turned back ‿
      and dis|graced who | wish me | evil.

3 Let them turn a|way for | shame:
    who | say to me · 'A|ha a|ha!'.

4 Let all who seek you be joyful and | glad be|cause of you:
    let those who love your salvation say | always | 'God is |
      great'.

5 As for me I am | poor and | needy:
    O | God be | swift to | save me.

6 You are my helper and | my de|liverer:
    O | Lord make | no de|lay.

Prayer: to know Jesus as Lord and Saviour.

71   *O God, you have taught me from my youth upward.*

1 To you Lord have I | come for | shelter:
    let me | never · be | put to | shame.

2 In your righteousness rescue | and de|liver me:
    incline your | ear to | me and | save me.

3 Be for me a rock of refuge * a fortress | to de|fend me:
    for you are my high | rock | and my | stronghold.

4 Rescue me O my God from the | hand · of the | wicked:
    from the grasp of the | piti · less | and un|just.

5 For you Lord | are my | hope:
    you are my confidence O | God · from my | youth | upward.

6 On you have I | leaned · since my | birth:
    you are he that brought me out of my mother's womb
      and my | praise · is of | you con|tinually.

7 I have become as a fearful | warning · to | many:
    but | you are · my | strength · and my | refuge.

8 My mouth shall be | filled · with your | praises:
    I shall sing of your | glory | all the · day | long.

9 Cast me not away in the | time of · old | age:
    nor forsake me | when my | strength | fails.

10 For my enemies | speak a|gainst me:
    and those that watch for my life ‿
      con|spire to|gether | saying,

†11 'God ᴵ has forᴵsaken him:
  pursue him   take him   for ᴵ there is ᴵ none to ᴵ save him.'

12 Be not far ᴵ from me·O ᴵ God:
  my ᴵ God make ᴵ haste to ᴵ help me.

13 Let my adversaries be confounded and ᴵ put to ᴵ shame:
  let those who seek my hurt‿
      be ᴵ covered·with ᴵ scorn·and disᴵgrace.

14 As for me   I will wait in ᴵ hope conᴵtinually:
  and I will ᴵ praise you ᴵ more and ᴵ more.

15 My mouth shall speak of your righteousness ᴵ all the ᴵ day
  and tell of your salvation ᴵ ‿
      though it·exᴵceeds my ᴵ telling.

16 I will begin with the mighty acts of the ᴵ Lord my ᴵ God:
  and declare your righteous ᴵ dealing   ᴵ yours aᴵlone.

17 O God you have taught me from my ᴵ youth ᴵ upward:
  and to this day I proᴵclaim your ᴵ marvel·lous ᴵ works.

18 Forsake me not O God in my old age
      when I am ᴵ grey-ᴵheaded:
  till I have shown the strength of your arm‿
      to future generations
      and your ᴵ might to ᴵ those that·come ᴵ after.

19 Your righteousness O God ᴵ reaches·to the ᴵ heavens:
  great are the things that you have done
      O ᴵ God ᴵ who is ᴵ like you?

20 You have burdened me with many and bitter troubles
      O ᴵ turn·and reᴵnew me:
  and raise me up aᴵgain·from the ᴵ depths·of the ᴵ earth.

21 Bless me beyond my ᴵ former ᴵ greatness:
  O ᴵ turn to me·aᴵgain and ᴵ comfort me.

22 Then will I praise you upon the lute‿
      for your faithfulness ᴵ O my ᴵ God:
  and sing your praises to the harp‿
      O ᴵ Holy ᴵ One of ᴵ Israel.

23 My lips shall reᴵjoice in·my ᴵ singing:
  and my soul ᴵ also·for ᴵ you have ᴵ ransomed me.

†24 My tongue shall speak of your righteous dealing|
 all the·day | long:
for they shall be put to shame and disgraced ⌣
 that | seek to | do me | evil.

Prayer: for the elderly.

72 (1) *God has appointed his Christ to judge the living and the dead.*

1 Give the king your | judgement·O | God:
 and your righteousness to the | son | of a | king,
2 That he may judge your | people | rightly:
 and the | poor·of the | land with | equity.
3 Let the mountains be laden with peace ⌣
 be|cause of·his | righteousness:
 and the hills also with pros|peri·ty | for his | people.
4 May he give justice to the poor a|mong the | people:
 and rescue the children of the | needy· ⌣
  and | crush·the op|pressor.
5 May he live while the | sun en|dures:
 and while the moon gives light ⌣
  through|out all | gener|ations.
6 May he come down like rain upon the | new-mown | fields:
 and as | showers·that | water·the | earth.
7 In his time shall | righteous·ness | flourish:
 and abundance of peace till the | moon shall | be no | more.
8 His dominion shall stretch from | sea to | sea:
 from the Great | River·to the | ends·of the | earth.
9 His adversaries shall bow | down be|fore him:
 and his | enemies·shall | lick the | dust.
10 The kings of Tarshish and of the isles ⌣
 shall | bring | tribute:
 the kings of Sheba and | Seba·shall | offer | gifts.
†11 All kings shall fall | down be|fore him:
 and all | nations | do him | service.

Thanksgiving: for Christ's reign.

(2)   Let all nations call Christ blessed.

12 He will deliver the needy | when they | cry:
    and the | poor man · that | has no | helper.

13 He will pity the helpless | and the | needy:
    and | save the | lives · of the | poor.

†14 He will redeem them from op|pression · and | violence:
    and their blood shall be | precious | in his | sight.

15 Long may he live
        and be given of the | gold of | Sheba:
    may prayer be made for him continually
        and men | bless him | every day.

16 Let there be abundance of | wheat · in the | land:
    let it | flourish · on the | tops · of the | mountains;

†17 Let its ears grow fat like the | grain of | Lebanon:
    and its sheaves | thicken · like the | grass · of the | field.

18 Let his name | live for | ever:
    and en|dure as | long · as the | sun.

19 Let all peoples use his | name in | blessing:
    and all | nations | call him | blessèd.

20 Blessèd be the Lord God the | God of | Israel:
    who a|lone does | great | wonders.

21 Blessèd be his glorious | name for | ever:
    and let the whole earth be filled with his glory |
    Amen | A—|men.

Prayer: for the fulfilment of Christ's kingdom.

73 (1)   *Truly God is good to his people.*

1 God is indeed | good to | Israel:
    to | those whose | hearts are | pure.

2 Nevertheless my feet were | almost | gone:
    my | steps had | well-nigh | slipped.

3 For I was filled with envy | at the | boastful:
    when I saw the un|godly · had | such tran|quillity.

4 For they | suffer · no | pain:
and their | bodies · are | hale and | fat.

5 They come to no mis|fortune · like | other folk:
nor | are they | plagued like | other men.

6 Therefore they put on | pride · as a | necklace:
and clothe themselves in | vio·lence | as · in a | garment.

7 Their eyes shine from | folds of | fatness:
and they have | all that | heart could | wish.

8 Their talk is | malice · and | mockery:
and they hand down | slanders | from on | high.

9 Their mouths blas|pheme a·gainst | heaven:
and their tongues go | to and | fro on | earth.

10 Therefore my | people | turn to them:
and | find in | them no | fault.

11 They say | 'How can · God | know:
is there under|standing · in the | Most | High?'

12 Behold | these are · the un|godly:
yet they | prosper · and in|crease in | riches.

13 Was it for nothing then that I | cleansed my | heart:
and | washed my | hands in | innocence?

14 Have I been stricken all day | long in | vain:
and re|buked | every | morning?

†15 If I had said | 'I will · speak | thus':
I should have betrayed the | fami·ly | of your | children.

16 Then I thought to under|stand | this:
but it | was too | hard | for me,

17 Till I went into the | sanctuary · of | God:
and then I under|stood · what their | end will | be.

18 For you set them in | slipper·y | places:
and cause them to | fall · ‿
from their | treacher·ous | footholds.

19 How suddenly they are | laid | waste:
they come to an | end they | perish · in | terror.

†20 As with a dream when | one a|wakes:
so when you rouse yourself O Lord| ‿
you will · de|spise their | image.

Prayer: for good people in adversity and the 'comfortable' in their arrogance.

(2)   *It is good for me to draw near to God.*

21 When my | heart was | soured:
and I was | wounded | to the | core,

22 I was but | brutish · and | ignorant:
no | better · than a | beast be|fore you.

23 Nevertheless I am | always | with you:
for you hold me | by my | right | hand.

24 You will guide me | with your | counsel:
and afterwards | you will | lead me · to | glory.

25 Whom have I in | heaven · but | you?:
and there is no one upon earth ‿
    that I de|sire · in com|parison · with | you.

26 Though my flesh and my | heart | fail me:
you O | God · are my | portion · for | ever.

27 Behold those who for|sake you · shall | perish:
and all who whore after other | gods you | will de|stroy.

28 But it is good for me to draw | near to | God:
I have made the Lord God my refuge
    and I will tell of | all that | you have | done.

Meditation: on Christ's call to take up the cross and follow him.

74 (1)   *Remember your congregation, Lord, whom you took to yourself of old.*

1 O Lord our God   why cast us | off so | utterly:
why does your anger burn ‿
    a|gainst the | sheep of · your | pasture?

2 Remember your congregation
    whom you took to your|self of | old:
the people that you redeemed to be your own possession
    and Mount | Zion · where | you have | dwelt.

3 Rouse yourself and go to the | utter | ruins:
to all the harm ‿
    that the | enemy · has | done · in the | sanctuary.

4 Your adversaries have made uproar
    in the place appointed | for your | praise:
  they have set | up their | standards·in | triumph.

5 They have destroyed on | every | side:
  like those who take axes | up·to a | thicket·of | trees.

6 All the carved woodwork they have | broken | down:
  and | smashed it·with | hammers·and | hatchets.

7 They have set | fire to·your | sanctuary:
  and defiled to the ground ⌣
    the | dwelling·place | of your | name.

8 They have said in their hearts
    'Let us make | havoc | of them':
  they have burned down ⌣
    all the holy | places·of | God·in the | land.

9 We see no signs * there is not one | prophet | left:
  there is none who knows ⌣
    how | long these | things shall | be.

10 How long shall the adversary | taunt you·O | God:
  shall the enemy blas|pheme your | name for | ever?

†11 Why do you hold | back your | hand:
  why do you keep your | right hand | in your | bosom?

  Prayer: for Christian unity.

  (2) *Lord our God, remember the covenant that you have made with us.*

12 [Yet] God is my | king·from of | old:
  who wrought de|liverance·up|on the | earth.

13 You divided the | sea·by your | might:
  you shattered the heads of the | dragons | in the | waters.

14 You crushed the | heads·of Le|viathan:
  and gave him as food ⌣
    to the | creatures·of the | desert | waste.

15 You cleft open | spring and | fountain:
  you dried up the | ever|flowing | waters.

16 The day is yours * and so also | is the | night:
  you have es|tablished·the | moon·and the | sun.

17 You set all the boundaries | of the | earth:
  you cre|ated | winter·and | summer.

18 Remember O Lord the | taunts · of the | enemy:
how a mindless | people · have blas|phemed your | name.

19 Do not give to the wild beasts the | soul that | praises you:
do not forget for ever the | life of | your af|flicted.

20 Look on all that | you have | made:
for it is full of darkness ⏜
　　and | violence · in|habits · the | earth.

21 Let not the oppressed and reviled turn a|way re|jected:
but let the poor and | needy | praise your | name.

22 Arise O God * plead your | own | cause:
remember how a mindless people |
　　taunt you | all day | long.

23 Do not forget the | clamour · of your | adversaries:
or how the shouting of your | enemies · as|cends con|tinually

Prayer: for Christians in difficulties.

75　*God has cast down the mighty from their thrones.*

1 We give you thanks O God we | give you | thanks:
we call upon your name
　　and tell of all the | wonders | you have | done.

2 'I will surely ap|point a | time:
when I the | Lord will | judge with | equity.

3 'Though the earth shake and | all who | dwell in it:
it is | I · that have | founded · its | pillars.

4 'I will say to the boasters | "Boast no | more":
and to the wicked | "Do not | flaunt your | horns;

†5 ' "Do not flaunt your | horns so | high:
or speak so | proud and | stiff-|necked".'

6 For there is none from the east or | from the | west:
or from the wilderness | who can | raise | up;

7 But it is God who | is the | judge:
who puts down | one · and ex|alts an|other.

8 For there is a cup in the | Lord's | hand:
and the wine | foams · and is | richly | mixed;

9   He gives it in turn⏝
      to each of the | wicked · of the | earth:
  they drink it and | drain it | to the | dregs.

10 But I will sing praises to the | God of | Jacob:
    I will | glorify · his | name for | ever.

11 All the horns of the | wicked · I will | break:
    but the horns of the | righteous · shall be | lifted | high.

Prayer: for humility.

76   *We shall see the Son of man coming on the clouds of heaven.*

1   In Judah | God is | known:
    his | name is | great in | Israel.

2   At Salem | is his | tabernacle:
    and his | dwelling | is in | Zion.

3   There he broke in pieces⏝
      the flashing | arrows · of the | bow:
  the shield the | sword · and the | weapons · of | battle.

4   Radiant in | light are | you:
    greater in majesty | than · the e|ternal | hills.

5   The valiant were dumbfounded   they | sleep their | sleep:
    and all the men of | war have | lost their | strength.

6   At the blast of your voice O | God of | Jacob:
    both horse and | chariot · were | cast a|sleep.

7   Terrible are | you Lord | God:
    and who may stand be|fore you · when | you are | angry?

8   You caused your sentence to be | heard from | heaven:
    the earth | feared | and was | still,

9   When God a|rose to | judgement:
    to | save · all the | meek · of the | earth.

10 For you crushed the | wrath of | man:
    you bridled the | remnant | of the | wrathful.

11 O make vows to the Lord your | God and | keep them:
    let all around him bring gifts
      to him that is | worthy | to be | feared.

12 For he cuts down the | fury · of | princes:
    and he is terrible to the | kings | of the | earth.

Prayer: that God's will may be done on earth as it is in heaven.

77 (1) *In the day of my distress I seek the Lord.*

1 I call to my God   I cry | out to|ward him:
   I call to my God   and | surely | he will | answer.

2 In the day of my distress I seek the Lord
       I stretch out my hands to | him by | night:
   my soul is poured out without ceasing
       it re|fuses | all | comfort.

3 I think upon God and | groan a|loud:
   I | muse · and my | spirit | faints.

4 You hold my | eyelids | open:
   I am so | dazed · that I | cannot | flee.

5 I consider the | times · that are | past:
   I remember the | years of | long a|go.

6 At night I am | grieved · to the | heart:
   I ponder | and my | spirit · makes | search;

7 'Will the Lord cast us | off for | ever:
   will he | show us · his | favour · no | more?

8 'Is his mercy clean | gone for | ever:
   and his promise come to an | end for | all · gener|ations?

9 'Has God for|gotten · to be | gracious:
   has he shut up his | pity | in dis|pleasure?'

10 And I say * 'Has the right hand of the Most High |
        lost its | strength:
    has the | arm · of the | Lord | changed?'

Prayer: for those who feel themselves abandoned by God.

(2) *Who is so great a god as our God?*

11 I will declare the mighty | acts · of the | Lord:
    I will call to | mind your | wonders · of | old.

12 I will think on all that | you have | done:
    and | meditate · up|on your | works.

13 Your way O | God is | holy:
    who is so | great a | god as | our God?

14 You are the God that | works | wonders:
    you made known your | power a|mong the | nations;

15 By your mighty arm you re|deemed your | people:
the | children · of | Jacob · and | Joseph.

16 The waters saw you O God
the waters saw you and | were a|fraid:
the | depths | also · were | troubled.

17 The clouds poured out water   the | heavens | spoke:
and your | arrows | darted | forth.

18 The voice of your thunder was | heard · ‿
in the | whirlwind:
your lightnings lit the world
the | earth | shuddered · and | quaked.

19 Your way was in the sea
your path in the | great | waters:
and your | footsteps | were not | seen.

20 You led your | people · like | sheep:
by the | hand of | Moses · and | Aaron.

Prayer: for those in great need.

78 (1)   *Our fathers have told us the glorious deeds of the Lord.*

1 Give heed to my teaching | O my | people:
incline your | ears · to the | words of · my | mouth;

2 For I will open my | mouth · in a | parable:
and expound the | mysteries · of | former | times.

3 What we have | heard and | known:
what | our fore|fathers · have | told us,

4 We will not hide from their children ‿
but declare to a generation | yet to | come:
the praiseworthy acts of the Lord
his | mighty · and | wonder·ful | works.

5 He established a law in Jacob
and made a de|cree in | Israel:
which he commanded our fore|fathers · ‿
to | teach their | children,

6 That future generations might know
and the children | yet un|born:
that they in turn might | teach it | to their | sons;

401

7 So that they might put their | confidence · in | God:
    and not forget his | works but | keep · his com|mandments,
8 And not be as their forefathers
        a stubborn and re|bellious · gener|ation:
    a generation that did not set their heart aright
        whose spirit | was not | faithful · to | God.

9 The children of Ephraim | armed · with the | bow:
    turned | back · in the | day of | battle.
10 They did not keep God's covenant
        they refused to | walk in · his | law:
    they forgot what he had done
        and the | wonders | he had | shown them.
11 For he did marvellous things‿
        in the | sight of · their | fathers:
    in the land of Egypt | in the | country · of | Zoan.
12 He divided the sea and | let them · pass | through:
    he made the | waters · stand | up · in a | heap.
13 In the daytime | he led them · with a | cloud:
    and all night | long · with the | light of | fire.
14 He cleft | rocks · in the | wilderness:
    and gave them drink in abundance|‿
        as from | springs of | water.
†15 He brought streams | out of · the | rock:
    and caused the waters to | flow | down like | rivers.

Prayer: for the covenant people, the Jews.

(2)   *God's people drank from the spiritual rock, and the rock was Christ.*

16 [But] for all this they sinned yet | more a|gainst him:
    and rebelled against the Most | High | in the | desert.
17 They wilfully put | God · to the | test:
    and de|manded | food · for their | appetite.
18 They spoke against | God and | said:
    'Can God prepare a | table | in the | wilderness?

19 'He indeed struck the rock
    so that the waters gushed ‿
    and the | streams · over|flowed:
but can he also give bread
    or provide | meat | for his | people?'

20 When the Lord heard it he was angry
    and a fire was kindled a|gainst | Jacob:
his wrath | blazed a|gainst | Israel.

21 For they put no | trust in | God:
nor would they be|lieve his | power to | save.

†22 Then he commanded the | clouds a|bove:
and | opened · the | doors of | heaven.

23 He rained down manna for | them to | eat:
and | gave them · the | grain of | heaven.

24 So men ate the | bread of | angels:
and he | sent them | food · in a|bundance.

25 He stirred up the south east | wind · in the | heavens:
and | guided · it | by his | power.

26 He rained down meat upon them | thick as | dust:
and winged | birds · like the | sands · of the | sea.

27 He made them fall into the | midst of · their | camp:
and | all a|bout their | tents.

28 So they ate and were | well | filled:
for he had | given · them | what · they de|sired.

29 But before they had | satisfied · their | craving:
while the | food was | still in · their | mouths,

30 The anger of God | blazed · up a|gainst them:
and he slew their strongest men
    and laid | low the | youth of | Israel.

Prayer: for communicants.

(3)   *Help us to remember that God is our Saviour and our Redeemer.*

31 [But] for all this they | sinned yet | more:
and | put no | faith · in his | wonders.

403

32 So he ended their | days · like a | breath:
and their | years with | sudden | terror.

33 When he struck them down | then they | sought him:
they turned and | sought | eagerly · for | God.

34 They remembered that | God · was their | rock:
that God Most | High was | their re|deemer.

35 But they lied to him | with their | mouths:
and dis|sembled | with their | tongues;

36 For their hearts were not | fixed up|on him:
nor | were they | true to · his | covenant.

37 Yet he being merciful
    forgave their iniquity and did | not de|stroy them:
many times he turned his anger aside
    and would not | wholly · a|rouse his | fury.

38 He remembered that they | were but | flesh:
like a wind that passes | and does | not re|turn.

Prayer: that God's people may learn from their mistakes.

(4)   *The Lord brought his people to his holy land.*

39 How often they rebelled against him | in the | wilderness:
and | grieved him | in the | desert!

40 Again and again they put | God · to the | test:
and provoked the | Holy | One of | Israel.

41 They did not re|member · his | power:
or the day when he re|deemed them | from the | enemy;

42 How he wrought his | signs in | Egypt:
his | wonders · in the | country · of | Zoan.

43 For he turned their | rivers · into | blood:
so that they | could not | drink · from the | streams.

44 He sent swarms of | flies · that de|voured them:
and | frogs that | laid them | waste.

45 He gave their | crops · to the | locust:
and the fruits of their | labour | to the | grasshopper.

46 He struck down their | vines with | hailstones:
and their | syco·more | trees with | frost.

404

47 He gave up their | cattle · to the | hail:
and their | flocks · to the | flash · of the | lightning.

48 He loosed on them the fierceness of his anger
his fury his indignation | and dis|tress:
and these were his | messen·gers | of de|struction.

49 He opened a | path · for his | fury:
he would not spare them from death
but gave | up their | lives · to the | pestilence.

50 He struck down the | firstborn · of | Egypt:
the first-fruits of their manhood | ⌣
in the | dwellings · of | Ham.

51 As for his own people   he led them | out like | sheep:
and guided them in the | wilder·ness | like a | flock.

52 He led them in safety   and they were | not a|fraid:
but the | sea | covered · their | enemies.

53 He brought them to his | holy | land:
to the mountains that his | own right | hand had | won.

54 He drove out the nations before them
and apportioned their lands | as a · pos|session:
and settled the tribes of | Israel | in their | tents.

Thanksgiving: for our salvation.

(5)   *The Lord chose David his servant to be the shepherd of his people.*

55 [But] they rebelled against God Most High ⌣
and | put him · to the | test:
they would | not o|bey · his com|mandments.

56 They turned back and dealt treacherously| ⌣
like their | fathers:
they turned aside | slack · as an | unstrung | bow.

57 They provoked him to anger with their | heathen | shrines:
and moved him to jealousy | with their | carved | images.

58 God heard and was angry * he utterly re|jected | Israel:
he forsook the tabernacle at Shiloh
the | tent · where he | dwelt a·mong | men.

59 He gave the ark of his might | into · cap|tivity:
and his glory | into · the | hands · of the | enemy.

60 He delivered his | people · to the | sword:
and was enraged a|gainst his | own pos|session.

61 Fire de|voured the · young | men:
there was | no one · to be|wail the | maidens;

62 Their priests | fell · by the | sword:
and there was | none to | mourn · for the | widows.

63 Then the Lord awoke like a | man · out of | sleep:
like a warrior that had been | over|come with | wine.

64 He struck the backs of his enemies | as they | fled:
and | put them · to per|petu·al | shame.

65 He rejected the | family · of | Joseph:
he re|fused the | tribe of | Ephraim.

66 But he chose the | tribe of | Judah:
and the hill of | Zion | which he | loved.

67 He built his sanctuary like the | heights of | heaven:
like the earth which | he had | founded · for | ever.

68 He chose | David · his | servant:
and | took him | from the | sheepfolds;

69 He brought him from | following · the | ewes:
to be the shepherd of his people Jacob
and of | Israel · his | own pos|session.

70 So he tended them with | upright | heart:
and | guided them · with | skilful | hand.

Prayer: that God's will may be done.

79 *Lord, teach us the things that make for our peace.*

1 O God the heathen have | come in·to your | land:
they have defiled your holy temple
they have made Je|rusalem · a | heap of | stones.

2 They have given the dead bodies of your servants⌣
as food to the | birds · of the | air:
and the flesh of your faithful ones⌣
to the wild | beasts | of the | earth.

3 Their blood they have spilt like water ⌣
    on every | side · of Je|rusalem:
and | there is | none to | bury them.

4 We have become a mockery | to our | neighbours:
the scorn and | laughing-stock · of | those a|bout us.

5 How long O Lord shall your anger be | so ex|treme:
will your jealous | fury | burn like | fire?

6 Pour out your wrath on the nations ⌣
    that | do not | know you:
on the kingdoms that have not | called up|on your | name.

7 For they have de|voured | Jacob:
and made his | dwelling-place · a | deso|lation.

8 Do not remember against us the sin of | former | times:
but let your compassion hasten to meet us
    for we are | brought | very | low.

†9 Help us O God our saviour ⌣
    for the | honour · of your | name:
O deliver us and expiate our | sins · ⌣
    for your | name's | sake.

10 Why should the heathen say | 'Where is · their | God?':
O let vengeance for the blood of your servants that is ⌣
    shed
be shown upon the | nations | in our | sight.

11 Let the sorrowful sighing of the prisoners |
    come be|fore you:
and as your power is great
reprieve | those con|demned to | die.

12 For the taunts with which our neighbours ⌣
    have taunted | you O | Lord:
repay them seven times | over | into · their | bosoms.

13 So we that are your people and the sheep of your pasture
    shall give you | thanks for | ever:
we will declare your praise in | every | gener|ation.

Prayer: for greater faithfulness in the church.

407

80   *Look down from heaven, Lord, bestow your care upon this vine.*

1 Hear O Shepherd of Israel
      you that led | Joseph · like a | flock:
   you that are enthroned upon the cherubim | ‿
      shine | out in | glory;

2 Before Ephraim Benjamin | and Man|asseh:
   stir up your | power and | come to | save us.

†3 *Restore us again O | Lord of | hosts:*
   show us the light of your countenance | ‿
         and we | shall be | saved.

4 O Lord | God of | hosts:
   how long will you be | angry · at your | people's | prayer?

5 You have fed them with the | bread of | tears:
   and given them tears to | drink in | good | measure.

6 You have made us the victim | of our | neighbours:
   and our | ene·mies | laugh us·to | scorn.

7 *Restore us again O | Lord of | hosts:*
   show us the light of your countenance | ‿
         and we | shall be | saved.

8 You brought a | vine·out of | Egypt:
   you drove out the | nations·and | planted·it | in.

9 You cleared the | ground be|fore it:
   and it struck | root and | filled the | land.

10 The hills were | covered·with its | shadow:
   and its boughs were like the | boughs· ‿
         of the | great | cedars.

11 It stretched out its | branches·to the | sea:
   and its tender | shoots·to the | Great | River.

12 Why then have you broken | down its | walls:
   so that every passer-|by can | pluck its | fruit?

13 The wild boar out of the woods | roots it | up:
   and the locusts from the | wild | places·de|vour it.

14 Turn to us again O | Lord of | hosts:
   look | down from | heaven·and | see.

15 Bestow your care up|on this | vine:
   the stock which your | own right | hand has | planted.

16 As for those that burn it with fire and | cut it | down:
   let them perish at the re|buke | of your | countenance.

17 Let your power rest on the man at your | right | hand:
   on that son of man ⌣
      whom you | made so | strong · for your|self.

18 And so we shall | not turn | back from you:
   give us life   and we will | call up|on your | name.

19 *Restore us again O | Lord of | hosts:*
   show us the light of your countenance | ⌣
      and we | shall be | saved.

   Prayer: for Christian unity.

81   *O that today we might hear God's voice.*

1 O sing joyfully to | God our | strength:
   shout in | triumph · to the | God of | Jacob.

2 Make music and | beat up·on the | drum:
   sound the | lute and · the mel|odi·ous | harp.

3 Blow the ram's horn at the | new | moon:
   and at the full moon | of our | day of | festival.

4 For this was a | statute · for | Israel:
   a com|mandment · of the | God of | Jacob,

†5 Which he laid on Joseph as a | solemn | charge:
   when he came | out of · the | land of | Egypt.

6 I heard a voice that I had not | known | saying:
   'I eased your shoulders of the burden
      and your | hands were | freed · from the | load.

7 'You called to me in trouble | and I | rescued you:
   I answered you from the secret place of my thunder
      I put you to the | test · at the | waters · of | Meribah.

8 'Listen my people and | I · will ad|monish you:
   O Israel if | only | you would | hear me.

9 'There shall be no strange | god a|mong you:
   nor shall you bow | down · to an | ali·en | god.

†10 'I am the Lord your God
      who brought you up from the | land of | Egypt:
   open wide your | mouth and | I will | fill it.

409

11 'But my people would not | listen · to my | voice:
and | Israel | would have | none of me.

12 'So I left them to the stubbornness | of their | hearts:
to walk ac|cording · to their | own de|signs.

13 'If only my | people · would | listen:
if Israel | would but | walk in · my | ways,

14 'I would soon put | down their | enemies:
and turn my | hand a|gainst their | adversaries.

15 'Those that hate the Lord would | cringe be|fore him:
and their | punishment · would | last for | ever.

16 'But Israel I would feed with the | finest | wheat:
and satisfy you with | honey | from the | rocks.'

Prayer: that we might heed God's voice in times of prosperity.

82 *The Lord our God is judge over all.*

1 God has stood up in the | council · of | heaven:
in the midst of the | gods | he gives | judgement.

2 'How long will you | judge un|justly:
and | favour · the | cause · of the | wicked?

3 'Judge for the | poor and | fatherless:
vindicate the af|flicted | and op|pressed.

4 'Rescue the | poor and | needy:
and | save them · from the | hands · of the | wicked.

5 'They do not know   they do not understand
they walk a|bout in | darkness:
all the found|ations · of the | earth are | shaken.

6 'Therefore I say | "Though · you are | gods:
and all of you | sons · of the | Most | High,

7 ' "Nevertheless you shall | die like | man:
and | fall like | one of · the | princes" '.

8 Arise O God and | judge the | earth:
for you shall take all | nations · as | your pos|session.

Prayer: for those who exercise great power.

410

83   *While we were yet sinners, Christ died for us.*

1 Hold not your | peace O | God:
O God be not | silent | or un|moved.

2 See how your | enemies · make | uproar:
how those that hate you have | lifted | up their | heads.

3 For they lay shrewd plots a|gainst your | people:
they scheme against | those whom | you have | cherished.

4 'Come' they say 'let us destroy them
    that they may no | longer · be a | nation:
that the very name of Israel ⏝
    may | be re|membered · no | more.'

5 With one mind they con|spire to|gether:
they | make al|liance · a|gainst you,

6 The tribes of Edom | and the | Ishmaelites:
the people of | Moab | and the | Hagarites,

7 Gebal and | Ammon · and | Amalek:
Philistia | and · the in|habitants · of | Tyre;

8 Asshur | also · is | joined with them:
and lends a friendly | arm · to the | children · of | Lot.

9 Do to them as you | did to | Midian:
as to Sisera and Jabin | at the | river · of | Kishon,

10 Who were de|stroyed at | Endor:
and be|came like | dung · for the | earth.

11 Make their leaders as | Oreb · and | Zeeb:
and all their princes like | Zebah | and Zal|munna,

12 Who said 'Let us | take pos|session:
let us | seize the | pastures · of | God.'

13 Make them like | thistledown · my | God:
or like chaff | blown be|fore the | wind.

14 As fire con|suming · a | thicket:
or as flame that | sets the | hillsides · a|blaze,

15 Pursue them | with your | tempest:
and | terrify · them | with your | storm-wind.

16 Cover their faces with | shame O | Lord:
that | they may | seek your | name.

17 Let them be disgraced and dis|mayed for | ever:
let them | be con|founded · and | perish,

411

18 That they may know that you ⌣
    whose | name · is the | Lord:
are alone the Most | High · over | all the | earth.

Prayer: for our country; and for freedom from all opposed to God's will.

84   *How I long to enter the·courts of the Lord.*

1 How lovely | is your | dwelling-place:
    O | Lord | God of | hosts!
2 My soul has a desire and longing ⌣
    to enter the | courts · of the | Lord:
my heart and my flesh re|joice · in the | living | God.
3 The sparrow has found her a home
    and the swallow a nest ⌣
    where she may | lay her | young:
even your altar   O Lord of | hosts ⌣
    my | King · and my | God.
4 Blessèd are those who | dwell in · your | house:
    they will | always · be | praising | you.
5 Blessèd is the man whose | strength · is in | you:
    in whose | heart · are the | highways · to | Zion;
6 Who going through the valley of dryness
    finds there a spring from | which to | drink:
till the autumn | rain shall | clothe it · with | blessings.
†7 They go from | strength to | strength:
    they appear every one of them ⌣
    before the | God of | gods in | Zion.

8 O Lord God of hosts | hear my | prayer:
    give | ear O | God of | Jacob.
9 Behold O God | him who · reigns | over us:
    and look upon the | face of | your a|nointed.
10 One day in your courts is | better · than a | thousand:
    I would rather stand at the threshold of the house of my ⌣
        God
    than | dwell · in the | tents of · un|godliness.

11 For the Lord God is a rampart and a shield
    the Lord gives | favour · and | honour:
  and no good thing will he withhold ⌣
    from | those who | walk in | innocence.

†12 O Lord | God of | hosts:
  blessèd is the man who | puts his | trust in | you.

Prayer: for the pilgrim people of God.

85   *Show us your mercy O Lord, and grant us your salvation.*

1 O Lord you were gracious | to your | land:
  you re|stored the | fortunes · of | Jacob.

2 You forgave the iniquity | of your | people:
  and | covered | all their | sin.

3 You put aside | all your | wrath:
  and turned away from your | fierce | indig|nation.

4 Return to us again O | God our | saviour:
  and | let your | anger | cease from us.

5 Will you be displeased with | us for | ever:
  will you stretch out your wrath
    from one gene|ration | to an|other?

6 Will you not give us | life a|gain:
  that your | people | may re|joice in you?

†7 Show us your | mercy · O | Lord:
  and | grant us | your sal|vation.

8 I will hear what the Lord | God will | speak:
  for he will speak peace to his people
    to his faithful ones whose | hearts are | turned to | him.

9 Truly his salvation is near to | those that | fear him:
  and his | glory · shall | dwell · in our | land.

10 Mercy and truth are | met to|gether:
  righteousness and | peace have | kissed each | other;

11 Truth shall flourish | out of · the | earth:
  and righteousness | shall look | down from | heaven.

12 The Lord will also give us | all · that is | good:
  and our | land shall | yield its | plenty.

13 For righteousness shall | go be|fore him:
and tread the | path be|fore his | feet.

Prayer: for people at war.

86 *In the day of my trouble I call upon you, for you will surely answer.*

1 Incline your ear to me O | God and | answer me:
for | I am | poor · and in | misery.
2 Preserve my life for | I am | faithful:
my God save your servant who | puts his | trust in | you.
3 Be merciful to | me O | Lord:
for I | call to · you | all the · day | long.
4 O make glad the | soul of · your | servant:
for I put my | hope in | you O | Lord.
5 For you Lord are | good · and for|giving:
of great and continuing kindness ‿
    to | all who | call up|on you.
6 Hear my | prayer O | Lord:
and give heed to the | voice · of my | suppli|cation.
†7 In the day of my trouble I | call up|on you:
for | you will | surely | answer.

8 Among the gods there is none like | you O | Lord:
nor are there | any | deeds like | yours.
9 All the nations you have made ‿
    shall come and | worship · be|fore you:
O Lord they shall | glori|fy your | name.
10 For you are great and do | marvel·lous | things:
and | you a|lone are | God.
11 Show me your way O Lord
    and I will | walk in · your | truth:
let my heart de|light to | fear your | name.
12 I will praise you O Lord my God with | all my | heart:
and I will | glorify · your | name for | ever.
13 For great is your abiding | love to|ward me:
and you have delivered my life ‿
    from the | lowest | depths · of the | grave.

14 Insolent men O God have | risen · a|gainst me:
a band of ruthless men seek my life
they have not set | God be|fore their | eyes.

15 But you Lord are a God | gracious · and com|passionate:
slow to anger | full of | goodness · and | truth.

16 Turn to me and be merciful
give your | strength · to your | servant:
and | save the | son of · your | handmaid.

17 Show me some token | of your | goodness:
that those who hate me may see it and be ashamed
because you Lord are my | helper | and my | comforter.

Prayer: for the underprivileged.

87   *Glorious things shall be spoken of you, city of our God.*

1 He has founded it upon a | holy | hill:
and the Lord loves the gates of Zion
more than | all the | dwellings · of | Jacob.

2 Glorious things shall be | spoken · of | you:
O Zion | city | of our | God.

3 I might speak of my kinsmen in Egypt | or in | Babylon:
in Philistia Tyre or Nubia | where | each was | born.

4 But of Zion it | shall be | said:
many were born in her
he that is Most | High | has es|tablished her.

5 When the Lord draws up the record | of the | nations:
he shall take note where | every | man was | born.

6 And the singers and the | dancers · to|gether:
shall | make their | song · to your | name.

Prayer: that all nations may come to know Christ as Lord.

88   *O Lord my God, I call to you for help.*

1 O Lord my God   I call for | help by | day:
and by night also I | cry | out be|fore you.

415

2 Let my prayer come | into · your | presence:
   and turn your | ear · to my | loud | crying.

†3 For my soul is | filled with | trouble:
   and my life has come | even · to the | brink · of the | grave.

4 I am reckoned among those that go | down · to the | Pit:
   I am a | man that | has no | help.

5 I lie among the dead
      like the slain that | sleep · in the | grave:
   whom you remember no more
      who are cut | off | from your | power.

6 You have laid me in the | lowest | Pit:
   in darkness and | in the | water·y | depths.

7 Your wrath lies | heavy · up|on me:
   and all your | waves are | brought a|gainst me.

8 You have put my | friends far | from me:
   and made me to | be ab|horred | by them.

9 I am so fast in prison I | cannot · get | free:
   my eyes fail be|cause of | my af|fliction.

10 Lord I call to you | every | day:
   I stretch | out my | hands to|ward you.

11 Will you work | wonders · for the | dead:
   or will the shades rise | up a|gain to | praise you?

12 Shall your love be de|clared · in the | grave:
   or your faithfulness | in the | place · of de|struction?

13 Will your wonders be made | known · in the | dark:
   or your righteousness‿
      in the land where | all things | are for|gotten?

14 But to you Lord | will I | cry:
   early in the morning my | prayer shall | come be|fore you.

15 O Lord why have | you re|jected me:
   why do you | hide your | face | from me?

16 I have been afflicted and wearied‿
      from my | youth | upward:
   I am tossed high and | low   I | cease to | be.

17 Your fierce anger has | over|whelmed me:
   and your | terrors · have | put me · to | silence.

18 They surround me like a flood | all the·day | long:
  they close up|on me·from | every | side.
19 Friend and acquaintance you have put | far | from me:
  and kept my com|panions | from my | sight.

  Prayer: for those who feel themselves deserted by God and man.

89 (1)   *Loving kindness and faithfulness attend your presence, Lord.*

1 Lord I will sing for ever of your | loving-|kindnesses:
  my mouth shall proclaim your faithfulness‿
      through|out all | gener|ations.
2 I have said of your loving-kindness‿
      that it is | built for | ever:
  you have established your | faithful·ness | in the | heavens.
3 The Lord said
      'I have made a covenant | with my | chosen:
  I have sworn an | oath·to my | servant | David.
4 'I will establish your | line for | ever:
  and build up your | throne for | all·gener|ations.'

5 Let the heavens praise your | wonders·O | Lord:
  and let your faithfulness be sung‿
      in the as|sembly | of the | holy ones.
6 For who amidst the clouds can be com|pared·‿
      to the | Lord:
  or who is like the Lord a|mong the | sons of | heaven?
7 A God to be feared in the council | of the | holy ones:
  great and terrible above | all that | are a|round him.
8 O Lord God of hosts | who is | like you?:
  your power and your | faithfulness·are | all a|bout you.
9 You rule the | raging·of the | sea:
  when its | waves | surge you | still them.
10 You crushed Rahab | like a | carcase:
  you scattered your enemies | by your | mighty | arm.
11 The heavens are yours * so also | is the | earth:
  you founded the | world and | all·that is | in it.

417

12 You created the | north · and the | south:
. Tabor and Mount | Hermon · shall | sing of · your | name.
13 Mighty | is your | arm:
   strong is your hand
      and your right | hand is | lifted | high.
14 Righteousness and justice‿
      are the foundation | of your | throne:
. loving-kindness and | faithfulness · at|tend your | presenc
15 Happy the people who know the tri|umphal | shout:
   who walk O | Lord · in the | light of · your | countenance.
16 They rejoice all the day long be|cause of · your | name:
   because of your | righteousness · they | are ex|alted.
17 For you are their glory | and their | strength:
   and our heads are up|lifted | by your | favour.
18 Our king be|longs · to the | Lord:
   he that rules over us to the | Holy | One of | Israel.

   Prayer: for confidence in the promises of God.

   (2)   *From the line of David God has given us a Saviour.*

19 You spoke | once · in a | vision:
   and | said | to your | faithful one,
20 'I have set a youth a|bove a | warrior:
   I have exalted a | young man | out of · the | people.
21 'I have found my | servant | David:
   and anointed him | with my | holy | oil.
22 'My hand | shall up|hold him:
   and my | arm | shall | strengthen him.
23 'No enemy | shall de|ceive him:
   no | evil | man shall | hurt him.
24 'I will crush his | adversaries · be|fore him:
   and | strike down | those that | hate him.
25 'My faithfulness and loving-kindness | shall be | with hi▸
   and through my name his | head · shall be | lifted | high.
26 'I will set the hand of his dominion‿
      upon the | Western | Sea:

418

and his right hand shall stretch⏝
   to the | streams of | Meso·po|tamia.

27 'He will call to me |"You·are my Father:
my God and the | Rock of | my sal|vation."

28 'I will make him my | first-born | son:
and highest a|mong the | kings·of the | earth.

29 'I will ever maintain my loving | kindness·to|ward him:
and my covenant | with him·shall | stand | firm.

30 'I will establish his | line for | ever:
and his | throne·like the | days of | heaven.

31 'If his children for|sake my | law:
and | will not | walk in·my | judgements;

32 'If they pro|fane my | statutes:
and | do not | keep·my com|mandments,

33 'Then I will punish their re|bellion·with the | rod:
and | their in|iquity·with | blows.

34 'But I will not cause my loving-|kindness· ⏝
   to | cease from him:
nor will | I be|tray my | faithfulness.

35 'I will not pro|fane my | covenant:
or alter | what has | passed from·my | lips.

36 'Once and for all I have | sworn·by my | holiness:
I will | not prove | false to | David.

37 'His posterity shall en|dure for | ever:
and his throne be | as the | sun be|fore me;

38 'Like the moon that is es|tablished·for | ever:
and stands in the | heavens·for | ever|more.'

Prayer: for all who work to spread the reign of Christ in inland Australia.

  (3)   *How long, O Lord? Raise up your power and come among us.*

39 [Yet] you have been enraged a|gainst·your an|ointed:
you have ab|horred him | and re|jected him.

40 You have spurned the covenant | with your | servant:
and de|filed his | crown·to the | dust.

41 You have broken down | all his | walls:
and | made his | strongholds | desolate.

42 All that pass | by | plunder him:
he has be|come the | scorn of · his | neighbours.

43 You have exalted the right hand | of his | adversaries:
and | gladdened | all his | enemies.

44 His bright sword you have | turned | backward:
you have not en|abled him · to | stand · in the | battle.

45 You have brought his | lustre · to an | end:
you have | cast his | throne · to the | ground.

46 You have cut short the | days of · his | youth:
and | clothed him | with dis|honour.

47 How long O Lord will you hide your|self so | utterly:
how long shall your | fury | burn like | fire?

48 Remember how I draw to my e|ternal | end:
have you created | all man|kind for | nothing?

49 Where is the man who can live and | not see | death:
who can deliver his | life · from the | power · of the | grave?

50 Where O Lord are your loving-|kindnesses · of | old:
which you have vowed to | David | in your | faithfulness?

51 Remember O Lord how your servant | is re|viled:
how I bear in my bosom ⏝
the | onslaught | of the | peoples;

52 Remember how your | ene·mies | taunt:
how they mock the | footsteps · of | your an|ointed.

†53 Blessèd be the | Lord for | ever:
A|men and | A—|men.

Prayer: for all who despise the name of Christ.

90 (1) *Teach us so to number our days that we may apply our hearts to wisdom.*

1 Lⁿrd you have | been our | refuge:
from one gener|ation | to an|other.

2 Before the mountains were born
or the earth and the world were | brought to | be:
from eternity to e|terni·ty | you are | God.

3 You turn man | back · into | dust:
saying 'Return to | dust you | sons of | Adam'.

4 For a thousand years in your sight ⌣
    are like | yester·day | passing:
or | like one | watch · of the | night.

5 You cut them | short · like a | dream:
like the fresh | grass | of the | morning;

6 In the morning it is | green and | flourishes:
at evening it is | withered · and | dried | up.

7 And we are con|sumed · by your | anger:
because of your indig|nation · we | cease to | be.

8 You have brought our in|iquities · be|fore you:
and our secret | sins · to the | light of · your | countenance.

9 Our days decline be|neath your | wrath:
and our years | pass a|way · like a | sigh.

10 The days of our life are three score years and ten
    or if we have | strength four | score:
the pride of our labours is but toil and sorrow
    for it passes quickly a|way and | we are | gone.

11 Who can know the | power of · your | wrath:
who can know your indig|nation · like | those that | fear you?

12 Teach us so to | number · our | days:
that we may ap|ply our | hearts to | wisdom.

Prayer: that we may be ready for death.

(2)   *Lord, you have been our refuge from one generation to another.*

13 Relent O Lord * how long will | you be | angry?:
take | pity | on your | servants.

14 O satisfy us early | with your | mercy:
that all our days we | may re|joice and | sing.

15 Give us joy for all the days you | have af|flicted us:
for the | years · we have | suffered · ad|versity.

16 Show your | servants · your | work:
and let their | children | see your | glory.

17 May the gracious favour of the Lord our | God · be up|on us:
prosper the work of our hands
    O | prosper · the | work · of our | hands!

Prayer: for the aged.

91   *The Lord will cover us with his wings: we shall not be afraid.*

1 He who dwells in the shelter of the | Most | High:
    who abides under the | shadow | of the · Al|mighty,

2 He will say to the Lord
      'You are my refuge | and my | stronghold:
    my | God in | whom I | trust.'

3 For he will deliver you from the | snare · of the | hunter:
    and | from the · des|troying | curse.

4 He will cover you with his wings
      and you will be safe | under · his | feathers:
    his faithfulness will | be your | shield · and de|fence.

5 You shall not be afraid of any | terror · by | night:
    or of the | arrow · that | flies by | day,

6 Of the pestilence that walks a|bout in | darkness:
    or the | plague · that des|troys at | noonday.

7 A thousand may fall beside you
      and ten thousand at your | right | hand:
    but | you it | shall not | touch;

8 Your own | eyes shall | see:
    and look on the re|ward | of the · un|godly.

9 The Lord him|self · is your | refuge:
    you have | made the · Most | High your | stronghold.

10 Therefore no | harm · will be|fall you:
    nor will any | scourge come | near your | tent.

11 For he will com|mand his | angels:
    to | keep you · in | all your | ways.

12 They will bear you | up · in their | hands:
    lest you dash your | foot a|gainst a | stone.

13 You will tread on the | lion · and the | adder:
    the young lion and the serpent⌣
      you will | trample | under | foot.

14 'He has set his love upon me
      and therefore I | will de|liver him:
    I will lift him out of danger⌣
      be|cause · he has | known my | name.

15 'When he calls upon me | I will | answer him:
  I will be with him in trouble
    I will | rescue him · and | bring him · to | honour.
16 'With long | life · I will | satisfy him:
  and | fill him · with | my sal|vation.'

Prayer: for all in danger.

92 *In all you have done, O Lord, you have made me glad.*

1 How good to give | thanks · to the | Lord:
  to sing praises to your | name | O Most | High,
2 To declare your | love · in the | morning:
  and at | night to | sing of · your | faithfulness,
†3 Upon the lute   upon the lute of | ten | strings:
  and to the | melo·dy | of the | lyre.
4 For in all you have done O Lord ‿
    you have | made me | glad:
  I will sing for joy be|cause of · the | works · of your | hands.
5 Lord how glorious | are your | works:
  your | thoughts are | very | deep.
6 The brutish do | not con|sider:
  and the | fool · cannot | under|stand
7 That though the wicked | sprout like | grass:
  and | all wrong|doers | flourish,
8 They flourish to be de|stroyed · for | ever:
  but you Lord are ex|alted · for | ever|more.
9 For behold   your enemies O Lord ‿
    your | enemies · shall | perish:
  and all the workers of | wicked·ness | shall be | scattered.
10 You have lifted up my head
    like the horns of the | wild | oxen:
  I am an|ointed · with | fresh | oil;
11 My eyes have looked | down · on my | enemies:
  and my ears have heard the ruin ‿
    of | those who · rose | up a|gainst me.
12 The righteous shall | flourish · like the | palm tree:
  they shall spread a|broad · like a | cedar · in | Lebanon;

13 For they are planted in the | house · of the | Lord:
and flourish in the | courts of | our | God.

14 In old age they shall be | full of | sap:
they shall be | sturdy · and | laden · with | branches;

15 And they will say that the | Lord is | just:
the Lord my Rock in | whom is | no un|righteousness.

Praise: to God the creator.

93   *The Lord our God the Almighty reigns.*

1 The Lord is King * and has put on | robes of | glory:
the Lord has put on his glory
he has | girded · him|self with | strength.

2 He has made the | world so | firm:
that it | cannot | be | moved.

3 Your throne is es|tablished · from of | old:
you | are from | ever|lasting.

4 The floods have lifted up O Lord
the floods have lifted | up their | voice:
the | floods lift | up their | pounding.

5 But mightier than the sound of many waters
than the mighty waters or the | breakers · of the | sea:
the | Lord on | high is | mighty.

6 Your decrees are | very | sure:
and holiness O Lord a|dorns your | house for | ever.

Praise: for the exaltation of Christ.

94   (1)   *The Lord vindicates the righteous.*

1 O Lord God to whom | vengeance · be|longs:
O God to whom vengeance be|longs
shine | out in | glory.

2 Arise | judge · of the | earth:
and requite the | proud as | they de|serve.

3 Lord how | long · shall the | wicked:
  how | long · shall the | wicked | triumph?

4 How long shall all evildoers | pour out | words:
  how | long · shall they | boast and | flaunt themselves?

5 They crush your | people · O | Lord:
  they op|press your | own pos|session.

6 They murder the | widow · and the | alien:
  they | put the | fatherless · to | death.

7 And they say 'The | Lord · does not | see:
  nor does the | God of | Jacob · con|sider it.'

8 Consider this   you senseless a|mong the | people:
  fools | when · will you | under|stand?

9 He who planted the ear   does | he not | hear:
  he who formed the | eye   does | he not | see?

10 He who disciplines the nations will | he not | punish:
   has the | teacher · of man|kind no | knowledge?

†11 The Lord knows the | thoughts of | man:
    he | knows · that they | are mere | breath.

Prayer: for those who suffer for righteousness' sake.

(2)   *The Lord is my stronghold.*

12 Blessèd is the man whom you | discipline · O | Lord:
   and | teach | from your | law,

13 Giving him rest from | days of | misery:
   till a | pit is | dug · for the | wicked.

14 The Lord will not cast | off his | people:
   nor | will he · for|sake his | own.

15 For justice shall return to the | righteous | man:
   and with him to | all the | true of | heart.

16 Who will stand up for me a|gainst the | wicked:
   who will take my part a|gainst the | evil|doers?

17 If the Lord had not | been my | helper:
   I would soon have | dwelt · in the | land of | silence.

18 But when I said 'My | foot has | slipped':
    your | mercy · O | Lord was | holding me.
19 In all the | doubts · of my | heart:
    your conso|lations · de|lighted · my | soul.
20 Will you be any friend to the | court of | wickedness:
    that contrives | evil · by | means of | law?
21 They band together against the | life · of the | righteous:
    and con|demn | inno·cent | blood.
22 But the | Lord · is my | stronghold:
    my | God · is my | rock · and my | refuge.
23 Let him requite them for their wickedness
        and silence them | for their | evil:
    the | Lord our | God shall | silence them.

Prayer: for all who witness to Christ.

95 *Let us come before the Lord with thanksgiving.*

1 O come let us sing | out · to the | Lord:
   let us shout in triumph to the | rock of | our sal|vation.
2 Let us come before his | face with | thanksgiving:
   and cry | out to · him | joyfully · in | psalms.
3 For the Lord is a | great | God:
   and a great | king a·bove | all | gods.
4 In his hand are the | depths · of the | earth:
   and the peaks of the | mountains · are | his | also.
†5 The sea is his and | he | made it:
   his hands | moulded | dry | land.
6 Come let us worship and | bow | down:
   and kneel be|fore the | Lord our | maker.
7 For he is the | Lord our | God:
   we are his | people · and the | sheep of · his | pasture.
8 Today if only you would hear his voice
       'Do not harden your | hearts · as at | Meribah:
   as on that day at | Massah | in the | wilderness;

9 'When your | fathers | tested me:
  put me to proof though | they had | seen my | works.
10 'Forty years long I loathed that gener|ation · and | said:
  "It is a people who err in their hearts
    for they | do not | know my | ways";
11 'Of whom I | swore · in my | wrath:
  "They | shall not | enter · my | rest." '

Prayer: that our worship may be acceptable to God.

96 *Heaven and earth are full of his glory.*

1 O sing to the Lord a | new | song:
  sing to the | Lord | all the | earth.
2 Sing to the Lord and bless his | holy | name:
  proclaim the good news of his sal|vation ·
    from | day to | day.
3 Declare his glory a|mong the | nations:
  and his | wonders · a|mong all | peoples.
4 For great is the Lord and | greatly · to be | praised:
  he is more to be | feared than | all | gods.
5 As for all the gods of the nations |
    they are · mere | idols:
  it is the | Lord who | made the | heavens.
6 Majesty and | glory · are be|fore him:
  beauty and | power are | in his | sanctuary.
7 Render to the Lord you families | of the | nations:
  render to the | Lord | glory · and | might.
8 Render to the Lord the honour | due · to his | name:
  bring offerings and | come in|to his | courts.
9 O worship the Lord in the beauty | of his | holiness:
  let the whole earth | stand in | awe of | him.
10 Say among the nations that the | Lord is | king:
  he has made the world so firm that it can never be
    moved
      and he shall | judge the | peoples · with | equity.

427

11 Let the heavens rejoice   and let the | earth be | glad:
    let the sea | roar and | all that | fills it;

12 Let the fields rejoice and | every·thing | in them:
    then shall all the trees of the wood⌣
       shout with | joy be|fore the | Lord;

†13 For he comes   he comes to | judge the | earth:
    he shall judge the world with righteousness
       and the | peoples | with his | truth.

Prayer: for the conversion of the nations.

97   *Light dawns for the righteous, and joy for the true of heart.*

1 The Lord is king   let the | earth re|joice:
    let the | multitude·of | islands·be | glad.

2 Clouds and darkness are | round a|bout him:
    righteousness and justice⌣
       are the found|ation | of his | throne.

3 Fire | goes be|fore him:
    and burns up his | enemies·on | every | side.

4 His lightnings | light the | world:
    the | earth | sees it·and | quakes.

5 The mountains melt like wax be|fore his | face:
    from before the face of the | Lord of | all the | earth.

6 The heavens have pro|claimed his | righteousness:
    and all | peoples·have | seen his | glory.

7 They are ashamed
       all those who serve idols⌣
       and glory in | mere | nothings:
    all | gods bow | down be|fore him.

8 Zion heard and was glad * and the daughters of | Judah
    ·re|joiced:
    be|cause of·your | judgements·O | God.

9 For you Lord are most high over | all the | earth:
    you are exalted | far a·bove | all | gods.

10 The Lord loves | those that·hate | evil:
    the Lord guards the life of the faithful
       and delivers them from the | hand of | the un|godly.

11 Light | dawns · for the | righteous:
  and | joy · for the | true of | heart.
12 Rejoice in the | Lord you | righteous:
  and give | thanks · to his | holy | name.

  Prayer: for non-Christians.

  98 *All the ends of the earth have seen the salvation of our God.*

1 O sing to the Lord a | new | song:
  for he has | done | marvel·lous | things;
2 His right hand and his | holy | arm:
  they have | got | him the | victory.
3 The Lord has made | known · his sal|vation:
  he has revealed his just de|liverance · ⌣
    in the | sight of · the | nations.
4 He has remembered his mercy and faithfulness ⌣
    towards the | house of | Israel:
  and all the ends of the earth ⌣
    have seen the sal|vation | of our | God.
5 Shout with joy to the Lord | all the | earth:
  break into | singing · and | make | melody.
6 Make melody to the Lord up|on the | harp:
  upon the harp and | with the | sounds of | praise.
7 With trumpets | and with | horns:
  cry out in triumph be|fore the | Lord the | king.
8 Let the sea roar and | all that | fills it:
  the good earth and | those who | live up|on it.
9 Let the rivers | clap their | hands:
  and let the mountains ring out to|gether · be|fore the |
    Lord;
10 For he comes to | judge the | earth:
  he shall judge the world with righteousness
    and the | peoples | with | equity.

  Praise: for the hope of Christ's coming in glory.

99   *The Lord our God is holy!*

1 The Lord is king   let the | nations | tremble:
  he is enthroned upon the cherubim |
      let the | earth | quake.
2 The Lord is | great in | Zion:
  he is | high a|bove all | nations.
3 Let them praise your great and | terri·ble | name:
  for | holy | is the | Lord.
4 The Mighty One is king and | loves | justice:
  you have established equity
      you have dealt | righteousness· and | justice·in | Jacob.
†5 *O exalt the | Lord our | God:*
  and bow down before his | footstool·for | he is | holy.
6 Moses and Aaron among his priests
      and Samuel among those who call up|on his | name:
  they called to the | Lord | and he | answered.
7 He spoke to them from the | pillar·of | cloud:
  they kept to his teachings |
      and the | law·that he | gave them.
8 You answered them O | Lord our | God:
  you were a forgiving God to them
      and | pardoned·their | wrong|doing.
9 *O exalt the | Lord our | God:*
  and bow down towards his holy hill
      for the | Lord our | God is | holy.

  Prayer: for those who lead us in praise of God.

100   *Let us come into his presence with thanksgiving.*

1 O shout to the Lord in triumph | all the | earth:
  serve the Lord with gladness
      and come before his | face with | songs of | joy.
2 Know that the Lord | he is | God:
  it is he who has made us and we are his
      we are his | people·and the | sheep of·his | pasture.

3 Come into his gates with thanksgiving,
   and into his | courts with | praise:
   give thanks to him and | bless his | holy | name.
4 For the Lord is good * his loving mercy | is for | ever:
   his faithfulness through|out all | gener|ations.

   Praise: for the privilege of prayer.

101   *God shall judge the world with righteousness*
      and the peoples with his truth.

1 My song shall be of | steadfastness · and | justice:
   to | you Lord | will I | sing.
2 I will be wise in the | way of | innocence:
   O | when | will you | come to me?
3 I will walk with|in my | house:
   in | puri|ty of | heart.
4 I will set nothing evil be|fore my | eyes:
   I hate the sin of backsliders
      it shall | get no | hold | on me.
†5 Crookedness of heart shall de|part | from me:
   I will | know | nothing · of | wickedness.
6 The man who secretly slanders his neighbour⌣
      I | will de|stroy:
   the proud look and the arrogant | heart ·⌣
      I will | not en|dure.
7 My eyes shall look to the faithful in the land
      and they shall | make their | home with me:
   one who walks in the way of innocence|⌣
      he shall | minis·ter | to me.
8 No man who practises deceit shall | live in · my | house:
   no one who utters | lies shall | stand in · my | sight.
9 Morning by morning I will destroy⌣
      all the | wicked · of the | land:
   and cut off all evildoers from the | city | of the | Lord.

   Prayer: for a deepening of our sense of justice and love.

102 (1) *Lord, let my cry come to you: do not hide your face from me.*

1 O Lord | hear my | prayer:
   and | let my | cry | come to you.

2 Do not hide your face from me⌣
      in the | day of·my | trouble:
   turn your ear to me
      and when I | call be | swift to | answer.

3 For my days pass a|way like | smoke:
   and my bones | burn as | in a | furnace.

4 My heart is scorched and | withered·like | grass:
   and I for|get to | eat my | bread.

5 I am weary with the | sound of·my | groaning:
   my | bones stick | fast to·my | skin.

6 I have become like an | owl·in the | wilderness:
   like a | screech-owl a|mong the | ruins.

7 I keep watch   and | flit·to and | fro:
   like a | sparrow·up|on a | housetop.

8 My enemies taunt me | all day | long:
   and those who | rave at me·make | oaths a|gainst me.

9 Surely I have eaten | ashes·for | bread:
   and | mingled·my | drink with | tears,

10 Because of your wrath and | indig|nation:
    for you have taken me | up and | tossed·me a|side.

†11 My days de|cline·like a | shadow:
    and I | wither·a|way like | grass.

Prayer: for true penitence.

(2) *Lord God our Father, you comfort us in all our afflictions.*

12 [But] you Lord are en|throned for | ever:
    and your name shall be known⌣
       through|out all | gener|ations.

13 You will arise and have | mercy up·on | Zion:
    for it is time to pity her
       the ap|pointed | time has | come.

14 Your servants love | even · her | stones:
  and her | dust moves | them to | pity.

15 Then shall the nations fear your | name O | Lord:
  and all the | kings · of the | earth your | glory,

16 When the Lord has | built up | Zion:
  when he | shows him|self · in his | glory,

17 When he turns to the | prayer · of the | destitute:
  and does not de|spise their | suppli|cation.

†18 Let this be written down for | those who · come | after:
  and a people yet un|born will | praise the | Lord.

19 For the Lord has looked down◡
    from the | height · of his | holiness:
  from heaven he has | looked up|on the | earth,

20 To hear the | groaning · of the | prisoner:
  to deliver | those con|demned to | die;

21 That they may proclaim the name of the | Lord◡
    in | Zion:
  and his | praises | in Je|rusalem,

22 When the nations are | gathered · to|gether:
  and the | kingdoms · to | serve the | Lord.

23 He has broken my strength be|fore my | time:
  he has | cut | short my | days.

24 Do not take me away O God in the | midst of · my | life:
  you whose years ex|tend through | all · gener|ations.

25 In the beginning you laid the foun|dations · of the | earth:
  and the | heavens · are the | work of · your | hands.

26 They shall perish   but | you · will en|dure:
  they shall all grow old like a garment
    like clothes you will change them◡
    and | they shall | pass a|way.

27 But you are the same | for | ever:
  and your | years will | never | fail.

28 The children of your servants shall | rest se|cure:
  and their seed shall be es|tablished | in your | sight.

Prayer: for those troubled in mind or spirit.

103 (1)   *Let all that is in me praise God's holy name.*

1 Praise the Lord | O my | soul:
   and all that is within me | praise his | holy | name.

2 Praise the Lord | O my | soul:
   and for|get not | all his | benefits,

3 Who forgives | all your | sin:
   and | heals | all · your in|firmities,

4 Who redeems your | life · from the | Pit:
   and crowns you with | mercy | and com|passion;

†5 Who satisfies your being with | good | things:
   so that your | youth · is re|newed · like an | eagle's.

6 The Lord | works | righteousness:
   and justice for | all who | are op|pressed.

7 He made known his | ways to | Moses:
   and his | works · to the | children · of | Israel.

8 The Lord is full of com|passion · and | mercy:
   slow to anger | and of | great | goodness.

9 He will not | always · be | chiding:
   nor will he | keep his | anger · for | ever.

10 He has not dealt with us ac|cording · to our | sins:
   nor rewarded us ac|cording | to our | wickedness.

11 For as the heavens are high a|bove the | earth:
   so great is his | mercy · over | those that | fear him;

12 As far as the east is | from the | west:
   so far has he | set our | sins | from us.

13 As a father is tender to|wards his | children:
   so is the Lord | tender · to | those that | fear him.

†14 For he knows of | what · we are | made:
   he re|members · that we | are but | dust.

Thanksgiving: for God's mercy in Christ and the forgiveness of sins.

(2)   *The merciful goodness of the Lord endures for ever.*

15 The days of man are | but as | grass:
   he flourishes | like a | flower · of the | field;

16 When the wind goes over it | it is | gone:
   and its | place will | know it · no | more.

17 But the merciful goodness of the Lord
   endures for ever and ever toward | those that | fear him:
   and his righteousness up|on their | children's | children;

18 Upon those who | keep his | covenant:
   and | remember · his com|mandments · to | do them.

19 The Lord has established his | throne in | heaven:
   and his | kingdom | rules · over | all.

20 Praise the Lord all you his angels
   you that ex|cel in | strength:
   you that fulfil his word
   and obey the | voice of | his com|mandment.

21 Praise the Lord all | you his | hosts:
   his | servants · who | do his | will.

22 Praise the Lord all his works
   in all places of | his do|minion:
   praise the | Lord | O my | soul!

Prayer: that we may act for the welfare of our children's children.

104 (1)   *O Lord my God, how great you are!*

1 Bless the Lord | O my | soul:
   O Lord my | God how | great you | are!

2 Clothed with | majesty · and | honour:
   wrapped in | light as | in a | garment.

3 You have stretched out the | heavens · like a | tent-cloth:
   and laid the beams of your | dwelling · up|on their | waters;

4 You make the | clouds your | chariot:
   and | ride up·on the | wings · of the | wind;

5 You make the | winds your | messengers:
   and | flames of | fire your | ministers;

6 You have set the earth on | its found|ations:
   so | that it · shall | never · be | moved.

435

7 The deep covered it | as·with a | mantle:
  the waters | stood a|bove the | hills.

8 At your re|buke they | fled:
  at the voice of your | thunder·they | hurried·a|way;

9 They went up to the mountains
    they went | down·by the | valleys:
  to the place which | you·had ap|pointed | for them.

10 You fixed a limit which they | may not | pass:
   they shall not return a|gain to | cover·the | earth.

11 You send springs | into·the | gullies:
   which | run be|tween the | hills;

12 They give drink to every | beast·of the | field:
   and the wild | asses | quench their | thirst.

13 Beside them the birds of the air | build their | nests:
   and | sing a|mong the | branches.

14 You water the mountains from your | dwelling·on |
     high:
   and the earth is | filled·by the | fruits of·your | work.

   Praise: for creation.

   (2)   *The Lord fills all things living with plenteousness.*

15 You cause the grass to | grow·for the | cattle:
   and all green things for the | servants | of man|kind.

16 You bring food | out of·the | earth:
   and wine that makes | glad the | heart of | man,

17 Oil to give him a | shining | countenance:
   and | bread to | strengthen·his | heart.

18 The trees of the Lord are | well-|watered:
   the cedars of | Lebanon·that | he has | planted,

19 Where the birds | build their | nests:
   and the stork | makes her | home·in the | pine-tops.

20 The high hills are a refuge for the | wild | goats:
   and the crags a | cover | for the | conies.

21 You created the moon to | mark the | seasons:
   and the sun | knows the | hour·of its | setting.

22 You make darkness | and it · is | night:
in which all the beasts of the | forest | move by | stealth.
23 The lions | roar · for their | prey:
seek|ing their | food from | God.
24 When the sun rises | they re|tire:
and | lay them·selves | down · in their | dens.
†25 Man goes | out · to his | work:
and to his | labour · un|til the | evening.

Praise: for God's providence.

(3)   *Praise the Lord, O my soul, and forget not all his benefits.*

26 Lord how various | are your | works:
in wisdom you have made them all
    and the | earth is | full of · your | creatures.
27 There is the wide im|measur·able | sea:
there move living things without | number |
    great and | small;
28 There go the ships | to and | fro:
and there is that Leviathan
    whom you | formed to | sport · in the | deep.
29 These all | look to | you:
to give them their | food in | due | season.
30 When you give it to | them they | gather it:
when you open your hand ⌣
    they are | satisfied · with | good | things.
31 When you hide your | face · they are | troubled:
when you take away their breath ⌣
    they | die · and re|turn · to their | dust.
†32 When you send forth your spirit they | are cre|ated:
and you re|new the | face · of the | earth.

33 May the glory of the Lord en|dure for | ever:
may the | Lord re|joice · in his | works.
34 If he look upon the | earth · it shall | tremble:
if he but touch the | mountains | they shall | smoke.

35 I will sing to the Lord as | long as · I | live:
   I will praise my | God · while I | have · any | being.
36 May my meditation be | pleasing | to him:
   for my | joy shall | be · in the | Lord.
†37 May sinners perish from the earth,
   let the wicked | be no | more:
   bless the Lord O my | soul*   O | praise | – the | Lord.

Prayer: that we may be good stewards of God's creation.

105 (1)   *Let us remember the wonderful works the Lord our God has done.*

1 O give thanks to the Lord   and call up|on his | name:
   tell among the | peoples · what | things · he has | done.
2 Sing to him O | sing | praises:
   and be telling of | all his | marvel · lous | works.
3 Exult in his | holy | name:
   and let those that seek the | Lord be | joyful · in | heart.
4 Seek the | Lord · and his | strength:
   O | seek his | face con|tinually.
5 Call to mind what wonders | he has | done:
   his marvellous acts
   and the | judgements | of his | mouth,
6 O seed of | Abraham · his | servant:
   O | children · of | Jacob · his | chosen one.
7 For he is the | Lord our | God:
   and his judgements | are in | all the | earth.
8 He has remembered his | covenant · for | ever:
   the word that he ordained for a | thousand | gener|ations,
9 The covenant that he | made with | Abraham:
   the | oath · that he | swore to | Isaac,
10 And confirmed it to | Jacob · as a | statute:
   to Israel as an | ever|lasting | covenant,
11 Saying   'I will give you the | land of | Canaan:
   to be the | portion · of | your in|heritance',
12 And that when they | were but | few:
   little in number   and | ali · ens | in the | land.

438

13 They wandered from | nation · to | nation:
   from one people and | kingdom | to an|other.

14 He suffered no man to | do them | wrong:
   but re|proved · even | kings · for their | sake,

†15 Saying 'Touch not | my an|ointed:
   and | do my | prophets · no | harm.'

16 Then he called down a | famine · on the | land:
   and destroyed the | bread that | was their | stay.

17 But he had sent a | man a|head of them:
   Joseph | who was | sold · into | slavery,

18 Whose feet they | fastened · with | fetters:
   and thrust his | neck in·to a | hoop of | iron.

19 Till the time that his | words proved | true:
   he was | tested · by the | Lord's com|mand.

20 Then the king | sent and | loosed him:
   the ruler of | nations | set him | free;

21 He made him master | of his | household:
   and ruler | over | all · his pos|sessions,

†22 To rebuke his | officers · at | will:
   and to | teach his | counsel·lors | wisdom.

   Prayer: for our nation.

   (2) *The Lord remembered his holy word and led out his people with rejoicing.*

23 [Then] Israel | came · into | Egypt:
   and Jacob | dwelt · in the | land of | Ham.

24 There the Lord made his | people | fruitful:
   too | numer·ous | for their | enemies,

25 Whose hearts he turned to | hate his | people:
   and to deal de|ceitful·ly | with his | servants.

26 Then he sent | Moses · his | servant:
   and | Aaron · whom | he had | chosen.

27 Through them he | manifested · his | signs:
   and his | wonders · in the | land of | Ham.

439

28 He sent darkness | and it · was | dark:
    yet they would | not o|bey · his com|mands.

29 He turned their | waters · into | blood:
    and | slew the | fish there|in.

30 Their country | swarmed with | frogs:
    even the inner | chambers | of their | kings.

31 He spoke the word
    and there came great | swarms of | flies:
    and | gnats with·in | all their | borders.

32 He sent them | storms of | hail:
    and darts of | fire | into · their | land.

33 He struck their | vines · and their | fig-trees:
    and shattered the | trees with|in their | borders.

34 He commanded   and there | came | grasshoppers:
    and young | locusts · with|out | number.

35 They ate up every green thing | in the | land:
    and de|voured the | fruit · of the | soil.

36 He smote all the first-born | in their | land:
    the | first-fruits · of | all their | manhood.

37 He brought Israel out with silver | and with | gold:
    and not one among their | tribes was | seen to | stumble.

38 Egypt was | glad · at their | going:
    for dread of | Israel · had | fallen · up|on them.

39 He spread out a | cloud · for a | covering:
    and | fire to | lighten · the | night.

40 The people asked and he | brought them | quails:
    and satisfied them | with the | bread from | heaven.

41 He opened a rock so that the | waters | gushed:
    and ran in the parched | land | like a | river.

42 For he had remembered his | holy | word:
    that he gave to | Abra|ham his | servant.

43 So he led out his | people · with re|joicing:
    his | chosen ones · with | shouts of | joy;

44 He gave them the | land · of the | nations:
    and they took possession of the | fruit ‿
       of | other · men's | toil,

†45 So that they might | keep his | statutes:
and faithfully obey his laws
    O | praise | – the | Lord.

Prayer: that the Church may be faithful to her vocation.

106 (1)   *Give thanks to the Lord for he is good, and his mercy endures for ever.*

1 Praise the Lord
    O give thanks to the Lord for | he is | good:
and his | mercy · en|dures for |ever.

2 Who can express the mighty | acts · of the | Lord:
or | fully | voice his | praise?

3 Blessèd are those who act ac|cording · to | justice:
who at | all times | do the | right.

4 Remember me O Lord
    when you visit your people | with your | favour:
and come to me | also · with | your sal|vation,

†5 That I may see the prosperity | of your | chosen:
that I may rejoice with the rejoicing of your people
    and exult with | those who | are your | own.

6 We have | sinned · like our | fathers:
we have acted per|versely · and | done | wrong.

7 Our fathers when they | were in | Egypt:
took no | heed | of your | wonders;

8 They did not remember‿
    the multitude of your | loving | kindnesses:
but they re|belled · at the | Red | Sea.

9 Nevertheless he saved them for his | name's | sake:
that he | might make | known his | power.

10 He commanded the Red Sea and it | dried | up:
and he led them through the | deep‿
    as | through a | desert.

11 He delivered them from the | hand ·‿
    of their | adversary:
and redeemed them | from the | power · of the | enemy.

12 The waters closed over | their op|pressors:
    so that not | one was | left a|live.

13 Then they be|lieved his | words:
    and | sang him | songs of | praise.

14 But in a little while they forgot what | he had | done:
    and would | wait · for his | counsel · no | more.

15 Greed took hold of them | in the | desert:
    and they put | God · to the | test · in the | wilderness.

16 So he gave them that which | they de|sired:
    but sent a | wasting | sickness · a|mong them.

17 Then they grew envious of Moses | in the | camp:
    and of Aaron the | holy · one | of the | Lord;

18 Whereupon the earth opened and | swallowed · up |
        Dathan:
    it closed over the | compan·y | of A|biram;

19 Fire flared out a|gainst their | number:
    and | flame de|voured · the un|godly.

20 At Horeb they | made themselves · a | calf:
    and bowed down in | worship | to an | image.

21 And so they exchanged the | glory · of | God:
    for the likeness of an | ox that | eats | hay.

22 They forgot God who | was their | saviour:
    that had done such | great | things in | Egypt,

23 Who had worked his wonders in the | land of | Ham:
    and his terrible | deeds · at the | Red | Sea.

†24 Therefore he | thought · to de|stroy them:
    had not Moses his servant stood before him in the ⌣
        breach
        to turn a|way his | wrath · from de|stroying them.

Thanksgiving: for our nation.

(2) *Deliver us, Lord, and be not angry with us for ever.*

25 [Then] they despised the | pleasant | land:
    and | put no | faith · in his | promise,

442

26 But murmured | in their | tents:
and would not o|bey the | voice · of the | Lord.

27 So he lifted his hand to swear an | oath a|gainst them:
that he would | strike them | down · in the | wilderness,

28 And cast out their children a|mong the | nations:
and | scatter them · through | all the | lands.

29 Then they joined themselves to the | Baal · of | Peor:
and ate things sacrificed to | gods that | have no | life.

30 They provoked him to anger with their | wanton | deeds:
and | plague broke | out a|mong them.

31 Then stood up Phinehas and | inter|posed:
and | so the | plague was | ended;

32 And that was counted to | him for | righteousness:
throughout all gener|ations · for | ever|more.

33 They angered God also at the | waters · of | Meribah:
so that Moses | suffered · for | their mis|deeds;

34 For they had em|bittered · his | spirit:
and he spoke | rashly | with his | lips.

Prayer: of penitence for our nation's failings.

(3) *Save us, Lord, and gather us from among the nations.*

35 They did not de|stroy the | peoples:
as the Lord had com|manded | them to | do,

36 But they mingled themselves | with the | heathen:
and | learned to | follow · their | ways.

37 They worshipped | foreign | idols:
and | these be|came their | snare,

38 So that they | sacrificed · their | sons:
and | their own | daughters · to | demons.

39 They shed | inno·cent | blood:
even the blood of their | own | sons and | daughters,

40 Whom they offered to the | idols · of | Canaan:
and the | land · was de|filed with | blood.

41 They made themselves | foul · by their | acts:
and with wanton deeds | whored · after | strange | gods.

42 Then was the wrath of the Lord kindled ⁀
  a|gainst his | people:
  and he | loathed his | own pos|session;

43 He gave them into the | hands · of the | nations:
  and their | adver·saries | ruled | over them.

44 Their enemies be|came · their op|pressors:
  and they were brought into sub|jection · ⁀
    be|neath their | power.

45 Many a | time he | saved them:
  but they rebelled against him to follow their own ⁀
    designs
    and were brought | down | by their | wickedness.

46 Nevertheless he looked on | their dis|tress:
  when he | heard their | loud | crying.

47 He remembered his | coven·ant | with them:
  and relented
    according to the a|bundance · of his | loving | kindness.

48 And he caused them | to be | pitied:
  even by | those that | held them | captive.

49 Save us O Lord our God
    and gather us from a|mong the | nations:
  that we may give thanks to your holy name
    and | make our | boast · in your | praises.

50 Blessèd be the Lord the God of Israel
    from everlasting to | ever|lasting:
  and let all the people say Amen|
    Praise| – the | Lord.

Prayer: for Australia's relations with the rest of the world.

107 (1)   *Give thanks to the Lord, for he is good.*

1 O give thanks to the Lord for | he is | good:
  for his loving | mercy | is for | ever.

2 Let the Lord's re|deemed | say so:
  whom he has redeemed from the | hand | of the | enemy,

†3 And gathered in from every land
    from the east and | from the | west:
  from the | north and | from the | south.

444

4 Some went astray in the wilderness and | in the | desert:
   and found no | path to·an in|habit·ed | city;
5 They were | hungry·and | thirsty:
   and their | heart | fainted·with|in them.
6 Then they cried to the Lord in | their dis|tress:
   and he | took them | out of·their | trouble.
7 He led them by the | right | path:
   till they | came to·an in|habit·ed | city.
8 *Let them thank the | Lord·for his | goodness:*
   and for the wonders that he | does·for the | children·of | men;
9 *For he | satisfies·the | thirsty:*
   and fills the | hungry·with | good | things.

10 Some sat in darkness and in | deadly | shadow:
    bound | fast·in af|fliction·and | iron,
11 Because they had rebelled against the | words of | God:
    and scorned the purposes | of the | Most | High.
12 So he bowed down their | hearts·with af|fliction:
    they tripped | headlong·with | none to | help them.
13 Then they cried to the Lord in | their dis|tress:
    and he | took them | out of·their | trouble.
†14 He brought them out from darkness ⌣
       and | deadly | shadow:
    and | broke their | chains in | two.
15 *Let them thank the | Lord·for his | goodness:*
    and for the wonders that he | does·for the | children·of | men;
16 *For he shatters the | doors of | bronze:*
    and | cleaves the | bars of | iron.

   Prayer: for refugees and for prisoners.

   (2)   *Give thanks to the Lord: his mercy endures for ever.*

17 Fools were far | gone·in trans|gression:
    and be|cause of·their | sins·were af|flicted.
18 They sickened at | any | food:
    and had | come·to the | gates of | death.

19 Then they cried to the Lord in | their dis|tress:
    and he | took them | out of · their | trouble.

20 He sent his | word and | healed them:
    and | saved their | life · from the | Pit.

21 *Let them thank the | Lord · for his | goodness:*
    and for the wonders that he | does · for the | children · of | men;

22 *Let them offer sacrifices of | thanks|giving:*
    and tell what he has | done with | shouts of | joy.

23 Those who go down to the | sea in | ships:
    and follow their | trade on | great | waters,

24 These men have seen the | works of | God:
    and his | wonders | in the | deep.

25 For he spoke and | raised the | storm-wind:
    and it lifted | high the | waves · of the | sea.

26 They go up to the sky   and down a|gain · to the | depths:
    their courage melts a|way · in the | face · of dis|aster.

27 They reel and stagger like | drunken | men:
    and are | at their | wits' | end.

28 Then they cried to the Lord in | their dis|tress:
    and he | took them | out of · their | trouble.

29 He calmed the | storm · to a | silence:
    and the | waves · of the | sea were | stilled.

30 Then they were glad be|cause · they were | quiet:
    and he | brought them · to the | haven · they | longed for.

31 *Let them thank the | Lord · for his | goodness:*
    and for the wonders that he | does · for the | children · of | men;

32 *Let them exalt him in the as|sembly · of the | people:*
    and | praise him · in the | council · of | elders.

Prayer: for the sick and for sailors.

(3)   *Give thanks to the Lord, for he is good.*

33 He turns the | rivers · into | desert:
    and springs of | water · into | thirsty | ground.

34 He makes of a fruitful land a | salty | waste:
    be|cause · its in|habitants · are | evil.

446

35 He turns the wilderness into a | pool of | water:
and parched | ground · into | flowing | springs.

36 And there he | settles · the | hungry:
and they | build a | city · to | live in.

37 They sow fields and | plant | vineyards:
which | give them | fruitful | harvest.

38 He blesses them   and they | multi·ply | greatly:
he does not | let their | cattle · dim|inish.

39 But he pours con|tempt up·on | princes:
and makes them | stray · in the | pathless | desert;

40 They are weakened and | brought | low:
through | stress of · ad|versity · and | sorrow.

41 But he lifts the | poor · out of | misery:
and increases their | families · like | flocks of | sheep.

42 The upright shall | see it · and re|joice:
and all | wickedness · shall | shut its | mouth.

†43 Whoever is wise   let him ob|serve these | things:
and consider the loving | kindness | of the | Lord.

Prayer: for farmers and primary producers, and for the needy.

108   *Let your glory, Lord, be over all the earth.*

1 My heart is fixed O God my | heart is | fixed:
I will | sing and | make | melody.

2 Awake my soul   awake | lute and | harp:
for | I · will a|waken · the | morning.

3 I will give you thanks O Lord a|mong the | peoples:
I will sing your | praise a|mong the | nations.

4 For the greatness of your mercy |
    reaches · to the | heavens:
and your | faithful·ness | to the | clouds.

5 Be exalted O God a|bove the | heavens:
and let your glory be | over | all the | earth;

6 That those whom you love may | be de|livered:
O save us by | your right | hand and | answer me.

447

7 God has said in his | holy | place:
'I will exult and divide Shechem
   I will parcel | out the | valley·of | Succoth.

8 'Gilead is mine and Man|asseh·is | mine:
Ephraim is my helmet⌣
   and | Judah·my | rod·of com|mand.

†9 'Moab is my wash-bowl
   over Edom will I | cast my | shoe:
against Philistia | will I | shout in | triumph.'

10 Who will lead me into the | forti·fied | city:
who will | bring me | into | Edom?

11 Have you not cast us | off O | God?:
you | go not | out·with our | armies.

12 Give us your help a|gainst the | enemy:
for | vain·is the | help of | man.

13 By the power of our God we | shall do | valiantly:
for it is he that | will tread | down our | enemies.

Prayer: for missionaries and all who spread the gospel.

109 (1)   *Forgive us our sins, as we forgive those who sin against us.*

1 O God of my praise do | not be | silent:
for evil and deceitful | mouths are | opened·a|gainst me.

2 They speak of me with | lying | tongues:
they surround me with words of hatred
   they fight a|gainst me·with|out | cause.

3 In return for my friendship | they op|pose me:
and | that for·no | fault of | mine.

4 They repay me | evil·for | good:
and | hatred·for | my af|fection.

5 Appoint an evil man to | stand a|gainst him:
and let an adversary | be at·his | right | hand.

6 When he is judged   let him be | found | guilty:
let his prayer for | help be | counted·as | sin.

7 Let his | days be | few:
  and let another | take what | he has | hoarded.

8 Let his children be | made | fatherless:
  and his | wife be|come a | widow.

9 Let his children be | vagabonds·and | beggars:
  let them seek alms | far·from their | own | homes.

10 Let the usurer exact | all·that he | has:
  and let strangers | plunder·the | fruit·of his | toil.

11 Let no man be | loyal·to | him:
  and let no one have | pity·on his | father·less | children.

12 Let his line be|come ex|tinct:
  in one generation let their | name be | blotted | out.

13 Let the sins of his fathers‿
    be re|membered·by the | Lord:
  and his mother's iniquity | not be | wiped a|way.

14 Let their sins be constantly be|fore the | Lord:
  may he root out their | memo·ry | from the | earth.

15 For he was a man that did not remember‿
    to | show | loyalty:
  but he persecuted the humble the poor and the crushed‿
    in spirit
  and | sought to | put them·to | death.

16 He loved to curse * let curses | fall on | him:
  he took no pleasure in blessing
    so let | it be | far from | him.

17 He clothed himself in cursing | like a | garment:
  so let it seep like water into his body
    and like | oil | into·his | bones.

18 Let it be as the clothes he | wraps a|bout him:
  or like the | girdle·that he | wears each | day.

19 This is the Lord's recompense to | those·that op|pose him:
  to | those that·speak | evil·a|gainst me.

Prayer: for the malicious and for deliverance from our own malice.

(2)   *Lord, save me for your mercy's sake.*

20 Act for me O Lord my God for your | name's | sake:
and deliver me   as your | steadfast | love is | good.

21 For I am | poor and | needy:
and my | heart | writhes with|in me.

22 I fade like a | lengthen·ing | shadow:
I am | shaken | off·like a | locust.

23 My knees are | weak from | fasting:
my | flesh grows | lean and | shrunken.

†24 I have become the | scorn of·my | enemies:
and when they see me⌣
they | toss their | heads·in de|rision.

25 Help me O | Lord my | God:
and save me | for your | mercy's | sake,

26 That men may know it was | your | hand:
that | you O | Lord have | done it.

27 Though they curse yet | give me·your | blessing:
and those that come against me will be put to shame
and your | servant | shall re|joice.

28 Let those that oppose me be | covered·with dis|grace:
let them | wear their | shame·as a | garment.

29 And I will give the Lord⌣
great | thanks·with my | mouth:
and | praise him·in the | midst·of a | multitude.

30 For the Lord will stand at the right | hand·of the | poor:
to save him from | those that | would con|demn him.

Prayer: for victims of hatred and injustice.

110   *You are the King of glory, Lord Christ.*

1 The Lord | said to | my lord:
'Sit at my right hand
until I | make your | enemies·your | footstool.'

2 The Lord commits to you the sceptre | of your | power:
reign from | Zion·in the | midst of·your | enemies.

3 Noble are you
      from the day of your birth upon the | holy | hill:
radiant are you even from the womb
      in the | morning | dew of·your | youth.

4 The Lord has sworn and will | not turn | back:
'You are a priest for ever
      after the | order | of Mel|chizedek.'

5 The king shall stand at your right | hand O | Lord:
and shatter | kings·in the | day of·his | wrath.

6 Glorious in majesty
      he shall judge a|mong the | nations:
and shatter heads | over·a | wide | land.

†7 He shall slake his thirst⌣
      from the brook be|side the | way:
therefore shall | he lift | up his | head.

Praise: to Christ as king, priest, and judge.

111   *Great and wonderful are your deeds, Lord God the Almighty.*

1 O praise the Lord
      I will praise the Lord with my | whole | heart:
in the company of the upright
      and a|mong the | congre|gation.

2 The works of the | Lord are | great:
and studied by | all who | take de|light in them.

3 His deeds are ma|jestic·and | glorious:
and his | righteous·ness | stands for | ever.

4 His marvellous acts have won him a name⌣
      to | be re|membered:
the | Lord is | gracious·and | merciful.

5 He gives food to | those that | fear him:
he re|members·his | covenant·for | ever.

6 He showed his people the | power·of his | acts:
in giving them the | herit·age | of the | heathen.

7 The works of his hands are | faithful·and | just:
and | all·his com|mandments·are | sure;

451

8 They stand firm for | ever · and | ever:
   they are done in | faithful·ness | and in | truth.
9 He sent redemption to his people
      he ordained his | covenant · for | ever:
   holy is his name and | worthy | to be | feared.
10 The fear of the Lord is the beginning of wisdom
      and of good understanding are those that | keep · his ⌣
   com|mandments:
   his | praise · shall en|dure for | ever.

Prayer: that we may prepare rightly to receive the holy communion.

112   *The children of the light walk in all that is good and right and*
         true.

1 O praise the Lord
      Blessèd is the man who | fears the | Lord:
   and greatly de|lights in | his com|mandments.
2 His children shall be | mighty · in the | land:
   a race of upright | men who | will be | blessed.
3 Riches and plenty shall be | in his | house:
   and his | righteous·ness | stands for | ever.
4 Light arises in darkness | for the | upright:
   gracious and merciful | is the | righteous | man.
5 It goes well with the man ⌣
      who acts | generously · and | lends:
   who | guides · his af|fairs with | justice.
6 Surely he shall | never · be | moved:
   the righteous shall be held in | ever|lasting · re|membrance.
7 He will not | fear bad | tidings:
   his heart is steadfast | trusting | in the | Lord.
8 His heart is confident and | will not | fear:
   he will see the | downfall | of his | enemies.
9 He gives | freely · to the | poor:
   his righteousness stands for ever
      his | head is · up|lifted · in | glory.

10 The wicked man shall see it | and be | angry:
he shall gnash his teeth and consume away
and the | hope · of the | wicked · shall | fail.

Prayer: for our friends.

113 *The Lord raises the lowly and lifts up the poor.*

1 Praise the Lord
O sing praises you that | are his | servants:
O | praise the | name · of the | Lord.
2 Let the name of the | Lord be | blessed:
from this time | forward | and for | ever.
3 From the rising of the sun to its | going | down:
let the | name · of the | Lord be | praised.
4 The Lord is exalted over | all the | nations:
and his | glory · is a|bove the | heavens.
5 Who can be likened to the | Lord our | God:
in | heaven · or up|on the | earth,
6 Who has his | dwelling · so | high:
yet condescends to | look on | things be|neath?
7 He raises the | lowly · from the | dust:
and lifts the | poor from | out of · the | dungheap;
8 He gives them a place a|mong the | princes:
even among the | princes | of his | people.
†9 He causes the barren woman to | keep | house:
and makes her a joyful mother of children|
Praise | –the | Lord.

Prayer: for social workers and those who work among the underprivileged.

114 *Now is the accepted time, now is the day of salvation.*

1 When Israel came | out of | Egypt:
and the house of Jacob ⌣
from among a | people · of an | alien | tongue,

2 Judah be|came his | sanctuary:
   and | Israel | his do|minion.
3 The sea saw | that and | fled:
   Jor|dan was | driven | back.
4 The mountains | skipped like | rams:
   and the little | hills like | young | sheep.
5 What ailed you O | sea · that you | fled:
   O Jordan that | you were | driven | back?
6 You mountains that you | skipped like | rams:
   and you little | hills like | young | sheep?
7 Tremble O earth at the | presence · of the | Lord:
   at the | presence · of the | God of | Jacob,
8 Who turned the rock into a | pool of | water:
   and the flint-stone | into · a | welling | spring.

Prayer: for those recently baptized.

115 *We are called to serve the one true God.*

1 Not to us O Lord not to us
      but to your name | give the | glory:
   for the sake of your faithfulness |
      and your | loving-|kindness.
2 Why should the heathen say | 'Where is · their | God?':
   our God is in heaven   he | does what|ever · he | wills.
3 As for their idols   they are | silver · and | gold:
   the | work · of a | man's | hand.
4 They have | mouths but | speak not:
   they have | eyes · but they | cannot | see.
5 They have ears yet | hear | nothing:
   they have | noses · but | cannot | smell.
6 Hands they have but handle nothing
      feet but they | do not | walk:
   they | make no | sound · with their | throats.
†7 Those who make them | shall be | like them:
   so shall | everyone · that | trusts in | them.

8 O Israel | trust · in the | Lord:
  he is your | help | and your | shield.

9 O house of Aaron | trust · in the | Lord:
  he is your | help | and your | shield.

10 You that fear the Lord | trust · in the | Lord:
  he is your | help | and your | shield.

11 The Lord has remembered us and | he will | bless us:
  he will bless the house of Israel
      he will | bless the | house of | Aaron.

12 He will bless all those that | fear the | Lord:
  both | high and | low to|gether.

13 May the Lord in|crease you | greatly:
  you | and your | children | after you.

14 The blessing of the | Lord · be up|on you:
  he that | made | heaven · and | earth.

15 As for the heavens | they · are the | Lord's:
  but the earth he has | given · to the | children · of | men.

16 The dead do not | praise the | Lord:
  nor do | any · that go | down to | silence.

17 But we will | bless the | Lord:
  both now and for evermore
      O | praise | – the | Lord.

Prayer: for those recently confirmed.

116   *The Lord delivers my life from death.*

1 I love the Lord because he | heard my | voice:
  the | voice of · my | suppli|cation;

2 Because he in|clined his | ear to me:
  in the | day | that I | called to him.

3 The cords of death encompassed me
      the snares of the | grave took | hold on me:
  I | was in | anguish · and | sorrow.

4 Then I called upon the | name · of the | Lord:
  'O | Lord · I be|seech you · de|liver me!'

5 Gracious and righteous | is the | Lord:
  full of com|passion | is our | God.

455

6 The Lord pre|serves the | simple:
  when | I was · brought | low he | saved me.

7 Return O my | soul · to your | rest:
  for the | Lord | has re|warded you.

8 For you O Lord have delivered my | soul from | death:
  my eyes from | tears · and my | feet from | falling.

†9 I will walk be|fore the | Lord:
  in the | land | of the | living.

Prayer: for the dying.

(2)   *How shall I repay the Lord for all his benefits to me?*

10 I believed that I would perish
  I was | brought · very | low:
  I said in my haste | 'All | men are | liars.'

11 How shall I re|pay the | Lord:
  for | all his | bene·fits | to me?

12 I will take up the | cup of · sal|vation:
  and | call up·on the | name · of the | Lord.

13 I will pay my | vows · to the | Lord:
  in the | presence · of | all his | people.

14 Grievous in the | sight · of the | Lord:
  is the | death | of his | faithful ones.

15 O Lord I am your servant
  your servant and the | son of · your | handmaid:
  you | have un|loosed my | bonds.

16 I will offer you a sacrifice of | thanks|giving:
  and | call up·on the | name · of the | Lord.

17 I will pay my | vows · to the | Lord:
  in the | presence · of | all his | people,

†18 In the courts of the | house · of the | Lord:
  even in your midst O Jerusalem |
  Praise | – the | Lord.

Prayer: of self-offering.

117   *The right hand of the Lord does mighty things.*

1 O praise the Lord | all you | nations:
  O | praise him | all you | peoples.

456

2 For great is his loving-|kindness · to|ward us:
and the faithfulness of the Lord endures for ever |
　　　Praise | — the | Lord.

Prayer: for the United Nations.

118 (1)　　*The right hand of the Lord does mighty things.*

1 O give thanks to the Lord for | he is | good:
his | mercy · en|dures for | ever.

2 Let Israel | now pro|claim:
that his | mercy · en|dures for | ever.

3 Let the house of | Aaron · pro|claim:
that his | mercy · en|dures for | ever.

4 Let those who fear the | Lord pro|claim:
that his | mercy · en|dures for | ever.

5 In my danger I | called · to the | Lord:
he | answered · and | set me | free.

6 The Lord is on my side　I | shall not | fear:
what can | man | do to | me?

7 The Lord is at my side | as my | helper:
I shall see the | downfall | of my | enemies.

8 It is better to take refuge | in the | Lord:
than to | put your | trust in | man;

†9 It is better to take refuge | in the | Lord:
than to | put your | trust in | princes.

10 All the | nations · sur|rounded me:
but in the name of the | Lord I | drove them | back.

11 They surrounded　they surrounded me on | every | side:
but in the name of the | Lord I | drove them | back.

12 They swarmed about me like bees
　　they blazed like fire a|mong the | thorns:
in the name of the | Lord I | drove them | back.

13 I was pressed so hard that I | almost | fell:
but the | Lord | was my | helper.

†14 The Lord is my | strength · and my | song:
and has be|come | my sal|vation.

457

15 The sounds of | joy · and de|liverance:
   are | in the | tents · of the | righteous.

16 The right hand of the Lord does | mighty | things:
   the right hand of the | Lord | raises | up.

17 I shall not | die but | live:
   and pro|claim the | works · of the | Lord.

18 The Lord has | disciplined · me | hard:
   but he has not | given · me | over · to | death.

Prayer: for the United Nations.

(2)   *The stone the builders rejected has become the head of the corner.*

19 Open me the | gates of | righteousness:
   and I will enter and give | thanks | to the | Lord.

20 This is the | gate · of the | Lord:
   the | righteous | shall | enter it.

21 I will praise you | for you | answered me:
   and have be|come | my sal|vation.

22 The stone that the | builders · re|jected:
   has be|come the | head · of the | corner.

23 This is the | Lord's | doing:
   and it is | marvel·lous | in our | eyes.

24 This is the day that the | Lord has | made:
   let us re|joice | and be | glad in it.

25 O Lord | save us · we | pray:
   O Lord | send | us pros|perity.

26 Blessèd is he who comes in the | name · of the | Lord:
   from the | house · of the | Lord we | bless you.

27 The Lord is God   and he has | given · us | light:
   guide the festal throng up to the | horns | of the | altar.

28 You are my God and | I will | praise you:
   you are my | God I | will ex|alt you.

†29 O give thanks to the Lord for | he is | good:
   and his | mercy · en|dures for | ever.

Meditation: on the Lord's day.

458

119 (1)   *Christ became obedient for us to death, even death on a cross.*

1 Blessèd are those whose | way is | blameless:
who | walk · in the | law · of the | Lord.

2 Blessèd are those who | keep · his com|mands:
and seek him | with their | whole | heart;

3 Those who | do no | wrong:
but | walk · in the | ways of · our | God.

4 For you Lord | have com|manded us:
to perse|vere in | all your | precepts.

5 If only my | ways · were un|erring:
towards the | keeping | of your | statutes!

6 Then I should | not · be a|shamed:
when I | looked on | all · your com|mandments.

7 I will praise you with sin|cerity · of | heart:
as I | learn your | righteous | judgements.

8 I will | keep your | statutes:
O for|sake me | not | utterly.

Prayer: for obedience to God's word and commandments.

(2)   *Happy are those who delight in the law of the Lord.*

9 How shall a young man's | path be | pure:
un|less he | keep to · your | word?

10 I have sought you with my | whole | heart:
let me not | stray from | your com|mandments.

11 I have treasured your | words · in my | heart:
that I | might not | sin a|gainst you.

12 Blessèd are | you Lord | God:
O | teach me | your | statutes.

13 With my lips I | have been | telling:
all the | judgements | of your | mouth;

14 And I find more joy in the way of | your com|mands:
than in | all | manner · of | riches.

15 I will meditate | on your | precepts:
and give | heed | to your | ways;

459

16 For my delight is wholly | in your | statutes:
  and I will | not for|get your | word.

Prayer: for young Christians.

(3)   *Your commands, Lord, are my delight.*

17 O be bountiful to your servant that | I may | live:
  in o|bedi·ence | to your | word.
18 Take away the | veil·from my | eyes:
  that I may see the | wonders | of your | law.
19 I am but a | stranger·on the | earth:
  do not | hide·your com|mandments | from me.
20 My soul is con|sumed with | longing:
  for your | judgements | day and | night.
21 You have re|buked the | proud:
  and cursed are those ͜
    who | stray from | your com|mandments;
22 Turn away from me their re|proach and | scorn:
  for | I have | kept·your com|mands.
23 Though princes sit and plot to|gether·a|gainst me:
  your servant shall | medi·tate | on your | statutes;
24 For your commands are | my de|light:
  and they are | counsellors·in | my de|fence.

Prayer: for spiritual joy.

(4)   *Out of the depths I call to you, O Lord.*

25 I am humbled | to the | dust:
  O give me life ac|cording | to your | word.
26 If I ex|amine·my | ways:
  surely you will answer me * O | teach me | your |
    statutes!
27 Make me to understand the | way of·your | precepts:
  and I shall meditate | on your | marvel·lous | works.
28 My soul pines a|way for | sorrow:
  O raise me up ac|cording | to your | word.

29 Keep me far from the | way of·de|ception:
    and | grant me·the | grace of·your | law.
30 I have chosen the | way of | truth:
    and have | set your | judgements·be|fore me.
31 I hold fast to | your com|mands:
    O Lord let me | never | be con|founded.
32 Let me run the way of | your com|mandments:
    for | you will | liberate·my | heart.

Prayer: for those in spiritual dryness.

(5)   *Let us live to the praise of your glory.*

33 Teach me O Lord the | way of·your | statutes:
    and I will | honour·it | to the | end.
34 Give me understanding   that I may | keep your | law:
    that I may keep it | with my | whole | heart.
35 Guide me in the path of | your com|mandments:
    for there|in is | my de|light.
36 Incline my heart to | your com|mands:
    and | not to | selfish | gain.
37 Turn away my eyes from | looking·on | vanities:
    as I walk in your | way | give me | life.
38 Make good your promise | to your | servant:
    the promise that en|dures for | all who | fear you.
39 Turn aside the | taunts·that I | dread:
    for your | judgements·are | very | good.
40 Lord I | long for·your | precepts:
    in your | righteous·ness | give me | life.

Prayer: of dedication.

(6)   *The Lord is my light and my salvation: of whom shall I be afraid?*

41 Let your loving mercy come to | me O | Lord:
    and your salvation ac|cording | to your | word.

461

42 Then I shall have an answer for | those·who re|proach me:
for I | trust | in your | word.

43 Do not take the word of truth ⌣
utterly | out of·my | mouth:
for in your | judgements | is my | hope.

44 Let me keep your | law con|tinually:
O | let me | keep it·for | ever.

45 And so I shall | walk at | liberty:
be|cause·I have | sought your | precepts.

46 I shall speak of your com|mands be·fore | kings:
and shall | not be | put to | shame.

47 My delight shall be in | your com|mandments:
which | I have | greatly | loved;

48 I shall worship you with | outstretched | hands:
and I shall | medi·tate | on your | statutes.

Prayer: for the bishops and church leaders.

(7)   *Let your loving mercy come to me, O Lord.*

49 Remember your | word·to your | servant:
on | which·you have | built my | hope.

50 This has been my comfort in | my af|fliction:
for your | word has | brought me | life.

51 Though the proud have | laughed me·to | scorn:
I have not | turned a|side from·your | law;

52 But I called to mind O Lord your | judgements·of | old:
and in | them·I have | found·consol|ation.

53 I am seized with indignation | at the | wicked:
for | they have·for|saken·your | law.

54 But your statutes have be|come my | songs:
in the | house | of my | pilgrimage.

55 I think on your name O | Lord·in the | night:
and | I ob|serve your | law;

56 This has | been·my re|ward:
be|cause·I have | kept your | precepts.

Prayer: for those in trouble.

(8)   *O worship the Lord in the beauty of holiness.*

57 The Lord | is my | portion:
I have | promised · to | keep your | words.

58 I have sought your favour with my | whole | heart:
O be gracious to me ac|cording | to your | word.

59 I have taken | stock of · my | ways:
and have turned back my | feet to | your com|mands.

60 I made haste and did | not de|lay:
to | keep | your com|mandments.

61 The snares of the | wicked · en|compassed me:
but I did | not for|get your | law;

62 At midnight I rise to | give you | thanks:
for the | righteous·ness | of your | judgements.

63 I am a friend to | all who | fear you:
to | those who | keep your | precepts.

64 The earth O Lord is full of your | loving | mercy:
O | teach me | your | statutes.

Prayer: for members of religious orders.

(9)   *Blessed be the God and Father of our Lord Jesus Christ.*

65 Lord you have done | good to · your | servant:
in ac|cordance | with your | word.

66 O teach me right | judgement · and | knowledge:
for I | trust in | your com|mandments.

67 Before I was afflicted I | went a|stray:
but | now I | keep your | word.

68 You are good and you | do | good:
O | teach me | your | statutes.

69 The proud have | smeared me · with | lies:
but I will keep your precepts | with my | whole | heart.

70 Their hearts are | gross like | fat:
but my de|light is | in your | law.

71 It is good for me that | I was · af|flicted:
so | I might | learn your | statutes.

72　The law of your mouth is | dearer · to | me:
　　than a | wealth of | gold and | silver.

　　　Prayer: of glad acceptance of the discipline of suffering.

　　(10)　*Father, my hope is in your word.*

73　Your hands have | made me · and | fashioned me:
　　O give me understanding ⏑
　　　　that | I may | learn · your com|mandments.
74　Those who fear you shall see me | and re|joice:
　　for my | hope is | in your | word.
75　I know Lord that your | judgements · are | right:
　　and that in | faithfulness · you | have af|flicted me.
76　Let your merciful kindness | be my | comfort:
　　according to your | promise | to your | servant.
77　O let your mercy come to me that | I may | live:
　　for your | law is | my de|light.
78　Let the proud be shamed
　　　　who steal my | rights · through their | lies:
　　but I will | medi·tate | on your | precepts.
79　Let those who fear you | turn to | me:
　　and | they shall | know · your com|mands.
80　O let my heart be | sound in · your | statutes:
　　that I may | never · be | put to | shame.

　　　Thanksgiving: for some deliverance.

　　(11)　*From the depths of my despair I call to you, O Lord.*

81　My soul languishes for | your sal|vation:
　　but my | hope is | in your | word;
82　My eyes fail with | watching · for your | promise:
　　saying 'O | when | will you | comfort me?'
83　I am parched as a wineskin | in the | smoke:
　　yet I do | not for|get your | statutes.
84　How many are the | days of · your | servant:
　　and | when · will you | judge my | persecutors?

85 The proud have dug | pitfalls | for me:
in de|fiance | of your | law.

86 All your com|mandments · are | true:
but they persecute me with lies * O come | to my | help!

87 They have almost made an end of me | on the | earth:
but I have | not for|saken · your | precepts.

88 In your merciful goodness | give me | life:
that I may keep the com|mands | of your | mouth.

Prayer: for those imprisoned or afflicted for the sake of the gospel.

(12) *Who is able to separate us from the love of God in Christ?*

89 Lord your | word · is for | ever:
it stands | firm | in the | heavens.

90 Your faithfulness abides from one gener|ation · to an|other:
firm as the | earth which | you have | made.

91 As for your judgements   they stand | fast this | day:
for | all things | are your | servants.

92 If your law had not been | my de|light:
I would have | perished · in | my af|fliction.

93 I will never for|get your | precepts:
for by | them · you have | given · me | life.

94 I am | yours O | save me:
for | I have | sought your | precepts.

95 The wicked have lain in wait for me | to de|stroy me:
but I | think on | your com|mands.

96 I have seen that all perfection | comes · to an | end:
only your com|mandment | has no | bounds.

Prayer: for those in despair.

(13) *I have set my heart to fulfil your statutes.*

97 Lord how I | love your | law:
it is my medi|tation | all the · day | long.

98 Your commandments have made me wiser | than my |
   enemies:
for they re|main with | me for | ever.

465

99 I have more understanding than | all my | teachers:
for I | study | your com|mands.

100 I am wiser | than the | agèd:
be|cause · I have | kept your | precepts.

101 I have held back my feet from every | evil | path:
that | I might | keep your | word;

102 I have not turned a|side from · your | judgements:
for | you your|self are · my | teacher.

103 How sweet are your | words · to my | tongue:
sweeter than | honey | to my | mouth.

104 Through your precepts I get | under|standing:
therefore I | hate all | lying | ways.

Prayer: for students of the Bible.

(14) *Your word is a light to my path.*

105 Your word is a lantern | to my | feet:
and a | light | to my | path.

106 I have vowed and | sworn an | oath:
to | keep your | righteous | judgements.

107 I have been afflicted be|yond | measure:
Lord give me life ac|cording | to your | word.

108 Accept O Lord the freewill offerings | of my | mouth:
and | teach me | your | judgements.

109 I take my life in my | hands con|tinually:
yet I do | not for|get your | law.

110 The wicked have | laid a | snare for me:
but I | have not | strayed from · your | precepts.

111 Your commands are my in|heritance · for | ever:
they | are the | joy of · my | heart.

112 I have set my heart to ful|fil your | statutes:
always | even | to the | end.

Prayer: for translators of the Bible, especially in remote places.

(15)   How I love your law; it is my meditation all the day long.

113 I loathe those who are | double-|minded:
but your | law | do I | love.

114 You are my shelter | and my | shield:
and in your | word | is my | hope.

115 Away from me all | you that·do | evil:
I will keep the com|mandments | of my | God.

116 Be my stay according to your word that | I may | live:
and do not disap|point me | in my | hope.

117 Hold me up and I | shall be | safe:
and I will ever de|light | in your | statutes.

118 You scorn all those who | swerve from·your | statutes:
for their | calumnies·a|gainst me·are | lies;

119 All the ungodly of the earth you | count as | dross:
therefore I | love | your com|mands.

120 My flesh | shrinks for | fear of you:
and I am a|fraid | of your | judgements.

Prayer: that our faithfulness may be deepened.

(16)   I am your servant, Lord; O give me understanding.

121 I have done what is | just and | right:
O do not give me | over·to | my op|pressors.

122 Stand surety for your | servant's | good:
let | not the | proud op|press me.

123 My eyes fail with watching for | your sal|vation:
for the fulfilment | of your | righteous | word.

124 O deal with your servant ‿
according to your | loving | mercy:
and | teach me | your | statutes.

125 I am your servant   O give me | under|standing:
that | I may | know·your com|mands.

126 It is time for the | Lord to | act:
for they | viol·ate | your | law.

127 Therefore I | love·your com|mandments:
more than gold | more·than the | finest | gold;

467

128 Therefore I straighten my paths by | all your | precepts:
     and I | hate all | lying | ways.

Prayer: for those facing moral dilemmas.

(17) *Lord, have mercy on us, and write your law in our hearts by your*
      Spirit.

129 Wonderful are | your com|mands:
     and | therefore · my | soul | keeps them.
130 The unfolding of your | word gives | light:
     it gives under|standing | to the | simple.
131 I open my mouth and draw | in my | breath:
     for I | yearn for | your com|mandments.
132 O turn to me and be | merci·ful | to me:
     as is your way with | those who | love your | name.
133 Order my steps according | to your | word:
     that no evil | may get | master·y | over me.
134 Deliver me from | man's op|pression:
     that | I may | keep your | precepts.
135 Make your face shine up|on your | servant:
     and | teach me | your | statutes.
136 My eyes gush out with | streams of | water:
     because they | pay no | heed to · your | law.

Prayer: for grace to respond to Christ's call.

(18) *The righteousness of your commands is everlasting.*

137 Righteous are | you Lord | God:
     and | just are | your | judgements;
138 The commands that | you · have com|manded:
     are ex|ceeding·ly | righteous · and | true.
139 Zeal and indignation have | choked my | mouth:
     because my enemies | have for|gotten · your | words.
140 Your word has been | tried · in the | fire:
     and | therefore · your | servant | loves it.

468

141 I am small and of | no ac|count:
     but I have | not for|gotten · your | precepts.
142 Your righteousness is an ever|lasting | righteousness:
     and your | law | is the | truth.
143 Trouble and anguish have | taken | hold on me:
     but your com|mandments · are | my de|light.
144 The righteousness of your commands is | ever|lasting:
     O give me under|standing · and | I shall | live.

Prayer: for those in trouble.

(19)   *Hear me, O Lord, I will keep your statutes.*

145 I call with my | whole | heart:
     hear me O Lord | I will | keep your | statutes.
146 I cry out to | you O | save me:
     and | I will | heed · your com|mands.
147 Before the morning light I | rise · and I | call:
     for in your | word | is my | hope.
148 Before the night watch my | eyes | wake:
     that I may | meditate · up|on your | words.
149 Hear my voice O Lord in your | loving | mercy:
     and according to your | judgements | give me | life.
150 They draw near to me who mal|icious·ly | persecute me:
     but | they are | far from · your | law.
151 You Lord are | close at | hand:
     and | all · your com|mandments · are | true.
152 I have known long since from | your com|mands:
     that you have | founded | them for | ever.

Prayer: of commitment to diligent prayer.

(20)   *In your mercy, Lord, give me life.*

153 Consider my affliction | and de|liver me:
     for I do | not for|get your | law.
154 Plead my cause and | set me | free:
     O give me life ac|cording | to your | word.

155 Salvation is | far·from the | wicked:
for they | do not | seek your | statutes.

156 Numberless O Lord are your | tender | mercies:
according to your | judgements | give me | life.

157 Many there are that persecute | me and | trouble me:
but I have not | swerved from | your com|mands.

158 I am cut to the heart when I | see the | faithless:
for they | do not | keep your | word.

159 Consider O Lord how I | love your | precepts:
and in your | mercy | give me | life.

160 The sum of your | word is | truth:
and all your righteous | judgements | stand for | ever.

Prayer: for those in urgent need.

(21)　　*Christ was obedient to death, even death on a cross.*

161 Princes have persecuted me with|out a | cause:
but my heart | stands in | awe of·your | word.

162 I am as | glad of·your | word:
as | one who | finds rich | spoil.

163 Lies I | hate·and ab|hor:
but your | law | do I | love.

164 Seven times a | day I | praise you:
be|cause of·your | righteous | judgements.

165 Great is the peace of those who | love your | law:
and | nothing·shall | make them | stumble.

166 Lord I have waited for | your sal|vation:
and I have | done | your com|mandments.

167 My soul has heeded | your com|mands:
and I | love them·be|yond | measure.

168 I have kept your precepts | and com|mands:
for all my | ways are | open·be|fore you.

Prayer: of praise and trust in God.

(22)   *I am yours, Lord, yours alone.*

169 Let my cry | come to you · O | Lord:
O give me understanding ac|cording | to your | word;

170 Let my supplication | come be|fore you:
and deliver me ac|cording | to your | promise.

171 My lips shall pour | forth your | praise:
be|cause you | teach me · your | statutes;

172 My tongue shall | sing of · your | word:
for | all · your com|mandments · are | righteousness.

173 Let your hand be | swift to | help me:
for | I have | chosen · your | precepts.

174 Lord I have longed for | your sal|vation:
and your | law is | my de|light.

175 O let my soul live that | I may | praise you:
and let your | judgements | be my | help.

176 I have gone astray like a | sheep · that is | lost:
O seek your servant
for I do | not for|get · your com|mandments.

Prayer: for all Christ's disciples.

120   *Let us know your presence, Lord God of our defence.*

1 I call to the | Lord · in my | trouble:
that | he may | answer | me.

2 O Lord deliver me from | lying | lips:
and | from the | treacher·ous | tongue.

3 What will he do to you
and what more will he do to you ⏝
O | treacher·ous | tongue?:
you are sharp as the arrows of a warrior
that are | tempered · in | coals of | juniper.

4 Alas for me * I am like a | stranger · in | Meshech:
like one who dwells a|midst the | tents of | Kedar.

5 My soul has | been too | long:
among | those · who are | enemies · to | peace.

6 I am for peace   but | when I | speak of it:
they | make them·selves | ready · for | war.

Prayer: for world peace.

121 *Here we have no lasting city; we seek the city which is to come.*

1 I lift up my | eyes · to the | hills:
  but | where · shall I | find | help?

2 My help | comes · from the | Lord:
  who has | made | heaven · and | earth.

3 He will not suffer your | foot to | stumble:
  and he who watches | over · you | will not | sleep.

4 Be sure he who has | charge of | Israel:
  will | neither | slumber · nor | sleep.

5 The Lord him|self is · your | keeper:
  the Lord is your defence up|on your | right | hand;

6 The sun shall not | strike you · by | day:
  nor | shall the | moon by | night.

7 The Lord will defend you from | all | evil:
  it is | he · who will | guard your | life.

8 The Lord will defend your going out ⌣
    and your | coming | in:
  from this time | forward · for | ever|more.

  Prayer: for all in anxiety, danger, tribulation.

122 *We have come to Mount Zion, the city of the living God.*

1 I was glad when they | said to | me:
  'Let us | go · to the | house · of the | Lord.'

2 And now our | feet are | standing:
  with|in your | gates · O Je|rusalem;

†3 Jerusalem which is | built · as a | city:
  where the | pilgrims | gather · in | unity.

4 There the tribes go up   the | tribes · of the | Lord:
  as he commanded Israel
    to give | thanks · to the | name · of the | Lord.

5 There are set | thrones of | judgement:
  the | thrones · of the | house of | David.

6 O pray for the | peace · of Je|rusalem:
  may | those who | love you | prosper.

7 Peace be with|in your | walls:
and pros|peri·ty | in your | palaces.
8 For the sake of my brothers | and com|panions:
I will | pray that | peace be | with you.
9 For the sake of the house of the | Lord our | God:
I will | seek | for your | good.

Prayer: for the unity of all Christian people.

123 *In you, Lord, have we trusted, let us never be confounded.*

1 To you I lift | up my | eyes:
you who are en|throned | in the | heavens.
2 As the eyes of servants⏑
look to the | hand of·their | master:
or as the eyes of a maid
to|ward the | hand of·her ⌐mistress,
†3 So our eyes look to the | Lord our | God:
un|til he | show us·his | mercy.
4 Have mercy upon us O Lord have | mercy·up|on us:
for we have | had our | fill·of de|rision.
5 Our souls overflow with the mockery of | those at | ease:
and with the con|tempt | of the | proud.

Prayer: that the Church may be obedient to God's call.

124 *Our help is in the name of the Lord
who has made heaven and earth.*

1 If the Lord had not been on our side⏑
now may | Israel | say:
if the Lord had not been on our side⏑
when | men rose | up a|gainst us,
2 Then they would have | swallowed us·a|live:
when their | anger·was | kindled·a|gainst us.
3 Then the waters would have overwhelmed us
and the | torrent·gone | over us:
the raging waters | would have | gone clean | over us.

473

4 But praised | be the | Lord:
who has not given us as a | prey | to their | teeth.
5 We have escaped like a bird
from the | snare · of the | fowler:
the snare is | broken · and | we have · gone | free.
6 Our help is in the | name · of the | Lord:
who has | made | heaven · and | earth.

Prayer: for those called to give an account of their faith.

125 *The Lord stands about his people for evermore.*

1 Those who put their trust in the Lord
shall | be as · Mount | Zion:
which cannot be | shaken · but en|dures for | ever.
2 As the mountains stand about Jerusalem
so stands the Lord a|bout his | people:
from this time | forward · for | ever|more.
3 For the sceptre of wickedness shall have no sway
over the land apportioned | to the | righteous:
lest the righteous | set their | hands to · do | evil.
4 Do good O Lord to | those · who are | good:
to | those · that are | upright · in | heart.
†5 As for those who turn aside to crooked ways
let the Lord lead them away with the | evil|doers:
and in | Israel | let there · be | peace.

Prayer: for our country.

126 *Those that sow in tears, shall reap with songs of joy.*

1 When the Lord turned again the | fortunes · of | Zion:
then were we like | men re|stored to | life.
2 Then was our mouth | filled with | laughter:
and | our | tongue with | singing.
3 Then said they a|mong the | heathen:
'The Lord has done great | things for | them'.

474

4 Truly the Lord has done great | things for | us:
and | therefore | we re|joiced.

5 Turn again our | fortunes · O | Lord:
as the streams re|turn · to the | dry | south.

6 Those that | sow in | tears:
shall | reap with | songs of | joy.

†7 He who goes out weeping | bearing · the | seed:
shall come again in gladness | ‿
    bringing · his | sheaves | with him.

Prayer: for refugees.

127   *Unless the Lord builds the house, their labour is but lost that build it.*

1 Unless the Lord | builds the | house:
their labour | is but | lost that | build it.

2 Unless the Lord | keeps the | city:
the | watchmen | watch in | vain.

3 It is in vain that you rise up early and go so late to rest
    eating the | bread of | toil:
for the Lord bestows honour | and on | those · whom
he | loves.

4 Behold   children are a heritage | from the | Lord:
and the | fruit · of the | womb is · his | gift.

5 Like arrows in the | hand · of a | warrior:
are the | sons · of a | man's | youth.

6 Happy the man who has his | quiver | full of them:
he will not be put to shame
    when he confronts his | enem·ies | at the | gate.

Prayer: for our parish and local community.

128   *Blessed is everyone who fears the Lord.*

1 Blessèd is everyone who | fears the | Lord:
and walks in the | confine | of his | ways.

2 You will eat the | fruit of · your | labours:
happy shall you | be and | all · shall go | well with you.

3 Your wife with|in your | house:
shall | be · as a | fruitful | vine;
4 Your children a|round your | table:
like the fresh | shoots | of the | olive.
5 Behold thus shall the | man be | blessed:
who | lives · in the | fear · of the | Lord.
6 May the Lord so | bless you · from | Zion:
that you see Jerusalem in prosperity | ⌣
all the | days of · your | life.
†7 May you see your | children's | children:
and in | Israel | let there · be | peace.

Prayer: for families, husbands, wives, children.

129 *In the world we have tribulation, but Christ has overcome the world.*

1 Many a time from my youth upward ⌣
have they | fought a|gainst me:
now | may | Israel | say,
2 Many a time from my youth upward ⌣
have they | fought a|gainst me:
but | they have | not pre|vailed.
3 They have scored my back as | with a | ploughshare:
they have | opened | long | furrows.
4 But the | Lord is | righteous:
and he has cut me | free · from the | thongs · of the | wicked.
5 They shall be confounded and | turned | backward:
all | those who | hate | Zion.
6 They shall be as the grass ⌣
that grows up|on the | housetops:
which withers before it | comes to | any | good,
7 With which no reaper may | fill his | hand:
nor the | binder · of | sheaves his | bosom.
8 And none who pass by shall say to them
'The blessing of the | Lord · be up|on you:
we | bless you · in the | name · of the | Lord.'

Prayer: for those who persecute the Church.

130 *Jesus, Lamb of God, have mercy on us.*

1 Out of the depths have I called to | you O | Lord:
Lord | hear | my | voice;
2 O let your ears con|sider | well:
the | voice · of my | suppli|cation.
3 If you Lord should note what | we do | wrong:
who | then O | Lord could | stand?
4 But there is for|giveness · with | you:
so that | you | shall be | feared.
5 I wait for the Lord * my | soul | waits for him:
and | in his | word · is my | hope.
6 My soul | looks · for the | Lord:
more than watchmen for the morning
more I say than | watchmen | for the | morning.
7 O Israel trust in the Lord
for with the | Lord · there is | mercy:
and with | him is | ample · re|demption.
8 He will re|deem | Israel:
from the | multi·tude | of his | sins.

Prayer: of trust in God.

131 *Jesus, Lamb of God, grant us your peace.*

1 O Lord my | heart is · not | proud:
nor | are my | eyes | haughty.
2 I do not busy myself in | great | matters:
or in | things too | wonder·ful | for me.
3 But I have calmed and quieted my soul
like a weaned child upon its | mother's | breast:
like a child on its mother's breast | ⌣
is my | soul with|in me.
4 O Israel | trust · in the | Lord:
from this time | forward | and for | ever.

Prayer: of childlike trust in God.

132 *God has given our Lord Jesus the throne of his father David.*

1 Lord remember David and | all his | trouble:
how he swore an oath to the Lord
    and vowed to the | Mighty | One of | Jacob;

2 'I will not enter the | shelter · of my | house:
nor climb into the | comfort | of my | bed;

3 'I will not give | sleep to · my | eyes:
or | slumber | to my | eyelids,

4 'Till I find out a place for the | ark · of the | Lord:
a dwelling for the | Mighty | One of | Jacob.'

5 Lo we | heard of it · at | Ephrathah:
we | found it · in the | fields of | Ja-ar.

6 Let us go to the | place of · his | dwelling:
let us fall upon our | knees be|fore his | footstool.

7 Arise O Lord | into · your | resting-place:
you | and the | ark of · your | might.

8 Let your priests be | clothed with | righteousness:
and let your | faithful · ones | shout for | joy.

†9 For the sake of | David · your | servant:
do not turn away the | face of | your an|ointed.

10 The Lord has | sworn to | David:
an | oath · which he | will not | break;

11 'One who is the | fruit of · your | body:
I will | set up|on your | throne.

12 'If your children will keep my covenant
    and the com|mands · which I | teach them:
their children also shall sit up|on your | throne for | ever.'

13 For the Lord has chosen | Zion · for him|self:
he has de|sired it · for his | habi|tation.

14 'This shall be my | resting-place · for | ever:
here will I dwell   for | my de|light · is in | her.

15 'I will bless her pro|visions · with a|bundance:
I will | satisfy · her | poor with | bread.

16 'I will clothe her | priests with · sal|vation:
   and her | faithful ones · shall | shout for | joy.

17 'There will I make a horn to sprout‿
      for the | family · of | David:
   I have prepared a | lamp for | my an|ointed.

†18 'As for his enemies   I will | cover them · with | shame:
   but upon his | head · shall his | crown be | bright.'

Prayer: that we may be built into a living temple for the Lord.

133   *Let us love one another, for love is of God.*

1 Behold how good and how | lovely · it | is:
   when brothers | live to|gether · in | unity.

2 It is fragrant as oil upon the head
      that runs down | over · the | beard:
   fragrant as oil upon the beard of Aaron
      that ran down over the | collar | of his | robe.

3 It is like a | dew of | Hermon:
   like the dew that falls up|on the | hill of | Zion.

4 For there the Lord has com|manded · his | blessing:
   which is | life for | ever|more.

Prayer: for fellow Christians.

134   *Praise God, all his servants; bless the Lord through the night.*

1 Come bless the Lord   all you | servants · of the | Lord:
   you that by night | stand · in the | house of · our | God.

2 Lift up your hands toward the holy place‿
      and | bless the | Lord:
   may the Lord bless you from Zion
      the | Lord who · made | heaven · and | earth.

Prayer: for night workers.

135   *Give thanks to the Lord for he is good, his mercy endures for ever.*

1 Praise the Lord
      praise the | name · of the | Lord:
   praise him you | servants | of the | Lord,

2 Who stand in the | house · of the | Lord:
   in the | courts · of the | house of · our | God.

3 Praise the Lord for the | Lord is | gracious:
   sing praises to his | name for | it is | good.

4 For the Lord has chosen Jacob | for him|self:
   and Israel | as his | own pos|session.

5 I know that the | Lord is | great:
   and that our | Lord · is a|bove all | gods.

6 He does whatever he wills
      in heaven and up|on the | earth:
   in the seas and | in the | great | depths.

7 He brings up clouds from the | ends · of the | earth:
   he makes lightning for the rain
      and brings the | wind | out of · his | storehouses.

8 He struck down the | firstborn · of | Egypt:
   both | man and | beast a|like.

9 He sent signs and wonders into your | midst O | Egypt:
   against Pharaoh and a|gainst | all his | servants.

10 He struck down | great | nations:
   and | slew | mighty | kings,

11 Sihon king of the Amorites
      and Og the | king of | Bashan:
   and | all the | princes · of | Canaan.

12 He made over their | land · as a | heritage:
   a | heritage · for | Israel · his | people.

13 O Lord your name shall en|dure for | ever:
   so shall your renown through|out all | gener|ations.

14 For the Lord will | vindicate · his | people:
   he will take | pity | on his | servants.

15 As for the idols of the nations
      they are but | silver · and | gold:
   the | work · of a | man's | hand.

16 They have | mouths but | speak not:
   they have | eyes · but they | cannot | see.

17 They have ears yet | hear | nothing:
   there is no | breath | in their | nostrils.

18 Those who make them | shall be | like them:
    so shall | every|one that | trusts in them.

19 Bless the Lord O | house of | Israel:
    bless the | Lord O | house of | Aaron.
20 Bless the Lord O | house of | Levi:
    you that | fear the · Lord | bless the | Lord.
21 Blessèd be the | Lord from | Zion:
    he that dwells in Jerusalem|
        Praise | – the | Lord.

Prayer: that we may be delivered from idolatry.

136 *Praise to the Lord, our creator and our redeemer!*

1 O give thanks to the Lord for | he is | good:
   for his | mercy · en|dures for | ever.
2 O give thanks to the | God of | gods:
   for his | mercy · en|dures for | ever.
3 O give thanks to the | Lord of | lords:
   for his | mercy · en|dures for | ever;

4 To him who alone does | great | wonders:
   for his | mercy · en|dures for | ever;
5 Who by wisdom | made the | heavens:
   for his | mercy · en|dures for | ever;
6 Who stretched out the earth up|on the | waters:
   for his | mercy · en|dures for | ever;
7 Who made the | great | lights:
   for his | mercy · en|dures for | ever,
8 The sun to | rule the | day:
   for his | mercy · en|dures for | ever,
9 The moon and the stars to | govern · the | night:
   for his | mercy · en|dures for | ever;

10 Who struck down Egypt | and its | firstborn:
    for his | mercy · en|dures for | ever;
11 Who brought out Israel | from a|mong them:
    for his | mercy · en|dures for | ever,

481

†12 With a strong hand and with | outstretched | arm:
　　for his | mercy·en|dures for | ever;

13 Who divided the Red Sea into | two | parts:
　　for his | mercy·en|dures for | ever,

14 And made Israel pass | through the | midst of it:
　　for his | mercy·en|dures for | ever;

15 Who cast off Pharaoh and his host into the | Red | Sea:
　　for his | mercy·en|dures for | ever;

16 Who led his people | through the | wilderness:
　　for his | mercy·en|dures for | ever;

17 Who struck down | great | kings:
　　for his | mercy·en|dures for | ever;

18 Who slew | mighty | kings:
　　for his | mercy·en|dures for | ever,

19 Sihon | king·of the | Amorites:
　　for his | mercy·en|dures for | ever,

20 And Og the | king of | Bashan:
　　for his | mercy·en|dures for | ever;

21 Who made over their | land·as a | heritage:
　　for his | mercy·en|dures for | ever,

22 As a heritage for | Israel·his | servant:
　　for his | mercy·en|dures for | ever;

23 Who remembered us in our hu|mili|ation:
　　for his | mercy·en|dures for | ever,

24 And delivered us | from our | enemies:
　　for his | mercy·en|dures for | ever;

25 Who gives food to | all that | lives:
　　for his | mercy·en|dures for | ever.

26 O give thanks to the | God of | heaven:
　　for his | mercy·en|dures for | ever.

Prayer: for those who do not know God's love.

482

137 *Let me never forget you, Jerusalem, city of my God.*

1 By the waters of Babylon we sat | down and | wept:
  when | we re|membered | Zion.
2 As for our harps we | hung them | up:
  upon the | trees · that are | in that | land.
3 For there those who led us away captive‿
  re|quired of us · a | song:
  and those who had despoiled us demanded mirth
  saying 'Sing us | one of · the | songs of | Zion'.
*4 How can we sing the Lord's | song · in a | strange | land?
5 If I forget you | O Je|rusalem:
  let my right | hand for|get its | mastery.
6 Let my tongue cling to the | roof of · my | mouth:
  if I do not remember you
  if I do not prefer Jerusalem a|bove my | chief | joy.
7 Remember O Lord against the Edomites‿
  the | day · of Je|rusalem:
  how they said 'Down with it   down with it |
  raze it · to | its found|ations.'
8 O daughter of Babylon | you that · lay | waste:
  happy shall he be who serves | you‿
  as | you have · served | us;
†9 Happy shall he be who | takes your | little ones:
  and | dashes them · a|gainst the | stones.

Prayer: for deliverance from worldliness.

138 *Praise the Lord, O my soul.*

1 I will give you thanks O Lord with my | whole | heart:
  even before the | gods · will I | sing your | praises.
2 I will bow down toward your holy temple
  and give | thanks to · your | name:
  because of your faithfulness and your loving-kindness
  for you have made your name and your | word‿
  su|preme · over | all things.

* sung to the last four bars of the chant.

3 At a time when I called to you you | gave me | answer:
    and put new | strength with|in my | soul.

4 All the kings of the earth shall | praise you · O | Lord:
    for they have | heard the | words of · your | mouth;

5 And they shall sing of the | ways · of the | Lord:
    that the | glory · of the | Lord is | great.

6 For though the Lord is exalted   he looks up|on the | lowl
    but he | humbles · the | proud · from a|far.

7 Though I walk in the midst of danger
        yet will you pre|serve my | life:
    you will stretch out your hand against the fury of my ⌣
        enemies * and | your right | hand shall | save me.

8 The Lord will complete his | purpose | for me:
    your loving-kindness O Lord endures for ever
        do not forsake the | work · of your | own | hands.

Thanksgiving: for God's providence and care.

139   *Search me out, O God, and know my heart.*

1 O Lord you have searched me | out and | known me:
    you know when I sit or when I stand
        you comprehend my | thoughts | long be|fore.

2 You discern my path   and the places | where I | rest:
    you are ac|quainted · with | all my | ways.

3 For there is not a | word · on my | tongue:
    but you Lord | know it | alto|gether.

4 You have encompassed me be|hind · and be|fore:
    and have | laid your | hand up|on me.

†5 Such knowledge is too | wonder·ful | for me:
    so | high · that I | cannot · en|dure it.

6 Where shall I | go · from your | spirit:
    or where shall I | flee | from your | presence?

7 If I ascend into heaven | you are | there:
    if I make my bed in the grave | you are | there | also.

8 If I spread out my wings to|wards the | morning:
   or dwell in the | utter·most | parts·of the | sea,

9 Even there your | hand shall | lead me:
   and | your right | hand shall | hold me.

10 If I say 'Surely the | darkness·will | cover me:
   and the | night | will en|close me',

11 The darkness is no darkness with you
   but the night is as | clear·as the | day:
   the darkness and the | light are | both a|like.

12 For you have created my | inward | parts:
   you knit me together | in my | mother's | womb.

13 I will praise you for | you are·to be | feared:
   fearful are your | acts and | wonderful·your | works.

14 You knew my soul
   and my bones were not | hidden | from you:
   when I was formed in secret
   and | woven·in the | depths·of the | earth.

15 Your eyes saw my limbs when they were | yet im|perfect:
   and in your book were | all my | members | written;

16 Day by | day·they were | fashioned:
   and not | one was | late in | growing.

17 How deep are your thoughts to | me O | God:
   and how | great | is the | sum of them!

18 Were I to count them
   they are more in number | than the | sand:
   were I to come to the | end·I would | still be | with you.

19 If only you would slay the | wicked·O | God:
   if only the men of | blood·would de|part | from me!

20 For they affront you | by their | evil:
   and your enemies ex|alt them|selves a|gainst you.

21 Do I not hate them O Lord that | hate | you:
   do I not loathe | those·who re|bel a|gainst you?

22 I hate them with a | perfect | hatred:
   they | have be|come my | enemies.

23 Search me out O God and | know my | heart:
put me to the | proof and | know my | thoughts.

24 Look well lest there be any way of | wicked·ness | in me:
and lead me in the | way·that is | ever|lasting.

Prayer: for all who try to escape from the loving demands of God.

140 *You, Lord, are my refuge and strength.*

1 Deliver me O Lord from | evil | men:
and pre|serve me·from | vio·lent | men,

2 Who devise mischief | in their | hearts:
who stir up | enmi·ty | day by | day.

3 They have sharpened their | tongues·like a | serpent's:
and the venom of | asps is | under·their | lips.

4 Keep me O Lord from the | power·of the | wicked:
preserve me from violent men
who think to | thrust me | from my | course.

5 The arrogant have laid a snare for me
and rogues have | stretched the | net:
they have set | traps a|long my | way.

6 But I have said to the Lord | 'You are·my | God':
hear O | Lord the | voice of·my | pleading.

7 O Lord my God and my | sure | stronghold:
you have covered my | head·in the | day of | battle.

8 Do not fulfil O Lord the de|sire·of the | wicked:
nor further the | evil·that he | has de|vised.

9 Let not those that beset me | lift their | heads:
but let the mischief that is | on their | lips | bury them.

10 Let hot burning coals be | poured up|on them:
let them be plunged into that miry pit⏝
from | which·they shall | never·a|rise.

†11 Let no man of evil tongue find | footing·in the | land:
the evil   the violent man
let him be | hunted | to the | end.

12 I know that the Lord will work justice |
for·the op|pressed:
and right | judgements | for the | poor.

486

13 Surely the righteous shall have cause⌣
        to | praise your | name:
    and the | just shall | dwell in · your | sight.

   Prayer: to know the power of the cross.

141 *Let the lifting up of my hands be before you as the evening sacrifice.*

1 O Lord I call to you   make | haste to | help me:
   and | hear my | voice · when I | cry.

2 Let my prayer be as | incense · be|fore you:
   and the lifting up of my | hands · as the | evening | sacrifice.

3 Set a guard O | Lord · on my | mouth:
   and | keep the | door · of my | lips.

4 Let not my heart incline to evil speech
        to join in wickedness with | wrong|doers:
   let me not taste the | pleasures | of their | table.

5 But let the righteous | man chas|tise me:
   and the | faithful | man re|buke me.

6 Let not the oil of the wicked an|oint my | head:
   for I pray to you | still a|gainst their | wickedness.

7 They shall be cast down⌣
        by that Mighty One who | is their | judge:
   and how pleasing shall my words | be to | them | then!

8 As when a farmer | breaks the | ground:
   so shall their bones lie | scattered · ⌣
        at the | mouth of | Sheol.

9 But my eyes look to you O | Lord my | God:
   to you I come for refuge |do not · pour | out my | life.

10 Keep me from the snare that | they have | laid for me:
    and from the | traps · of the | evil|doers.

11 Let the wicked fall together into their | own | nets:
    whilst | I pass | safely | by.

   Prayer: for patience in affliction.

142 *All things work for good for those who love God.*

1 I call to the Lord with a | loud | voice:
   with loud | voice · I en|treat his | favour.

2 I pour out my com|plaint be|fore him:
   and | tell him | all my | trouble.

3 When my spirit is faint within me you | know my | path:
   in the way where I walk | ⌣
      they have | hidden · a | snare for me.

4 I look to my right | hand and | see:
   but | no | man will | know me;

5 All es|cape is | gone:
   and | there is | no one · who | cares for me.

6 I call to you O Lord   I say | 'You are · my | refuge:
   you are my | portion · in the | land · of the | living.'

7 Heed my loud crying   for I am | brought · very | low:
   O save me from my persecutors| ⌣
      for they | are too | strong for me.

8 Bring me | out of · the | prison-house:
   that | I may | praise your | name.

†9 When you have given me | my re|ward:
   then will the | righteous | gather · a|bout me.

   Prayer: for those on the way back to God.

143 *Hide not your face from me, Lord, for my trust is in you.*

1 Hear my | prayer O | Lord:
   in your faithfulness consider my petition
      and in your | righteous·ness | give me | answer.

2 Bring not your servant | into | judgement:
   for in your sight can | no man | living · be | justified.

3 For the enemy has pursued me
      he has crushed my | life · to the | ground:
   he has made me dwell in darkness ⌣
      like | those for | ever | dead.

4 Therefore my | spirit · grows | faint:
   and my | heart · is ap|palled with|in me.

5 I remember the days of old
    I think on all that | you have | done:
I con|sider · the | works of · your | hands.
6 I stretch out my | hands to|ward you:
my soul yearns for you | like a | thirsty | land.
7 Be swift to hear me O Lord   for my | spirit | fails:
hide not your face from me
    lest I be like | those who · go | down · to the | Pit.
8 O let me hear of your merciful kindness in the morning
    for my | trust · is in | you:
show me the way that I should go
    for | you | are my | hope.
9 Deliver me from my | enemies · O | Lord:
for I | run to | you for | shelter.
10 Teach me to do your will   for | you are · my | God:
let your kindly spirit | lead me · in an | even | path.
11 For your name's sake O Lord pre|serve my | life:
and for the sake of your righteousness |
    bring me | out of | trouble.
12 In your merciful goodness slay my enemies
    and destroy all those that | come a|gainst me:
for | truly · I | am your | servant.

Prayer: for the discouraged and the despairing.

144   *I can do all things in God who strengthens me.*

1 Blessèd be the | Lord my | Rock:
who teaches my hands to | war · and my | fingers · to | fight;
2 My strength and my stronghold
    my fortress and | my de|liverer:
my shield to whom I come for refuge
    who sub|dues the | peoples | under me.
3 Lord what is man
    that you should be | mindful | of him:
or the son of man | that you | should con|sider him?

4 Man is but a | breath of | wind:
   his days are like a | shadow · that | passes · a|way.

5 Part the heavens O Lord and | come | down:
   touch the | mountains · and | they shall | smoke.

6 Dart forth your lightnings
      and scatter them on | every | side:
   let loose your | arrows · with the | roar · of the | thunderbolt.

7 Reach down your hand from on high
      rescue me   and pluck me out of the | great | waters:
   out of the | hands | of the | aliens,

8 Whose | mouths speak | perjury:
   and their right hand | is a · right | hand of | falsehood.

9 I will sing you a new | song O | God:
   on the ten-stringed | lute · will I | sing your | praises.

10 You have given | victory · to | kings:
   and de|liverance · to | David · your | servant.

11 O save me from the | peril · of the | sword:
   pluck me out of the | hands | of the | aliens,

12 Whose | mouths speak | perjury:
   and their right hand | is a · right | hand of | falsehood.

13 Our sons in their youth shall be like | sturdy | plants:
   and our daughters as the | carved | corners · of | palaces.

14 Our barns shall be full   and give food of | every | kind:
   the sheep shall lamb in our fields ⌣
      in | thousands · and | tens of | thousands.

15 Our cattle shall be heavy with calf
      there shall be no miscarriage or un|timely | birth:
   and no loud | crying | in our | streets.

16 Happy the people whose lot is | such as | this:
   happy that people who | have the | Lord for · their |
      God!

   Prayer: for confidence to do as God wills.

145 *Your loving kindness will follow me all the days of my life.*

1 I will exalt you O | God my | king:
  I will bless your | name for | ever · and | ever.

2 Every|day · will I | bless you:
  and praise your | name for | ever · and | ever.

3 Great is the Lord
      and wonderfully | worthy · to be | praised:
  his greatness is | past | searching | out.

4 One generation shall praise your | works · to an|other:
  and de|clare your | mighty | acts.

5 As for me * I will be talking ⌣
      of the glorious splendour | of your | majesty:
  I will tell the | story · of your | marvel·lous | works.

6 Men shall recount the power of your | terri·ble | deeds:
  and | I will · pro|claim your | greatness.

†7 Their lips shall flow ⌣
      with the remembrance of your a|bundant | goodness:
  they shall | shout for | joy at · your | righteousness.

8 The Lord is | gracious · and com|passionate:
  slow to anger | and of | great | goodness.

9 The Lord is | loving · to | every man:
  and his mercy is | over | all his | works.

10 All creation | praises you · O | Lord:
  and your faithful | servants | bless your | name.

11 They speak of the glory | of your | kingdom:
  and | tell of · your | great | might,

†12 That all mankind may know your | mighty | acts:
  and the glorious | splendour | of your | kingdom.

13 Your kingdom is an ever|lasting | kingdom:
  and your dominion en|dures through | all · gener|ations.

14 The Lord upholds all | those who | stumble:
  and raises up | those · that are | bowed | down.

15 The eyes of all look to | you in | hope:
  and you give them their | food in | due | season;

16 You open | wide your | hand:
  and fill all things | living · with your | bounte·ous | gift.

491

17 The Lord is just in | all his | ways:
and | faithful · in | all his | dealings.

18 The Lord is near to all who | call up|on him:
to all who | call up|on him · in | truth.

19 He will fulfil the desire of | those that | fear him:
he will | hear their | cry and | save them.

20 The Lord preserves all | those that | love him:
but the wicked | he will | utterly · de|stroy.

†21 My mouth shall speak the | praises · of the | Lord:
and let all flesh bless his holy | name
for | ever · and | ever.

Praise: to God for the bounty of the earth.

146 *While I have any being I will sing praises to my God.*

1 Praise the Lord *   praise the Lord | O my | soul:
while I | live · I will | praise the | Lord;

2 While I | have · any | being:
I will sing | praises | to my | God.

3 Put not your | trust in | princes:
nor in the sons of | men who | cannot | save.

4 For when their breath goes from them
they return a|gain · to the | earth:
and on that day | all their | thoughts | perish.

5 Blessèd is the man whose help is the | God of | Jacob:
whose hope is | in the | Lord his | God,

6 The God who made | heaven · and | earth:
the sea and | all | that is | in them,

†7 Who keeps | faith for | ever:
who deals justice to | those that | are op|pressed.

8 The Lord gives | food · to the | hungry:
and | sets the | captives | free.

9 The Lord gives | sight · to the | blind:
the Lord lifts up | those · that are | bowed | down.

10 The Lord | loves the | righteous:
the Lord cares for the | stranger | in the | land.

11 He upholds the | widow · and the | fatherless:
      as for the way of the wicked he | turns it | upside | down.

†12 The Lord shall be | king for | ever:
      your God O Zion ⌣
          shall reign through all generations |
          Praise | – the | Lord.

Prayer: to praise God in our lives.

147 *Cry out with joy to the Lord, all the earth: Alleluia.*

1 O praise the Lord
      for it is good to sing praises | to our | God:
      and to | praise him · is | joyful · and | right.

2 The Lord is re|building · Je|rusalem:
      he is gathering together ⌣
          the | scattered | outcasts · of | Israel.

3 He heals the | broken · in | spirit:
      and | binds | up their | wounds.

4 He counts the | number · of the | stars:
      and | calls them | all by | name.

5 Great is our Lord and | great · is his | power:
      there is no | measuring · his | under|standing.

6 The Lord re|stores the | humble:
      but he brings down the | wicked | to the | dust.

7 O sing to the Lord a | song of | thanksgiving:
      sing praises to our | God up|on the | harp.

8 He covers the heavens with cloud
          and prepares | rain · for the | earth:
      and makes the grass to | sprout up|on the | mountains.

9 He gives the | cattle · their | food:
      and feeds the young | ravens · that | call | to him.

10 He takes no pleasure in the | strength · of a | horse:
      nor does he de|light in | any · man's | legs,

†11 But the Lord's delight is in | those that | fear him:
      who | wait in | hope · for his | mercy.

493

12 Praise the | Lord · O Je|rusalem:
    sing | praises · to your | God O | Zion.

13 For he has strengthened the | bars of · your | gates:
    and | blessed your | children · with|in you.

14 He makes peace with|in your | borders:
    and satisfies you | with the | finest | wheat.

15 He sends his com|mand · to the | earth:
    and his | word runs | very | swiftly.

16 He gives | snow like | wool:
    and | scatters · the | hoar-frost · like | ashes.

17 He sprinkles his ice like | morsels · of | bread:
    and the waters | harden | at his | frost.

†18 He sends out his | word and | melts them:
    he blows with his | wind · and the | waters | flow.

19 He made his word | known to | Jacob:
    his | statutes · and | judgements · to | Israel.

20 He has not dealt so with any | other | nation:
    nor have they knowledge of his laws |
        Praise | – the | Lord.

Thanksgiving: for the Church.

148 *To him who sits on the throne and to the Lamb be blessing and glory
    for ever.*

1 Praise the Lord
    praise the | Lord from | heaven:
    O | praise him | in the | heights.

2 Praise him | all his | angels:
    O | praise him | all his | host.

3 Praise him | sun and | moon:
    praise him | all you | stars of | light.

4 Praise him you | highest | heaven:
    and you waters that | are a|bove the | heavens.

5 Let them praise the | name · of the | Lord:
    for he com|manded · and | they were | made.

6 He established them for | ever · and | ever:
    he made an ordinance which | shall not | pass a|way.

7 O praise the | Lord · from the | earth:
  praise him you sea-|monsters · and | all | deeps;

8 Fire and hail | mist and | snow:
  and storm-wind ful|filling | his com|mand;

9 Mountains and | all | hills:
  fruiting | trees and | all | cedars;

10 Beasts of the wild and | all | cattle:
   creeping | things and | winged | birds;

11 Kings of the earth and | all | peoples:
   princes and all | rulers | of the | world;

12 Young | men and | maidens:
   old | men and | children · to|gether.

13 Let them praise the | name · of the | Lord:
   for | his · name a|lone · is ex|alted.

14 His glory is above | earth and | heaven:
   and he has lifted | high the | horn · of his | people.

†15 Therefore he is the praise of | all his | servants:
   of the children of Israel
     a people that is near him |
     Praise | – the | Lord.

Prayer: for farmers, and the right use of natural resources.

149 *Throughout the world the holy Church acclaims you.*

1 O praise the Lord
    and sing to the Lord a | new | song:
  O praise him in the as|sembly | of the | faithful.

2 Let Israel rejoice in | him that | made him:
  let the children of Zion be | joyful | in their | king.

3 Let them praise him | in the | dance:
  let them sing his praise with | timbrel | and with | harp.

4 For the Lord takes de|light · in his | people:
  he adorns the | meek with | his sal|vation.

5 Let his faithful ones ex|ult · in his | glory:
  let them sing for | joy up|on their | beds.

6 Let the high praises of God be | in their | mouths:
  and a | two-edged | sword · in their | hands,

7 To execute vengeance ǀ on the ǀ nations:
and ǀ chastisement · upǀon the ǀ peoples,

8 To bind their ǀ kings in ǀ chains:
and their ǀ nobles · with ǀ fetters · of ǀ iron,

†9 To visit upon them the judgement that ǀ is deǀcreed:
such honour belongs ⌣

    to all his faithful servants ǀ
    Praise ǀ – the ǀ Lord.

Thanksgiving: for the spread of the gospel.

150   *Praise God in the firmament of his power.*

1 Praise the Lord
    O praise ǀ God · in his ǀ sanctuary:
praise him in the ǀ firma·ment ǀ of his ǀ power.

2 Praise him for his ǀ mighty ǀ acts:
praise him according to ǀ his aǀbundant ǀ goodness.

3 Praise him in the ǀ blast · of the ǀ ram's horn:
praise him upǀon the ǀ lute and ǀ harp.

4 Praise him with the ǀ timbrel · and ǀ dances:
praise him upǀon the ǀ strings and ǀ pipe.

5 Praise him on the ǀ high-· sounding ǀ cymbals:
praise him upǀon the ǀ loud ǀ cymbals.

6 Let everything that has breath ǀ praise the ǀ Lord:
O ǀ praise ǀ –the ǀ Lord!

Praise God: for himself.

Baptism and Pastoral Services

Eupomatia laurina
Copper laurel

Thanksgiving for the Birth
of a Child,
before the Baptism

This service may be used in the church either apart from other services or
during a service, or immediately before the child is baptized. It may be used,
at the discretion of the minister, in the hospital or at the child's home.

1   *The minister says*

N and N wish to give thanks to God for the birth of their
son/daughter. They ask us to pray with them for God's guidance and blessing on them all as *he* grows up.

Let us therefore say together

2   Psalm 127.1-4

1 Unless the Lord | builds the | house:
   their labour | is but | lost that | build it.

2 Unless the Lord | keeps the | city:
   the | watchmen | watch in | vain.

3 It is in vain that you rise up early and go so late to rest
      eating the | bread of | toil:
   for the Lord bestows | honour | and on | those · whom
      he | loves.

4 Behold   children are a heritage | from the | Lord:
   and the | fruit · of the | womb is · his | gift.

   Glo|ry to | God: Father | Son and | Holy | Spirit;
   As in the be|ginning · so | now: and for | ever | A|men

3   *The minister says*

Let us pray.

God our heavenly Father, we thank you and praise your
glorious Name, because you have blessed these your servants
and given them the gift of a *son/daughter*. Grant that they
may lead their child into the christian way of life, so that
your will may be done and your glory made known; through
Jesus Christ our Lord.   **Amen.**

4   Or this general thanksgiving may be said by all

Almighty God, Father of all mercies,

we your unworthy servants give humble and hearty thanks

for all your goodness and loving kindness to us and to all men;

and especially to your servants N and N for the gift of a *son/daughter*.

We bless you for our creation, preservation, and all the blessings of this life;

but above all for your amazing love

in the redemption of the world by our Lord Jesus Christ;

for the means of grace;

and for the hope of glory.

And, we pray, give us that due sense of all your mercies,

that our hearts may be truly thankful and that we may declare your praise

not only with our lips, but in our lives,

by giving up ourselves to your service,

and by walking before you in holiness and righteousness all our days;

through Jesus Christ our Lord,

to whom, with you and the Holy Spirit, be all honour and glory,

now and for ever. Amen.

5   All say the Lord's Prayer together.

6   The minister concludes the service with the Blessing or the Grace.

NOTE

§§4, 5, and 6 may be omitted if the service is used just before the baptism. If the service is used at Morning or Evening Prayer or at The Holy Communion, it may be used immediately after the entrance of the minister, after the Collects, or before the Intercession.

A SERVICE FOR THE
Public Baptism of Infants
TO BE USED IN THE CHURCH
FIRST ORDER

Baptism ought, whenever possible, to be administered at a public service on Sundays (see Note 2 on page 505), not only so that the whole congregation may witness the admission of the newly-baptized into Christ's Church and welcome them, but also so that Christians may be reminded of the profession of faith and obedience to God which they made in their own baptism.

Before the service begins, the priest shall ask the child's parents and godparents whether or not the child has already been baptized. If the infant has been baptized privately (see Note 1 on page 505), the priest shall assure himself that the baptism was carried out in due form, and proceed to use the Lord's Prayer and §§4, 5, 6, 7, 10, 11, and 13 of this service.

If it is stated that the child was baptized, but the priest is not satisfied that the child was baptized with water 'In the name of the Father, and of the Son, and of the Holy Spirit', he shall use the whole service with this form of words at §9, 'If you are not already baptized, N, I baptize you in the name of the Father, and of the Son, and of the Holy Spirit.'

Parents and godparents are to be instructed, either privately or openly, as to their duties regarding the Christian upbringing of those baptized.

It is desirable that the child's parents associate themselves with the godparents and make the answers with them in this service.

A male child shall have two godfathers and one godmother.
A female child shall have two godmothers and one godfather.

1   The priest welcomes those who have brought children to be baptized.
2   The priest addresses the congregation

God in his love has acted through Jesus Christ to free us from our slavery to sin. When Jesus had risen from the dead, he said to his disciples, 'All authority in heaven and on earth has been given to me. Go therefore and make all nations my disciples, baptizing them in the name of the Father and of the Son and of the Holy Spirit, teaching them to observe all I have commanded you.'

500

Soon after, the apostle Peter began preaching, 'Repent, and be baptized every one of you in the name of the Lord Jesus for the forgiveness of sins; and you will receive the gift of the Holy Spirit. For the promise is to you, and to your children, and to every one whom the Lord our God calls to him.'

Let us then pray that God will grant to *this child* that which by nature *he* cannot have, that *he* may be baptized with water and the Holy Spirit, and received into Christ's holy church, and be made *a* living *member* of his body.

3 The minister and congregation pray this prayer together, all standing

Lord God, our heavenly Father,
we thank you for your great goodness
in calling us to know you and to put our trust in you.
Increase this knowledge and strengthen our faith.
Give your Holy Spirit to *this child*,
that *he* may be born again and made *an heir* of everlasting
   salvation;
through Jesus Christ our Lord,
who lives and reigns with you and the Holy Spirit,
one God, now and for ever.   Amen.

4 The Gospel which follows, or one or more of the readings given on page 528, is read

Hear the Gospel of our Lord Jesus Christ according to Saint Mark, chapter ten, beginning at verse thirteen.

And they were bringing children to Jesus, that he might touch them; and the disciples rebuked them. But when Jesus saw it he was indignant, and said to them, 'Let the children come to me, do not hinder them; for to such belongs the kingdom of God. Truly, I say to you, whoever does not receive the kingdom of God like a child shall not enter it.' And he took them in his arms and blessed them, laying his hands upon them.

5   The congregation may be seated, and the minister continues

We read in the gospel the love of Jesus towards the children
of God's people, and his readiness to bless them. The love
of Jesus is still the same, and in the power of his resurrection
he stands ready to give the blessing of eternal life to our children whom we bring to him in faith. Children must indeed
make their own response of faith and obedience towards God
when they are able to do so. The rejection of sin and the confession of faith in Jesus Christ which *this child* must one day
make for *himself* are the conditions required for baptism, and
it is proper that they be declared in *his* name. Those of you
who already trust in Christ, and are willing to teach and encourage *him* in the same faith, are invited to make the baptismal promises on *his* behalf.

6   The minister invites the godparents to stand, and he addresses
them as follows

Are you yourself a follower of Jesus Christ and a member
of his church, sincerely believing the promises of God?

The godparents answer

I am.

Are you willing to sponsor this child, answering for *him* now,
and accepting responsibility for *his* Christian upbringing?

I am willing.

I ask you now to answer in the name of this child:

7   The baptismal vows of repentance, faith, and obedience, are made
in each child's name by *his* godparents

Do you renounce the devil and all his works,
the empty display and false values of the world,
and the sinful desires of the flesh,
so that you will not follow nor be led by them?

I renounce them all.

Do you believe in God, the Father almighty,
maker of heaven and earth?

Do you believe in Jesus Christ, his only Son our Lord?
And that he was conceived by the Holy Spirit,
born of the virgin Mary;
that he suffered under Pontius Pilate,
was crucified, dead, and buried;
that he went down to the place of the dead,
and also rose again the third day?
That he ascended into heaven,
and is seated at the right hand of God the Father
almighty,
and from there shall come to judge the living and the
dead?
And do you believe in the Holy Spirit;
the holy catholic church;
the communion of saints;
the forgiveness of sins;
the resurrection of the body,
and the life everlasting?

All this I firmly believe.

Will you keep God's holy will and commandments, and serve
him faithfully throughout your life?

With his help I intend to do so.

8   All standing, the priest says

Let us pray.

Lord, our merciful God, of your infinite love you have made
a covenant with us in your dear Son our Saviour Jesus
Christ, in which you have promised to be our God, and the
God and Father of our children. Fulfil your promise to us,
good Lord. Enable us who are baptized in your name to live
the holy life of the people whom you have bound to yourself
by covenant. And now we pray for *this child*. For Jesus
Christ's sake receive *him* into the number of your children.
Sanctify this water for the mystical washing away of sin; and
grant that *he* who *is* now to be baptized in it may

receive the new birth from above; may *he* die to sin and rise again to righteousness. May all things belonging to the Spirit live and grow in *him*, and mark *him* as yours for ever; through Jesus Christ our Lord. **Amen.**

9　The priest then takes the child and, having asked *his* name, he baptizes *him*. He dips *him* in the water, or pours water on *him*, saying

N, I baptize you in the name of the Father, and of the Son, and of the Holy Spirit. **Amen.**

10　The priest continues; he makes a cross on the child's forehead at the words sign *him* with the sign of the cross.

We receive this child into the congregation of Christ's flock and sign *him* with the sign of the cross, to show that *he* will not be ashamed to confess the faith of Christ crucified, and to fight bravely under his banner against sin, the world, and the devil, and to continue Christ's faithful soldier and servant until *his* life's end. **Amen.**

11　For each child, or when all have been baptized and received, the minister says

Blessed be the God and Father of our Lord Jesus Christ for birth from above and for the remission of sins. May almighty God, according to his gracious promise, finish the work of salvation begun in you, bringing you to the joyful resurrection and to the fulfilment of his eternal kingdom. **Amen.**

‡12　A hymn of praise or of dedication to discipleship may be sung.

13　These prayers are said now, or later in the service

Almighty God, our heavenly Father, whose Son Jesus Christ shared at Nazareth the life of an earthly home: bless our homes, we pray. Help parents to impart the knowledge of you and of your love; and children to respond with love and obedience. May our homes be blessed with peace and joy; through Jesus Christ our Lord. **Amen.**

O God, by whose Spirit the whole body of the church is governed and sanctified: preserve in the new-born children of your family the fulness of your grace. Grant that, having died and been buried with Christ, they may know the power of his risen life in their daily living. Keep us all fervent in the faith, and strong to endure to the end in your service, through Jesus Christ our Lord.   **Amen.**

‡14   If it is not used elsewhere in the service, the Lord's Prayer should now be said.

‡15   If the baptism is administered apart from another service, it may conclude with the congregation saying

The grace of our Lord Jesus Christ, and the love of God, and the fellowship of the Holy Spirit, be with us all evermore.   Amen.

NOTES

1 When need compels parents to ask that their children be baptized privately, baptism is to be administered in this way: Prayer, including the Lord's Prayer, should be offered as the time and circumstances permit. Then the child shall be named, and the minister shall pour water upon *him*, saying, 'N, I baptize you in the name of the Father, and of the Son, and of the Holy Spirit.   **Amen.**' The minister may add the prayer at §11.

2 This service may be inserted into Morning or Evening Prayer to replace the second reading with its canticle and the creed, or it may be inserted into The Holy Communion so as to replace the Gospel and creed. On Sundays and red letter days the collect and readings should be those of the day, but on other days the readings provided in the other Service for the Public Baptism of Infants (page 519) may be used.

3 When this order is used apart from the public service on Sundays, it is desirable that representatives of the congregation should attend the service, so that they may welcome the newly-baptized and be put in mind of their own baptism.

4 The godparents should be reminded that it is their duty to see that the baptized infant is taught to say the Creed, the Lord's Prayer, and the Ten Commandments, and receives further instruction in them according to the Church-Catechism; and that when *he* is ready to make *his* own response, *he* shall do so openly before the Church, when the bishop shall confirm *him*, laying hands on *him* with prayer. The priest may read the substance of the explanation printed as §4 on page 518.

A SERVICE FOR THE

Public Baptism of Adults

AND THOSE ABLE TO ANSWER
FOR THEMSELVES

FIRST ORDER

The bishop is to be notified beforehand concerning such candidates so that he may, if he so determine, be present at the baptism to confirm them as provided in §10. In this case either the bishop or the priest may administer the baptism.

The candidates are to be instructed and examined in the principles of the Christian faith, and also exhorted to prepare themselves by prayer and self-discipline for the receiving of baptism.

A candidate for baptism must have at least one godparent as sponsor and witness.

Before the service begins, the priest shall satisfy himself that the candidate has not previously been baptized. If it is stated that the candidate was baptized, but the priest is not satisfied that *he* was baptized with water 'In the name of the Father, and of the Son, and of the Holy Spirit', he shall use this form of words at §7, 'If you are not already baptized, N, I baptize you in the name of the Father, and of the Son, and of the Holy Spirit.'

Baptism ought, whenever possible, to be administered at the public service on Sundays (see Note 1 on page 511).

1 The priest addresses the congregation

God in his love has acted through Jesus Christ to free us from our slavery to sin. When Jesus had risen from the dead, he said to his disciples, 'All authority in heaven and on earth has been given to me. Go therefore and make all nations my disciples, baptizing them in the name of the Father and of the Son and of the Holy Spirit.'

Soon after, the apostle Peter began preaching, 'Repent, and be baptized every one of you in the name of Jesus Christ for the forgiveness of sins; and you will receive the Holy

506

Spirit. For the promise is to you and to your children, and to every one whom the Lord our God calls to him.'

Let us then pray that God will grant to *this person* that which by nature *he* cannot have, that *he* may be baptized with water and the Holy Spirit, and received into Christ's holy Church, and be made *a* living *member* of his body.

2   The minister and congregation pray this prayer together, all standing

Almighty God,
who delivered your chosen people from slavery in Egypt
through the waters of the Red Sea
and established with them a covenant of your unfailing
     love;
mercifully grant that *this person*
may be delivered from the slavery of sin through the new
     covenant,
and obtain the promise of eternal life
which you have given us in your Son our Saviour Jesus
     Christ,
who lives and reigns with you and the Holy Spirit,
one God, now and for ever.   Amen.

3   The Gospel which follows, or one or more of the readings given on page 528, is read

Hear the Gospel of our Lord Jesus Christ, according to Mark, chapter one, beginning at verse four.

John the baptizer appeared in the wilderness, preaching a baptism of repentance for the forgiveness of sins. And there went out to him all the country of Judea, and all the people of Jerusalem; and they were baptized by him in the river Jordan, confessing their sins . . . And he preached, saying, 'After me comes he who is mightier than I, the thong of whose sandals I am not worthy to stoop down and untie. I have baptized you with water; but he will baptize you with the Holy Spirit.'

507

In those days Jesus came from Nazareth of Galilee and was baptized by John in the Jordan. And when he came up out of the water, immediately he saw the heavens opened and the Spirit descending upon him like a dove; and a voice came from heaven, 'You are my beloved Son; with you I am well pleased.'

4   The congregation may be seated as the minister expounds the reading and exhorts the candidates for baptism, at the end of which he says to them

I ask you now to stand and, in the presence of your sponsors and of this whole congregation, to make your response to the promise of forgiveness of sins and eternal life held out to you by Jesus Christ.

5   The baptismal vows of repentance, faith, and obedience are made. The bishop or minister says

Do you renounce the devil and all his works,
the empty display and false values of the world,
and the sinful desires of the flesh,
so that you will not follow nor be led by them?

I renounce them all.

Do you believe in God, the Father almighty,
maker of heaven and earth?
Do you believe in Jesus Christ, his only Son our Lord?
And that he was conceived by the Holy Spirit,
born of the virgin Mary;
that he suffered under Pontius Pilate,
was crucified, dead, and buried;
that he went down to the place of the dead,
and also rose again the third day?
That he ascended into heaven,
and is seated at the right hand of God the Father
    almighty,
and from there shall come to judge the living and the
    dead?

And do you believe in the Holy Spirit;
the holy catholic church;
the communion of saints;
the forgiveness of sins;
the resurrection of the body,
and the life everlasting?

All this I firmly believe.

Will you keep God's holy will and commandments, and serve
him faithfully throughout your life?

With his help I intend to do so.

6　The candidates kneel. The congregation stands, and the bishop or
　　priest says

Let us pray.

Merciful God, grant that the old nature in *this person* may
be so buried that the new nature may be raised up in *him*.
Amen.

Grant that all sinful desires may die in *him*, and that all
things belonging to the Spirit may live and grow in *him*.
Amen.

Grant that *he* may have strength to triumph over the devil,
the world, and the flesh.　**Amen.**

Grant that *he*, who *is* here dedicated to you by our office and
ministry, may also be equipped with spiritual virtues, and
receive the eternal crown of life, through your mercy, blessed
Lord God; for you live and govern all things, now and for
ever.　**Amen.**

Almighty, everliving God, whose own dear Son Jesus Christ
shed his blood for the forgiveness of our sins, and opened the
gate of everlasting life to all believers, hear the prayer of this
congregation; sanctify this water for the mystical washing
away of sin; and grant that *he* who *is* now to be baptized
in it may receive the fulness of your grace, and for ever
remain in the number of your faithful and elect children,
through Jesus Christ our Lord.　**Amen.**

7   The minister who baptizes takes each candidate by the right hand and brings *him* to the font, and, having asked the godparents *his* name, baptizes *him*. He dips *him* in the water, or pours water on *him*, saying

N, I baptize you in the name of the Father, and of the Son, and of the Holy Spirit.
Amen.

8   The minister continues; he makes a cross on the forehead of the newly-baptized at the words **sign you with the sign of the cross**.

We receive you into the congregation of Christ's flock and sign you with the sign of the cross, to show that you will not be ashamed to confess the faith of Christ crucified, and to fight bravely under his banner against sin, the world, and the devil, and to continue Christ's faithful soldier and servant to your life's end.   Amen.

9   For each person, or when all have been baptized and received, the minister says

Blessed be the God and Father of our Lord Jesus Christ for birth from above and for the remission of sins. May almighty God, according to his gracious promise, finish the work of salvation begun in you, bringing you to the joyful resurrection and to the fulfilment of his eternal kingdom.   Amen.

‡10   If the bishop is present, he confirms the newly-baptized. The Confirmation service continues here.

      When only the newly-baptized are to be confirmed, the Confirmation service begins at §5 (page 513).

      When there are others besides the newly-baptized to be confirmed, the Confirmation service begins at §2 (page 512).

‡11   A hymn of praise or dedication to discipleship may be sung, and this prayer said now or later in the service, the congregation kneeling.

O God, by whose Spirit the whole body of the Church is governed and sanctified: preserve in the new-born children of your family the fulness of your grace. Grant that, having died and been buried with Christ, they may know the power of his risen life in their daily living. Keep us all fervent in

the faith, and strong to endure to the end in your service, through Jesus Christ our Lord. **Amen.**

‡12 If it has not been used elsewhere in the service, the Lord's Prayer should now be said.

‡13 If the baptism is administered apart from another service, it may conclude with the congregation saying

The grace of our Lord Jesus Christ, and the love of God, and the fellowship of the Holy Spirit, be with us all ever-more. Amen.

NOTES

1 This service may be inserted into Morning or Evening Prayer to replace the second reading with its canticle and the creed, or it may be inserted into The Holy Communion so as to replace the Gospel and the creed. On Sundays and red-letter days the collect and readings should be those of the day, but on other days the readings provided in the other Service for the Public Baptism of Adults (page 528) may be used.

2 When an adult has been baptized, and the bishop has not been present to confirm *him* at *his* baptism, *he* shall appear before the bishop as soon as convenient in order that the bishop may confirm *him* laying hands on *him* with prayer.

3 It is the responsibility of godparents to remind those whom they have sponsored at baptism what a solemn undertaking they have made before the congregation and especially before them, their chosen witnesses. They should urge them to make sure they are rightly instructed in God's word, so that they may grow in grace and in the knowledge of our Lord Jesus Christ, and live their lives accordingly.

An Order for Confirmation

FIRST FORM

1   This order for Confirmation may be used after the first reading
    at Morning or Evening Prayer, or after the first reading or Gospel
    at The Holy Communion.
    If this order is used as a separate service, it may begin with a hymn
    or psalm, and the bishop may greet the people. This order may
    also fittingly follow at once upon the baptism of those who answer
    for themselves (see §10 on page 510). When this occurs, §4 is not
    used if the congregation were present at the baptism.

2   The following is read

We have come together to pray for those who seek the blessing of God in Confirmation; they will first affirm their faith
in God and their desire to serve him throughout their lives.
In Confirmation, the bishop lays hands on those who have
been baptized and instructed in the Christian faith, praying
over them that God's indwelling Spirit will strengthen and
guide them.

Our Church requires that all who are to be confirmed
should first know and understand the Creed, the Lord's
Prayer, and the Ten Commandments, and be able to answer
the other questions in the Church-Catechism.

This rule enables those who have been baptized as infants,
when they are of age to do so, openly before the church, to
take upon themselves and confirm the promises made on
their behalf by their godparents.

Those who at their baptism have already made a profession of faith for themselves also seek the continuing grace
and strength of the Holy Spirit in the laying on of hands.

It is for us as the people of God to hear the response to
God's call of those who have come to be confirmed, to support them now and always with our prayer, and to renew
our own commitment to the gospel of our Lord Jesus
Christ.

3   The bishop may address the congregation and candidates. He then says to those who were baptized as infants

At your baptism, your godparents made three promises in your name: first, that you would renounce the devil and all his works, the empty display and false values of the world, and the sinful desires of the flesh; secondly, that you would believe the Christian faith as set out in the Apostles' Creed; and thirdly, that you would keep God's holy will and commandments, and walk in them all the days of your life.

Do you now, in the presence of God and of this congregation, renew these promises and take them upon yourself?

    The candidates answer

I do.

‡4   The bishop next addresses those who have already answered for themselves at baptism

Do you stand firmly to the confession and commitment you made at your baptism?

    Each one answers

I do.

5   When all have answered the bishop continues

Let us now pray that God will enrich with his Holy Spirit each one of these who have been baptized and confessed Christ.

    All kneel, and the bishop continues

Our help is in the name of the Lord,

  who has made heaven and earth.

Blessed be the name of the Lord

  now and for evermore.

Lord, hear our prayers,

  and let our cry come to you.

6 The bishop continues

Almighty and everliving God,
whose Son Jesus Christ was crucified and rose again
to break the power of sin and death:
we give you thanks and praise for the gift of your Holy
 Spirit
by whom these your servants have been born again
and made your children.
Grant that in the power of the same Holy Spirit
they may continue to grow in the knowledge and likeness of
 Christ.
Increase in them your gracious gifts,
the spirit of wisdom and understanding,
the spirit of counsel and inward strength,
the spirit of knowledge and godly living,
and fill them, O Lord, with the spirit of true reverence for you,
now and always.

Amen.

7 Those to be confirmed kneel before the bishop, who lays his hand
upon the head of each and says the following prayer

Defend, O Lord, this your child/servant [N]
with your heavenly grace,
that *he* may continue yours for ever,
and daily increase in your Holy Spirit
until *he* comes to your everlasting kingdom.

And each one of them answers with the congregation

Amen.

8 When he has laid his hands on all to be confirmed, the bishop
says

The Lord be with you.

And also with you.

Let us pray.

‡9 If the Lord's Prayer is not used elsewhere in the service, it is now
said.

Our Father in heaven,
   hallowed be your Name,
   your kingdom come,
   your will be done
     on earth as in heaven.
Give us today our daily bread.
Forgive us our sins
   as we forgive those who sin against us.
Lead us not into temptation,
   but deliver us from evil.
For the kingdom, the power, and the glory are yours
   now and for ever.   **Amen.**

10   The bishop says this prayer

Almighty and everlasting God,
by your Holy Spirit you are at work in us,
inspiring us both to will and to do those things that are good
   and pleasing in your sight;
we pray for your servants upon whom we have now laid our
   hands,
following the example of your holy apostles,
to assure them, by this sign, of your favour and gracious
   goodness.
Let your fatherly hand always be over them;
let your Holy Spirit always be with them;
lead them in the knowledge and obedience of your word,
so that in the end they may obtain eternal life;
through our Lord and Saviour Jesus Christ.
Amen.

‡11   This prayer may be added, in which all may join

Almighty and everlasting God,
we pray that you will direct, sanctify, and govern
our hearts and bodies in the ways of your command-
   ments,
that through your mighty protection, here and ever,
we may be kept safe in body and soul,

**and joyfully serve you in the work of the gospel
to which you have called us;
through our Lord and Saviour Jesus Christ. Amen.**

12 The bishop then blesses those who have been confirmed, saying

**The blessing of God almighty, the Father, the Son, and the
Holy Spirit, be upon you, and remain with you for ever.
Amen.**

‡13 A reading from the New Testament (see Note 4 below) may follow.

‡14 A sermon may be preached here.

‡15 Morning or Evening Prayer may resume at the Apostles' Creed or
at the prayers. The Holy Communion resumes in the First Order
of The Holy Communion at the offertory and in the Second Order
at §14.

NOTES

1 At §3, the bishop may put the question to each candidate individually.
He may address them by name, or their names may be read out.

2 At §7, the minister presenting the candidates may tell the bishop their
christian names, or a sponsor accompanying the candidate may do so, or
the candidates may tell him their christian names themselves.

3 On Sundays and red-letter days, the collect and readings are normally
those of the day. On other days one of the collects listed below may be used,
and the readings chosen from those listed below.

4 The following prayers and readings are suitable at a Confirmation service. The collects for Whitsunday, Trinity 1,2,4,7, or 18, or this prayer

> Almighty and merciful God,
> we pray that your Holy Spirit
> who comes to us and dwells in us
> may make us temples of your glory;
> we ask this through Christ our Lord.

Exodus 20.1-17	Romans 8.11-17	1 Peter 1.22-2.3	Luke 9.18-26
Deut. 30.11-20	Galatians 5.16-25	1 Peter 2.1-10	Luke 6.20-31(-38)
Joshua 24.14-24	Ephesians 6.10-20		John 14.15-17
Jeremiah 31.31-34	Philippians 1.3-11		John 14.25-27 and
Ezekiel 36.26-28	Colossians 3.1-11	Matthew 5.1-10	15.12-17, 26-27
	Colossians 3.12-17	Mark 10.35-45	John 15.1-11
	Hebrews 10.19-25	Luke 2.41-51	John 16.4b-15

516

Public Baptism of Infants

SECOND ORDER

Baptism ought, wherever possible, to be administered at a public service on Sundays (see Note 2 on page 525), not only so that the whole congregation may witness the admission of the newly-baptized into Christ's Church and welcome them, but also so that Christians may frequently be reminded of the profession of faith and obedience to God which they made in their own baptism.

Before the service begins, the priest shall ask the child's parents and godparents whether or not the child has already been baptized. If the infant has been baptized privately (see Note 1 on page 525), the priest shall assure himself that the baptism was carried out in due form, and proceed to use the Lord's Prayer, §§ 4, 5, and 6 (omitting the last sentence), the questions in § 8, the Apostles' Creed and the first and third questions in § 12, and §§ 14, 15, 16, and 18 of this service.

If it is stated that the child was baptized, but the priest is not satisfied that the child was baptized with water 'In the name of the Father and of the Son and of the Holy Spirit', he shall use the whole service with this form of words at §13, 'If you are not already baptized, N, I baptize you in the name of the Father, and of the Son, and of the Holy Spirit.'

The priest explains to the parents and godparents their duties either in the words set out in this order (§4) or in his own words. If he does not do this privately, he should do so in church at the beginning of the service or in a sermon.

It is desirable that the child's parents associate themselves with the godparents and make the answers with them in this service.

A male child shall have two godfathers and one godmother. A female child shall have two godmothers and one godfather.

INTRODUCTION

‡1 A hymn or psalm may be sung.

‡2 The priest welcomes those who bring the child for baptism.
He may say **The Lord be with you. And also with you.**

‡3 The priest may read one of the following or other Sentences of Scripture.

Our Lord Jesus Christ said, Go and make disciples of all nations, baptizing them in the name of the Father, and of the Son, and of the Holy Spirit, teaching them to observe all that I have commanded you.   Matthew 28.19-20

Our Lord Jesus Christ said, Let the children come to me; do not hinder them; for to such belongs the kingdom of God.   Mark 10.14

4 If he has not previously done so, the priest explains their duties to parents and godparents in these or similar words

Children are baptized on the understanding that they will be brought up as faithful members of the Church, to follow Christ and to fight against evil; and that they will be brought to the bishop to be confirmed by him, when they are of age to take upon themselves the promises you are about to make on their behalf.

As they grow up they need encouragement, teaching, and the help of a good example, so that they may learn to worship God, to pray to him, to put their faith and trust in him, and to take their place in the life of the Church.

Parents and godparents, *this child depends* chiefly on you for the help and encouragement *he needs*. Are you willing to give *him* this help and encouragement by every means in your power?

The parents and godparents answer

I am willing.

THE MINISTRY OF THE WORD

‡5 If the baptism does not take place at Morning or Evening Prayer or at The Holy Communion, one or more passages from the Old and New Testaments may be read; the readings should always include at least one reading from the Gospels.

Genesis 9.1-17; Exodus 14.19-31; 1 Samuel 1.12-18; Jeremiah 1.4-8.
Acts 2.37-42; 1 Corinthians 12.12-13; Colossians 2.9-15 (*and* 3.1-4); 1 Peter 3.18-21.
Mark 10.13-16; Matthew 28.13-16; Mark 1.1-11; John 3.1-8.

Each reading is announced A/The reading from . . ., chapter . . ., beginning at verse . . .

After the last reading the reader may say This is the word of the Lord. And all answer **Thanks be to God.**

Readings from the Gospels may be announced The gospel of our Lord Jesus Christ according to . . ., chapter . . ., beginning at verse . . . All may respond **Glory to you, Lord Christ.** At the end of a reading from a Gospel, the reader may say This is the gospel of the Lord. All may answer **Praise to you, Lord Christ.**

‡6   If there is no sermon declaring the purposes of Christian baptism, the following may be read

God is the creator of all things, and he gives to parents the work and joy of bringing children to birth and nurturing them. Yet, Jesus tells us, those who are born of human parents need to be born anew. 'What is born of flesh,' he says, 'is flesh; and what is born of the Spirit is spirit.' And again he says, 'Unless one is born from above he cannot see the kingdom of God.' Because of our sinfulness, God calls us to a new birth and life in union with himself. Baptism is the sign and seal of this new birth. Jesus commanded his disciples to preach the gospel to all nations and to baptize those who believe. They obeyed this command, and we read of Saint Peter preaching in these words, 'Repent, and be baptized in the name of Jesus Christ for the forgiveness of your sins; and you shall receive the gift of the Holy Spirit. For the promise is to you and to your children and to all that are afar off, every one whom the Lord our God calls to him.' In obedience to that same command we ourselves were baptized and now bring *this child* to baptism.

7 The priest continues

Let us pray to God through our Lord Jesus Christ, that he will grant to *this child* that which by nature *he* cannot have; that *he* may be baptized with water and the Holy Spirit, received into Christ's holy Church, and made *a* living *member* of the same.

All join the priest in saying

Heavenly Father,
we thank you that in your great love
you have called us to know you
and to trust in you.
Increase this knowledge and strengthen our faith.
Give your Holy Spirit to *this child*
that *he* may be born again
and may inherit your eternal Kingdom.
We ask this through Jesus Christ our Lord. Amen.

THE DECISION

8 The godparents stand, and the priest says to them

Those who bring young children to be baptized must declare, on behalf of the children, allegiance to Christ and rejection of all that is evil: the devil and all his works, the empty display and false values of the world, and the sinful desires of the flesh.

Therefore I ask you to answer on behalf of this child,

Do you turn to Christ?

The godparents answer

I turn to Christ.

Do you repent of your sins?

I repent of my sins.

Do you renounce evil?

I renounce evil.

520

9 Then the priest says

Almighty God deliver you from the powers of darkness, and
lead you in the light of Christ to his everlasting kingdom.
Amen.

THE BAPTISM

‡**10** A hymn or psalm may be used. Psalms 23; 27.1-9; 34.2-8; and
36.5-10 are suitable.

11 The priest says the following prayer either here or after §12

Almighty God, whose Son Jesus Christ was baptized in the
River Jordan,
we thank you for the gift of water to cleanse and revive us:
we thank you that you delivered your people from slavery
and led them through the waters of the Red Sea
to freedom in the promised land;
we thank you that you brought your Son through the deep
waters of death and raised him to life in triumph.
Hear now the prayers of your faithful people;
sanctify this water for the mystical washing away of sin,
that your *servant* who *is* to be baptized in it
may be made one with Christ in his death and in his
resurrection;
send your Holy Spirit upon *him*
to bring *him* to new birth in the family of your Church,
and raise *him* with Christ to full and eternal life.
For all might, majesty, authority, and power are yours,
now and for ever.
Amen.

12 The priest says

This child has been brought for baptism. Let us all now profess
the faith into which *he is* to be baptized and in which *he is*
to be brought up.

521

All join in saying the Apostles' Creed

I believe in God, the Father almighty,
maker of heaven and earth;
and in Jesus Christ, his only Son our Lord,
who was conceived by the Holy Spirit,
born of the virgin Mary,
suffered under Pontius Pilate,
was crucified, dead, and buried.
He descended into hell.
The third day he rose again from the dead.
He ascended into heaven,
and is seated at the right hand of God the Father almighty;
from there he shall come to judge the living and the dead.
I believe in the Holy Spirit;
the holy catholic church;
the communion of saints;
the forgiveness of sins;
the resurrection of the body,
and the life everlasting.   Amen.

The priest says to the godparents

I now ask you to answer in the name of this child,
Do you profess this faith?

The godparents answer
I do.

Do you ask for baptism in this faith?
I do.

Will you, with God's help, strive to keep his holy will and commandments and serve him faithfully throughout your life?
I will.

If he has not already done so, the priest then says the prayer at §11.

13　The priest then takes the child and, having asked *his* name, he baptizes *him*. He dips *him* in the water, or pours water on *him*, saying

N, I baptize you in the name of the Father, and of the Son, and of the Holy Spirit.

And all answer

Amen.

14　The priest continues

God has called you into his Church.

The congregation joins the priest in saying

**We therefore receive and welcome you
as a fellow member of the body of Christ,
as a child of the same heavenly Father,
and as an inheritor with us of the kingdom of God.**

15　The priest makes a cross on the child's forehead and says to *him*

**I sign you with the sign of the cross
to show that you are to be true to Christ crucified
and that you are not to be ashamed
to confess your faith in him.**

The congregation joins the priest in saying

**Fight bravely under his banner
against sin, the world, and the devil,
and continue Christ's faithful soldier and servant
to your life's end.**

The priest says

God has called you out of darkness into his marvellous light.

The congregation joins the priest in saying

**Shine as a light in the world
to the glory of God the Father.**

16   The priest says

Let us pray.

Lord God our Father, maker of heaven and earth, we thank you that you have been pleased to give *this child* new birth with your Holy Spirit, to adopt *him* for your own, and to receive *him* into the fellowship of your Church. Being buried with Christ in his death, may *he* die to sin, walk in newness of life, and be united with Christ in his resurrection. May *he* grow in the faith into which *he has* been baptized, and come to profess it for *himself*; and may all things belonging to the Spirit live and grow in *him*.   **Amen.**

Heavenly Father, we pray for the parents of *this child*; give them the spirit of wisdom and love, that their children may grow up to love and reverence you and their *home* may share in the joy of your eternal kingdom.   **Amen.**

God of truth and love, we pray for the godparents of *him* whom we have baptized in your name, that they may desire to share with their *godchild* what you have revealed to us in your holy gospel. We ask this through Jesus Christ our Lord. **Amen.**

17   All say together

Our Father in heaven,
  hallowed be your Name,
  your kingdom come,
  your will be done
    on earth as in heaven.
Give us today our daily bread.
Forgive us our sins
  as we forgive those who sin against us.
Lead us not into temptation,
  but deliver us from evil.
For the kingdom, the power, and the glory are yours
  now and for ever.   Amen.

18 The priest says

The grace of our Lord Jesus Christ, and the love of God, and
the fellowship of the Holy Spirit, be with us all evermore.
Amen.

NOTES

1 When need compels parents to ask that their children be baptized
privately, baptism is to be administered in this way:
Prayer, including the Lord's Prayer, should be offered as the time and
circumstances permit. Then the child shall be named, and the minister
shall pour water upon *him*, saying, 'N, I baptize you in the name of the
Father, and of the Son, and of the Holy Spirit. Amen.' The minister may
add the first of the prayers at §16.

2 When the baptism is at Morning or Evening Prayer, it should take place
before the Second Reading, or after the hymn following the third collect.
The Intercessions of Morning Prayer may follow §17 of this service, or
the service may end with §18. When Morning or Evening Prayer are
resumed at the Second Reading, the Apostles' Creed should be omitted
from that service. The readings may be taken from those provided at
§5.
When the baptism is at The Holy Communion:
The Sentence may be one from §3 above. On Sundays and red-letter
days, the readings for the day are normally used. On other days, the readings given at §5 and the Psalms given at §11 are suitable. The baptism
takes place after any of the readings or immediately after the sermon.
The Nicene Creed may be omitted from The Holy Communion; §§1-3
and 17-18 may be omitted from this service.

3 At §15 a minister may give to a parent or godparent for each child a
lighted candle when the priest says, 'God has called you out of darkness
into his marvellous light'.

4 When this order is used apart from the public service on Sundays, it is
desirable that representatives of the congregation should attend the service, so that they may welcome the newly-baptized and be put in mind
of their own baptism. It is also necessary that there should be at least
one reading at §5.

5 The godparents should be reminded that it is their duty to bring the children to the bishop to be confirmed, and to see that the children are taught
the Creed, the Lord's Prayer, and the Ten Commandments, and receive
further instruction in them according to the Church-Catechism (pages
541-547).

A SERVICE FOR THE

Public Baptism of Adults

AND THOSE ABLE TO ANSWER
FOR THEMSELVES

SECOND ORDER

It is desirable that the bishop be present in order to confirm the candidates as provided in §15.

When some who are already baptized are to be confirmed with the newly-baptized, the readings at §5 may be chosen from those provided at §6 of the Confirmation service. The bishop may preach after the readings. After §14 of this service, a hymn or psalms may be used, and the service of Confirmation continue from §12 on page 537.

A candidate for baptism must have at least one godparent as sponsor and witness.

The directions on page 506 also apply to this service.

INTRODUCTION

‡1   A hymn or psalm may be sung.

‡2   The priest welcomes those who come for baptism.
     He may say
     The Lord be with you.
     and all answer
     And also with you.

‡3   The priest may read this or another sentence from the Bible.
     Our Lord Jesus Christ said, Truly, truly, I say to you, unless one is born of water and the Holy Spirit, he cannot enter the kingdom of God.   John 3.5

4   The priest says

Dearly beloved in Christ, seeing that God wills all men to
be saved, and that our Saviour Christ says, 'Unless one is
born anew he cannot see the kingdom of God', let us pray
to God the Father through our Lord Jesus Christ that he will
grant to *this person* that which by nature *he* cannot have, that
he may be baptized with water and the Holy Spirit, received
into Christ's holy Church, and be made *a* living *member* of
the same.

> All join the priest in saying

Heavenly Father,
we thank you that in your great love
you have called us to know you
and to trust in you.
Increase this knowledge and strengthen our faith.
Give your Holy Spirit to *this* your *servant*
that *he* may be born again
and may inherit your eternal kingdom.
We ask this through Jesus Christ our Lord.   Amen.

> If there are any who have already been baptized and are to be con-
> firmed, the bishop or priest adds

Let us pray for those who have already been baptized and are
to be confirmed.

Almighty God, our heavenly Father,
by your Holy Spirit you have called *these* your *servants*
and made *them* your *children* by adoption and grace;
mercifully grant that, being strengthened by the same Spirit,
they may continue your *servants* and receive your promises;
through our Lord Jesus Christ your Son,
who lives and reigns with you and the Holy Spirit,
one God, for ever and ever.
Amen.

THE MINISTRY OF THE WORD

‡5   If the baptism does not take place at Morning or Evening Prayer or at The Holy Communion, one or more passages from the Old and New Testaments are read; the readings should always include at least one reading from the New Testament. The following passages are suitable.

Genesis 9.1-17; Exodus 14.19-31; Isaiah 8.1-8; Ezekiel 36.25-28. Acts 2.37-42; Romans 6.1-11. Matthew 28.18-20; Mark 1.1-11; John 3.1-8.

Each reading is announced **A/The reading from . . . , chapter . . . , beginning at verse . . . .**

After the last reading, the reader may say **This is the word of the Lord.** And all answer **Thanks be to God.**

Readings from the Gospels may be announced **The gospel of our Lord Jesus Christ according to . . . , chapter . . . , beginning at verse . . . .** All may respond **Glory to you, Lord Christ.**

At the end of a reading from a Gospel, the reader may say **This is the gospel of the Lord.** All may answer **Praise to you, Lord Christ.**

THE DECISION

6   Those to be baptized stand, and, if there are any who have already been baptized and are now to be confirmed, they stand with them, and the bishop or priest says to them

Those who are to be baptized [and confirmed] must declare their allegiance to Christ and their rejection of all that is evil: the devil and all his works, the empty display and false values of the world, and the sinful desires of the flesh.

Therefore I ask
Do you turn to Christ?

The candidates answer

I turn to Christ.

Do you repent of your sins?
I repent of my sins.

Do you renounce evil?
I renounce evil.

7   Then the bishop or priest says

**Almighty God deliver you from the powers of darkness, and lead you in the light of Christ to his everlasting kingdom.
Amen.**

THE BAPTISM

‡8   A hymn or psalm may be used. Psalms 23; 27.1-9; 34.2-8; and 36.5-10 are suitable.

9   The bishop or priest says the following prayer either here or after §10.

Almighty God, whose Son Jesus Christ was baptized in the
    River Jordan,
we thank you for the gift of water to cleanse and revive us:
we thank you that you delivered your people from slavery
    and led them through the waters of the Red Sea
    to freedom in the promised land;
we thank you that you brought your Son through the deep
    waters of death
    and raised him to life in triumph.
Hear now the prayers of your faithful people;
    sanctify this water for the mystical washing away of sin,
    that your *servant* who *is* to be baptized in it
    may be made one with Christ in his death and in his resur-
    rection;
send your Holy Spirit upon *him*
    to bring *him* to new birth in the family of your Church,
    and raise *him* with Christ to full and eternal life.
For all might, majesty, authority, and power are yours
    now and for ever.
Amen.

529

10 The bishop or priest says to those who are to be baptized, and, if there are any who have already been baptized and are now to be confirmed, he addresses them also

You have come here to be baptized [and confirmed]. You must now profess the faith into which you are to be baptized [or into which you were baptized].

Therefore I ask you to say the Apostles' Creed.

The candidates and congregation say together

I believe in God, the Father almighty,
maker of heaven and earth;
and in Jesus Christ, his only Son, our Lord,
who was conceived by the Holy Spirit,
born of the virgin Mary,
suffered under Pontius Pilate,
was crucified, dead, and buried.
He descended into hell.
The third day he rose again from the dead.
He ascended into heaven,
and is seated at the right hand of God the Father
almighty;
from there he shall come to judge the living and the dead.
I believe in the Holy Spirit;
the holy catholic church;
the communion of saints;
the forgiveness of sins;
the resurrection of the body,
and the life everlasting.   Amen.

The bishop or priest says to the candidates for baptism and confirmation

I now ask you
Do you profess this faith?

The candidates answer

I do.

Will you, with God's help, strive to keep his holy will and commandments and serve him faithfully throughout your life?

I will.

> The bishop or priest says to those to be baptized

Do you ask for baptism in the faith you have professed?

I do.

> If he has not already done so, the bishop or priest says the prayer at §9.

11 Each person to be baptized comes to the font and the bishop or priest, having asked *his* name, baptizes *him*. He dips *him* in the water, or pours water on *him*, saying

N, I baptize you in the name of the Father, and of the Son, and of the Holy Spirit.

> And each one of them answers with the congregation

Amen.

12 The bishop or priest continues

God has called you into his Church.

> The congregation joins with him in saying

We therefore receive and welcome you
as a fellow member of the body of Christ,
as a child of the same heavenly Father,
and as an inheritor with us of the kingdom of God.

13 The bishop or priest makes a cross on the candidate's forehead and says to him

I sign you with the sign of the cross
to show that you are to be true to Christ crucified
and that you are not to be ashamed
to confess your faith in him.

> The congregation joins with him in saying

Fight bravely under his banner
against sin, the world, and the devil,
and continue Christ's faithful soldier and servant
to your life's end.

The bishop or priest says

God has called you out of darkness into his marvellous light.

The congregation joins with him in saying

**Shine as a light in the world
to the glory of God the Father.**

14   The bishop or priest continues

Let us pray.

Lord God our Father, maker of heaven and earth, we thank you that you have been pleased to give your *servant* new birth with your Holy Spirit, to adopt *him* for your own, and to receive *him* into the fellowship of your Church. Being buried with Christ in his baptism, may *he* die to sin, walk in newness of life, and be united with Christ in his resurrection. May *he* grow in the faith into which *he* has been baptized, and may all things belonging to the Spirit live and grow in *him*.
Amen.

‡15   When the bishop is present, and he is to confirm, a hymn may be sung and the service continues at §12 of the Confirmation service on page 537.

16   When there is to be no Confirmation service, these prayers are said.

The priest says

Almighty God, we thank you for our fellowship in the household of faith with all those who have been baptized in your name. Help us to live in obedience to the promises made in our baptism, and hasten that day when the whole creation shall be made perfect in your Son, our Saviour, Jesus Christ.
Amen.

All say together

**Our Father in heaven,
hallowed be your Name,
your kingdom come,**

your will be done
on earth as in heaven.
Give us today our daily bread.
Forgive us our sins
as we forgive those who sin against us.
Lead us not into temptation,
but deliver us from evil.
For the kingdom, the power, and the glory are yours
now and for ever.   Amen.

17   The priest says

The grace of our Lord Jesus Christ, and the love of God, and
the fellowship of the Holy Spirit, be with us all evermore.
   Amen.

NOTES

1 When the baptism is at Morning or Evening Prayer, or at The Holy Communion, the directions given in Note 2 on page 525 should be observed;
§§16 and 17 may be omitted from this service.

2 At §13 a minister may give a lighted candle to each newly-baptized person when the priest says, 'God has called you out of darkness into his marvellous light.'

A SERVICE OF
Confirmation

SECOND FORM

‡1 A psalm or hymn may be sung.

2 The bishop says

The Lord be with you.
And all answer
And also with you.

‡3 This sentence, or another sentence from the Bible at the bishop's
choice, may be read.

> **We were buried with Christ by baptism into death, so that
> as Christ was raised from the dead to the glory of the
> Father, we too might walk in newness of life.**   Romans 6.4

‡4 If the bishop so direct, the address on page 512 may be read here.
The priest may present the candidates to the bishop.

5 The bishop continues

Let us pray

Almighty God, our heavenly Father,
by your Holy Spirit you have called *these* your *servants*
and made *them* your *children* by adoption and grace;
mercifully grant that, being strengthened by the same
**   Spirit,**
***they* may continue your *servants* and receive your promises;**
through our Lord Jesus Christ your Son,
who lives and reigns with you and the Holy Spirit,
one God, for ever and ever.   Amen.

THE MINISTRY OF THE WORD

6 One or more passages from the Bible are read; the readings shall
always include at least one from the New Testament.

The following passages are suitable.

Exodus 20.1-17; Deut. 30.11-20; Joshua 24.14-24; Jeremiah 31.31-34.

Romans 8.11-17; Gal. 5.16-25; Eph. 6.10-20; Philippians 1.3-11.

Matthew 5.1-16; Mark 10.35-45; Luke 2.41-51; Luke 6.20-31 (-38); John 14.25-27 and 15.12-17, 26-27; John 16.4b-15.

Each reading is announced **A/The reading from . . . chapter . . ., beginning at verse . . .**

After the last reading the reader may say **This is the word of the Lord.** And all answer **Thanks be to God.**

Readings from the Gospel may be announced **The gospel of our Lord Jesus Christ according to . . . ., chapter . . . ., beginning at verse . . . . .** All may respond **Glory to you, Lord Christ.** At the end of a reading from a Gospel, the reader may say **This is the gospel of the Lord.** All may answer **Praise to you, Lord Christ.**

A Psalm (Psalms 1; 119.169-176; 122; 130 are suitable) may be said or sung between any two readings.

7 The bishop preaches the sermon.

THE DECISION

8 A hymn may be sung.

The candidates and congregation stand.

The bishop says to the candidates

Those who are to be confirmed come to make for themselves the promises made on their behalf at their baptism [or to reaffirm the promises they have made in their own name]. You must therefore declare your allegiance to Christ and your rejection of all that is evil: the devil and all his works, the empty display and false values of the world, and the sinful desires of the flesh.

Therefore I ask you,

Do you turn to Christ?

The candidates answer

I turn to Christ.

Where several candidates are to be confirmed, the bishop may put this question to each candidate individually. He may address them by name, or their names may be read out.

Do you repent of your sins?

I repent of my sins.

Do you renounce evil?

I renounce evil.

9   The bishop continues

You who are to be confirmed must now yourselves profess before God and his Church the christian faith into which you were baptized.

Therefore I ask you to say the Apostles' Creed.

I believe in God, the Father almighty,
maker of heaven and earth;
and in Jesus Christ, his only Son our Lord,
who was conceived by the Holy Spirit,
born of the virgin Mary,
suffered under Pontius Pilate,
was crucified, dead, and buried.
He descended into hell.
The third day he rose again from the dead.
He ascended into heaven,
and is seated at the right hand of God the Father
**   almighty;**
from there he shall come to judge the living and the dead.
I believe in the Holy Spirit;
the holy catholic church;
the communion of saints;
the forgiveness of sins;
the resurrection of the body,
and the life everlasting. Amen.

10   The bishop says to the candidates

Will you, with God's help, strive to keep his holy will and commandments and serve him faithfully throughout your life?

        The candidates answer

I will

536

11   The bishop then says to the congregation

You have heard *these* our *brothers and sisters* respond to God's call to love and serve him. Will you support *them* in this high calling?

The congregation answers

We will do so.

THE CONFIRMATION

12   The bishop says

Our help is in the name of the Lord,
  who has made heaven and earth.

Blessed be the name of the Lord,
  as in the beginning, so now, and for ever.   Amen.

Let us pray that God will enrich with his Holy Spirit each of these who have been baptized and confessed Christ.

Almighty and everliving God,
you have been pleased to grant to your *servants*
new birth by water and the Holy Spirit
and have given *them* forgiveness of *their* sins;
strengthen *them*, we pray, with the Holy Spirit;
grant that *they* may grow in grace;
and give *them* the spirit of wisdom and understanding,
the spirit of discernment and inner strength,
the spirit of knowledge and true godliness,
and fill *them*, Father, with wonder and awe in your presence,
now and for ever.   **Amen.**

13   Those to be confirmed kneel before the bishop.
      The bishop lays his hand on each of them individually.
      The priest presenting them may tell the bishop the candidates'
      names, or the sponsor accompanying the candidates may do so,
      or the candidates may do so themselves.

While laying his hand on each candidate the bishop says

Strengthen, Lord, your servant [N] with your Holy Spirit.

And each one of them answers with the congregation

Amen.

The congregation joins with the bishop in saying the following prayer, which may be said for each candidate, for groups of candidates, or when all have received the laying on of hands.

Defend, O Lord, *these* your *children*
with your heavenly grace,
that *they* may continue yours for ever,
and daily increase in your Holy Spirit
until *they* come to your everlasting kingdom. Amen.

The bishop himself may use this prayer instead of the prayer Strengthen, Lord, when laying hands on each candidate

Defend, O Lord, this your child/servant [N]
with your heavenly grace,
that *he* may continue yours for ever
and daily increase in your Holy Spirit
until *he* comes to your everlasting kingdom.

And each one of them answers with the congregation

Amen.

14 If the Holy Communion follows, the prayer in §15 may be said, the Nicene Creed may be omitted, and the service continues with or after the Intercession. Otherwise the order of Confirmation concludes with these prayers.

15 The bishop says

The Lord be with you.
And also with you.

Let us pray.

And all say together

Our Father in heaven,
hallowed be your Name,
your kingdom come,
your will be done
on earth as in heaven.

Give us this day our daily bread.
Forgive us our sins
  as we forgive those who sin against us.
Lead us not into temptation,
  but deliver us from evil.
For the kingdom, the power, and the glory are yours
  now and for ever. Amen.

The bishop continues

Almighty and everliving God,
we pray for *these* your *servants*
upon whom, after the example of the apostles, we have now
  laid our hands
to assure *them* of your love for *them.*
May your fatherly hand ever protect *them.*
Let your Holy Spirit ever be with *them*
to lead *them* into all truth
and to uphold *them* in obedience to your word.
Strengthen *them* with the body and blood of your Son
and keep *them* in eternal life;
through our Lord and Saviour Jesus Christ.   **Amen.**

16   The bishop may add other prayers at his discretion.

‡17   The bishop may say to the congregation

Those who have been baptized and confirmed, and desire
to acknowledge the obligation of membership in the church,
are called to study and seek to understand the Bible and the
christian faith more fully, to take their part in the life of the
Church, to hear the word of God and share in the holy communion, and to pray faithfully and regularly both publicly
and privately.

They are called to share with others, by word and
example, the love of Christ and his gospel of reconciliation
and hope.

And they are called to love their neighbour as themselves,
to honour all men, and to pray and work for peace and
justice.

539

I invite all of you to commit yourselves to this calling.

We gladly do so.
May the Holy Spirit strengthen us
for the work he calls us to do.

> When the Communion Service continues after the Confirmation
> the bishop may use this address with its reply immediately before
> the Blessing. If the Second Order for the Holy Communion is used
> it may replace §27 in that service.

18   The bishop then dismisses the congregation with the blessing

The peace of God which passes all understanding keep your
hearts and minds in the knowledge and love of God, and of
his Son, Jesus Christ our Lord; and the blessing . . .

or

Go forth into the world in peace; be of good courage;
hold fast that which is good; render to no man evil for evil;
strengthen the fainthearted; support the weak; help the
    afflicted;
honour all men; love and serve the Lord,
rejoicing in the power of the Holy Spirit;

and the blessing of God almighty, the Father, the Son, and
the Holy Spirit, be amongst you and remain with you
always. **Amen.**

Go in peace to love and serve the Lord:
  In the name of Christ.   Amen.

NOTES

1 When The Holy Communion is to follow the Confirmation, the Communion service is used as far as the Gospel; then the Confirmation service
from §§7 to 13; after which the Communion service resumes in the First
Order of The Holy Communion at the offertory and in the Second Order
at §14.

On Sundays and red-letter days the collect and readings at the Communion are normally those of the day. The prayer at §5 should be said
after the collect for the day.

On other days, the collect shall be that at §5 above, and the readings
and psalm chosen from those given at §6.

The Catechism

*Instruction in christian faith and conduct
for those who are to be confirmed
and for those who are to answer for themselves in baptism.*

THE COVENANT OF BAPTISM

This section is for those who were baptized as infants.

Question

What is your christian name?

Answer

My name is . . .

Question

Who called you by this name?

Answer

My godparents, at my baptism in which I was made a member of Christ, the child of God, and an inheritor of the kingdom of heaven.

Question

What did your godparents do for you at your baptism?

Answer

They promised and vowed three things in my name: first, that I would renounce the devil and all his works, the empty display and false values of the world, and the sinful desires of the flesh;

secondly, that I would believe the christian faith as set out in the Apostles' Creed;

and thirdly, that I would keep God's holy will and commandments, and walk in them all the days of my life.

Question

Do you agree that you are bound to believe and to do as they have promised for you?

Answer

Yes, certainly; and by God's help I will. And I heartily thank our heavenly Father that he has called me to this state of salvation through Jesus Christ our Saviour. And I pray to God to give me his grace, that I may continue in this state to the end of my life.

THE CHRISTIAN FAITH

Catechist

Recite the articles of your belief, the Apostles' Creed.

Answer

I believe in God, the Father almighty,
maker of heaven and earth;
and in Jesus Christ, his only Son our Lord,
who was conceived by the Holy Spirit,
born of the virgin Mary,
suffered under Pontius Pilate,
was crucified, dead, and buried.
He descended into hell.
The third day he rose again from the dead.
He ascended into heaven,
and is seated at the right hand of God the Father
     almighty;
from there he shall come to judge the living and the dead.
I believe in the Holy Spirit;
the holy catholic church;
the communion of saints;
the forgiveness of sins;
the resurrection of the body,
and the life everlasting.   Amen.

Question

What do you chiefly learn from this creed?

Answer

First I learn to believe in God the Father, who has made me
and all the world;

secondly, in God the Son, who has redeemed me and all
mankind;

thirdly, in God the Holy Spirit, who sanctifies me and all
the elect people of God.

THE COMMANDMENTS

Question

When we speak of keeping God's commandments, which
commandments do we specially refer to?

542

Answer

Those which God spoke in the twentieth chapter of Exodus, saying: I am the Lord your God, who brought you out of the land of Egypt, out of the house of bondage;

1 You shall have no other gods but me.

2 You shall not make for yourself a graven image, or any likeness of anything that is in heaven above, or on the earth beneath, or in the water under the earth. You shall not bow down to them or worship them. For I the Lord your God am a jealous God, visiting the iniquity of the fathers upon the children to the third and fourth generation of those who hate me, but showing steadfast love to thousands of those who love me and keep my commandments.

3 You shall not take the name of the Lord your God in vain. For the Lord will not hold him guiltless who takes his name in vain.

4 Remember the sabbath day, to keep it holy. Six days you shall labour, and do all your work; but the seventh day is a sabbath to the Lord your God; in it you shall not do any work, you, or your son, or your daughter, your manservant, or your maidservant, or your cattle, or the sojourner who is within your gates; for in six days the Lord made heaven and earth, the sea, and all that is in them, and rested the seventh day; therefore the Lord blessed the seventh day, and hallowed it.

5 Honour your father and your mother, that your days may be long in the land which the Lord your God gives you.

6 You shall do no murder.

7 You shall not commit adultery.

8 You shall not steal.

9 You shall not bear false witness against your neighbour.

10 You shall not covet your neighbour's house; you shall not covet your neighbour's wife, or his servant, or his maid, or his ox, or his ass, or anything that is his.

Question

What do you chiefly learn from God's commandments?

Answer

I learn two things: my duty towards God, and my duty towards my neighbour.

Question

What is your duty towards God?

Answer

My duty towards God is,

to believe in him, to fear him, and to love him, with all my heart, with all my mind, with all my soul, and with all my strength;

to worship him, to give him thanks, to put my whole trust in him, to pray to him;

to honour his holy name and his word;

and to serve him truly all the days of my life.

Question

What is your duty towards your neighbour?

Answer

My duty towards my neighbour is,

to love him as myself, and to do to others whatever I wish they would do to me;

to love, honour, and care for my parents; to honour and obey the Queen and all who are in authority under her; to submit myself to my teachers and spiritual pastors; to be respectful and courteous to all;

to hurt no one by word or deed; to bear no malice or hatred in my heart;

to keep my body in temperance, soberness, and chastity; to be true and just in all my dealings;

to keep my hands from pilfering and stealing, and my tongue from evil speaking, lying, and slandering;

not to covet or desire things that belong to other people but to learn to work honestly for my own living, and to do my duty in that state of life to which it shall please God to call me.

PRAYER

Catechist

You know that you are not able to do these things by yourself, or to walk in the commandments of God, or to serve him, without his special grace, which you must learn at all times to ask for by diligent prayer. Let me hear therefore if you can say the Lord's Prayer.

Answer

> Our Father in heaven,
> > hallowed be your Name,
> > your kingdom come,
> > your will be done
> > > on earth as in heaven.
> Give us today our daily bread.
> Forgive us our sins
> > as we forgive those who sin against us.
> Lead us not into temptation,
> > but deliver us from evil.
> For the kingdom, the power, and the glory are yours
> > now and for ever.   Amen.

Question

What do you ask of God in this prayer?

Answer

I ask my Lord God our heavenly Father, who is the giver of all goodness, to send his grace to me, and to all people, that we may worship him, serve him, and obey him, as we ought to do. And I pray to God that he will send us all that we need both for our souls and bodies; and that he will be merciful to us and forgive us our sins; and that it will please him to save and defend us in all dangers to body and spirit; and that he will keep us from all sin and wickedness, and from our spiritual enemy, and from everlasting death.

And this I trust he will do, of his mercy and goodness, through our Lord Jesus Christ. And therefore I say, 'Amen', 'So be it'.

THE SACRAMENTS

Question

How many sacraments has Christ ordained in his Church?

Answer

Two only, as generally necessary to salvation; that is to say, baptism and the Lord's Supper (which is the Holy Communion).

Question

What do you mean by this word 'sacrament'?

Answer

I mean an outward and visible sign of an inward and spiritual grace, given to us, ordained by Christ himself, as a means by which we receive that grace, and a pledge to assure us of it.

Question

How many parts are there in a sacrament?

Answer

Two: the outward visible sign, and the inward spiritual grace.

Question

What is the outward visible sign, or form, in baptism?

Answer

Water, in which the person is baptized 'in the name of the Father, and of the Son, and of the Holy Spirit'.

Question

What is the inward and spiritual grace?

Answer

A death to sin and a new birth to righteousness; for, being born with a sinful nature, we are by this new birth made the children of grace.

Question

What is required of persons to be baptized?

Answer

Repentance, by which they forsake sin; and faith, by which they firmly believe the promises of God made to them in this sacrament.

Question

Why then are infants baptized, when by reason of their age they can neither repent nor believe?

Answer

Because they promise them both by their sponsors, and they must take this responsibility upon themselves when they are old enough to do so.

Question

Why was the sacrament of the Lord's Supper ordained?

Answer

For the continual remembrance of the sacrifice of the death of Christ, and of the benefits we receive by it.

Question

What is the outward part, or sign, of the Lord's Supper?

Answer

Bread and wine, which the Lord has commanded to be received.

Question

What is the inward part, or thing signified?

Answer

The body and blood of Christ, which are truly and indeed taken and received by the faithful in the Lord's Supper.

Question

What benefits do we partake of by this?

Answer

We are strengthened and inwardly refreshed by the body and blood of Christ, as our bodies are by the bread and wine.

Question

What is required of those who come to the Lord's Supper?

Answer

It is required that they examine themselves to see if they truly repent of their sins, and that they firmly intend to lead a new life. They must have a living faith in God's mercy through Christ with a thankful remembrance of his death and resurrection, and they must be in charity with all men.

A Service for Marriage

FIRST FORM

1   At the day and time appointed for solemnization of matrimony, the persons to be married come into the church with their friends and neighbours; and there standing together, the man on the right hand, and the woman on the left, the priest says

We have come together here in the sight of God, and in the presence of this congregation, to join together this man and this woman in holy matrimony; which is an honourable state of life, instituted from the beginning by God himself, signifying to us the spiritual union that is between Christ and his Church.

Christ adorned and beautified matrimony with his presence, and with the first sign by which he revealed his glory, at the marriage in Cana of Galilee; and holy scripture commands that all should hold it in honour.

It is therefore not to be entered upon unadvisedly, lightly, or merely to satisfy physical desires; but prayerfully, with careful thought, and with reverence for God, duly considering the purposes for which it was ordained.

It was ordained for the procreation of children and that they might be brought up in the nurture and instruction of the Lord, to the praise of his holy name.

It was ordained so that those to whom God has granted the gift of marriage might live a chaste and holy life, as befits members of Christ's body.

And it was ordained for the mutual companionship, help, and comfort, that the one ought to have of the other, both in prosperity and adversity.

Into this holy manner of life N and N come now to be joined. Therefore if anyone can show any just cause why they may not lawfully be joined together, let him speak now, or hereafter remain silent.

548

2   Speaking to the persons to be married, the priest says

I charge you both, as you will answer before God, who is the
judge of all and from whom no secrets are hidden, that if
either of you know any reason why you may not lawfully
be joined together in matrimony, you now confess it. For be
assured that those who marry otherwise than God's word
allows are not joined together by God, neither is their matrimony lawful in his sight.

THE CONSENT

3   If no impediment be alleged, the priest says to the man

N, will you have N as your wife,
to live together, as God has ordained,
in the holy state of matrimony?
Will you love her, cherish her,
honour and protect her,
in sickness and in health;
and, forsaking all others,
be faithful to her, as long as you both shall live?

The man answers

I will.

4   Then the priest says to the woman

N, will you have N as your husband,
to live together, as God has ordained,
in the holy state of matrimony?
Will you love him, obey him,
honour and protect him,
in sickness and in health;
and, forsaking all others,
be faithful to him, as long as you both shall live?

The woman answers

I will.

‡5 If the bride is to be given away, the priest says

Who gives this woman to be married to this man?

> And he receives her at her father's or friend's hands, taking her by the right hand.

THE BETROTHAL AND WEDDING

6 They give their troth to each other in this manner.
They face each other, and the minister causes the man with his right hand to take the woman by her right hand and to say

I N take you N to be my wife,
according to God's holy ordinance:
to have and to hold
from this day forward,
for better for worse,
for richer for poorer,
in sickness and in health,
to love and to cherish,
until we are parted by death.
And to this I pledge you my word.

7 Then they loose their hands; and the woman, with her right hand taking the man by his right hand, says

I N take you N to be my husband,
according to God's holy ordinance:
to have and to hold
from this day forward,
for better for worse,
for richer for poorer,
in sickness and in health,
to love and to obey,
until we are parted by death.
And to this I pledge you my word.

8 They again loose their hands, and the man gives the woman a ring, placing it on the book*. The priest takes it and gives it to the man to put it on the fourth finger of the woman's left hand. The man holds the ring there, and says

With this ring I wed you,
with my body I worship you;
with all that I am and all that I have
I honour you:
in the name of the Father,
and of the Son,
and of the Holy Spirit.
Amen.

9 They both kneel. The minister says

Let us pray.

Eternal God,
creator and preserver of all mankind,
giver of all spiritual grace
and author of everlasting life:
send your blessing upon this man and this woman
whom we bless in your name;
that as Isaac and Rebecca lived faithfully together,
so N and N may surely perform and keep
the vow and covenant made between them,
of which this ring given and received is a token and pledge,
and may ever remain in perfect love and peace together,
and live according to your laws;
through Jesus Christ our Lord.   **Amen.**

---

* At §8 while the ring is on the book the priest may say
    Lord, we pray that this ring may be to your servants
    a token of their solemn vows,
    and a pledge of pure and abiding love;
    through Jesus Christ our Lord.   **Amen.**

If the bride is to give the bridegroom a ring, she does so after §8.

10   Then the priest joins their right hands together and says

Those whom God has joined together
let not man put asunder.

THE DECLARATION OF THE MARRIAGE

11   The priest addresses the people

N and N have now witnessed to their mutual consent
before God and this company;
they have pledged their solemn word to each other;
and they have confirmed it
by the giving and receiving of a ring
and by the joining of hands.
I therefore declare them to be husband and wife:
in the name of the Father,
and of the Son,
and of the Holy Spirit.
   Amen.

And he adds this blessing

God the Father,
God the Son,
God the Holy Spirit,
bless, preserve, and keep you;
the Lord mercifully with his favour look upon you
and fill you with all spiritual blessing and grace,
that you may so live together in this life,
that in the world to come you may have life everlasting.
   Amen.

THE PRAYERS

12 One of the following psalms is said or sung. The minister, followed
by the man and the woman, may go to the Lord's table during
the reading or singing of the psalm.

Psalm 128

1 Blessed is everyone who | fears the | Lord:
   and walks in the | confine | of his | ways.
2 You will eat the | fruit of · your | labours:
   happy shall you | be and | all · shall go | well with you.
3 Your wife with|in your | house:
   shall | be · as a | fruitful | vine;
4 Your children a|round your | table:
   like the fresh | shoots | of the | olive.
5 Behold thus shall the | man be | blessed:
   who | lives · in the | fear · of the | Lord.
6 May the Lord so | bless you · from | Zion:
   that you see Jerusalem in prosperity |⌣
      all the | days · of your | life.
7 May you see your | children's | children:
   and in | Israel | let there · be | peace.

   Glo|ry to | God: Father | Son and | Holy | Spirit;
   As in the be|ginning · so | now: and for | ever | A|men.

Psalm 37.3-7

3 Trust in the | Lord and · do | good:
   and you shall dwell in the land |⌣
      and | feed in | safe | pastures.
4 Let the Lord be | your de|light:
   and he will | grant you · your | heart's de|sire.
5 Commit your | way · to the | Lord:
   trust | him and | he will | act.

6 He will make your righteousness
    shine as | clear · as the | light:
  and your | inno·cence | as the | noonday.

7 Be still | before | the Lord:
  and wait | patient|ly for | him.

  Glo|ry to | God: Father | Son and | Holy | Spirit;
  As in the be|ginning · so | now: and for | ever | A|men

Psalm 67

1 Let God be gracious to | us and | bless us:
  and make his | face | shine up|on us,

2 That your ways may be | known on | earth:
  your liberating | power · a|mong all | nations.

3 Let the peoples | praise you · O | God:
  let | all the | peoples | praise you.

4 Let the nations be | glad and | sing:
  for you judge the peoples with integrity
    and govern the | nations · up|on | earth.

5 Let the peoples | praise you · O | God:
  let | all the | peoples | praise you.

6 Then the earth will | yield its | fruitfulness:
  and | God our | God will | bless us.

†7 God | shall | bless us:
  and all the | ends · of the | earth will | fear him.

  Glo|ry to | God: Father | Son and | Holy | Spirit;
  As in the be|ginning · so | now: and for | ever | A|men

13 One or more passages of scripture may be read (see Note 4) and
    a sermon declaring the duties of husband and wife may be
    preached here or later in the service. If no sermon is preached,
    Ephesians 5.20-33 at least must be read.

Hear now the teaching of Saint Paul on the duties of husband and
wife.

Always give thanks for everything to God the Father, in
the name of our Lord Jesus Christ. Submit yourselves to one
another, because of your reverence for Christ.

Wives, submit yourselves to your husbands, as to the Lord. For a husband has authority over his wife in the same way that Christ has authority over the church; and Christ is himself the Saviour of the church, his body. And so wives must submit themselves completely to their husbands, in the same way that the church submits itself to Christ.

Husbands, love your wives in the same way that Christ loved the church and gave his life for it. He did this to dedicate the church to God, by his word, after making it clean by the washing in water, in order to present the church to himself, in all its beauty, pure and faultless, without spot or wrinkle, or any other imperfection.

Men ought to love their wives just as they love their own bodies. A man who loves his wife loves himself. (No one ever hates his own flesh. Instead, he feeds it and takes care of it, just as Christ does the church; for we are members of his body.) As the scripture says, 'For this reason, a man will leave his father and mother, and unite with his wife, and the two will become one.' There is a great truth revealed in this scripture, and I understand it applies to Christ and the church. But it also applies to you: every husband must love his wife as himself, and every wife must respect her husband.

Ephesians 5.20-33 (TEV)

14   Then, the people kneeling, and the man and the woman kneeling before the Lord's Table, the priest stands at the Table and, turning towards them says

The Lord be with you.
   And also with you.

Let us pray.

**Our Father in heaven,
   hallowed be your Name,
   your kingdom come,
   your will be done
      on earth as in heaven.**

555

Give us today our daily bread.
Forgive us our sins
  as we forgive those who sin against us.
Lead us not into temptation,
  but deliver us from evil.
For the kingdom, the power, and the glory are yours
  now and for ever.   Amen.

Lord, save your servants,
  who put their trust in you.

Lord, send them help from your holy place,
  and evermore defend them.

Be to them a tower of strength,
  against every enemy.

Father, hear our prayer,
through Jesus Christ our Lord.

A prayer for the blessing of eternal life

God of Abraham,
God of Isaac,
God of Jacob,
bless these your servants
and sow the seed of eternal life in their hearts,
that whatever they learn in your holy word
they may indeed fulfil.
Look in love upon them, Father,
and bless them with the blessing you sent on Abraham and
    Sarah
that, obeying your will and secure in your protection,
they may abide in your love to their lives' end;
through Jesus Christ our Lord.
  Amen.

A prayer for the blessing of children

We praise you, Father,
for creating us in your own image
and for your gracious gift whereby mankind is increased;
give to N and N the blessing of children,
and grant them the wisdom and grace to bring them up
in the discipline and instruction of the Lord,
to your praise and honour;
through Jesus Christ our Lord.
   Amen.

A prayer for the blessing of mutual love and faithfulness

Almighty God,
who by joining man and woman together
taught us from the beginning
that we should not separate what you have joined as one;
we praise you that you have consecrated the state of
      matrimony to such an excellent purpose
that in it is signified the spiritual marriage and unity
      between Christ and his Church.
Look mercifully on these your servants,
that this man may love his wife, according to your word,
as Christ loved his bride the Church,
and gave himself for it,
cherishing it as himself;
and also that this woman may be loving and generous,
responsive and faithful to her husband.
O Lord, bless them both,
and grant them to inherit your everlasting kingdom;
through Jesus Christ our Lord.
   Amen.

or

Lord God,
you have consecrated marriage
to be a sign of the spiritual unity between Christ and his
      Church;

557

bless these your servants
that they may love, honour, and to cherish each other
in faithfulness, patience, wisdom, and true godliness;
may their home be a place of love and peace;
through Jesus Christ our Lord.

Amen.

15   Then the priest says

Almighty God,
who created our first parents
and sanctified and joined them together in marriage,
pour upon you the riches of his love,
sanctify and bless you,
that you may please him both in body and soul,
and live together in holy love to your lives' end.

Amen.

or

God the Father enrich you with his grace,
God the Son make you holy in his love,
God the Holy Spirit strengthen you with his joy.
The Lord bless you and keep you in eternal life.

Amen.

16   If there is no Communion, the minister concludes

And the grace of our Lord Jesus Christ, and the love of God,
and the fellowship of the Holy Spirit, be with us all evermore.   **Amen.**

NOTES

1 It is fitting that the newly-married persons should receive the holy communion at the time of their marriage or at the first opportunity after their marriage.

2 If the Holy Communion is celebrated at the time of the marriage, the priest may incorporate the Marriage service as is most appropriate in the circumstances.

The Psalm (§12), readings (§13), and the Lord's Prayer (from §14) may be omitted from the Marriage service;

the Prayers (§§14-15) may replace the Intercession in the Communion service;

the Marriage service may begin after the Gospel and Sermon of the Communion service, and the Communion service resume at the Preparation for the Lord's Supper; or the Communion service may begin after §11;

one or more of the prayers at §§14-15 may be said before the Blessing of the Communion service.

3 The Marriage service may be preceded by the ministry of the word from the Communion service even when the Holy Communion is not celebrated.

4 Collects and readings appropriate for reading at a Marriage are to be found on page 292.

5 Only those impediments to a marriage can be alleged which are recognized by God's law or the laws of this Commonwealth. Any person alleging an impediment on the occasion of a marriage must give an indemnity against any pecuniary loss, in the event of his allegation failing, which his action brings upon the parties. If such an allegation is made and an indemnity is given, the marriage must be deferred until the truth has been tried.

6 The placing of hymns and directions regarding posture, other than those noted in the rubrics of the order of service, may be determined by the priest.

7 The marriage certificates are to be signed at the conclusion of the service or after §11 at the discretion of the priest.

8 Where the couple are unable to have children, the prayer for the blessing of children at §14 is omitted.

A Service for Marriage

SECOND FORM

THE PREFACE

1 When all are assembled in the church, with the bridegroom and the bride standing before the priest, the priest greets them all, and then says

We have come together in the sight of God for the joining in marriage of this man N and this woman N.

Our Lord Jesus Christ said of marriage that 'From the beginning of creation God made them male and female. "For this reason a man shall leave his father and mother and be joined to his wife, and the two shall become one." So they are no longer two but one. What therefore God has joined together, let not man put asunder'.

Marriage is the symbol of God's unending love for his people, and of the union between Christ and his Church. So Saint Paul teaches that the husband must love his wife as Christ loved the Church, and that the wife must give due honour to her husband.

Marriage should be honoured by all, and is not to be entered into lightly or carelessly, but with reverent and serious respect for those purposes for which it was instituted by God.

Marriage is a gift from God for the well-being of mankind, and for the proper expression of natural instincts and affections with which he has endowed us.

It is a life-long union in which a man and a woman are called so to give themselves in body, mind, and spirit, and so to respond, that from their union will grow a deepening knowledge and love of each other. In the joys and sorrows of life, in prosperity and adversity, they share their companionship, faithfulness, and strength.

In marriage a new family is established in accordance with God's purpose, so that children may be born and nurtured in secure and loving care, for their well-being and instruction, and for the good order of society, to the glory of God.

N and N have now come here to be joined in this holy union to which God has led them. They seek his blessing on their life together, that they may fulfil his purpose for them; and they ask us to support them in this prayer. If any person here can show why they may not lawfully be joined in marriage he should speak now, or hereafter remain in silence.

Speaking to the persons to be married, the priest says

I charge you both, as you will answer before God, that if either of you know any reason why you may not lawfully be joined together in matrimony, you now confess it. For be assured that those who marry otherwise than God's word allows are not joined together by God, neither is their matrimony lawful in his sight.

THE CONSENT

2 *There being no objection lodged, the priest then says to the man*

N, will you take N to be your wife,
to live together according to God's law?
Will you give her the honour
due to her as your wife
and, forsaking all others,
love and protect her,
as long as you both shall live?

The man answers

I will.

3   The priest says to the woman

N, will you take N to be your husband,
to live together according to God's law?
Will you give him the honour
due to him as your husband
and, forsaking all others,
love and protect him,
as long as you both shall live?

The woman answers

I will.

[‡4   The priest may ask

Who brings this woman to be married to this man?

Answer

I do.

The priest receives the woman's right hand from her
father or her friend.]

5   The priest causes the man to take the woman's right hand.
The priest, together with all the people, says

God our Father, in your great love for mankind
you have given us the gift of marriage;
so bless these two persons as they pledge their lives to each
other,
that their love may evermore grow
to be the true reflection of your love for us all;
through Jesus Christ our Lord.   Amen.

THE WEDDING

6   The man, holding the woman's right hand in his, says

I N, in the presence of God,
take you N to be my wife;
to have and to hold
from this day forward,
for better for worse,
for richer for poorer,
in sickness and in health,
to love and to cherish,
as long as we both shall live.
This is my solemn vow and promise.

7   The woman, taking the man's right hand in hers, says

I N, in the presence of God,
take you N to be my husband;
to have and to hold
from this day forward,
for better for worse,
for richer for poorer,
in sickness and in health,
to love and to cherish,
as long as we both shall live.
This is my solemn vow and promise.

‡**8**   The priest receives the wedding ring[s], and may then say

Grant, Lord, that *this ring* may be a token and constant sign
of the pledge of love and faithfulness which these two persons
make to each other; through Christ our Lord.

      All say

Amen.

9   The man places the ring on the ring-finger of the woman, and holding it there, says

N, with this ring I wed you;
with all that I am and all that I have
I honour you;
in the name of God.   Amen.

‡10   Before they loose hands, the woman may respond

N, I receive this ring
in token of our marriage.
May God enable us to grow in love together.

‡11   If the woman gives a ring to the man, this procedure is to be repeated appropriately.

12   The man and the woman then kneel. The priest joins their right hands and says

Those whom God has joined together
let not man put asunder.

13   The priest addresses the people

Before God and in the presence of us all,
by solemn consent and promise,
by the giving and receiving of a ring,
and by the joining of hands,
N and N have now accepted each other in marriage.
In the name of God,
I declare them to be husband and wife.

14   The priest then addresses the husband and wife, saying

God the Father enrich you with his grace,
God the Son make you holy in his love,
God the Holy Spirit strengthen you with his joy.
The Lord bless you and keep you in eternal life.
**Amen. Blessed be the Father, Son, and Holy Spirit;
one God, to be praised for ever.**

THE PRAYERS

15 One or more passages from Scripture (See Note 4 on page 567) may be read; and an address may follow.

16 This or another psalm is said or sung.

Psalm 67

1 Let God be gracious to | us and | bless us:
 and make his | face | shine up|on us,

2 That your ways may be | known on | earth:
 your liberating | power · a|mong all | nations.

3 Let the peoples | praise you · O | God:
 let | all the | peoples | praise you.

4 Let the nations be | glad and | sing:
 for you judge the peoples with integrity
  and govern the | nations · up|on | earth.

5 Let the peoples | praise you · O | God:
 let | all the | peoples | praise you.

6 Then the earth will | yield its | fruitfulness:
 and | God our | God will | bless us.

†7 God | shall | bless us:
 and all the | ends · of the | earth will | fear him.

 Glo|ry to | God: Father | Son and | Holy | Spirit;
 As in the be|ginning · so | now: and for | ever | A|men.

17 The priest (standing at the Lord's Table) says

The Lord be with you.
 And also with you.

 All kneel

Our Father in heaven,
 hallowed be your Name,
 your kingdom come,
 your will be done
  on earth as in heaven.

Give us today our daily bread.
Forgive us our sins
 as we forgive those who sin against us.
Lead us not into temptation,
 but deliver us from evil.
For the kingdom, the power, and the glory are yours
 now and for ever. Amen.

18 The priest continues

Almighty Father, giver of life and love, look in favour on all who are made one in marriage, and especially on these your servants as they enter into their new life together. In your love deepen their love; strengthen their wills to keep the promises they have made; that they may live to your glory and to the good of mankind; through Jesus Christ our Lord. **Amen.**

19 The priest says

Almighty Father, you have created us in your own image, and by your gracious gift mankind is increased. To N and N grant the blessing of children; and such wisdom and loving care in the nurture of their family, that they and their children may come to know you in their lives and give you praise and honour; through Jesus Christ our Lord. **Amen.**

20 The priest and congregation say

Almighty God, Lord of the universe,
all love, strength, and understanding come from you;
so direct and govern us in body and soul
that we may strive to live according to your word
and to do everything that is agreeable to your will:
through Jesus Christ our Lord. Amen.

The grace of our Lord Jesus Christ, and the love of God, and the fellowship of the Holy Spirit, be with us all evermore. Amen.

NOTES

1   If the Holy Communion is celebrated at the time of the marriage, the priest may incorporate the Marriage service as is most appropriate in the circumstances.

The psalm, the Lord's Prayer and readings (§§15-17) may be omitted from the Marriage service;

the Prayers (§§18-20) may replace the Intercession in the Communion service;

the Marriage service may begin after the Gospel and Sermon of the Communion service, and the Communion service resume at the Preparation for the Lord's Supper;

or the Communion service may begin after §14;

one or more of the prayers at §§18, 19, and 20 may be said before the Blessing of the Communion service.

2   The Marriage service may be preceded by the ministry of the word from the Communion service even when the Holy Communion is not celebrated.

3   The priest's greeting at the commencement of the service may be given in the manner he considers appropriate.

4   Collects and readings appropriate for reading at a marriage are to be found on page 292. One or more passages from Scripture should be read at a Marriage.

5   Only those impediments to a marriage can be alleged which are recognized by God's law or the laws of this Commonwealth. Any person alleging an impediment on the occasion of a marriage must give an indemnity against any pecuniary loss, in the event of his allegation failing, which his action brings upon the parties. If such an allegation is made and an indemnity is given, the marriage must be deferred until the truth has been tried.

6   The placing of hymns or psalms and directions regarding posture, other than those noted in the rubrics of the order of service, may be determined by the priest.

7   The marriage certificates are to be signed at the conclusion of the service or after §14.

8   Where the couple are unable to have children, the prayer §19 is omitted.

Ministration to the Sick

Pastoral care as a ministry of the Gospel occurs when the love of God sustains people experiencing specific needs and stresses. The relation between the pastor and the sick person is of the first importance in this ministry. He should, therefore, be sensitive to the situation of the sick person and choose from the following liturgical forms what he believes most appropriately meets the needs of the sick person.

The word 'Minister' in the directions of §§1-4 includes any authorized lay person.

‡1   When a minister calls on a sick person at home or in hospital he may use the greeting

The peace of God be with you.

     And the sick person may respond

And also with you.

2   At the discretion of the minister the following form may be used wholly or in part with the sick person, save that the absolution and the forms for a blessing are used by a priest only.

The Lord's Prayer

A reading from the Bible

The Apostles' Creed (page 26)

One or more of the Prayers

A confession of sins and absolution

A blessing.

SUITABLE READINGS FROM THE BIBLE

3   The following selections of readings from the Bible may be used
by the minister or by the sick person privately. They may also be
used as alternative readings at the Communion of the Sick.

Faith and confidence in God

Psalms 27; 46; 71; 91; 121
Proverbs 3.11-26
Isaiah 26.1-9; 40.1-11; 55.6-11
Lamentations 3.22-26
Matthew 5.1-12
Mark 10.46-52
Luke 10.38-42; 22.14-20; 24.36-48
John 6.47-58; 11.20-27; 14.1-27; 15.1-11
Romans 8.31-end
Philippians 4.6-7
James 5.13-18
Revelation 7.9-17; 21.1-7; 22.1-7

Our Lord's works of healing

Mark 2.1-12; 5.22-43; 9.14-29; 10.46-52
Matthew 8.14-17
Luke 17.11-19
John 5.2-9;   9

The apostles' healing ministry

Mark 6.7-13
Acts 3.1-10; 9.32-42

Penitence

Psalms 51; 130; 143
Luke 15
John 3.14-21

Prayer for God's help

Psalms 43; 86; 143

Praise and thanksgiving

Psalms 34; 40; 103; 145

Christ the Good Shepherd

Psalm 23
John 10.1-18

God's love to man

Romans 5.6-11
1 John 3.1-7

Man's love to God and to his fellow-man

1 Corinthians 13
1 John 4.7-end.

PRAYERS

4 The following prayers are for use by the minister with sick people,
or as occasional prayers. In addition, the sick person may adapt
the prayers for private use.

For healing

God of grace, power, and mercy;
look on your servant N with compassion.
Give *him* courage and complete confidence in your protection,
and keep *him* in peace,
through Jesus Christ our Lord.   **Amen.**

Almighty God, giver of life and health,
hear our prayers for N
that by your blessing on *him* and on those who minister to
him,
he may be restored to health of body and mind according
to your will,
and in the presence of your people give thanks to you;
through Jesus Christ our Lord.   **Amen.**

Lord and heavenly Father,
the strengthener of those who suffer in body, mind, and
    soul;
lay your healing hands on N
that *he* may be restored to health
and show *his* thankfulness in love to you
and service to *his* fellows,
through Jesus Christ our Lord. **Amen.**

Lord of compassion, your hand is always stretched out in
blessing and healing of the sick; we pray for those whom we
have named before you, that they may be set free from the
sickness which afflicts them and healed by your power, for
the honour and glory of your name; through Jesus Christ our
Lord. **Amen.**

For a sick child

Lord Jesus Christ, you received and blessed the children
brought to you; give your blessing to your child N; and according to your gracious will, deliver *him* from *his* bodily
pain, that *he* may live to serve you for your glory. **Amen.**

Heavenly Father, you are watching with us over this sick
child for whom our prayers are offered; grant that *he* may
be restored to that perfect health which is yours alone to give;
through Jesus Christ our Lord. **Amen.**

Thanksgiving for healing

Almighty God, Father of all mercies,
we thank you for all your gifts of healing and forgiveness:
for the grace to love and care for each other,
for your hidden blessings,
and for all you have still in store for us;
for everything, whether joy or sorrow,
whereby you are drawing us to yourself
through Jesus Christ our Lord. **Amen.**

For a dying child

Lord Jesus Christ,
for our sake you became a baby in Bethlehem;
we commend to your loving care this child N,
lead *him* gently to those heavenly places
where those who sleep in you have continual peace and
     joy,
and fold *him* in the arms of your unfailing love;
as you live and reign with the Father and the Holy Spirit,
one God, world without end.   **Amen.**

For one troubled in conscience

Lord, Father of compassion and God of all comfort:
look in mercy on N whose heart and mind are troubled.
Give *him* a right understanding of *himself*
and a knowledge of your will for *him*,
that *he* may lose neither *his* confidence in you,
nor place it anywhere but in your purposes;
deliver *him* from the fear of evil;
and give *him* your continual peace;
through the merits and mediation of Jesus Christ our Lord.
     Amen.

For one facing an operation

Father of compassion and mercy,
you never fail to help and comfort those who seek your
     aid;
give strength and peace to this your *son*,
and enable *him* to know that you are near.
Give wisdom and care to those who minister to *him*
and especially . . . (surgeon and theatre staff);
grant that *he* may have no fear
since you are with *him*;
through Jesus Christ our Lord.   **Amen.**

For one distressed in mind

Almighty Father, in your love and wisdom you know the anxieties and fears of your children. Grant that N may be enabled to cast all *his* care on you, for you care for *him*. Give *him* quietness of mind, an unshaken trust in you, and guide *his* feet into the way of peace, through Jesus Christ our Lord. **Amen.**

For the dying

Lord Jesus Christ, in your last hour you commended your spirit into the hands of your heavenly Father; have mercy on your servant N. Give *him* the assurance of your presence even in the dark valley, and may death be to *him* the gate of paradise; for you are the Resurrection and the Life, to whom be glory for ever and ever. **Amen.**

For the handicapped

Loving Father,
we pray for the blind,
the deaf, the dumb, the frail,
those worn with sickness,
and all who are permanently injured.
May they know the presence of Christ on the road of
    suffering.
Show them the service they can render you
and grant that by their example we may be strengthened.
We ask this in the name of Jesus our Saviour
who took our infirmities on himself
and who now lives and reigns with you and the Holy
    Spirit,
one God, world without end. **Amen.**

For one believed to be suffering from an incurable disease

Father, we pray for N
and for all who suffer from diseases for which we know no
    cure.

Give them the victory of trust and hope
that they may never lose their faith in your loving purpose.
Grant your wisdom to all who are working
to discover the causes and the cures of disease,
and the realisation that in you all things are possible.
We ask this in the name of him
who went about doing good and healing all manner of
    disease,
even your Son Jesus Christ our Lord.   **Amen.**

For a convalescent

Lord, your compassion does not fail
and your mercies are new every morning;
we thank you that you have given N
both relief from pain and the hope of renewed health.
Continue in *him* the good work that has begun,
that, daily increasing in bodily strength,
and humbly rejoicing in your goodness,
he may so order *his* life as to think and do
always such things as shall please you,
through Jesus Christ our Lord.   **Amen.**

For submission to the will of God

God our heavenly Father, in whom we live and move and
have our being: grant to your servant N grace to desire only
your most holy will, that, whether living or dying *he* may be
yours; for the sake of Jesus Christ who loved us and gave
himself for us. **Amen.**

The almighty God, who is a most strong tower to all that
put their trust in him, and to whom all things in heaven and
earth do bow and obey; be now and always your defence,
and make you know and feel that there is no other name
under heaven given to man, in whom and through whom
you may receive health and salvation, but only the name of
our Lord Jesus Christ. **Amen.**

For commendation into God's keeping

To you, Lord, we commend the soul of your servant N that,
dying to the world, *he* may live to you, and whatever sins
he has committed through the frailty of earthly life, we ask
you to blot out by your most loving and merciful forgiveness;
through Jesus Christ our Lord. **Amen.**

Go forth, Christian soul, on your journey from this world,
in the name of God the Father who created you;
in the name of Jesus Christ who suffered for you;
in the name of the Holy Spirit who strengthens you;
in communion with the blessed saints,
and aided by angels and archangels and all the heavenly
    host.
May your portion this day be in peace,
and your dwelling in the heavenly Jerusalem. **Amen.**

Receive *him*, Lord, as a lamb of your own flock,
as a child of your own creating;
as a soul of your own redeeming;
and grant that whatever sins *he* may have committed
through the weakness of *his* earthly nature
may be forgiven;
and that *he* may for ever enjoy
the clear shining light of paradise. **Amen.**

Forms for a blessing

To God's gracious mercy and protection we commit you.
The Lord bless you and keep you.
The Lord make his face to shine on you
and be gracious to you.
The Lord lift up his countenance on you and give you peace,
both now and evermore. **Amen.**

The peace of God, which passes all understanding, keep your heart and mind in the knowledge and love of God, and of his Son Jesus Christ our Lord: and the blessing of God almighty, the Father, the Son, and the Holy Spirit, be on you and remain with you always. **Amen.**

The grace of our Lord Jesus Christ, and the love of God, and the fellowship of the Holy Spirit, be with us all evermore. Amen.

A FORM OF CONFESSION OF SINS AND ABSOLUTION

5   When the priest examines the sick person as to his faith, and as to whether he truly repents of his sins and is in love and charity with all, the sick person is then moved to make a special confession of his sins if he feels his conscience troubled with any weighty matter. The following form may be used.

The priest invites the sick person to have trust in God.

The Lord Jesus welcomes you. He came to call sinners. Have confidence in him.

and/or

The Lord be in your heart and on your lips, and help you to make a true confession of your sins, in the name of the Father and of the Son and of the Holy Spirit.
Amen.

The penitent may make confession of sins in his own words; and/or use the following form:

Merciful God, my maker and my judge,
I have sinned against you in thought, word, and deed:
I have not loved you with my whole heart;
I have not loved my neighbour as myself;
I repent, and am sorry for all my sins.
Father, forgive me.

Strengthen me to love and obey you in newness of life;
through Jesus Christ our Lord.   Amen.

or this form:

Lord and heavenly Father,
I confess that I have sinned in thought, word,
    and deed through my own fault;
and especially I have sinned in this way ...
For these sins I am truly sorry,
and firmly purpose to amend my life.
I ask for your forgiveness,
for Jesus' sake.   Amen.

After this confession the priest absolves him (if he humbly and heartily desires it) in this manner:

Our Lord Jesus Christ, who has left power to his Church to absolve all sinners who truly repent and believe in him, of his great mercy forgive you your offences: and by his authority committed to me I absolve you from all your sins, in the name of the Father, and of the Son, and of the Holy Spirit.   **Amen.**

Then the priest says this collect:

Let us pray

Most merciful God, in the fulness of your mercy you so put away the sins of those who truly repent, that you remember them no more. Be gracious to your servant who has earnestly asked your pardon and forgiveness. Renew in *him*, most loving Father, whatever has been corrupted by the deceits of the devil, or by *his* own sinful will and frailty. Keep *him* securely in the unity of the church. And because *he* puts *his* full trust only in your mercy, do not impute to *him his* former sins, but strengthen *him* with your blessed Spirit; through the merits of your dear Son, Jesus Christ our Lord.
   Amen.   His mercy endures for ever.

The priest adds

To God's gracious mercy and protection we commit you:
the Lord bless you and keep you.
The Lord make his face to shine on you
and be gracious to you.
The Lord lift up his countenance on you, and give you
peace,
both now and evermore. **Amen.**

THE COMMUNION OF THE SICK

6 The Minister of the parish shall carefully instruct the
people to receive the holy communion when it is administered in
the church. But if a sick person is unable to come to the church
he may receive the holy communion (at home or in the hospital
or wherever he is being cared for) where he is. In this case there
should normally be at least two or three to communicate with him.
However, where it is difficult for others to join with him, and when
the sick person specially requests it, the minister alone may communicate with him.

With all things necessary prepared so that he may reverently
minister, the priest may celebrate The Holy Communion according to either of the forms in this book (pages 114 and 134), beginning with the Collect, Epistle and Gospel which follows here (or
those of the day; or from the readings set out in §3), and proceeding
at §20 of the first order, or §15 of the second order.

In case of extreme illness, the priest may use his discretion concerning other omissions from the order, provided that he shall
always use, in the first order, that part of §28 beginning 'Hear us,
merciful Father', or, in the second order, that part of §20 beginning
'Merciful Father, we thank you' and concluding 'Do this, as often
as you drink it, in remembrance of me', together with the full words
of administration, the Lord's Prayer, and the blessing. The forms
which follow are printed for the convenience of the communicant.

If for good reason it is not possible for the sick person to receive the sacrament of Christ's body and blood, the minister shall counsel him that if he truly repents of his sins, and steadfastly believes that Jesus Christ has died on the cross for him and shed his blood for his redemption, earnestly remembering the benefits he has by this, and giving heartfelt thanks to the Lord Jesus for it, he eats and drinks the body and blood of our Saviour Christ profitably to his soul's health, even though he does not receive the sacrament with his mouth.

The prayer of preparation

Almighty God,
to whom all hearts are open,
all desires known,
and from whom no secrets are hidden:
cleanse the thoughts of our hearts
by the inspiration of your Holy Spirit,
that we may perfectly love you,
and worthily magnify your holy name,
through Christ our Lord.   **Amen.**

A collect, epistle, and gospel suitable for use with the sick

God of grace, power, and mercy;
look on your servant N with compassion,
give *him* courage and complete confidence in your protec-
    tion, and keep *him* in peace,
through Jesus Christ our Lord.
Amen.

Since we have a great high priest who has passed through the heavens, the Son of God, let us hold fast our confession. For we have not a high priest who is unable to sympathize with our weaknesses, but one who in every respect has been tempted as we are, yet without sin. Let us then with confidence draw near to the throne of grace, that we may receive mercy and find grace to help in time of need.

Hebrews 4.14-16

I am the good shepherd; I know my own and my own know
me, as the Father knows me and I know the Father; and I
lay down my life for the sheep. My sheep hear my voice, and
I know them, and they follow me; and I give them eternal
life, and they shall never perish, and no one shall snatch
them out of my hand.

John 10.14-15, 27-28

The Prayer of Approach

**We do not presume
to come to your table, merciful Lord,
trusting in our own righteousness,
but in your manifold and great mercies.
We are not worthy
so much as to gather up the crumbs under your table.
But you are the same Lord
whose nature is always to have mercy.
Grant us, therefore, gracious Lord,
so to eat the flesh of your dear Son Jesus Christ,
and to drink his blood,
that we may evermore dwell in him
and he in us.   Amen.**

The General Confession

**Merciful God,
our maker and our judge,
we have sinned against you in thought, word, and deed:
we have not loved you with our whole heart,
we have not loved our neighbours as ourselves,
we repent and are sorry for all our sins.
Father, forgive us.
Strengthen us to love and obey you in newness of life;
through Jesus Christ our Lord.   Amen**

The priest pronounces the Absolution.

Almighty God,
who has promised forgiveness to all who turn to him in
    faith,
pardon you and set you free from all your sins,
strengthen you to do his will,
and keep you in eternal life;
through Jesus Christ our Lord.
Amen

When the minister gives the holy communion he says

The body of our Lord Jesus Christ, which was given for you,
preserve your body and soul to everlasting life; take and eat
this in remembrance that Christ died for you, and feed on
him in your heart by faith with thanksgiving.

The blood of our Lord Jesus Christ, which was shed for you,
preserve your body and soul to everlasting life; drink this in
remembrance that Christ's blood was shed for you, and be
thankful.

After the Communion, the Lord's Prayer is said.

A prayer of thanksgiving after holy communion

Father, we thank you
that you feed us who have received these holy mysteries
with the spiritual food of the body and blood of our
    Saviour, Jesus Christ.
We thank you for this assurance of your goodness and
    love;
that we are living members of his body
and heirs of his eternal kingdom.
Accept this our sacrifice of praise and thanksgiving,
and help us to grow in love and obedience,
that with all your saints we may worship you for ever;
through Jesus Christ our Lord.
Amen.

The priest pronounces the Blessing.

Funeral Services

To the congregation

We come together —
to mourn a relative
to honour a departed friend
to dispose reverently of the mortal body
and to show sympathy with the bereaved.

We believe that those who die in Christ share eternal life
with him.

Therefore in faith and hope
we offer our prayer of thanksgiving and trust to God,
in whose loving care we leave our friend;
we recall the certainty of our own coming death and
judgment; and we proclaim that Christ is risen, that those
who believe in him will rise with him, and that we are
united with them in him.

A PRAYER

God our Father,
you alone are holy.
Forgive us all our sins and failures.
Uphold us by your Spirit.
Enable us to show your compassion.
Give us in our sorrow the calm of your peace.
May our grief give way to joy;
through Jesus Christ our Lord.
Amen.

The Service begins on the next page.

A SERVICE IN CHURCH

to be used when the body of the deceased has
been brought to the church prior to the interment
or cremation.

Alternatively, this service may be used in the cemetery or crematorium
chapel in conjunction with The Burial, in which case the minister may omit
§§11, 12, and 13, and may use sentences from §13 at §1.

If the body is brought to the church before the time of this service, the
priest should meet it at the entrance and reverently accompany it into the
church. He may say some of the sentences appointed at §§1 and 13.

In the absence of the priest, the funeral services may be conducted by
a deacon or an authorized lay person.

1   If the body has not already been brought into the church, the priest
    meets it at the entrance and says the sentences as he goes before
    it into the church. Otherwise, standing at the prayer desk or some
    other convenient place, he says

I am the resurrection and the life, says the Lord; he who
believes in me, though he die, yet shall he live, and whoever
lives and believes in me shall never die.   John 11.25-6

He may add one or more of these or other Sentences of Scripture:

The Lamb in the midst of the throne will be their shepherd,
and he will guide them to springs of living water; and God
will wipe away every tear from their eyes.   Revelation 7.17

The Lord God will feed his flock like a shepherd,
he will gather the lambs in his arms,
he will carry them in his bosom.   Isaiah 40.11

God is our refuge and strength,
a very present help in trouble.   Psalm 46.1

Blessed are those who mourn, for they shall be comforted.
                                                    Matthew 5.4

Jesus said: Let not your hearts be troubled; believe in God,
believe also in me. In my Father's house are many rooms;

if it were not so, would I have told you that I go to prepare
a place for you? And when I go and prepare a place for you,
I will come again and take you to myself, that where I am
you may be also.

John 14.1-3

I am sure that neither death, nor life, nor angels, nor prin-
cipalities, nor things present, nor things to come, nor powers,
nor height, nor depth, nor anything else in creation, will be
able to separate us from the love of God in Christ Jesus our
Lord.

Romans 8.38-39

What no eye has seen, nor ear heard, nor the heart of man
conceived, God has prepared for those who love him.

1 Corinthians 2.9

2   All standing, the minister says

Let us say together:

Heavenly Father,
in your Son Jesus Christ
you have given us a true faith and a sure hope.
Help us to live as those who believe in the communion of
**   saints,**
the forgiveness of sins,
and the resurrection to eternal life;
through your Son Jesus Christ our Lord.

3   One or more psalms is said or sung.

Psalm 90

1 Lord you have | been our | refuge:
   from one gener|ation | to an|other.
2 Before the mountains were born
        or the earth and the world were | brought to | be:
   from eternity to e|terni·ty | you are | God.

3 You turn man | back · into | dust:
    saying 'Return to | dust you | sons of | Adam'.

4 For a thousand years in your sight‿
    are like | yester·day | passing:
    or | like one | watch · of the | night.

5 You cut them | short · like a | dream:
    like the fresh | grass | of the | morning;

6 In the morning it is | green and | flourishes:
    at evening it is | withered · and | dried | up.

10 The days of our life are three score years and ten
    or if we have | strength four | score:
    the pride of our labours is but toil and sorrow
    for it passes quickly a|way and | we are | gone.

11 Who can know the | power of · your | wrath:
    who can know your indig|nation · like | those that | fear
    you?

12 Teach us so to | number · our | days:
    that we may ap|ply our | hearts to | wisdom.

13 Relent O Lord * how long will | you be | angry?:
    take | pity | on your | servants.

14 O satisfy us early | with your | mercy:
    that all our days we | may re|joice and | sing.

15 Give us joy for all the days you | have af|flicted us:
    for the | years · we have | suffered · ad|versity.

16 Show your | servants · your | work:
    and let their | children | see your | glory.

†17 May the gracious favour of the Lord our | God · be up|on
    us:
    prosper the work of our hands
        O | prosper | the | work | of our | hands!

    Glo|ry to | God: Father | Son and | Holy | Spirit;
    As in the be|ginning · so | now: and for | ever | A|men

Psalm 23

1 The Lord | is my | shepherd:
  therefore | can I | lack | nothing.
2 He will make me lie down in | green | pastures:
  and | lead me · be|side still | waters.
3 He will re|fresh my | soul:
  and guide me in right pathways | for his | name's | sake.
4 Though I walk through the valley of the shadow of
    death
    I will | fear no | evil:
  for you are with me
    your | rod · and your | staff | comfort me.
5 You spread a table before me
    in the face of | those who | trouble me:
  you have anointed my head with oil | and my | cup · will
    be | full.
6 Surely your goodness and loving-kindness ‿
    will follow me * all the | days · of my | life:
  and I shall dwell in the | house · of the | Lord for | ever.

Glo|ry to | God: Father | Son and | Holy | Spirit;
As in the be|ginning · so | now: and for | ever | A|men.

Psalms 39.1-8; 121; and 130 are also suitable.

4   The congregation sits.
    The reading from 1 Corinthians 15 is read, or else one or more of
    the passages listed.

1 Corinthians 15.20

Saint Paul declares the resurrection of the dead through Jesus
Christ.

Christ has been raised from the dead, the first fruits of
those who have fallen asleep. For as by a man came death,
by a man has come also the resurrection of the dead. For as
in Adam all die, so also in Christ shall all be made alive. But

each in his own order: Christ the first fruits, then at his coming those who belong to Christ. Then comes the end, when he delivers the kingdom to God the Father after destroying every rule and every authority and power. For he must reign until he has put all his enemies under his feet. The last enemy to be destroyed is death.

But some will ask, 'How are the dead raised? With what kind of body do they come?' You foolish man! What you sow does not come to life unless it dies. And what you sow is not the body which is to be, but a bare kernel, perhaps of wheat or of some other grain. But God gives it a body as he has chosen, and to each kind of seed its own body.

So it is with the resurrection of the dead. What is sown is perishable, what is raised is imperishable. It is sown in dishonour, it is raised in glory. It is sown in weakness, it is raised in power. It is sown a physical body, it is raised a spiritual body. If there is a physical body, there is also a spiritual body. Thus it is written, 'The first man Adam became a living being'; the last Adam became a life-giving spirit. But it is not the spiritual which is first but the physical, and then the spiritual. The first man was from the earth, a man of dust; the second man is from heaven. As was the man of dust, so are those who are of the dust; and as is the man of heaven, so are those who are of heaven. Just as we have borne the image of the man of dust, we shall also bear the image of the man of heaven. I tell you this, brethren, flesh and blood cannot inherit the kingdom of God, nor does the perishable inherit the imperishable.

Lo! I tell you a mystery. We shall not all sleep, but we shall all be changed, in a moment, in the twinkling of an eye, at the last trumpet. For the trumpet will sound, and the dead will be raised imperishable, and we shall be changed. For this perishable nature must put on the imperishable, and this mortal nature must put on immortality. When the perishable puts on the imperishable, and the mortal puts on immortality, then shall come to pass the saying that is written:

> 'Death is swallowed up in victory.'
> 'O death, where is your victory?
> O death, where is your sting?'

Thanks be to God who gives us the victory through our Lord Jesus Christ.

Therefore, my beloved brethren, be steadfast, immovable, always abounding in the work of the Lord, knowing that in the Lord your labour is not in vain.

1 Corinthians 15.20-26,35-38,42-55,57-58

John 14.1

Jesus promises his followers a place in his Father's house.

He said to them, 'Let not your hearts be troubled; believe in God, believe also in me. In my Father's house are many rooms; if it were not so, would I have told you that I go to prepare a place for you? And when I go and prepare a place for you, I will come again and will take you to myself, that where I am you may be also. And you know the way where I am going.' Thomas said to him, 'Lord, we do not know where you are going; how can we know the way?' Jesus said to him, 'I am the way, and the truth, and the life; no one comes to the Father, but by me.'

John 14.1-6

John 5.19-29 The Son of God has power to give life
John 6.35-40 Jesus the Bread of life
John 11.17-27 Jesus the Resurrection and the Life
Romans 8.31-39 God's love in Christ Jesus
Romans 14.7-9 We belong to the Lord
2 Corinthians 1.3-5 All our help comes from God
2 Corinthians 4.7-15 Death and life at work in us
2 Corinthians 4.16-5.10 Living by faith
Philippians 3.8-21 God's purposes for us
1 Thessalonians 4.13-18 The coming of the Lord
Revelation 21.1-7 The new heaven and the new earth
Mark 10.13-16 Jesus blesses little children

5 | A sermon may be preached.

‡6 | All stand, and this hymn or another may be said or sung

8 You Lord Christ are the | King of | glory:
the e|ternal | Son of the | Father.

9 When you became man to | set us | free:
you did not dis|dain the | Virgin's | womb.

10 When you overcame the | sting of | death:
you opened the kingdom of | heaven · to | all be|lievers.

11 You are seated at God's right | hand in | glory:
we believe that you will | come and | be our | judge.

12 Come then Lord and | help your | people:
bought with the | price of | your own | blood;

13 and bring us | with your | saints:
to | glory | ever|lasting.   From the hymn Te Deum

7 | The minister says

Let us pray.

Lord, have mercy on us.

Christ, have mercy on us.

Lord, have mercy on us.

and all say together

Our Father in heaven,
hallowed be your Name,
your kingdom come,
your will be done
on earth as in heaven.
Give us today our daily bread.
Forgive us our sins
as we forgive those who sin against us.
Lead us not into temptation,
but deliver us from evil.
For the kingdom, the power, and the glory are yours
now and for ever.   Amen.

8   The minister continues

Holy and loving Father,
you gave us life when you created us,
and in your redeeming love you have given us new life in
    Christ Jesus.
We give you thanks for your servant, N.
In faith and trust we leave *him* in your keeping;
through Jesus Christ your Son our Lord,
who died and rose again to save us,
and now lives and reigns with you and the Holy Spirit
    in glory for ever.
    Amen.

or, at the funeral of a child, he says

Holy God and loving Father,
we give thanks for the gift of your child, N.
In faith and trust we leave *him* in your keeping,
praying that in your good purpose
we may rejoice with *him* in your eternal kingdom;
through Jesus Christ our Lord.
    Amen.

9   The minister adds these prayers

Almighty God,
Father of all mercies and giver of all comfort;
deal graciously, we pray, with those who mourn,
that, casting all their care on you,
they may know the consolation of your love;
through Jesus Christ our Lord.
    Amen.

O God,
the maker and redeemer of all mankind,
we pray for the coming of your kingdom,
that in the last day,
when you bring together all things in Christ,

591

we with all who have died in him
may enjoy the fulfilment of your promises;
through Jesus Christ our Lord.

Amen.

Additional prayers (see §§21ff on pages 598-601) may be said here.

‡10   The minister may say

Help us, Lord, to receive and understand your gospel,
so that we may find light in our darkness,
strength in our grief,
and hope and comfort in your saving words.
We ask this through Christ our Lord.

Amen.

or this

Lord, you alone are the source of life.
May your life-giving Spirit flow through us.
Grant us your compassion one for the other.
In our sorrow give us the calm of your peace.
Kindle our hope,
and let our grief give way to joy;
through Jesus Christ our Lord.

Amen.

11   The minister says

May God in his infinite love and mercy bring the whole Church, living and departed in the Lord Jesus, to a joyful resurrection and the fulfilment of his eternal kingdom.

Amen.

or

May the God of peace who brought again from the dead our Lord Jesus, the great shepherd of the sheep, by the blood of the eternal covenant, equip you with everything good that you may do his will, working in you that which is pleasing in his sight, through Jesus Christ; to whom be glory for ever and ever.

Amen.   Hebrews 13.20,21

12   A hymn may be sung.

592

THE BURIAL

13   When the body is brought to the cemetery, or to the crematorium,
      the minister meets it at the entrance. He says one or more of the
      following sentences, either as he goes before the body towards the
      grave or into the chapel, or when all have come together.

If we live, we live to the Lord, and if we die, we die to the
Lord; so then, whether we live or whether we die, we are the
Lord's. For to this end Christ died and rose again, that he
might be Lord of the dead and of the living.   Romans 14.8-9

Blessed be the God and Father of our Lord Jesus Christ! By
his great mercy we have been born anew to a living hope
through the resurrection of Jesus Christ from the dead.

1 Peter 1.3

We believe that Jesus died and rose again. Through Jesus,
God will bring with him those who have fallen asleep.

1 Thessalonians 4.14

We brought nothing into the world, and we can take nothing
out of the world. The Lord gave, and the Lord has taken
away; blessed be the name of the Lord. 1 Timothy 6.7; Job 1.21

14   At the place of burial or cremation these words are said:

Man that is born of woman is of few days, and full of
    trouble.
He comes forth like a flower, and withers.
He passes like a shadow and does not stay.

In the midst of life we are in death.
From whom may we seek for help, but from you, Lord God,
though you are justly displeased on account of our sins?
And yet, Lord God almighty, most holy and most merciful
    Saviour,
deliver us from the bitterness of eternal death.

You know the secrets of our hearts;
mercifully hear us, most worthy judge eternal;
keep us, at our last hour, in the consolation of your love.

or he may read Psalm 103.8,13-17

The Lord is full of compassion and mercy:
slow to anger and of great goodness.
As a father is tender towards his children:
so is the Lord tender to those who fear him.
For he knows of what we are made:
he remembers that we are but dust.
The days of man are but as grass:
he flourishes like a flower of the field;
when the wind goes over it, it is gone:
and its place will know it no more.
But the merciful goodness of the Lord endures for ever and
    ever towards those that fear him:
and his righteousness upon their children's children.

15   At a burial while earth is cast on the body, or at a cremation while
      the body is removed, the priest says

Almighty God, our heavenly Father,
you have given us a sure and certain hope of the resurrection
    to eternal life;
in your keeping are all those who have departed in Christ;
we here commit the body of our dear *brother* N to the
    ground/to be cremated:
earth to earth, ashes to ashes, dust to dust;
in the name of our Lord Jesus Christ,
who died, and was buried, and rose again for us,
and who shall change our mortal body
that it may be like his glorious body.
Thanks be to God who gives us the victory
through Jesus Christ our Lord!
Amen.

594

16   Then the following prayers are said.
At a funeral they are said at the graveside.
At a cremation they may be said in the chapel; or they may be said later after the interment of the ashes.

The minister first says

Saint John the Divine tells us: I heard a voice from heaven, saying, 'Blessed are the dead who die in the Lord henceforth.' 'Blessed indeed,' says the Spirit, 'that they may rest from their labours.'   Revelation 14.13

He may add

Let us say the Lord's Prayer together.

Our Father in heaven,
  hallowed be your Name,
  your kingdom come,
  your will be done
    on earth as in heaven.
Give us today our daily bread.
Forgive us our sins
  as we forgive those who sin against us.
Lead us not into temptation,
  but deliver us from evil.
For the kingdom, the power, and the glory are yours
  now and for ever.   Amen.

17   The minister continues

Merciful God, Father of our Lord Jesus Christ, who is the resurrection and the life of all who believe in him, and who has taught us not to grieve, as people without hope, for those who sleep in him: raise us, we pray, from the death of sin to the life of righteousness, that when we depart this life we may rest in him as, our hope is, our *brother* does, and that at the resurrection on the last day we may be found acceptable to you, and receive the kingdom prepared for all who love and fear you; grant this, merciful Father, through Jesus Christ, our mediator and redeemer.   **Amen.**

or he may use this prayer

Eternal Father,
God of all consolation,
in your unending love and mercy for us
you turn the darkness of death into the dawn of new life.
Be our refuge and strength in sorrow.
As your Son, our Lord Jesus Christ,
by dying for us conquered death,
and by rising again restored us to life,
so may we go forward in faith to meet him
and after our life on earth
be united with our dear brothers and sisters in Christ
where every tear will be wiped away.
We ask this through Jesus Christ our Lord.
Amen.

Additional prayers (see §§21ff on pages 598-601) may be said
here.

18   The minister concludes

Now to him who is able to keep us from falling, and to
present us faultless before the presence of his glory with
everlasting joy, to the only wise God our Saviour, be glory
and majesty, dominion and power, both now and ever.
Amen.   Jude 24 and 25

or

The grace of our Lord Jesus Christ, and the love of God, and
the fellowship of the Holy Spirit, be with us all.
Amen.   1 Corinthians 13.13

or he may use one of the prayers at §11.

THE INTERMENT OF THE ASHES

19   The minister may use such prayers and readings from §§1-10 as
are suitable to each occasion.

At the interment of the ashes he says

Almighty God, our heavenly Father,
you have given us a sure and certain hope of the resurrection
    to eternal life;
in your keeping are all those who have departed in Christ;
we here commit the ashes of our dear *brother* N to their
    resting place:
earth to earth, ashes to ashes, dust to dust;
in the name of our Lord Jesus Christ,
who died, and was buried, and rose again for us,
and who shall change our mortal body
that it may be like his glorious body.
Thanks be to God who gives us the victory
through Jesus Christ our Lord!
Amen.

Almighty God,
grant that we, with all who have believed in you,
may be united in the full knowledge of your love
and the unclouded vision of your glory;
through Jesus Christ our Lord.
Amen.

      The prayers, §§16-18, may follow.
      If they were not used at the cremation, they shall be used here.

A SERVICE WHICH MAY BE USED
IN THE CHURCH OR IN THE HOME
BEFORE A FUNERAL

20 If the body is brought to the church before the funeral, §§1-12 or the following may be used.

A sentence or sentences from §1
Psalm 27.1-8 or 139.1-11,17-18
Romans 8.31b-39 or another reading from §4
The Lord's Prayer
Other prayers taken from §§21ff
The Grace (2 Corinthians 13.13, §18).

[If §§1-12 are subsequently to be used before the funeral, §1 may be omitted.]

Alternatively, this service may be said in the home before the body is taken to church.

A SELECTION OF
ADDITIONAL PRAYERS

21
Merciful Father and Lord of life,
we praise you that mankind is made in your image
and is called to reflect your truth and light;
we thank you for the life of your *son*, N,
for the love and mercy *he* received from you
and showed among us.
Above all we rejoice in your gracious promise
to all your servants, living and departed;
that we shall be made one again at the coming of Christ.
And we ask that in due time we may share with them
that clearer vision of your heavenly glory;
through Jesus Christ our Lord.   **Amen.**

22

Almighty God,
with whom the souls of the faithful departed who die in the
Lord
are in joy and felicity,
we give thanks that it has pleased you to deliver this our
brother, N,
from the troubles of this sinful world,
beseeching you, of your goodness, to hasten your kingdom;
that we, with all who are departed in the true faith of your
holy name,
may have our perfect consummation and bliss,
both in body and soul,
in your eternal glory;
through Jesus Christ our Lord.   **Amen.**

23

Almighty God,
Father of all mercies and giver of all comfort;
deal graciously, we pray, with those who mourn,
that, casting all their care on you,
they may know the consolation of your love;
through Jesus Christ our Lord.   **Amen.**

24

Grant us, Lord, wisdom and grace
to use aright the time that is left to us here on earth.
While we have time lead us to repent of our sins,
and to do what we have left undone.
Strengthen us to follow in the steps of your Son Jesus
Christ
along the way of your eternal kingdom;
through Jesus Christ our Lord.   **Amen.**

25

O God, in whose mighty power it lies to bring good out of
    evil,
and to raise up life from the dead;
grant us a patient faith in time of darkness,
and enlighten our understanding with the knowledge of your
    ways;
through Jesus Christ our Lord. **Amen.**

26

O Lord, support us all the day long of this troublous life,
until the shadows lengthen and the evening comes,
the busy world is hushed,
the fever of life is over,
and our work is done.
Then, Lord, in your mercy,
grant us a safe lodging,
a holy rest,
and peace at the last;
through Christ our Lord. **Amen.**

27

Almighty and merciful Father,
we give you thanks for the life of your servant, N.
We pray that you will preserve among us the good of *his*
    example,
and keep us in the way of truth until we come to your eternal
    kingdom;
through Jesus Christ our Lord. **Amen.**

28

O Lord our God,
from whom neither life nor death
can separate those who trust in your love,
and whose love holds in its embrace
your children in this world and the next;

so unite us to yourself,
that in our fellowship with you
we may be always united to our loved ones,
whether here or there;
give us courage, constancy, and hope;
through him who died and was buried and rose again for
    us,
Jesus Christ our Lord.   **Amen.**

29

Almighty God,
grant that we, with those who have believed in you,
may be united in the full knowledge of your love
and the unclouded vision of your glory;
through Jesus Christ our Lord.   **Amen.**

NOTES

1   Collects and readings which may be used if there is a celebration of the Holy Communion on the day of the funeral are given on page 295.

2   At a *Burial at Sea*, §§1 or 13 or Psalm 107.23-24 may be read. The service may be shortened, but should always include §§1 or 13 and §15 (as below), the Lord's Prayer, and the Grace (see §18). The prayer of committal (§15) is said as follows:

> Almighty God, our heavenly Father,
> you have given us a sure and certain hope of the resurrection
>   to eternal life;
> in your keeping are all those who have departed in Christ;
> we here commit the body of our dear *brother* N to the sea:
> in the name of our Lord Jesus Christ,
> who died, and was buried, and rose again for us,
> and who shall change our mortal body
> that it may be like his glorious body.
> Thanks be to God who gives us the victory
> through Jesus Christ our Lord!
>   **Amen.**

The Ordinal

Eucalyptus camaldulensis
River red gum

The Making of Deacons

1   On the day appointed by the bishop, after Morning Prayer, there is a sermon on the duties of deacons, the necessity of this office in Christ's Church, and how the people ought to esteem those who hold it.

2   First, the archdeacon (or one appointed in his place) presents to the bishop sitting in his chair near the holy table those who are to be made deacons that day.

The archdeacon says

Reverend Father in God, I present to you these persons, N and N, to be admitted to the Order of Deacons.

The bishop says

Take care that the persons you present are, by their learning and godly way of life, suitable to exercise their ministry to the glory of God and the building up of his church.

The archdeacon

I have enquired concerning them, and I have examined them [*or* and they have been examined]. I believe them to be fit for this office.

3   Then the bishop says to the people

Good people, if you know of any obstacle or notorious offence in any of these persons presented to be ordered deacon, such as would bar him from being received into this holy ministry, come forward in the name of God and reveal what the offence or obstacle is.

If any offence or obstacle is alleged against a candidate, the bishop shall postpone his ordination until such time as he is cleared of the charge.

4   The bishop then commends them to the prayers of the congregation. The Litany may be sung or said.

5   Then shall be said or sung the service for The Holy Communion,
with the collect as follows.

Almighty God, by your divine providence you have appointed various orders of ministers in your church, and you
inspired your apostles to choose for the order of deacons the
first martyr Saint Stephen together with others: look in
mercy on these your servants now called to this office and
administration; so fill them with the truth of your doctrine,
and clothe them with holiness of life, that by word and good
example they may faithfully serve you in this office, to the
glory of your name, and the building up of your Church;
through the merits of our Saviour Jesus Christ, who lives and
reigns with you and the Holy Spirit, now and for
ever. **Amen.**

6   The Readings are selected from those printed in The Book of Common Prayer or those printed on page 293.

7   Before the Gospel, the bishop, sitting in his chair, examines in the
presence of the people each one of those who are to be ordained.

Do you believe that you are inwardly moved by the Holy
Spirit to take upon you this office and ministry, to serve God,
for the promoting of his glory, and the edifying of his
people?

    Answer

I believe so.

    The bishop

Do you think that you are truly called according to the will
of our Lord Jesus Christ and the order of the Church of
England in Australia to the ministry of the church?

    Answer

I think so.

The bishop

Do you unreservedly believe all the canonical scriptures of the Old and New Testament, as given by God to convey to us in many and varied ways the revelation of himself which is fulfilled in our Lord Jesus Christ?

Answer

I do believe them.

The bishop

Will you diligently read them to the people assembled in the church where you will be appointed to serve?

Answer

I will.

8 The bishop says

It pertains to the office of a deacon, in the church where he is appointed to serve, to assist the priest in divine service, and help him in the administration of the holy communion; to read the holy scriptures in the church; to give instruction to young people in the Christian faith as contained in the Church-Catechism; to baptize infants when the priest is absent; and to preach, if he is licensed to do so by the bishop. In addition, it is his duty, where provision is so made, to seek out the sick and needy of the parish and inform the priest so that they may be assisted by the parishioners and others. Will you do this gladly and willingly?

Answer

I will do so, by the help of God.

The bishop

Will you strive to live according to the teaching of Christ so that you and your family will be good examples to the flock of Christ?

Answer

I will, the Lord being my helper.

The bishop

Will you reverently obey your ordinary and other chief ministers set over you in the church, gladly and willingly following their godly counsel?

Answer

I will, the Lord being my helper.

9 Then the bishop lays his hands on the head of each one who is to be ordained, the candidates kneeling, and the bishop saying

[N,] Take authority to execute the office of a Deacon in the church of God, now committed to you; in the name of the Father, and of the Son, and of the Holy Spirit. **Amen.**

Then the bishop delivers to every one of them the New Testament saying

Take authority to read the Gospel in the Church of God, and to preach the same if you are so licensed by the bishop.

10 Then one of them, appointed by the bishop, reads the Gospel.

11 The bishop proceeds with the service of Holy Communion, and those who have been ordained shall receive the communion with him.

12 Before the blessing the bishop says this prayer.

Almighty God, giver of all good things, of your great goodness you have accepted these your servants into the office of deacons in your church. Make them, we ask you, O Lord, modest, humble, and faithful in their ministry, ready to observe every spiritual discipline. Give them the testimony of a good conscience, and enable them to continue steadfast and strong in your Son, Jesus Christ, to whom be glory and honour, now and for ever. **Amen.**

The Ordering of Priests

1   On the day appointed by the bishop, after Morning Prayer, there is a sermon on the duties of priests, the necessity of this office in Christ's church, and how the people ought to esteem those who hold it.

2   First, the archdeacon (or one appointed in his place) presents to the bishop sitting in his chair near the holy table those who are to be ordained priests that day.

The archdeacon says

Reverend Father in God, I present to you these persons, N and N, to be admitted to the Order of Priests.

The bishop says

Take care that the persons you present are, by their learning and godly way of life, suitable to exercise their ministry to the honour of God and the building up of his church.

The archdeacon

I have enquired concerning them, and I have examined them [*or* and they have been examined]. I believe them to be fit for this office.

3   *Then the bishop says to the people*

Good people, these are the candidates whom we propose, God willing, to receive this day into the holy office of the priesthood; for after due examination I find that they are lawfully called to this function and ministry, and that they are persons fit for this office. However, if you know of any obstacle or notorious offence in any of these persons, such as would bar him from being received into this holy ministry, come forward in the name of God and reveal what the offence or obstacle is.

If any offence or obstacle is alleged against a candidate, the bishop shall postpone his ordination until such time as he is cleared of the charge.

4 The bishop then commends them to the prayers of the congregation. The Litany may be said or sung.

5 Then shall be said or sung the service for The Holy Communion, with the collect as follows.

Almighty God, giver of all that is good, by your Holy Spirit you have appointed various orders of ministers in your church: look in mercy on these your servants now called to the office of priesthood. So fill them with the truth of your doctrine and clothe them with holiness of life, that they may faithfully minister to the glory of your name and the benefit of your Church. We ask this through Jesus Christ our Lord, who lives and reigns with you and the Holy Spirit, one God, now and for ever. **Amen.**

6 The Readings are selected from those printed in The Book of Common Prayer or those printed on page 293.

7 After the Gospel, the bishop, sitting in his chair, says to the candidates

You have heard, my brothers, in your private examination, in the sermon, and in the readings from holy scripture, how great is the dignity and importance of this office to which you are called. And now again I exhort you, in the name of our Lord Jesus Christ, that you remember the dignity of the high office and charge to which you are called: that is to say, to be messengers, watchmen, and stewards of the Lord; to teach and forewarn, to feed and provide for the Lord's family; to seek for Christ's sheep who are scattered abroad, and for his children who are surrounded by temptation in this world, that they may be saved through Christ for ever.

Have always therefore printed in your mind how great a treasure is committed to your care. For they are the sheep of Christ, whom he bought with his death, and for whom he shed his blood. The church and congregation whom you

609

must serve is his bride and his body. And if it should come about that the church, or any of its members, is hurt or hindered as a result of your negligence, you know the greatness of the fault and the judgment that will follow. Accordingly, consider within yourselves the purpose of your ministry to the children of God; and see that you never cease your labour, your care, and diligence, until you have done all that lies in you, according to your bounden duty, to bring all such as are or will be committed to your care, to that understanding in the faith and knowledge of God, and to that maturity in Christ, which leaves no place among you for error in religion or viciousness in life.

Since your office is of such excellence and such difficulty, you can see how much care and study you need, to show yourselves dutiful and thankful to the Lord, who has placed you in so great a dignity with so great a responsibility. Take care therefore that neither you yourselves offend, nor be the cause of others' offending. You cannot have such a mind and will by yourselves; for that will and ability is given by God alone. Therefore you ought to pray earnestly for his Holy Spirit. And because you cannot perform the difficult task of leading men to salvation without the doctrine and guidance of the holy scriptures, you should read and study them well, and shape your life and the lives of those for whom you are responsible, according to their teaching. And for the same reason you should put away, as much as possible, all worldly preoccupations and pursuits.

We have good reason to believe that you have carefully considered these things already; and that you have decided, by God's grace, to give yourselves wholly to this office to which God has been pleased to call you: so that to the best of your ability you will devote yourselves completely to this.

You will continually pray to God the Father, by the mediation of our Saviour Jesus Christ, for the assistance of the Holy Spirit; so that, by daily reading and meditating on the scriptures, you may grow in your ministry; and that you may so strive to sanctify the lives of you and yours and to shape them according to the teaching of Christ, that you may be godly patterns for the people to follow.

And now, in order that this present congregation of Christ's people may also be assured of your intentions in these things, and in order that your public profession may strengthen your resolve to do your duties, you shall plainly answer these questions which I, in the name of God, and of his Church, now put to you:

Do you think in your heart that you are truly called, according to the will of our Lord Jesus Christ, and the order of this Church of England in Australia, to the order and ministry of priesthood?

Answer

I do.

The bishop

Are you convinced that the holy scriptures contain all doctrine required of necessity for eternal salvation through faith in Jesus Christ? And will you instruct the people committed to your care from the scriptures, and teach nothing (as required of necessity to eternal salvation) except what you are convinced may be proved by the scriptures?

Answer

I am convinced, and will do so, by God's grace.

The bishop

Will you always faithfully minister the doctrine and sacraments, and the discipline of Christ, as the Lord has commanded, and as this Church has received them, according to the commandments of God? Will you teach the people committed to your charge to keep and observe them diligently?

Answer

I will do so, by the help of the Lord.

611

The bishop

Will you be ready to drive away all false and strange doctrines that are contrary to God's word; and to this end both publicly and privately to warn and encourage all within your care, both the sick and the well, as often as the occasion demands?

Answer

I will, the Lord being my helper.

The bishop

Will you be diligent in prayer, and in the reading of the scriptures, undertaking studies that help to a fuller knowledge of them, and turning aside from the pursuit of studies for self-indulgence and worldly gain?

Answer

I will do so, the Lord being my helper.

The bishop

Will you strive to live according to the teaching of Christ, so that you and your family may be good examples to the flock of Christ?

Answer

I will, the Lord being my helper.

The bishop

Will you maintain and promote, to the best of your ability, quietness, peace, and love among all Christian people, especially among those who are committed to your care?

Answer

I will, the Lord being my helper.

The bishop

Will you reverently obey your ordinary and other chief ministers set over you in the church, gladly and willingly following their godly counsel?

Answer

I will, the Lord being my helper.

8   The bishop stands and says

Almighty God, who has given you the will to do all these things, grant you the strength and power to perform them; that he may complete his work which he has begun in you; through Jesus Christ our Lord.   **Amen.**

9   A short period of silence is kept, during which the congregation is asked to pray silently for those to be ordained that they may perform faithfully what they have promised.

10   The candidates kneel, and the hymn *Veni Creator Spiritus* (or a similar hymn to the Holy Spirit) is said or sung.

11   Then the bishop says

Let us pray.

Almighty God and heavenly Father, by your infinite love and goodness you have given us your only Son Jesus Christ to be our redeemer and the author of eternal life.

After he had ascended into heaven, he sent into the world his apostles, prophets, evangelists, teachers and pastors, by whose ministry he gathered together a great flock in all parts of the world to proclaim the praise of your holy Name.

For these great benefits, and because you have called these your servants to the same office and ministry appointed for the salvation of mankind, we give you most hearty thanks, and we praise and worship you. We humbly ask that we and all who call upon your name may be continually thankful for these and all your benefits; and that we may daily increase in the knowledge and love of you, Father, with your Son and the Holy Spirit.

And we pray that through these your ministers, and those whom they serve, your Name may be for ever glorified and your kingdom enlarged; through Jesus Christ our Lord, who lives and reigns with you and the Holy Spirit, one God, for ever and ever. **Amen.**

12   When this prayer is finished, the bishop and the priests present lay their hands on the head of each one who is to receive the Order of Priesthood, the candidates kneeling, and the bishop saying

[N,] Receive the Holy Spirit for the office and work of a Priest in the church of God, now committed to you by the laying on of our hands. Whose sins you forgive they are forgiven: whose sins you retain they are retained; and be a faithful dispenser of the word of God and of his holy sacraments; in the name of the Father, and of the Son, and of the Holy Spirit. **Amen.**

The bishop delivers to each of them the Bible, saying

Take authority to preach the word of God, and to administer the holy sacraments in the congregation in which you shall be lawfully appointed to do so.

13   After this, the Nicene Creed is said or sung; and the bishop proceeds with the service of Holy Communion, and those who have been ordained receive the communion together.

14   At the end of the service of Holy Communion, before the blessing, the following collect is used.

Most merciful Father, we beseech you to send your blessing on these your servants, that they may be clothed with righteousness, and that your word spoken through them may be of such effect that it may never be spoken in vain. Grant also that we may always have grace so to hear and receive their proclamation of your holy word that in all our words and deeds we may seek your glory, and the increase of your kingdom; through Jesus Christ our Lord. **Amen.**

15   If on the same day the Order of Deacons is given to some and the Order of Priesthood to others, the deacons shall be presented first and then the priests. It is sufficient that the Litany be said once for both. The following joint Collect shall be used:

Almighty God, giver of all that is good, by your Holy Spirit you have appointed various orders of ministers in your church; look in mercy on these your servants now called to the office of deacons and of priests. So fill them with the truth of your doctrine and clothe them with holiness of life, that they may faithfully minister to the glory of your name and the benefit of your church. We ask this through Jesus Christ our Lord, who lives and reigns with you and the Holy Spirit, one God, now and for ever.   **Amen.**

Immediately after the Epistle the candidates for the diaconate shall be examined and ordained, as prescribed above.

One of the newly-ordained deacons shall read the Gospel.

Then those who are to be ordained priest shall likewise be examined and ordained.

The prayers in conclusion (§12 on page 607 and §14 above) are both said before the Blessing.

The Consecrating of a Bishop

1   This service shall take place on a Sunday or a Holy Day.

2   Morning Prayer being ended, the archbishop (or some other bishop) begins the service of Holy Communion, with the collect as follows.

Almighty God, by your Son Jesus Christ you gave many excellent gifts to your apostles, and ordered them to feed your flock; bless all bishops, the pastors of your church, that they may diligently preach your word and rightly instruct from it your people; and grant that your people may follow it faithfully, so that all may receive the crown of eternal glory; through Jesus Christ our Lord.   **Amen.**

3   The readings are selected from those printed in The Book of Common Prayer or those printed on page 293, and are read by two other bishops at least.

4   After the Nicene Creed and the sermon, the bishop-elect wearing his rochet is presented by two other bishops to the archbishop of the province (or some other bishop lawfully appointed) who is seated in his chair near the holy table. These bishops say

Most reverend Father in God, we present to you this godly and learned man to be ordained and consecrated bishop.

5   The authority for the consecration shall be read, and the bishop-elect shall take the necessary oaths and declarations, including the customary oath of due obedience to the archbishop.

6   Then the archbishop says

Brethren, it is written in the Gospel of Saint Luke that our Saviour Christ spent the whole night in prayer before he chose and sent out his twelve apostles. It is written also in the Acts of the Apostles that the disciples who were at Antioch fasted and prayed before they laid hands on Paul and Barnabas and sent them out. Let us therefore, following the examples of our Saviour and his apostles, commit ourselves to prayer before we admit and send out this person presented to us to the work to which we trust the Holy Spirit has called him.

The Litany may then be sung or said.

7   The archbishop says this prayer.

Almighty God, giver of all that is good, by your Holy Spirit you have appointed various orders of ministers in your Church; bless your servant N now called to the work and ministry of a bishop. So fill him with the truth of your doctrine and clothe him with holiness of life, that he may faithfully minister in this office to the glory of your name and the benefit of your Church. We ask this through our Lord Jesus Christ, who lives and reigns with you and the Holy Spirit, one God, now and for ever.   **Amen.**

8   The archbishop, sitting in his chair, says to the bishop-elect

My brother, the holy scripture and the ancient canons command that we should not be hasty in laying on hands and admitting anyone to government in the church of God. Therefore, before I admit you to this ministry, I must examine you in certain matters so that the congregation present may hear how you are determined to act in the Church of God.

Are you convinced that you are truly called to this office, according to the will of our Lord Jesus Christ, and the order of the Church of England in Australia?

Answer

I am.

The archbishop

Are you convinced that the holy scriptures contain all doctrine required of necessity for eternal salvation through faith in Jesus Christ? And will you instruct the people committed to your care from the scriptures, and teach nothing (as required of necessity for eternal salvation) except what you are convinced may be proved by the scriptures?

Answer

I am convinced, and will do so, by God's grace.

The archbishop

Will you then study the scriptures and pray for a true understanding of them so that you may be able to teach and exhort with sound doctrine, and be able to withstand and convince those who speak against them?

Answer

I will do so, by the help of God.

The archbishop

Are you ready to drive away all false and strange doctrine which is contrary to God's word; and privately and publicly to call upon and encourage others to do likewise?

Answer

I am, the Lord being my helper.

The archbishop

Will you forsake ungodliness and worldliness, and live moderately, righteously, and in a godly manner; so that by your example and good works you may show forth the love of God to others?

Answer

I will, the Lord being my helper.

The archbishop

Will you maintain and promote (as much as lies in your power) quietness, peace, and love among all men; and will you correct and discipline, according to the authority you have by God's word, the disorderly and disobedient and those guilty of offence within your jurisdiction?

Answer

I will, by the help of God.

The archbishop

Will you be faithful in ordaining, commissioning, and laying hands upon others?

Answer

I will, by the help of God.

The archbishop

Will you be gentle, and merciful for Christ's sake, to the poor and needy, and all strangers who need your help?

Answer

I will, by God's help.

9   The archbishop, standing up, says

Almighty God, who has given you the will to do all these things, grant you the strength and power to perform them; that he may finish the work he has begun in you; through Jesus Christ our Lord. **Amen.**

10   Then the bishop-elect puts on the rest of the episcopal vesture; he kneels down, and the hymn *Veni Creator Spiritus* (or another hymn to the Holy Spirit) is sung or said.

11   The archbishop then says

Let us pray.

Almighty God and heavenly Father, by your infinite love and goodness you have given us your only Son Jesus Christ to be our redeemer and the author of eternal life. After he had ascended into heaven, he poured down his gifts abundantly on men, making some apostles, some prophets, some evangelists, some pastors and teachers, to the building up of his church. Grant, O Lord, we beg you, to this your servant N grace that he may always be ready to proclaim the good news of salvation and reconciliation. May he be a wise and faithful steward of your mysteries, so that at the last he may be received into eternal joy; through Jesus Christ our Lord, who lives and reigns with you and the Holy Spirit, one God, for ever and ever. **Amen.**

12   Then the archbishop and bishops present lay their hands on the head of the bishop-elect, as he kneels before them, the archbishop saying

Receive the Holy Spirit for the office and work of a bishop in the church of God, now committed to you by the laying on of our hands, in the name of the Father, and of the Son, and of the Holy Spirit. Amen. Remember to stir up the grace of God which is given you, by this laying on of our hands, for God has not given us the spirit of fear, but of power and love and self-control.

Then the archbishop gives him a Bible, saying

Give your attention to reading, exhortation, and teaching. Think upon the things contained in this book. Practise them that what you learn may be evident to all men. Apply these things to yourself, teach them, and practise them diligently, for in so doing you will save yourself and those who hear you. Be to the flock of Christ a shepherd, and not a wolf; feed them, devour them not. Support the weak, heal the sick, bind up the broken, restore the outcasts, seek the lost. Be merciful, without being remiss; administer discipline with mercy. When the Chief Shepherd appears may you receive the never-fading crown of glory; through Jesus Christ our Lord. **Amen.**

13   Then the archbishop proceeds with the service of Holy Communion. The newly-consecrated bishop receives the communion with him and the others present.

14   Immediately before the blessing, this prayer is said.

Most merciful Father, we beg you to send your heavenly
blessing upon this your servant. So clothe him with your
Holy Spirit that, faithfully fulfilling his ministry, he may at
the last receive the crown of righteousness from him who
lives and reigns with you and the Holy Spirit, one God, now
and for ever.   **Amen.**

Acknowledgments

The Publishers are grateful to the following for permission to reproduce copyright material:

David L Frost, John Emerton, and Andrew Macintosh, for the translation of the Psalms, and to William Collins and Sons for the pointing of the Psalms, taken from *The Psalms, a New Translation for Worship*, © 1976, 1977, David L Frost, John Emerton, and Andrew Macintosh, published by William Collins and Sons; the pointing of the Psalms © 1976, 1977, William Collins and Sons.

The Registrars of the Provinces of Canterbury and York, for the text and pointing of the canticles The Song of Zechariah, The Song of Mary, A Song of Creation, The Song of the Three Young Men, The Song of Simeon, A Song of Christ's Glory, Saviour of the World, A Song to the Lamb, Great and Wonderful, and the Easter Anthems, taken from *Morning and Evening Prayer* (Alternative Services Series 3) © 1974, 1975, Registrars of the Provinces of Canterbury and York, and published by Cambridge University Press, Eyre and Spottiswoode, Oxford University Press, and S.P.C.K. Source material for Baptism of Infants and of Adults, Second Order, and Confirmation, Second Form, and the Funeral Services is also gratefully acknowledged.

International Committee on English in the Liturgy, Inc., for the alternative collects in the Three Year Series of Collects and Readings at The Holy Communion, taken from the English translation of the Prayers from the Roman Missal, © 1973. All rights reserved.

American Bible Society, New York, for the translation of Ephesians 1.3-6, Hebrews 10.19-22, and the reading from Ephesians 5 in A Service for Marriage, Second Form, and those passages of Scripture used in this Book marked 'TEV', taken from *Good News for Modern Man*, © 1966.

Oxford and Cambridge University Presses, for the translation of Judith 16.13-15, taken from *The New English Bible*, second edition © 1970.

International Consultation on English Texts, for the text of Gloria in excelsis, Sanctus, and Benedictus qui venit printed in The Holy Communion, taken from *Prayers We Have In Common* published and © 1970, 1971, 1975.

Division of Christian Education and Ministry of the National Council of the Churches of Christ in the U.S.A., for the translations of the other

622

passages of Scripture used in this Book, taken from the *Revised Standard Version*, copyrighted 1946, 1952, © 1971, 1973.

The first prayer on page 173 is by Dr David L Frost, from Alternative Series 3, An Order for Holy Communion, and is reproduced by permission of S.P.C.K. on behalf of the Registrars of the Provinces of Canterbury and York.

The form of the Lord's Prayer printed on page 41 and elsewhere in this Book is that published by the International Consultation on English Texts, 1970, except for lines 2 and 9 where the traditional translation is retained pending a more general agreement as to how these petitions should be rendered in modern English.

The practical needs of common prayer have prompted a number of minor revisions in the translations, particularly the amendment of 'thee' to 'you'.

A CONFESSION OF THE CHRISTIAN FAITH
commonly called
THE CREED OF SAINT ATHANASIUS

Whosoever will be saved: before all things it is necessary that he hold the Catholick Faith.

Which Faith except every one do keep whole and undefiled: without doubt he shall perish everlastingly.

And the Catholick Faith is this: That we worship one God in Trinity, and Trinity in Unity;

Neither confounding the Persons: nor dividing the Substance.

For there is one Person of the Father, another of the Son: and another of the Holy Ghost.

But the Godhead of the Father, of the Son, and of the Holy Ghost, is all one: the Glory equal, the Majesty co-eternal.

Such as the Father is, such is the Son: and such is the Holy Ghost.

The Father uncreate, the Son uncreate: and the Holy Ghost uncreate.

The Father incomprehensible, the Son incomprehensible: and the Holy Ghost incomprehensible.

The Father eternal, the Son eternal: and the Holy Ghost eternal.

And yet they are not three eternals: but one eternal.

As also there are not three incomprehensibles, nor three uncreated: but one uncreated, and one incomprehensible.

So likewise the Father is Almighty, the Son Almighty: and the Holy Ghost Almighty.

And yet they are not three Almighties: but one Almighty.

So the Father is God, the Son is God: and the Holy Ghost is God.

And yet they are not three Gods: but one God.

So likewise the Father is Lord, the Son Lord: and the Holy Ghost Lord.

And yet not three Lords: but one Lord.

For like as we are compelled by the Christian verity: to acknowledge every Person by himself to be God and Lord;

So are we forbidden by the Catholick Religion: to say, There be three Gods, or three Lords.

The Father is made of none: neither created, nor begotten.

The Son is of the Father alone: not made, nor created, but begotten.

The Holy Ghost is of the Father and of the Son: neither made, nor created, nor begotten, but proceeding.

So there is one Father, not three Fathers; one Son, not three Sons: one Holy Ghost, not three Holy Ghosts.

And in this Trinity none is afore, or after other: none is greater, or less than another;

But the whole three Persons are co-eternal together: and co-equal.

So that in all things, as is aforesaid: the Unity in Trinity, and the Trinity in Unity is to be worshipped.

He therefore that will be saved: must thus think of the Trinity.

Furthermore, it is necessary to everlasting salvation: that he also believe rightly the Incarnation of our Lord Jesus Christ.

For the right Faith is, that we believe and confess: that our Lord Jesus Christ, the Son of God, is God and Man;

God, of the Substance of the Father, begotten before the worlds: and Man, of the Substance of his Mother, born in the world;

Perfect God, and perfect Man: of a reasonable soul and human flesh subsisting;

Equal to the Father, as touching his Godhead: and inferior to the Father, as touching his Manhood.

Who although he be God and Man: yet he is not two, but one Christ;

One; not by conversion of the Godhead into flesh: but by taking of the Manhood into God;

One altogether; not by confusion of Substance: but by unity of Person.

For as the reasonable soul and flesh is one man: so God and Man is one Christ;

Who suffered for our salvation: descended into hell, rose again the third day from the dead.

He ascended into heaven, he sitteth on the right hand of the Father, God Almighty: from whence he shall come to judge the quick and the dead.

At whose coming all men shall rise again with their bodies: and shall give account for their own works.

And they that have done good shall go into life everlasting: and they that have done evil into everlasting fire.

This is the Catholick Faith: which except a man believe faithfully, he cannot be saved.

THE ARTICLES OF RELIGION

Agreed upon by the
Archbishops, Bishops,
and the whole clergy
of the Provinces of Canterbury and York,
London, 1562.

I. *Of Faith in the Holy Trinity.*

There is but one living and true God, everlasting, without body, parts, or passions; of infinite power, wisdom, and goodness; the Maker, and Preserver of all things both visible and invisible. And in unity of this Godhead there be three Persons, of one substance, power, and eternity; the Father, the Son, and the Holy Ghost.

II. *Of the Word or Son of God, which was made very Man.*

The Son, which is the Word of the Father, begotten from everlasting of the Father, the very and eternal God, and of one substance with the Father, took Man's nature in the womb of the blessed Virgin, of her substance: so that two whole and perfect Natures, that is to say, the Godhead and Manhood, were joined together in one Person, never to be divided, whereof is one Christ, very God, and very Man; who truly suffered, was crucified, dead and buried, to reconcile his Father to us, and to be a sacrifice, not only for original guilt, but also for all actual sins of men.

III. *Of the going down of Christ into Hell.*

As Christ died for us, and was buried, so also is it to be believed, that he went down into Hell.

IV. *Of the Resurrection of Christ.*

Christ did truly rise again from death, and took again his body, with flesh, bones, and all things appertaining to the perfection of Man's nature; wherewith he ascended into Heaven, and there sitteth, until he return to judge all Men at the last day.

V. *Of the Holy Ghost.*

The Holy Ghost, proceeding from the Father and the Son, is of one substance, majesty, and glory, with the Father and the Son, very and eternal God.

VI. *Of the Sufficiency of the Holy Scriptures for salvation.*

Holy Scripture containeth all things necessary to salvation: so that whatsoever is not read therein, nor may be proved thereby, is not to be required of any man, that it should be believed as an article of the Faith, or be thought requisite or necessary to salvation. In the name of the Holy Scripture we do understand those Canonical Books of the Old and New Testament, of whose authority was never any doubt in the Church.

Of the Names and Number of the Canonical Books.

Genesis,	*The First Book of Chronicles,*
Exodus,	*The Second Book of Chronicles,*
Leviticus,	*The First Book of Esdras,*
Numbers,	*The Second Book of Esdras,*
Deuteronomy,	*The Book of Esther,*
Joshua,	*The Book of Job,*
Judges,	*The Psalms,*
Ruth,	*The Proverbs,*
The First Book of Samuel,	*Ecclesiastes or Preacher,*
The Second Book of Samuel,	*Cantica, or Songs of Solomon,*
The First Book of Kings,	*Four Prophets the greater,*
The Second Book of Kings,	*Twelve Prophets the less.*

And the other Books (as *Hierome* saith) the Church doth read for example of life and instruction of manners; but yet doth it not apply them to establish any doctrine; such are these following:

The Third Book of Esdras,	*Baruch the Prophet,*
The Fourth Book of Esdras,	*The Song of the Three Children,*
The Book of Tobias,	*The Story of Susanna,*
The Book of Judith,	*Of Bel and the Dragon,*
The rest of the Book of Esther,	*The Prayer of Manasses,*
The Book of Wisdom,	*The First Book of Maccabees,*
Jesus the Son of Sirach,	*The Second Book of Maccabees.*

All the Books of the New Testament, as they are commonly received, we do receive, and account them Canonical.

VII. *Of the Old Testament.*

The Old Testament is not contrary to the New: for both in the Old and New Testament everlasting life is offered to Mankind by Christ, who is the only Mediator between God and Man, being both God and Man. Wherefore they are not to be heard, which feign that the old Fathers did look only for transitory promises. Although the Law given from God by Moses, as touching Ceremonies and Rites, do not bind Christian men, nor the Civil precepts thereof ought of necessity to be received in any commonwealth; yet notwithstanding, no Christian man whatsoever is free from the obedience of the Commandments which are called Moral.

VIII. *Of the Three Creeds.*

The Three Creeds, *Nicene* Creed, *Athanasius's* Creed, and that which is commonly called the *Apostles'* Creed, ought thoroughly to be received and believed: for they may be proved by most certain warrants of Holy Scripture.

IX. *Of Original or Birth-sin.*

Original Sin standeth not in the following of *Adam*, (as the *Pelagians* do vainly talk;) but it is the fault and corruption of the Nature of every man, that naturally is ingendered of the offspring of Adam; whereby man is very far gone from original righteousness, and is of his own nature inclined to evil, so that the flesh lusteth always contrary to the spirit; and therefore in every person born into this world, it deserveth God's wrath and damnation. And this infection of nature doth remain, yea in them that are regenerated; whereby the lust of the flesh, called in the Greek, *phronema sarkos*, which some do expound the wisdom, some sensuality, some the affection, some the desire, of the flesh, is not subject to the Law of God. And although there is no condemnation for them that believe and are baptized, yet the Apostle doth confess, that concupiscence and lust hath of itself the nature of sin.

X. *Of Free-Will.*

The condition of Man after the fall of *Adam* is such, that he cannot turn and prepare himself, by his own natural strength and good works, to faith, and calling upon God: Wherefore we have no power to do good works pleasant and acceptable to God, without the grace of God by Christ preventing us, that we may have a good will, and working with us, when we have that good will.

XI. *Of the Justification of Man.*

We are accounted righteous before God, only for the merit of our Lord and Saviour Jesus Christ by Faith, and not for our own works or deservings: Wherefore, that we are justified by Faith only is a most wholesome Doctrine, and very full of comfort, as more largely is expressed in the Homily of Justification.

XII. *Of Good Works.*

Albeit that Good Works, which are the fruits of Faith, and follow after Justification, cannot put away our sins, and endure the severity of God's Judgement; yet are they pleasing and acceptable to God in Christ, and do spring out necessarily of a true and lively Faith; insomuch that by them a lively Faith may be as evidently known as a tree discerned by the fruit.

XIII. *Of Works before Justification.*

Works done before the grace of Christ, and the Inspiration of his Spirit, are not pleasant to God, forasmuch as they spring not of faith in Jesus Christ, neither do they make men meet to receive grace, or (as the School-authors say) deserve grace of congruity: yea rather, for that they are not done as God hath willed and commanded them to be done, we doubt not but they have the nature of sin.

XIV. *Of Works of Supererogation.*

Voluntary Works besides, over and above, God's Commandments, which they call Works of Supererogation, cannot be taught without arrogancy and impiety: for by them men do declare, that they do not only render unto God as much as they are bound to do, but that they do more for his sake, than of bounden duty is required: whereas Christ saith plainly, When ye have done all that are commanded to you, say, We are unprofitable servants.

XV. *Of Christ alone without Sin.*

Christ in the truth of our nature was made like unto us in all things, sin only except, from which he was clearly void, both in his flesh, and in his spirit. He came to be the Lamb without spot, who, by sacrifice of himself once made, should take away the sins of the world, and sin, as Saint *John* saith, was not in him. But all we the rest, although baptized, and born again in Christ, yet offend in many things; and if we say we have no sin, we deceive ourselves, and the truth is not in us.

XVI. *Of Sin after Baptism.*

Not every deadly sin willingly committed after Baptism is sin against the Holy Ghost, and unpardonable. Wherefore the grant of repentance is not to be denied to such as fall into sin after Baptism. After we have received the Holy Ghost, we may depart from grace given, and fall into sin, and by the grace of God we may arise again, and amend our lives. And therefore they are to be condemned, which say, they can no more sin as long as they live here, or deny the place of forgiveness to such as truly repent.

XVII. *Of Predestination and Election.*

Predestination to Life is the everlasting purpose of God, whereby (before the foundations of the world were laid) he hath constantly decreed by his counsel secret to us, to deliver from curse and damnation those whom he hath chosen in Christ out of mankind, and to bring them by Christ to everlasting salvation, as vessels made to honour. Wherefore, they which be endued with so excellent a benefit of God be called according to God's purpose by his Spirit working in due season: they through Grace obey the calling: they be justified freely: they be made sons of God by adoption: they be made like the image of his only-begotten Son Jesus Christ: they walk religiously in good works, and at length, by God's mercy, they attain to everlasting felicity.

As the godly consideration of Predestination, and our Election in Christ, is full of sweet, pleasant, and unspeakable comfort to godly persons, and such as feel in themselves the working of the Spirit of Christ, mortifying the works of the flesh, and their earthly members, and drawing up their mind to high and heavenly things, as well because it doth greatly establish and confirm their faith of eternal Salvation to be enjoyed through Christ, as because it doth fervently kindle their love towards God: So, for curious and carnal persons, lacking the Spirit of Christ, to have continually before their eyes the sentence of God's Predestination, is a most dangerous down-fall, whereby the Devil doth thrust them either into desperation, or into wretchlessness of most unclean living, no less perilous than desperation.

Furthermore, we must receive God's promises in such wise, as they be generally set forth to us in Holy Scripture: and, in our doings, that Will of God is to be followed, which we have expressly declared unto us in the Word of God.

XVIII. *Of obtaining eternal Salvation only by the Name of Christ.*

They also are to be had accursed that presume to say, That every man shall be saved by the Law or Sect which he professeth, so that he be diligent to frame his life according to that Law, and the light of Nature. For Holy Scripture doth set out unto us only the Name of Jesus Christ, whereby men must be saved.

XIX. *Of the Church.*

The visible Church of Christ is a congregation of faithful men, in the which the pure Word of God is preached, and the Sacraments be duly ministered according to Christ's ordinance in all those things that of necessity are requisite to the same.

As the Church of *Jerusalem, Alexandria,* and *Antioch,* have erred; so also the Church of *Rome* hath erred, not only in their living and manner of Ceremonies, but also in matters of Faith.

XX. *Of the Authority of the Church.*

The Church hath power to decree Rites or Ceremonies, and authority in Controversies of Faith: And yet it is not lawful for the Church to ordain any thing that is contrary to God's Word written, neither may it so expound one place of Scripture, that it be repugnant to another. Wherefore, although the Church be a witness and a keeper of Holy Writ, yet, as it ought not to decree any thing against the same, so besides the same ought it not to enforce any thing to be believed for necessity of Salvation.

XXI. *Of the Authority of General Councils.*

General Councils may not be gathered together without the commandment and will of Princes. And when they be gathered together, (forasmuch as they be an assembly of men, whereof all be not governed with the Spirit and Word of God,) they may err, and sometimes have erred, even in things pertaining unto God. Wherefore things ordained by them as necessary to salvation have neither strength nor authority, unless it may be declared that they be taken out of Holy Scripture.

XXII. *Of Purgatory.*

The Romish Doctrine concerning Purgatory, Pardons, Worshipping and Adoration, as well of Images as of Reliques, and also invocation of Saints, is a fond thing vainly invented, and grounded upon no warranty of Scripture, but rather repugnant to the Word of God.

XXIII. *Of Ministering in the Congregation.*

It is not lawful for any man to take upon him the office of publick preaching, or ministering the Sacraments in the Congregation, before he be lawfully called, and sent to execute the same. And those we ought to judge lawfully called and sent, which be chosen and called to this work by men who have publick authority given unto them in the Congregation, to call and send Ministers into the Lord's vineyard.

XXIV. *Of speaking in the Congregation in such a tongue as the people understandeth.*

It is a thing plainly repugnant to the Word of God, and the custom of the Primitive Church, to have publick Prayer in the Church, or to minister the Sacraments in a tongue not understood of the people.

XXV. *Of the Sacraments.*

Sacraments ordained of Christ be not only badges or tokens of Christian men's profession, but rather they be certain sure witnesses, and effectual signs of grace, and God's good will towards us, by the which he doth work invisibly in us, and doth not only quicken, but also strengthen and confirm our Faith in him.

There are two Sacraments ordained of Christ our Lord in the Gospel, that is to say, Baptism, and the Supper of the Lord.

Those five commonly called Sacraments, that is to say, Confirmation, Penance, Orders, Matrimony, and extreme Unction, are not to be counted for Sacraments of the Gospel, being such as have grown partly of the corrupt following of the Apostles, partly are states of life allowed in the Scriptures; but yet have not like nature of Sacraments with Baptism, and the Lord's Supper, for that they have not any visible sign or ceremony ordained of God.

The Sacraments were not ordained of Christ to be gazed upon, or to be carried about, but that we should duly use them. And in such only as worthily receive the same they have a wholesome effect or operation: but they that receive them unworthily purchase to themselves damnation, as Saint *Paul* saith.

XXVI. *Of the Unworthiness of the Ministers, which hinders not the effect of the Sacrament.*

Although in the visible Church the evil be ever mingled with the good, and sometimes the evil have chief authority in the Ministration of the Word and Sacraments, yet forasmuch as they do not the same in their own name, but in Christ's, and do minister by his commission and authority, we may use their Ministry, both in hearing the Word of God, and in receiving of the Sacraments. Neither is the effect of Christ's ordinance taken away by their wickedness, nor the grace of God's gifts diminished from such as by faith and rightly do receive the Sacraments ministered unto them; which be effectual, because of Christ's institution and promise, although they be ministered by evil men.

Nevertheless, it appertaineth to the discipline of the Church, that inquiry be made of evil Ministers, and that they be accused by those that have knowledge of their offences; and finally being found guilty, by just judgement be deposed.

XXVII. *Of Baptism.*

Baptism is not only a sign of profession, and mark of difference, whereby Christian men are discerned from others that be not christened, but it is also a sign of Regeneration or new Birth, whereby, as by an instrument, they that receive Baptism rightly are grafted into the Church; the promises of forgiveness of sin, and of our adoption to be sons of God by the Holy Ghost, are visibly signed and sealed; Faith is confirmed, and Grace increased by virtue of prayer unto God. The Baptism of young Children is in any wise to be retained in the Church, as most agreeable with the institution of Christ.

XXVIII. *Of the Lord's Supper.*

The Supper of the Lord is not only a sign of the love that Christians ought to have among themselves one to another; but rather is a Sacrament of our Redemption by Christ's death: insomuch that to such as rightly, worthily, and with faith, receive the same, the Bread which we break is a partaking of the Body of Christ; and likewise the Cup of Blessing is a partaking of the Blood of Christ.

Transubstantiation (or the change of the substance of Bread and Wine) in the Supper of the Lord, cannot be proved by Holy Writ; but is repugnant to the plain words of Scripture, overthroweth the nature of a Sacrament, and hath given occasion to many superstitions.

The Body of Christ is given, taken, and eaten, in the Supper, only after an heavenly and spiritual manner. And the mean whereby the Body of Christ is received and eaten in the Supper is Faith.

The Sacrament of the Lord's Supper was not by Christ's ordinance reserved, carried about, lifted up, or worshipped.

XXIX. *Of the Wicked which eat not the Body of Christ in the use of the Lord's Supper.*

The Wicked, and such as be void of a lively faith, although they do carnally and visibly press with their teeth (as Saint *Augustine* saith) the Sacrament of the Body and Blood of Christ, yet in no wise are they partakers of Christ: but rather, to their condemnation, do eat and drink the sign or Sacrament of so great a thing.

XXX. *Of both kinds.*

The Cup of the Lord is not to be denied to the Lay-people: for both the parts of the Lord's Sacrament, by Christ's ordinance and commandment, ought to be ministered to all Christian men alike.

XXXI. *Of the one Oblation of Christ finished upon the Cross.*

The offering of Christ once made is that perfect redemption, propitiation, and satisfaction, for all the sins of the whole world, both original and actual; and there is none other satisfaction for sin, but that alone. Wherefore the sacrifices of Masses, in the which it was commonly said, that the Priest did offer Christ for the quick and the dead, to have remission of pain or guilt, were blasphemous fables, and dangerous deceits.

XXXII. *Of the Marriage of Priests.*

Bishops, Priests, and Deacons, are not commanded by God's Law, either to vow the estate of single life, or to abstain from marriage: therefore it is lawful for them, as for all other Christian men, to marry at their own discretion, as they shall judge the same to serve better to godliness.

XXXIII. *Of excommunicate Persons, how they are to be avoided.*

That person which by open denunciation of the Church is rightly cut off from the unity of the Church, and excommunicated, ought to be taken of the whole multitude of the faithful, as an Heathen and Publican, until he be openly reconciled by penance, and received into the Church by a Judge that hath authority thereunto.

XXXIV. *Of the Traditions of the Church.*

It is not necessary that Traditions and Ceremonies be in all places one, and utterly like; for at all times they have been divers, and may be changed according to the diversities of countries, times, and men's manners, so that nothing be ordained against God's Word. Whosoever through his private judgement, willingly and purposely, doth openly break the traditions and ceremonies of the Church, which be not repugnant to the Word of God, and be ordained and approved by common authority, ought to be rebuked openly, (that others may fear to do the like,) as he that offendeth against the common order of the Church, and hurteth the authority of the Magistrate, and woundeth the consciences of the weak brethren.

Every particular or national Church hath authority to ordain, change, and abolish, ceremonies or rites of the Church ordained only by man's authority, so that all things be done to edifying.

XXXV. *Of the Homilies.*

The second Book of Homilies, the several titles whereof we have joined under this Article, doth contain a godly and wholesome Doctrine, and necessary for these times, as doth the former Book of Homilies, which were set forth in the time of *Edward* the Sixth; and therefore we judge them to be read in Churches by the Ministers, diligently and distinctly, that they may be understanded of the people.

Of the Names of the Homilies.

1 *Of the right Use of the Church.*
2 *Against peril of Idolatry.*
3 *Of repairing and keeping clean of Churches.*
4 *Of good Works: first of Fasting.*
5 *Against Gluttony and Drunkenness.*
6 *Against Excess of Apparel.*
7 *Of Prayer.*
8 *Of the Place and Time of Prayer.*
9 *That Common Prayers and Sacraments ought to be ministered in a known tongue.*
10 *Of the reverend estimation of God's Word.*
11 *Of Alms-doing.*
12 *Of the Nativity of Christ.*
13 *Of the Passion of Christ.*
14 *Of the Resurrection of Christ.*
15 *Of the worthy receiving of the Sacrament of the Body and Blood of Christ.*
16 *Of the Gifts of the Holy Ghost.*
17 *For the Rogation Days.*
18 *Of the State of Matrimony.*
19 *Of Repentance.*
20 *Against Idleness.*
21 *Against Rebellion.*

XXXVI. *Of Consecration of Bishops and Ministers.*

The Book of Consecration of Archbishops and Bishops, and Ordering of Priests and Deacons, lately set forth in the time of *Edward* the Sixth, and confirmed at the same time by authority of Parliament, doth contain all things necessary to such Consecration and Ordering: neither hath it any thing, that of itself is superstitious and ungodly. And therefore whosoever are consecrated or ordered according to the Rites of that Book, since the second year of the forenamed King *Edward* unto this time, or hereafter shall be consecrated or ordered according to the same Rites; we decree all such to be rightly, orderly, and lawfully consecrated and ordered.

XXXVII. *Of the Civil Magistrates.*

The King's Majesty hath the chief power in this Realm of *England*, and other his Dominions, unto whom the chief Government of all Estates of this Realm, whether they be Ecclesiastical or Civil, in all causes doth appertain, and is not, nor ought to be, subject to any foreign Jurisdiction.

Where we attribute to the King's Majesty the chief government, by which Titles we understand the minds of some slanderous folks to be offended; we give not to our Princes the ministering either of God's Word, or of the Sacraments, the which thing the Injunctions also lately set forth by *Elizabeth* our Queen do most plainly testify; but that only prerogative, which we see to have been given always to all godly Princes in Holy Scriptures by God himself; that is, that they should rule all estates and degrees committed to their charge by God, whether they be Ecclesiastical or Temporal, and restrain with the civil sword the stubborn and evildoers.

The Bishop of *Rome* hath no jurisdiction in this Realm of *England*.

The Laws of the Realm may punish Christian men with death, for heinous and grievous offences.

It is lawful for Christian men, at the commandment of the Magistrate, to wear weapons, and serve in the wars.

XXXVIII. *Of Christian men's Goods, which are not common.*

The Riches and Goods of Christians are not common, as touching the right, title, and possession of the same, as certain Anabaptists do falsely boast. Notwithstanding, every man ought, of such things as he possesseth, liberally to give alms to the poor, according to his ability.

XXXIX. *Of a Christian man's Oath.*

As we confess that vain and rash Swearing is forbidden Christian men by our Lord Jesus Christ, and *James* his Apostle, so we judge, that Christian Religion doth not prohibit, but that a man may swear when the Magistrate requireth, in a cause of faith and charity, so it be done according to the Prophet's teaching, in justice, judgement, and truth.

Set and printed in Australia in Baskerville
on Geisha Corona paper by John Sands Pty. Ltd.
Artarmon, N.S.W.
a.d. 1978